STUDIA INDICA

Volume 1 (2024) Part 2

Special Issue in Memory of Professor DUAN Qing

梵 学

第一辑（2024）下卷

段晴教授纪念专号

Editors:
YE Shaoyong, ZHANG Xing and FAN Jingjing

主编
叶少勇 张幸 范晶晶

RESEARCH INSTITUTE OF SANSKRIT MANUSCRIPTS & BUDDHIST LITERATURE

中西書局

图书在版编目（CIP）数据

梵学. 第一辑，段晴教授纪念专号：汉文、英文 / 叶少勇，张幸，范晶晶主编. —上海：中西书局，2024

ISBN 978-7-5475-2233-2

I. ①梵… II. ①叶… ②张… ③范… III. ①梵一文集一汉、英 IV. ①B351-53

中国国家版本馆 CIP 数据核字（2024）第 045144 号

CONTENTS
目 录

Part 2
下 卷

Papers in English 英文文章

English Abstracts of Papers in Chinese 中文文章的英文摘要

The Diversity and Commonality of the Buddhist Invocation Prayers from Dunhuang

CHEN Huaiyu

Abstract: Drawing upon two sets of liturgical texts in the Dunhuang manuscripts, this study analyses diversity and commonality within the Buddhist invocation rituals in the Dunhuang manuscripts and between these manuscripts and traditional canonical Buddhist literature. In the first case, I suggest that there are differences between the generic invocation prayer models and the historical prayers that refer to the ritual of invocation. In the second case, there are also differences between the invocation ritual in the Buddhist scriptural sources and that in the Dunhuang manuscripts. These differences indicate a substantial regional diversity of invocation rituals, from Central China to the frontier regions, such as Dunhuang. This study demonstrates that, although rituals used to invoke the hierarchical gods and deities varied from one tradition to another and from one region to another, in canonical texts and liturgical prayers the invocation ritual in medieval Chinese Buddhism shared specific essential components, including invocation, supplication, dedication, benediction, and confession.

Keywords: Invocation; prayer; Dunhuang manuscripts, Diversity, Commonality

1 Introduction

Since the discovery of the cave library in Dunhuang, contemporary scholarship has produced numerous publications on its manuscripts and artifacts, most of which are Buddhist texts. Canonical texts have been studied more thoroughly than non-canonical texts in traditional scholarship. However, the latter are often more appealing due to their unique academic merits that cannot be found in the canonical texts, particularly as they appear in the most widely used modern edition of the Taishō canon, Taishō Shinshū Daizōkyō (大正新修大藏經). Many of the non-canonical Buddhist manuscripts from Dunhuang may have been produced locally in family-patronized temples in Dunhuang, especially during the period when the local Returning-to-Righteousness Army (*guiyijun*, 歸義軍 c. 851–1036 CE) government ruled. Among these manuscripts, a group of prayers has attracted considerable attention from contemporary scholars due to their value in contribututing to the understanding of Buddhist ritual structure and procedures (Huang and Li 1997, 363–370; Zhang Guangda 1997, 60–73; Hao 1996, 64–71; Wang Sanqing 2008, 1–40; Teiser 2009, 201–237; Teiser 2007a, 295–308; Teiser 2007b, 284–307; Chen 2008, 167–85; Chen 2014, 233–257; Chen 2021, 1–36; Ding 2020).

This paper focuses on a particular genre of texts, the "invocation prayer" (*qiqingwen*, 啓請文), which refers to the prayers for invoking gods and deities in the context of

CHEN Huaiyu, Arizona State University.

liturgical ritual. On the one hand, these texts were mainly produced locally in Dunhuang in the 9th–10th centuries CE, as a marginal borderland far away from the Central Plain of the Chinese Empire, which was the center of East Asian Buddhism at that time. On the other hand, the rituals reflected in these texts follow some basic structures and conventions which are found in the texts from the Central Plains. Therefore, here I examine the diversity and commonality of the invocation rituals in the Dunhuang manuscripts compared to similar sources in the Buddhist canonical literature.

While reading the invocation prayers from Dunhuang, this paper benefited from Lewis Doney's article "Text, Act and Subject: A Proposed Approach to the Future Study of the Old Tibetan Prayer," (Doney 2021, 49–83). Doney highlights exciting ways to interpret and understand Tibetan prayers from the 8th to 10th centuries based on Sam Gill and Armin Geetz's theoretical framework on religious prayers and rituals. In this paper, I cover three dimensions in the invocation ritual in the Dunhuang manuscripts—text, act, and subject. My sources are prayers that were primary textual documents for performing invocation rituals in medieval China. I agree with Sam Gill's definitions of prayer, which include, "a collection of words that cohere as a human communication directed toward a spiritual entity," and "the human act of communicating with deities, including not only or exclusively language but especially the elements of performance that constitute the act" (Gill 2005, 7367). In this paper, the prayers I am concerned with deal with the communication of the ritual hosts with sacred presences through verbal acts for the sake of sacred transformation. A host's verbal act invokes the sacred presences, mostly Buddhist saints and worthies, and brings them to the ritual space to transform it into a sacred space and attest to the virtues of the host. This can also be called consecration. The verbal calling for gods and deities to witness the host's virtues and merits, manifests the performativity of the invocation ritual in the Dunhuang manuscripts. If the gods and deities do not accept a host's performance, it would not be possible to attest to the efficacy of the ritual performance.

Two sets of Dunhuang's manuscripts directly touch upon the invocation liturgies: generic invocation prayer models and historical prayers that refer to the particular invocation ritual. Hosted by historical figures. The first set is the group of texts titled *qiqingwen*, "the texts of invocation." For example, there are at least three manuscripts in this group, including S. 5957, S. 3875, and S. 5456, in the Stein Collection of the British Library (Huang and Wu 1995, 407–408, 416–418). They all contain the term "*qiqingwen*" in the title of the text. Manuscript S. 5957 is the longest and most complete one without any broken sentences. This manuscript has 28 lines, and each line has 23 characters. Manuscript S. 3875 contains two texts, and the *qiqingwen* one is damaged at the beginning. Manuscript S. 5456 preserved three texts. The invocation text is in the middle. In terms of format, they are all pamphlets. The second manuscript, S. 3875, indicates that it was one of the various feast texts (*zhaiwen*, 齋文) by its title, "*qiqingwen*." These three texts were likely model texts for generic use. We know this because they did not specify the names and titles of the patrons who offered the rituals and the beneficiaries who received the blessings and merits, nor did they mention any particular historical and geographical information.

The second set of invocation texts did not use the title "*qiqingwen*" on the manuscripts, but the contents contain the procedures of a specific historical invocation ritual. However, these manuscripts focus on other liturgical rituals, such as creating the ritual space (Wang 2018, 23–50), distributing food, and turning the dharma wheel. This group also has three manuscripts, including S. 2144, S. 3427 in the Stein Collection, and BD07677 at the National Library of China in Beijing (Huang and Wu 1995, 562–576). These manuscripts did not use the title "*qiqingwen*;" instead, their titles are written as "Jietan Sanshi Huixiang Fayuanwen," (結壇散食迴向發願文, lit., *Prayer for Creating Ritual Space, Distributing Food, and Transferring Merits*). The content of this text explains the detailed procedures for invoking various Buddhist saints and deities, creating ritual space, feeding ghosts, etc. The patrons of the ceremony and the recipients of the merits, whose names and titles were given in this passage, were mentioned. A specific historical and geographical context is also given and may be used to analyze this work.

Since we have both general model prayers and particular prayers from Dunhuang, we may compare them to other texts preserved in the canonical literature and, in some cases, trace the differences and similarilties of the invocation ritual's structure and practices back in time. Here I take account of two sets of differences: those between the Dunhuang texts generally and the cannonical literature; and those between the two types of Dunhuang invocation texts. This study will also note the similarities and shared elements between different genres and rituals, which I propose as the commonalities between the invocation ritual texts.

2 The Invocation Prayer as the Text and the Act

As I briefly noted above, the generic invocation prayers differ from those that focus on a specific invocation ritual. The former are contained in three manuscripts, including S. 5957, S. 3875, and S. 5456, and the latter in other three manuscripts, S. 2144, S. 3427, and BD07677. Although they both mention the invocation ritual, the invocation ritual was the central theme in the generic prayer model texts. In the historical prayers, the invocation ritual was mentioned as the cornerstone for performing other rituals, such as creating ritual space (*jietan*, 結壇) and distributing food (*sanshi*, 散食) to feed gods, deities, and ghosts. The generic invocation prayers did not specify any historical figures and places. They merely claimed that a Buddhist disciple (*dizi*, 弟子) performed the invocation ritual to bring various Buddhist saints and worthies to the ritual space and to attest the virtues of the host, whilst also performing the confession ritual. The main section of these generic invocation liturgy texts just listed various Buddhas,

Bodhisattvas, Buddhist saints, deities, guardians, and other gods. These prayers often clarified what the host should expect from each group of Buddhist saints and worthies.

The generic prayers in the Dunhuang manuscripts are more concise than many other canonical texts introducing invocation rituals. Usually, they list the names and titles of Buddhist saints and worthies. For instance, manuscript S. 5957 listed several groups of invoked targets. The first group referred to the highest class of Buddhist saints-Buddhas, including all the Buddhas from the ten directions; Tathāgatas of three ages; Dharma-body of the Thusness; ten billion Tathāgatas in the Lotus-womb Realm; one thousand manifested Buddhas from the great Bhadrakalpa; Vimalakīrti who wore white robes; the Tathāgata under the Bodhi tree who subdued the demons; the Great Awakened One who lived in the Tuṣita Palace and transformed the devas; Śākyamuni and his five hundred disciples; Akṣobhya Buddha of the eastern world; Candrasūryapradipa Buddha of the southern world; Amitāyuṣ Buddha of the western world; and Duṃdubhisvaranirghoṣa Buddha of the northern world. The ritual host, a layperson, prayed to them for descending to the ritual space to attest his merits and virtues while confessing (Skt. *kṣama āpatti pratideśana*).

The second group included five-vehicle hidden classics of the celestial realm and nāga palace; twelve divisions of scriptures; the great Nirvana mountains; and the great Prajñāpāramitā seas. Apparently, these are various divisions of Mahāyāna Buddhist texts. Furthermore, the *pratyekabuddha* without learning; the *arhat* without delusion; three worthies; and ten saints were also invoked. They were called by the host in order to inspire their compassionate minds. They would thus stand up from their meditation and come to the ritual space.

The next group included four heavenly kings, such as Dhṛtarāṣṭra of the east; Virūḍhaka of the south; Virūpākṣa of the west and Vaiśravaṇa of the north. Their attendants, including various demons and Yakṣa groups, were also called upon. In addition, Śakro devānām of the upper realm was invoked to bring his attendants, including the sun and moon lords; five officers of constellations; thirty-two deities; and four great guardians. Then, the Prthivi from the lower realm was invoked to bring all-mountain and river deities. Other invoked beings include deities of three realms and nine *bhūmi*s; twenty-eight sections; Nārāyaṇa deity; Pāñcika general; Guhyapāda Vajra; the saint king of wheel-turning; the kind god of stupa protection; the god of protecting saṃghārāma; various Bodhisattvas from three refuges and five precepts, Yama King, man-eating Rākṣasa, demonic king of spreading disease, the great god of five paths, the Lord of Mount Tai, the officer of the Lifespan and the Controller of the Emoluments, and other petty demons. These are various guardians of Buddhism. Many of them are demons who were transformed and tamed by the Buddha. They were invoked to appear in the ritual space to attest to the merits and virtues of the host.

Looking into this list, the Buddhist saints and worthies differ significantly from what we see in other canonical texts. First, the Chinese names for the first three Buddhas of the east, south, and west precisely matched those that appeared in the *Amitabha Sūtra* but not in other canonical texts. However, this does not mean that the *Amitābha Sūtra* was the scriptural foundation for the generic invocation prayers from Dunhuang. The list of Buddhas in the *Amitābha Sūtra* is much more comprehensive. For example, in the *Amitābha Sūtra*, in the east, there were Akṣobhya, Merudhvaja, Mahāmeru, Meruprabhāsa, and Mañjughoṣa Buddhas; in the south, there were Candrasūryapradipa, Yaśḥprabha, Mahārciskaṃdha, Merupradipa, and Arantavirya; in the west, there were Amitāyuṣ, Amitaskṃdha, Amitadhvaja, Mahāprabha, Mahāraśmiprabha, Mahāratnaketu, and Śuddharaśmi; and in the north, there were Mahārcislaṃdha, Duṃdubhisvaranirghoṣa, Duṣpradharṣa, Ādityasaṃbhava, and Jaleniprabha (T 12, no. 366, 347b18–348a6). In addition, these Buddhas appearing the *Amitābha Sūtra* were the objects being praised, not invoked.

Given that the generic invocation prayers from Dunhuang served as models, these prayers seem not to fall into any specific sectarian tradition of Chinese Buddhism and Buddhist communites in the Dunhuang area showed little sectarian inclination at that time. Supposedly, the model prayers, which might have been prepared by the ritual specialists—the monks from local temples—could be easily modified to fit various occasions.

Now I will compare the generic invocation prayers and the particular historical liturgical prayers that mentioned the invocation ritual in the Dunhuang texts. The manuscript S. 2144 is titled, *Prayer for Creating the Ritual Space, Distributing Food, and Fransferring Merits*. In this case, various Buddhist saints and worthies were invoked to the ritual space for protecting the ritual space and attesting the virtues and merits of the ritual hosts. The manuscript S. 2144 seems to be a prayer used in a historical ritual event, and it describes specific hosts, length, associated activities, and goals of the ritual. S. 2144 tells us that the Grand Mentor (Taifu, 太傅) and his family were the hosts. According to Rong Xinjiang (榮新江), Taifu was the title of Cao Yuanzhong (r. 944–974,) who received this title in 947. He was the powerful military commander of the Guiyijun Circuit in Dunhuang in the 10th century (Rong 2015; Rong 2004, 57–62). The manuscript said that the Grand Mentor hosted a ritual space for five days and five nights in the southeast corner of Dunhuang county. While serving the ritual, the Grand Mentor offered pure food (vegetarian food); incense and lamps; money and wealth; five grains; flowers and fruits; and music, six times to the Buddhist saints.

Once the ritual space was set up, the Grand Mentor respectfully invited various Buddhist saints and worthies. Interestingly, manuscript S. 2144 does not use the term *qiqing*, (啓請) that appeared in S. 5957. *Qiqing* in Chinese literarily means "invite with the petition," indicating a complete formal request with written text. Instead, S. 2144 uses the term *fengqing* (奉請) which literarily means "invite with respect" in Chinese. Focusing on Greek religious texts, Chrysi Kotsifou notes that there were two different genres in Greek literature: prayers and petitions. He explains that: "Petitions were letters sent to the king or other civil authorities requesting redress, while in the same fashion, a prayer on papyrus was sent to a deity appealing for justice" (Kotsifou 2016, 168). This might help us understand why the generic invocation prayers used the word *qiqing*.

The list of invoked saints and worthies was also hierarchically ordered in the liturgical prayers from Dunhuang. This hierarchical order is reminiscent of the seminal study of Arthur Wolf on the Chinese system of hierarchical gods, (Wolf 1974, 131–182). In his study, Wolf argues that the hierarchical god system in the Chinese religious tradition, from the kitchen god to the Jade Emperor, mirrored the hierarchical political order of the Chinese empire, from the household to the central court. Given the host's actions, as the manuscript described, such as offering money and wealth, vegetarian food, etc., *qiqing* could also mean "invite with offerings or presenting offerings to the saints." Nevertheless, inviting with respect was to bring the saints to the ritual space, similar to the action described in the generic invocation prayer. Thus, it was also an invocation ritual.

The list of the Buddhist saints and worthies in manuscript S. 2144 was far more comprehensive than that in the generic invocation prayers such as S. 5957, and it covered all figures that appeared in S. 5957, though it used different names. The list in manuscript S. 2144 begins with numerous Buddhas, including, the three bodies of the Buddhas and the Buddhas of four cardinal realms; and the Buddhas of the ten directions and the three ages. The host invited them to the ritual space in the southeastern corner of Dunhuang to receive numerous offerings and protect the host, his princess wife, and his entire family. The host family was the primary receiver of the blessings and protection, indicating that the ritual was largely a family event. The wife of the ritual host is called the princess, referred to as the princess of Khotan. This further confirms that the ritual host was Cao Yuanzhong because Cao was married to the princess of the Khotan Kingdom.

The Buddhas in the first group of the long list in S. 2144 starts with three bodies of the Buddha, including Dharma-body (Skt. *dharmakāya*), i.e. Vairocana; subtle body of limitless form (Skt. *saṃbhogakāya*), i.e. Locanabuddha; and manifested-body (Skt. *nirmā ṇakāya*), i.e. Śākyamuni. These three-body Buddhas do not explicitly appear in the list of manuscript S. 5957. However, the following group of Buddhas from four cardinal realms appear in both S. 2144 and S. 5957. Yet, only two names in S. 2144 and S. 5957 are the same: Candrasūryapradipa Buddha of the southern world and Duṃdubhisvara-nirghoṣa Buddha of the northern world. S. 2144 invited Bhaiṣajyaguru Buddha of the twelve upper vows of the eastern world and the Amitabha Buddha of the western paradise realm. The Bhaiṣajyaguru Buddha of the twelve upper vows seems to first appear in the *Consecration Sūtra* (*Guanding jing*, 灌頂經, Skt. *Mahābhiṣekamantra*, juan 12) translated by Śrīmitra in the early 4th century CE, (T 21, no. 1331, 532b07–533a20). Yet the Amitabha Buddha, of course, is the prominent figure in the *Amitābha Sūtra*. Therefore, manuscript S. 2144 more explicitly refers to the *Amitābha Sūtra* tradition, even though it also briefly mentions all Buddhas of the ten directions and the three ages, in contrast to manuscript S. 5957. According to some other manuscripts indicated, Cao Yuanzhong indeed sponsored the copying and spreading of the *Amitābha Sūtra* and the making of the *Amitābha Sūtra* transformation tableau (*Amituo jing bian*, 阿彌陀經變) on the southern wall of the Yulin Cave 19 for making merits.

Then, the second group in the list of manuscript S. 2144 refers to various Bodhisattvas, which could not be found in manuscript S. 5957. These Bodhisattvas were numerous, coming from all the ten directions and the three ages. Yet, the manuscript lists Mañjuśrī, the great saint from the top of the Clear and Cool Mountains (Qingliangshan, Mount Wutai), as the first Bodhisattva in this group. It is followed by the great saint Samantabhadra; the great saint and great compassionate Cintāmaṇicakra Bodhisattva; the great benevolent and suffering-saving Avalokiteśvara Bodhisattva; the great compassionate Mahāsthāmaprāpta Bodhisattva; and the great saint and great benevolent Kṣitigarbha Bodhisattva. Many paintings of these Bodhisattvas, also discovered in the Dunhuang cave library, provide evidence for their visual existence during the Guiyijun dynasty (Chen 2021, 1–36). To this group, the host prayed to protect the entire family and the people he ruled in Dunhuang, which demonastrates a clear locality of this historical invocation prayer.

The third group in the list includes those who did not need further learning (*wuxue*, 無學); *pratyekas*; *arhats* who entered the dhyana; and other saints who possessed six supernatural powers (divine eye, divine ear, telepathy, etc.). These saints also appeared in manuscript S. 5957, though named differently. The fourth group includes four heavenly kings; Śakro devānām; Pṛthivī; their attendants; and other gods and deities such as the twenty-eight sections; Nārāyaṇa deity; Pāñcika general; Guhyapāda vajra; the saint king of wheel-turning; the kind god of protecting stupas; the god of protecting *saṃghārāma*; Yama King; man-eating Rākṣasa; the demonic king of spreading disease; the great god of five paths; the Lord of Mount Tai; the officer of the Lifespan and the Controller of the Emoluments; and other petty demons, etc. These names are mostly identical to those in manuscript S. 5957 but there are slightly more in number in the former than the latter. The fifth group includes various demons and ghosts. The sixth group refers to the gods of the river and *nāga* kings in the seas. All of these groups received the offerings of food, flowers, incense, lamps, candles, five grains, fruits, music, etc. They were expected to bring merit and blessings to the entire Cao family and all people under the regime of the Guiyijun circuit.

The detailed comparison above regarding the lists of Buddhist saints and worthies between two manuscripts, S. 5957 and S. 2144, reveals that only the first and second groups of the Buddhist saints are different. The historical prayer S. 2144 has a lengthier and more detailed list. Thus, it might be concluded that the original generic invocation prayer only served as a model for hosts to enrich if they preferred. The local temple's monks who tried to interact with the area's lay patrons may have originated the idea of it being a model. During the Guiyijun period, the Cao family was the most influential in the Dunhuang region, and they prayed to a vast array of Buddhist saints and worthies. The listings of the Buddhas and Bodhisattvas in the manuscript S. 5957 are thus more detailed and explicit. While comparing the lists of Buddhas, Bodhisattvas, gods, demons, and deities in several different manuscripts from Dunhuang, it seems that the lists of Buddhas and Bodhisattvas were slightly different, depending on the different hosts; yet the lists of gods, demons, and deities were similar. In other words, the lists for gods, demons, and deities were more generic, rather than specific. This difference might reflect that the local ritual host paid attention to the hierarchy within the Buddhist cosmological order.

3 Understanding the Invocation Ritual in the Prayers from Dunhuang

Beyond comparing various types of Dunhuang manuscripts with each other, it is also interesting to compare the prayers from Dunhuang with the canonical texts. This might help us understand the canonicity and locality of the ritual prayers. Although the generic invocation and historical liturgical prayers did not reflect many features of particular sectarian inclinations, the canonical materials often limited themselves to a specific doctrinal tradition, such as the Pure Land tradition. One of the most popular texts in the Pure Land tradition for performing rituals was the *Eulogy for the Dharma Events of Turning Scriptures and Circumambulating for Vowing to be Reborn in the Pure Land* (*zhuanjing xingdao yuan wangsheng jingtu fashi zan*, 轉經行道願往生净土法事贊, T no. 1979). This text was written by Shandao (善導, 613–681 CE). This eulogy shows that the central icon that could be respectfully invited was the Amitabha Buddha. Nonetheless, at the outset of this text, it is stated that the host and donor of the ritual would like to welcome all World-honored Ones and the Buddhas of the ten directions. Then it says that the eighty-four thousand scriptures of the treasury will be invited, followed by the relics of whole and dismembered bodies. These invitees will emit divine lights in the ritual space to attest to the virtues and merits of the host.

The next group of invitees includes the *śrāvaka*s and *pratyeka*s of the ten directions and the enlightened saints. Then, the next group has Samantabhadra, Mañjuśrī, Avalokiteśvara, and Mahāsthāmaprāpta, according to the order of appearance in the text. This Pure Land eulogy mentions *arhats* and *pratyeka*s, Buddhist saints with six supernatural powers, as well as other gods and deities, such as officers from heavenly and underground realms; gods of Mount Tai and the Five Paths; and various mountain and river deities (T 47, no. 1979, 430b20–24). But the list in this eulogy is far briefer than those in the Dunhuang manuscripts. However, all lists from the prayers and the eulogy include the deities of Mount Tai, which were from the indigenous Chinese tradition, rather than from the earlier Buddhist tradition in South Asia. This is not surprising since these texts were produced in the Chinese cultural sphere. Shandao's text is more specific when highlighting the Amitabha Buddha out of all Buddhas in the cosmic world. In contrast, Cao Yuanzhong's prayer is from Dunhuang is neither exclusively nor explicitly associated with the Pure Land tradition.

Shandao's eulogy text mentions the relics of the Buddha, which is worth noting since neither of the Dunhuang's prayers mention them. Even though relics played essential roles in many of the activities of the Buddhist community in the Central Plain, it's possible that no relics were ever discovered or recovered in the Dunhuang region. Additionally, local adherents may never have cared whether relics were present in their ritual practices (Kieschnick 2003, 48–52; Chen 2002, 33–150; Chen 2007, 57–92). It might be the case that in the Dunhuang area when the ritual space was created, some visual images of the Buddhas and Bodhisattvas were used to symbolize the presence of these saints. Since so many Buddhas and Bodhisattvas were mentioned, this ritual would have no main icon, which makes it different from other Buddhist rituals, such as the ordination ritual. The relics and images of the Buddhas were used in the ordination ritual, as indicated in the *Illustrated Scripture for Establishing the Ordination Platform within the Pass* (*Guanzhong chuangli jietan tujing*, 關中創立戒壇圖經) by Daoxuan (道宣, 596–667CE). According to this text, the ordination ritual was performed by three principal masters and seven witness masters who would ascend onto the ordination platform. These ten masters performed the invocation ritual that brought cosmic Buddhas and Bodhisattvas to the ordination platform (T 45, no. 1892, 815a6–816b20). Daoxuan also observed that the Buddha' images were erected on the platform during the ceremonial performance. Their relics were honored there, indicating the Buddhas' presence in a symbolic gesture. Although Daoxuan traced the rise of the ordination platform and ritual back to the historical Buddha, his text explains that all cosmic Buddhas and Bodhisattvas would be invoked to attend this ritual performance. Daoxuan seemed to value images and relics symbolizing Buddhist divine figures.

Daoxuan's ordination ritual was designed to ordain monks. Huisi (515–577), a master honored by his followers as the second patriarch in the Tiantai tradition, wrote a text to serve as the manual for ordaining the Bodhisattva precept. There is also a ritual of invocation in this ritual of the Bodhisattva ordination. The Bodhisattva precept receiver would respectfully invite various Buddhist saints and worthies. The list begins with three principal masters such as Śākyamuni, Nāgarāja Buddha, and Maitreya Buddha. It also mentions present Buddhas from the ten directions as witness masters and the Bodhisattvas of the ten directions as companions. In addition to these Buddhas and Bodhisattvas, the list of invitees they have also includes every other Buddha in the three ages and the twelve divisions of scriptures; numerous guardians and the eight-sections beings; officers from the celestial and underground palaces; the lord of Mount Tai; other officers in charge of registers and lifespan; the general of five paths; the messengers of the path; the gods and deities of the five mountains and the four rivers; city gods; earth gods, etc. All of these guests were summoned to the ritual area to observe the qualities and virtues of the Bodhisattva ordination recipient (X 59, no. 1085, 350a3–351b23 // R 105, 1a1–4a08; Oka 2005, 27–44). This text mentions neither images nor relics. The three Buddhas often appear individually in other texts but do not appear in the same text elsewhere. The rest of the gods and deities in Huisi's list seem aligned with some of the other lists in the Dunhuang prayers that I have discussed above. The differences and similarities again attested to the fact that the invocation rituals in various traditions were similar in structure. Still, they were diverse in terms of which of the the highest class of Buddhist saints—the Buddhas—appeared as main characters.

It is unclear if there would have been one image depicting many Buddhas or several images depicting each Buddha used in the ritual events in the Dunhuang area. However, in other traditions in the Central Plain, the case might be different. This difference may be regarded as the difference between the canonical tradition and the vernacular tradition. For instance, in his study of a medieval Chinese Buddhist text entitled *Treasure Store Treatise* (*Baozang lun* 寶藏論, 5th century CE), Robert H. Sharf noted that in the Mahāyāna tradition, sentient beings can stimulate the Buddhas and Bodhisattvas who appear in resonant bodies to offer the grace and blessings to the invocators. He also concludes that these invocation practices, ritual empowerment, and divine grace are not associated with any single Buddhist tradition or movement. He writes that,

> Buddhist invocation rites—the mainstay of Mahāyāna praxis—involve the ritual transformation of the physical sanctuary into a buddha-realm populated by one or more Buddhist deities, followed by confession, vows, offerings, recitation of scripture, transference of merit, and so on. The entire rite is performed before the principal icon (*pen-tsun* 本尊)—the manifest body of a buddha, bodhisattva, or other divine being that functions as the central object of devotion, the primary recipient of offerings, and a major source of the rite's efficacy (Sharf 2002, 116).

For the principal icon, Sharf links the invocation rites with the ritual worship of icons such as in the *Scripture on the Production of Buddha Images* (*Zuo fo xingxiang jing*, 作佛形像經, T no. 692) and the *Scripture on Consecrating and Washing an Image of the Buddha* (*Guanxi fo xingxiang jing*, 灌洗佛形像經, T no. 695). The *Lotus Sutra*'s veneration of stupas, Buddhas (both past and present), and celestial Bodhisattvas is further evidence of this idolatry of images. Sharf also wrote: "The ultimate goal of such invocation rites, particularly in a monastic context, is to discern (*kuan*, 觀) or see (*chien*, 見) the body of the buddha being invoked." (Sharf 2002, 117) However, this is not the case in the Dunhuang area during the Guiyijun period. The generic invocation prayers had no principal icon, such as in S. 5957. In the meantime, the cosmic worlds in the invocation prayers and historical prayers were complicated since there were not only Buddhas, Bodhisattvas, and other divine beings present but also various gods, deities, and even demons, including local ones from the Dunhuang area. In addition, besides the *Scripture on the Production of Buddha Images* and the *Scripture on Consecrating and Washing an Image of the Buddha,* as Sharf mentions, another text entitled the *Scripture of Making Images for Merits and Virtues* (*Zaoxiang gongde jing,* 造像功德經) was also prevalent in the medieval period, as both the Chinese and Khotanese versions attested. This might be due to the promotion of the text by Emperor Wu Zetian (see Duan 2013, 109–168).

The Huayan (Skt. Avataṃsaka) perspective on the invocation ritual appeared in the *Manual for Cultivation and Verification in the Ritual Space of the Perfect Enlightenment Sutra* (*Yuanjuejing daochang xiuzheng yi,* 圓覺經道場修證儀) by Zongmi (宗密, 780–841CE, see X 74, no. 1475, 379c). This ritual manual preserved many liturgical texts, including one entitled, *The Repentance Liturgy for the Cultivation and Verification in the Ritual Space of the Perfect Enlightenment Sutra,* which offered eight ways of performing the repentance ritual. This text claims that, though all Buddhas and holy beings are omnipotently present everywhere, they do not manifest themselves if a Buddhist practitioner does not demonstrate sincerity of devotion. Therefore, the practitioner should always contemplate the Buddhas clearly in mind to invoke them. This claim has its scriptural foundation in the *Avataṃsakasūtra* (T 10, no. 279, 276b). Zongmi further explains the doctrinal foundation of the Huayan tradition for invoking the Buddha. He insists that the practitioner must understand the mutual relationship between the principle and phenomenon for purifying the mind in order to have the fortune to receive a response from the Buddha and for the Buddha to manifest himself following the performance of the invocation ritual.

Some details about the invocation ritual in the Huayan tradition reveals that the procedure was not so different from the rituals in other traditions. Several steps in the rituals—such as the one from the Dunhuang invocation prayers—could be compared to those in other traditions. The ceremonial space was set up and decorated, and the Buddhist saints were invoked. Countless offerings were made to the saints, the saints were eulogized, and the saints were circumcised to pay reverence, etc. Nonetheless, the Huayan invocation rite included several unique elements that set it apart from other cultures. Zongmi's text mentions that the practitioners should kneel in the ritual space and eulogise the saints by reciting Sanskrit syllables as mantra, or true words. His text also suggests that the ritual performer should call the names of the Buddhas and Bodhisattvas to bring them to the ritual space. This might be called "the invocation of addressing names" (*chengming qiqing,* 稱名啓請). This verbal invocation technique does not explicitly appear in the invocation prayers from Dunhuang. However, the prayer manuscripts offered a list of the Buddhas and Bodhisattvas in written form.

Zongmi's text highlights the centrality of the Vairocana Buddha, which could be regarded as the principal icon (*benzun* ,本尊) in the invocation ritual here. According to Zongmi's liturgical text, the Vairocana Buddha was *both* the *dharmakāya* (the actual Dharma body) and *saṃbhogakāya* (the retribution body) of the Buddha. He served as the only principle for the ritual; the wisdom of the ten directions; the principal origin of sentient and holy beings manifested by entering the Great Light Store in the *Scripture of Perfect Enlightenment*. Following the manifestation of Vairocana Buddha, all the other millions of Buddhas in the *Scripture of Perfect Enlightenment* would be invoked to the ritual space. For example, there was Śākyamuni Buddha, who has great compassion and benevolence and will manifest himself by sympathetic resonance in billions of different forms. There was also the Prabhūtaratna (多寶如來); the Bhaiṣajyaguruvaiḍūrya-prabhāsa Buddha (藥師琉璃光如來); and Amitābha Buddha. After a long list of Buddhas in the text, the next group of Buddhist saints lists numerous Bodhisattvas whose names are found in the *Scripture of Perfect Enlightenment*, including Mañjuśrī, Samantabhadra, and Avalokiteśvara. The heavenly kings and their attendants; numerous guardians; demigods, and deities follow. Interestingly, Zongmi also mentioned the names of two divine deities from local mountains—the divine king of the Mountain Guifeng (*Guifeng shanshen wang* 圭峰山神王) and the deity of the Mountain Purple Pavilion (*Zige shanshen* 紫閣山神). These local mountain gods are listed alongside other gods who guarded the ritual space, such as the god who guarded the Dharma; the god who guarded the temple; the god of the ritual space; the god of the region; the god of the land; the god of fire; the god of wind; the god of the mountain; the god of emptiness; and the god of medicine. The names of these deities differ slightly from those in Dunhuang's invocation prayers.

In this Huayan ceremonial text, the non-Buddhist saints and worthies are hardly any different from those in other customs. Consequently, here again, this demonstrates that the Buddhas or the main icons are the primary distinction between the Huayan tradition and other traditions in terms of their invocation ceremonies. The invocation ritual is called Āvāhana in Sanskrit. It has a long history in ancient South Asia as a ritual of "calling" the deity to be present in the image (skt. *mūrti*) worship. The Āvāhana was one of sixteen offerings/services (Skt. *upacāras*) as parts of puja in ancient Vedic religion. In the ancient South Asian culture, the *mūrti* could indicate a concretion, personification, and manifestation of the deity (Parmeshwaranand 2001, 328; Czerniak-Drożdżowicz 2017, 171–197; Mishra 2019, 290). In two ways, the invocation ritual in the prayer from Dunhuang followed a pattern similar to the Āhvān rite in ancient South Asia: first, it used an image to signify the presence of holy beings, and second, it called for gods and deities to appear as images. A great abundance of offerings were made to these gods and deities. Yet, different lineages and geographical sites of Chinese Buddhism had different lists of gods and deities who were called upon. In some traditions, their central gods were highlighted. Yet in the generic prayers, there was space for a ritual host to choose different icons.

The ritual, as it appears in the generic invocation prayer, includes the following steps: the ritual host invokes the gods and deities; gods and deities descend to the ritual space; they receive the offerings provided by the host; the gods and deities protect the ritual space; the host confesses; and the gods and deities witness the virtues and merits of the host. However, this is the simplest structure of the invocation ritual, as manifested in the prayer. Historical prayers would add new elements to this list of steps, such as making vows and feeding ghosts. Armin W. Geertz attempted to develop a more general structure of the prayer (Geertz 2008, 137–138). According to him, a prayer should contain the following things: a petition; an invocation; a supplication; an intercession; a thanksgiving; an act of worship; a dedication; a benediction; an act of repentance; and a confession. Further components of prayer as a language and speech act are the acts that Invoke, name, commit, promise, declare, affirm, convince, intend, command, and move (Geertz 2008, 137–138). The historical prayers indeed have more elements than the generic invocation prayers. The host, the host's family, the subjects under his rule, etc., were recorded as the recipients of the blessings in the ancient prayers of the Cao family. Consequently, it may be possible to condense Geertz's list so that his framework can also be used to comprehend the invocation prayers from Dunhuang. The invocation, supplication, benediction, repentance, and confession are the main components of invocation prayers from Dunhuang.

4 Conclusions

As a ritual for inviting gods and divine beings to communicate with the hosts, the invocation ritual played a crucial role in medieval Chinese Buddhism, spanning from the Central Plain to the frontier regions, especially Dunhuang. The invocation ritual called the divine beings to the ritual space to witness the virtues and merits of the host, protecting the ritual space and bestowing blessings upon the sentient beings who worshiped the divine beings. This study has illustrated that these divine beings varied between traditions and between regions. Some traditions, such as Tiantai, Pure Land, Huayan, and Vinaya traditions in medieval China, developed their own particular Buddhas as the principal icons, choosing from numerous Buddhas of the ten directions and the three ages which fall under the massive umbrella of the Mahāyāna tradition. This is evidence for the diversity of the invocation ritual.

In medieval Dunhuang, there were two sets of liturgical prayers directly related to the invocation ritual: the generic and the historical liturgical prayers. They were not explicitly associated with a particular sectarian or learning tradition. However, when comparing the texts of these two sets of prayers, one notes that the first group of divine beings to be invoked (i.e. the Buddhas) differ substantially. The generic invocation prayers are written models for the ritual hosts to perform. The historical liturgical prayers supported by the Military Governor of the Guiyijun regime reveal the host's individual preferences for particular Buddhas. For the host, his family, and those who lived under his dominion to receive more merit and benefit, the highest divine beings were the most important. The lists of secondary groups, including the Bodhisattvas and the less powerful divine beings, have more similarities and familiar features in different invocation ritual layouts, which may indicate the commonality of the invocation ritual throughout the Chinese Empire during the medieval period. However, the location of the flexible invocation topics is reflected in the fact that the mountain deities in the final group frequently shifted between regions.

Appendix: The English Translation of S. 5957: The Generic Invocation Prayer in the Dunhuang Manuscripts (Huang and Wu 1995, 407–408)

A Disciple, someone, and all participants at present in this ritual space invoke spectacular minds. We take refuge and invoke the Buddhas of the ten directions, the *tathāgatas* of the three ages, whose profundity was like the emptiness, and was the same as the thusness and the Dharma Body. In the lotus womb realm, there were ten billion *tathāgatas*. In the great Bhadrakalpa, there were one thousand manifested Buddhas. The one who swore to reside in the three realms was the king of Virtue Mountain. The companion who wore white robes was Vimalakīrti. The *tathāgata* who conquered Mara was present under the Bodhi Tree. The great enlightened one who changed heaven resided at the Tusita Palace. There were sixteen princes and Mahbhijnbhibh before the endless kalpas. After the kalpas, as numerous as the sands of the Ganges River, there were Śākyamuni and his five hundred disciples. Akṣobhya came from the eastern world. Candrasūryapradipa came from the southern world. Amitāyus came from the western world. Duṃdubhisvaranirghoṣa came from the northern world. Around all four cardinal dimensions, all Buddhas came like this. All Dharma Bodies came from various infinite realms. In each of these infinite worlds, there were hundreds and thousands of *tathāgatas*. For each of these infinite *tathāgatas*, the great assembly was as numerous as tiny dust particles; and each one in the assembly was a Bodhisattva. All Bodhisattvas possessed six supernatural powers, and they swore to save all sentient beings in the three realms. [We] only vow that these Buddhas and Bodhisattvas will depart from their diamond seats and leave Mount Cakravāḍa to come to the ritual space, witnessing the disciple perform repentance and confession.

Furthermore, [we] also invoke the mysterious classics of five vehicles in the heavenly and *nāga* palaces, and twelve-divisions of scriptures from Mount Gṛdhrakūṭa in the human world, from the Mahāparinirvana Mountain and the Mahāprājñāpāramitā

Sea. [We] invoke them to bestow their vitality for saving those who sunk. [We] also invoke the *pratyekas* without further learning, the *arhats* who detached from delusions, the three worthies and the ten saints (Mahāyāna Bodhisattvas), and those who possessed five eyes and six supernatural powers, hoping for them to aspire for their compassionate minds to rise from their meditations, in order to come to this ritual space.

Moreover, [we] invoke Dhṛtarāṣṭra, the heavenly king in the east, and all Gandharva deities and Piśācā demons as well as their attendants under his leadership, to this ritual space. [We] invoke Virūḍhaka, the heavenly king in the south, and all Kumbhāṇḍa deities and *preta* demons, as well as their attendants under his leadership, to this ritual space. [We] invoke Virūpakṣa, the heavenly king in the west, and all heavenly poisonous *nāgas* and *pūtana* demons and their attendants under his leadership to this ritual space. [We] invoke Vaiśravaṇa, the heavenly king in the north, and all *yakṣa* and *rākṣasa* as well as twenty-eight-section *yakṣa* generals and their attendants to this ritual space. [We] invoke Śakra Devānām Indra in the upper realm, Sūrya and Candra, five officers of constellations, thirty-two gods, four *vajras*, and their attendants to this ritual space.

Again, [we] invoke Prthivi in the lower realm, to lead all deities of mountains and rivers and their attendants to this ritual space. [We] invoke deities from the three realms and the nine earths, the twenty-eight divisions of deities, Nārāyaṇa, Pañcika, Guhyapāda, Cakravarti-raja, the kind deity for protecting stupas, the deity for protecting *saṁghārāma*, the deity for protecting the three refuges and five precepts, the deity for protecting the Bodhisattva treasury, Yama-rāja, the human-biting *rākṣasa*, the demonic king of plague, the five-path God, the lord of Mount Tai, the officer in charge of lifespan and register controller, the eight kings of five offices, the six houses of three months, the messenger of memorial for investigating documents, the judges for judging good and evil, the *kumāra*, *avīci*, *yakṣa*, and *rākṣasa*, *niraya*, and ox-head demons, and all deities with incredible divine and mighty powers like these. [We] implore them to fly in the sky and rain quickly like lighting and clouds running, coming to this ritual space, witnessing our virtues and merit cultivated in this ritual space. [We] vow to aspire the delighted minds to swear, confess and repent. Since we have all worthies and saints in this ritual space, with ultimate sincerity, we sincerely aspire to repentance and an ultimate mind for taking refuge, paying homage to the constant Three Jewels.

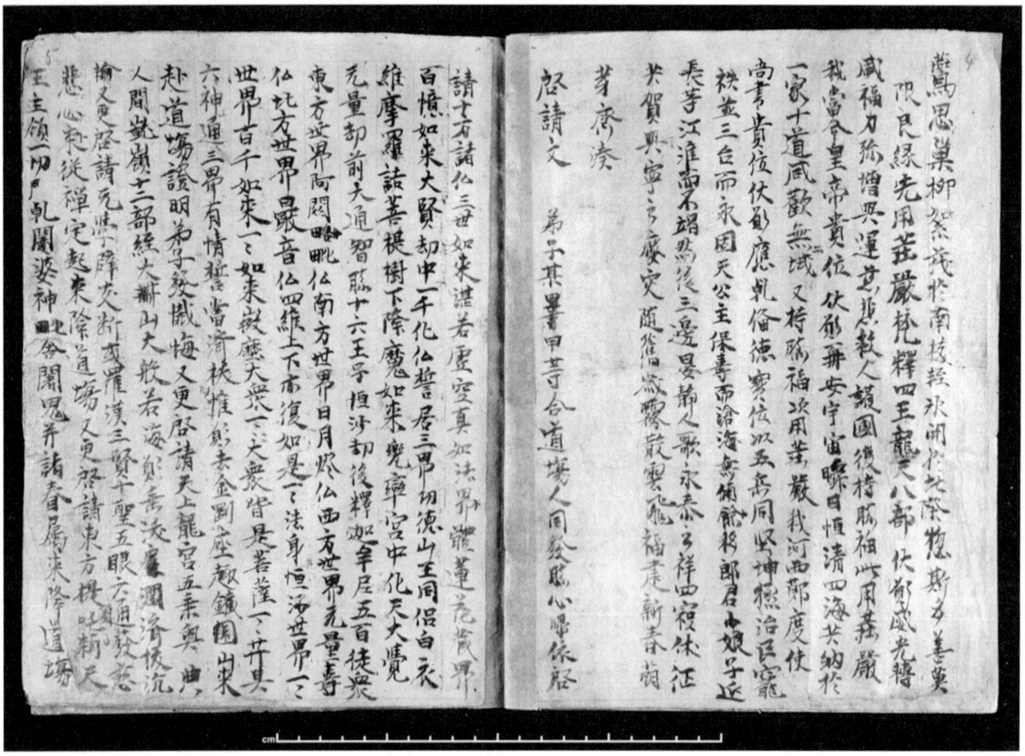

Dunhuang manuscript S. 5957
The picture is taken from the International Dunhuang Project website. © the British Library

Abbreviations

T *Taishō shinshū daizōkyō* 大正新修大藏經. Edited by Takakusu, Junjirō 高楠順次郎, and Watanabe Kaigyoku 渡邊海旭. Tokyo: Taishō issaikyō kankōkai 大正一切經刊行會, 1924–1932.

X *Manji shinsan zoku zōkyō* 卍新纂續藏經. Tokyo: Kokusho Kankokai, 1905–1912.

References

Chen 2021 Huaiyu Chen. "Making Four Buddhist Worlds: A Reading of the Liturgies for Creating Ritual Spaces in Dunhuang Manuscripts." *Hualin International Journal of Buddhist Studies* 4/2: 1–36.

2014 "Multiple Traditions in one Ritual: A Reading of the Lantern Prayers in Dunhuang Manuscripts." In: Tansen Sen, ed., *Buddhist across Asia: Networks of Material, Intellectual and Cultural Exchange*, 233–257. Singapore: Institute for South East Asian Studies and New Delhi: Manohar Publishers.

2008 "Dunhuang P. 2058v wenshu Zhong de Jie Dasuiqiu tan fayuanwen 敦煌P. 2058v文書中的結大隨求壇發願文." *Dunhuangxue* 敦煌學 27: 167–185.

2007 *The Revival of Buddhist Monasticism in Medieval China*. New York: Peter Lang.

Chen 2002 Jinhua Chen. "Sarira and Scepter: Empress Wu's Political Use of Buddhist Relics." *Journal of International Association of Buddhist Studies* 25/1–2: 33–150.

Czerniak-Drożdżowicz
2017 Marzenna Czerniak-Drożdżowicz. "At the Crossroads of Art and Religion: Image Consecration in the Pāñcarātrika Sources." In: Istvan Keul, ed., *Consecration Rituals in South Asia*, 171–197. Leiden: Brill.

Ding 2020 Ding Yi. "Divine Transactions: The Transformation of Buddhist Communal Liturgies at Dunhuang (8th–10th Centuries)." Ph.D. thesis, Stanford University.

Doney 2021 Lewis Doney. "Text, Act and Subject: A Proposed Approach to the Future Study of Old Tibetan Prayer." *Revue d'Etudes Tibétaines* 60: 49–83.

Duan 2013 Duan Qing 段晴. *Yutian, Fojiao, gujuan* 于闐，佛教，古卷. Shanghai: Zhongxi shuju.

Geertz 2008 Armin W. Geertz. "Comparing Prayer: On Science, Universals, and the Human Condition." In: Willi Braun and Russell T. McCutcheon eds., *Introducing Religion: Essays in Honor of Jonathan Z. Smith*, 113–139. London: Equinox.

Gill 2005 Sam Gill. "Prayer." In: Mircea Eliade, ed., *The Encyclopedia of Religion*, 489–493. New York: Macmillan.

Hao 1996 Hao Chunwen 郝春文. "Guanyu Dunhuang xieben zhaiwen de jige wenti 關於敦煌寫本齋文的幾個問題." *Shoudu shifan daxue xuebao* 首都師範大學報, no. 2: 64–71.

Huang and Li
1997 Huang Zheng 黄徵 and Li Danhe 李丹禾. "Dunhuang bianwen zhong de yuanwen 敦煌變文中的願文 [Prayers in the Transformation Texts from Dunhuang]." In: Xiang Chu, ed., *Dunhuang wenxue lunji* 敦煌文學論集 [Collected Papers on Dunhuang Literature], 363–370. Chengdu: Sichuan renmin chubanshe.

Huang and Wu
1995 Huang Zheng 黄徵 and Wu Wei 吴偉. *Dunhuang yuanwen ji* 敦煌願文集, Changsha: Yuelu shushe.

Kieschnick 2003 John Kieschnick. *The Impact of Buddhism on Chinese Material Culture*. Princeton: Princeton University Press.

Kotsifou 2016 Chrysi Kotsifou. "Prayers and Petitions for Justice: Despair and the 'Crossing of Boundaries' between Religion and Law." In: Thomas Corsten, Bernhard Palme, Hans Taeuber, eds., *Tyche: Beiträge zur Alten Geschichte, Papyrologie und Epigraphik*, 167–199. Wien: Holzhausen Verlag.

Mishra 2019 Ashok Mishra. *Hinduism: Ritual, Reason and Beyond*. Mumbai: StoryMirror Infotech Ltd.

Oka 2005 Oka Sumiaki 阿純章. "Jubosatsu kaigi no hensen: Shōjō sanbō no sahō o chūshin ni 受菩薩戒儀の変遷: 召請三宝の作法を中心に." *Higa ajia bukkyō kenkyū* 東アジア仏教研究 3: 27–44.

Parmeshwaranand
2001 Swami Parmeshwaranand. ed. *Encyclopaedic Dictionary of Purāṇas*. New Delhi, Sarup and Sons.

Rong 2015 Rong Xinjiang 榮新江. *Guiyijun shi yanjiu: Tang Song shidai Dunhuang lishi kaosuo* 歸義軍史研究：唐宋時代敦煌歷史考索. Shanghai: Shanghai guji chubanshe.

	2004	"Official Life at Dunhuang in the Tenth Century: The Case of Cao Yuanzhong." In: Susan Whitfield and Ursula Sims-Williams, eds., *The Silk Road: Trade, Travel, War and Faith*, 57–62. Chicago: Serindia Publications.
Sharf	2002	Robert H. Sharf. *Coming to Terms with Chinese Buddhism: A Reading of the Treasure Store Treatise*. Honolulu: University of Hawaii Press.
Teiser	2009	Stephen F. Teiser. "Ornamenting the Departed: Notes on the Language of Chinese Buddhist Ritual Texts." *Asia Major* 3rd series, 22/1: 201–237.
	2007a	"Shilun zhaiwen de biaoyanxing 試論齋文的表演性." *Dunhuang tulufan yanjiu* 敦煌吐魯番研究 10: 295–308.
	2007b	"Wei wangzhe yuan: Dunhuang yishi wenlei dingyi chutan 爲亡者願: 敦煌儀式文類定義初探." In: Li Fengmao 李豐楙 and Liao Zhaoheng 廖肇亨, eds., *Shengzhuan yu chanshi: Zhongguo wenxue yu zongjiao lunji* 聖傳與禪詩: 中國文學與宗教論集, 284–307. Taipei: Zhongyanyuan zhongguo wenzhe yanjiusuo.
Wolf	1974	Arthur Wolf. "Gods, Ghosts, and Ancestors." In: Arthur Wolf, ed., *Religion and Ritual in Chinese Society*, 131–182. Stanford: Stanford University Press.
Wang	2018	Michelle C. Wang. *Maṇḍalas in the Making: The Visual Culture of Esoteric Buddhism at Dunhuang*. Leiden: Brill.
Wang	2008	Wang Sanqing 王三慶. "Cong Dunhuang zhaiyuan wenxian kan Fojiao de zaidihua yinying 從敦煌齋願文獻看佛教的在地化因應." *Chengda zhongwen xuebao* 成大中文學報 21: 1–40.
Zhang	1997	Zhang Guangda 張廣達. "Tanfo yu tanzhai: Guanyu Dunhuang wenshu zhong de Zhaiwanwen de jige wenti '歎佛' 與 '歎齋': 關於敦煌文書中的齋琬文的幾個問題." In: Benshu bianweihui 本書編委會, ed., *Qingzhu Deng Guangming jiaoshou jiushi huadan lunweji* 慶祝鄧廣銘教授九十華誕論文集, 60–73. Shijiazhuang: Hebei jiaoyu chubanshe.

A Spicy Etymology

Remarks on Tocharian AB *śāñcapo*

CHEN Ruixuan and Chams Benoît BERNARD

Abstract: This paper argues that Tocharian AB *śāñcapo* is not a loanword from Sanskrit *śiṃśapā-* "*Dalbergia sissoo* Roxb.," as is traditionally assumed; but is the word for "mustard (seed)" corresponding to Sanskrit *sarṣapa-* "id." Having established this meaning, i.e., "mustard (seed)," on the basis of philological evidence, we put forward a new hypothesis of the etymology of the Tocharian word by tracing it back to the antecedent of Khotanese *śśaśvāna-* "mustard seed." It is thus likely that the word originated in a region where Pre-Khotanese was spoken, and found its way into Tocharian through language contact along the ancient Silk Routes.

Keywords: Tocharian, (Pre-)Khotanese, language contact, Central Asian Buddhism

In the past, spices were special.[1] That is to say, this generic term conveyed an aura of mystery, uniqueness, and rarity, which is no longer discernible today, when an array of spices becomes a plain-vanilla accessory in any quotidian kitchen. In the pre-modern world, however, there was no cheap and easily available spices in the European markets, as the spice trade across the Indian Ocean was still a costly enterprise.[2] At that time, spices had dazzling glamour, and their identification was sometimes not an easy task. In a different, but not irrelevant context, the present paper deals with the Tocharian word for a spicy substance, which has been misidentified by Western scholars since the very first attempt at its decipherment. Like the spice it designates, the word is as beguiling as it is opaque. Based on an exhaustive scrutiny of the occurrences of this word, we try to pin down its real meaning and venture a new hypothesis of its etymology. We offer this spicy etymology as a tribute to the late Professor Duan Qing, whose "spicy" scholarship gave a special, glamorous, and invaluable boost to many fields, such as Indology, Middle Iranian philology, Buddhist Studies, and beyond.

1.1 Received Meaning and Etymology

Tocharian A *śāñcapo*, B *śāñcapo* have been mostly identified as a loanword from Skt. *śiṃśapā-* f. "*Dalbergia sissoo* Roxb." (Filliozat 1948, 137; Adams 2013, 681), designating a kind of rosewood indigenous to North India, the knowledge of which in the West can be traced back to antiquity. Gerd Carling (2007, 331) points out that "[t]he A form is most

CHEN Ruixuan, Peking University. Chams Benoît BERNARD, Leiden University.

[1] As a matter of fact, both of the two words etymologically go back to Latin *speciēs* "aspect, appearance, kind" (later also pl. "goods, wares"); see Partridge 2006, 646, s.v. *special*.

[2] For a collection of essays dealing with the history of the spice trade from the 15th to the 17th century CE, see Pearson 1996.

likely a borrowing from B, but the B form remains obscure." In other words, how the Indic word was borrowed into Tocharian is not adequately clarified.

The putative Indic etymon is a *Kulturwort* of Ṛgvedic antiquity (EWAia II 633, s.v. *śiṃśápā-*). Elamite [GIŠ]*še-iš-šá-ba-ut* /šeššap°/[1] "sissoo" is attested in an Achaemenid inscription (6th cent. BC),[2] and is likely to be of the same origin as Skt. *śiṃśapā-* given the close resemblance (Gershevitch 1958, 174). Aramaic *sysm* סיסם "sissoo" is attested in the Samaritan Pentateuch (Löw 1881, 65), which, according to some experts, emerged sometimes between the late 2nd century BC and the early 1st century AD (Anderson and Giles 2012, 22). Slightly later in time, the Indic word also found its way into Greek as σησάμ- or σασάμ-,[3] from which an adjective in -ινος is derived, by the 1st century AD.[4] The latter form might be the source of Arabic *sāsam* "sissoo." Etymologically relevant is also New Persian *šīšam* "sissoo,"[5] which, in its turn, became the source of Hindi *śīśam*. Panjabi *sīsam*, Gujarati *sisam*, etc. should go back to a western Middle Indic prototype

---

[1] Note that Elamite ‹š› can render Old Persian /ç/ or /s/ (cf. Abedi 2020, 7–8).

[2] For an edition of the Elamite version of this inscription of Darius I (522–486 BC) at Susa [DS*f*], see Hinz 1950, 1–7. The word in question occurs in line 30 (p. 2), and Hinz's rendering of it as "teak" (pp. 3, 6) is not tenable.

[3] Both Aramaic *sysm* and Greek σησάμ- seem to have been borrowed through an early western Middle Indic intermediary such as Prakrit *sīsama* (< *sīsavā* < *śiṃśapā*; PSM 909a). For the nasalised -*ṽ*- and the nasalisation of secondary -*v*- (-*m*- < -*v*- < -*p*-/-*b*-) in Middle Indic, see von Hinüber 2001, 173, §§210–211. The alternation -η- : -α- is to be regarded as an inner-Greek development.

[4] See anonymous (ca. 40–70 AD), *Periplus Maris Erythraei*, §36 (ed. Casson 1989, 12, lines 4–7): ἐξαρτίζεται δὲ είς αὐτὴν συνήθως ἀπὸ μὲν Βαρυγάζων είς ἀμφότερα ταῦτα τῆς Περσίδος ἐμπόρια πλοῖα μεγάλα χαλκοῦ καὶ ξύλων σαγαλίνων καὶ δοκῶν καὶ κεράτων καὶ **φαλάγγων σασαμίνων** καὶ ἐβενίνων "Customarily the merchants of Barygaza [i.e., Broach; cf. Skt. Bhṛgukaccha] deal with it, sending out big vessels to both of Persis's ports of trade (sc. Apologos and Omana), with supplies of copper, teakwood, and beams, saplings, and **logs of sissoo** and ebony; [...]" (tr. Casson 1989, 13; annotation added). Dioscorides (ca. 40–80 AD), *De Materia Medica*, I.98 (ed. Wellmann 1907, 89, lines 13–14): ἔνιοι δὲ τὰ ἀκάνθινα ἢ καὶ συκάμινα [v.l. **σησάμινα**] **καλούμενα ξύλα**, ἐμφερῆ ὄντα, ἀντὶ ἐβένου πωλοῦσι "Some try to sell wood of the shittah tree and even **the wood called [sissoo]** as ebony, since they are similar; [...]" (tr. Beck 2005, 69; with modification). For a 6th-century reference to the sissoo wood in the *Christian Topography* by Cosmas Indicopleustes, see Wolska-Conus 1973, 346–347.

[5] This is not an inherited Iranian word, and probably does not predate New Persian. The inherited word for "sissoo" is Old Persian *yakā* > Middle/New Persian *jay* (MacKenzie 1971, 46); see Gershevitch 1957, 317–320. Balochi *jak* "sissoo" should be regarded as a Persian loanword; see Elfenbein 1990, II, 71. Brahui *jag* "id." is a borrowing from another Iranian language (ultimately from Middle/New Persian); see Rossi 1979, 81 [C5]. Turner traced New Persian *šīšam* back to a hypothetical Indic prototype **śīśampā* (CDIAL 719, §12424), which is to our mind not plausible. On the one hand, such a prototype is not borne out by any evidence from Old Indic materials; on the other, it fails to account for its relatively late emergence in the Persian-speaking world. Given that the sibilants *ś*, *ṣ*, *s* converge as *s* in the western Middle Indic languages, it is only possible to derive the New Persian word, which presupposes **śīśam(a)* < **śīśavā*, from the eastern languages or from Gāndhārī; see von Hinüber 2001, 177, §219. Geographically speaking, a Gāndhārī origin is more likely, despite the absence of textual evidence.

(e.g. Prakrit *sīsama*-; PSM 909a).[1] An unattested Middle Indic form **sīhava*- (< Prakrit *sīsavā*-)[2] seems to have been the source of some loanwords in Dardic and Eastern Iranian languages, e.g. Pashai *šəwa* "sissoo," Pashto *šəwə* "id." (Morgenstierne 2003, 80), while the other New Indic forms result from the contraction of Prakrit *sīsavā*- (> **sīsava* > **sīso* or **sisso*).[3]

Skt. *śiṃśapā*- and its cognates are thus both archaic and widespread. The question arises, however, whether TochAB *śāñcapo* can be assigned to the ample group of loanwords related to them.

1.2 Tocharian Occurrences

To begin with, we examine whether or not the received identification of TochAB *śāñcapo* as "sissoo" is philologically sound. The word occurs twice in Tocharian A and seven times in Tocharian B, and all nine occurrences will be classified and translated below.[4]

1.2. a) Or. 6402A/2.14 = W 26, b2 (ed. Filliozat 1948, 74): *(ṣa)lyp(e) ok=traunta se (ṣalype)* ***śāñcapotse*** **•** *misa* /// "... 8 *traus*[5] of oil, this oil **of *śāñcapo***, flesh ..."[6]

---

[1] Turner proposed to connect this group of words, together with Hindi *śīśam*, to New Persian *šīšam* (CDIAL 719, §12424). However, since a form such as Prakrit *sīsama* is well established in the western branch of Middle Indic, it is not a parsimonious theory to assume a Persian origin for this lexical group.

[2] Turner (CDIAL 719, §12424), following Morgenstierne (1956, 169), reconstructed **śīhava* as the source of the Pashai and Pashto words. To posit an initial *ś*- is perhaps unnecessary given the palatalising effect of the -*ī*- vowel. For the not fully clarified sound change -*s*- > -*h*- in Middle Indic, see von Hinüber 2001, 178, §221.

[3] See von Hinüber 2001, 133, §138.

[4] The transcription of the Tocharian passages follows CEToM unless indicated otherwise. Among the Tocharian names of *materia medica* and technical terms, only those stemming from Indic are denoted by their Sanskrit counterparts, which are given in round brackets.

[5] TochB *trau* ~ *troᵤ* (archaic) seems to be a measure of capacity, the size and etymology of which remain obscure; see Adams 2013, 342 ("about 2 teaspoonful?"). In a bilingual manuscript (U 5208 + 5207), it is glossed with Old Uighur *täŋ*; see Peyrot, Pinault, and Wilkens 2019, 82, §29. According to Wilkens (2021, 694), Old Uighur *täŋ* ~ *t(ä)ŋ* "equal, equivalent; scales; equanimity (Skt. *upekṣā*)" is a loanword from Late MChin. **təə̆ŋ* > *deng* 等 (Pulleyblank 1991, 74). But neither the Old Uighur lexeme nor the Chinese etymon seems to have been used as a measure of capacity. Alternatively it might be possible to consider it a variant of Old Uighur *taŋ* ~ *t(a)ŋ*, mostly attested as a measure of capacity for raw cotton (Yamada 1971, 496–498), which, in its turn, is presumably a loanword from Sogdian *δnk* /*θang*/ "id." (Yoshida 2003, 159); see also Khot. *thaṃga*- "id." (Bailey 1979, 148). The Khotanese word is also attested as a unit of measurement for cotton; however, in a bilingual document, it corresponds to Chin. *cheng* 秤 "a measurement of weight, ca. 15 catties (*jin* 斤) ≈ 3.38 kilograms (1 catty ≈ 225 grams; Chavannes 1897, 103, n. 2);" see Yoshida 2007, 470. Yamada (1971, 498), albeit with some reservation, proposed to relate Old Uighur *taŋ* to Chin. *dan* 擔, a larger unit of weight than *cheng* and *jin*.

[6] See also the French translation by Filliozat (1948, 85): "... huile, huit *trau*. Cette huile de Dalbergia sisu, viande ..."

1.2. b) i. PK AS 3B, b4–6: ‖ *ñake Bhūtatanträ weñau* ‖ *kayast vayast* • ***śāñcapo*** *– /// -po ṣp karañcapij • aṅwaṣṭ • pippāl mrañco • tvāṅkaro • kurkamäṣṣi ptsāñ okaro • śiriṣ toṃ saṃtkenta – /// -ne astare nanāṣṣusa klyiye tkācer wāltsoy se curṇ kuse salturna yāmu tākoy tesa nāṣṣi istak ast(are) ///* "Now I will speak of a *Bhūtatantra*[1] (lit. doctrine of spirits): cardamom (*kāyasthā*), small cardamom (*vayaḥsthā*), ***śāñcapo***, ... and ... seed of *Pongamia glabra* (*karañja-bīja*), *Asa foetida*, long pepper (*pippalī*), black pepper, ginger, saffron stigmas, sweet flag/*Acorus calamus*, siris/*Acacia lebbeck* (*śirīṣa*): These remedies (*śāntaka*) ... pure; a cleansed woman [or] daughter should crush [them]. This [is] the powder. If someone has been made bewitched,[2] he should bathe with it (i.e., the powder). Immediately [he will become] pure (i.e., cured) ..."[3]

ii. PK AS 3A, a1: *(ampo)ño mändrākka ṣamāṃ* ‖ *kuñcit wawāltsau* • ***śāñcapo*** • *ki – sintāp te śār yamaṣṣälle ampoñaṃtse sātke* ‖ "... just so the abscess sits down (i.e., goes away). Crushed sesame, [***śāñcapo***], ... rock salt (*saindhava*): This has to be put over [it] as a remedy (*śāntaka*) against abscess."[4]

---

[1] The *Bhūtatantra* refers to a genre rather than a specific scripture or treatise. This genre developed from the *Bhūtavidyā* (lit. "knowledge of spirits; demonology") as a system of exorcistic learning, which was well known in ancient India, particularly from the Āyurvedic tradition. Texts subsumed under the rubric of *Bhūtatantra* deal with ritualised procedures for the curing of demonic possession etc., and were systematised and incorporated into the Tantric corpus of Śaivism. For canonical lists of some twenty *Bhūtatantras* in later Śaiva works, see Sanderson 2001, 14, n. 13. Unfortunately, none of the listed titles are known to have survived in extant manuscripts. A fragmentary Sanskrit manuscript in Kathmandu, probably dating from the end of the 9th century AD, is so far the only known textual witness of this genre; see Acharya 2016, 157–179. We have not seen any evidence elsewhere for the Buddhist appropriation of this class of Śaiva literature. Viewed in this light, the historical significance of the brief allusion in a TochB fragment, which is linguistically categorised as "classical-late" (7th/8th cent. AD) and thus probably predates the aforesaid Sanskrit manuscript of "a" (rather than "the") *Bhūtatantra*, has yet to be fully appreciated.

[2] The word *salturna* is an obscure *hapax*, and the received meaning "bewitched" is very provisional. Sieg (1954, 69) read the *akṣaras* as *sal [ṣa]rn[e]*, and translated the clause in question as "Wer sich die Hände schmutzig(?) gemacht haben sollte, [...];" see also Schwentner 1955, 117. However, after close scrutiny of this fragment, Filliozat's reading *salturna* seems to us impeccable.

[3] See also the French translation by Filliozat (1948, 52f.): "Maintenant je vais exposer le livre des êtres (démoniaques). Coque du Levant, (variété de) coque de Levant, Dalbergia sisu ... et tout, graine de Pongamia glabra, Ferula asa foetida, poivre long, poivre noir, gingembre, stigmates de safran, Acorus calamus, Acacia Lebbek; ces remèdes ... dans ... purs avec ... femme, fille, mélanges, cette poudre, celui qui ... fait, qu'il soit ... aussitôt ..."

[4] See also the French translation by Filliozat (1948, 50): "... ainsi. Dalbergia sisu combinée au sésame, ... sel gemme; cela, à préparer en abondance, est le remède des *ampoña*." Sieg (1954, 67f.) first suggested to restore *(ampo)ño* and to derive the noun from the TochB verb *ampᵃ*- "to rot, decay" (hence "festering abscess"), which underlies his rendition of the first sentence as "[so] vergeht das faulige Geschwür." For a probable Late Khotanese origin of *ampᵃ*- and *ampoño/a*, see most recently Dragoni 2021, 307–308, §§3.1–3.2; 2023, 34–36.

1.2. c) i. PK AS 8C, a5–6: || *kete ā(ñm)e (t)ākaṃ lāntämpa larauwñe y(ā)mtsī • rājavṛkṣä stamatse arwāmeṃ koṣkīye yamaṣlya •* ***śāñcapo*** *ṣukt lykwarwa nässait yamaṣlya • pūwarne hom yamaṣlya • lānte rinale parkälle mäsketrä 1* || "1. One who has the [wish] to associate with a king should make a fire-pit[1] out of pieces of wood of a *Cassia fistula* tree (*rājavṛkṣa*), cast a spell on ***śāñcapo*** seven times, and put it as an oblation (*homa*) into the fire; [then] one is worth to be searched out and asked for by the king."[2]

ii. PK AS 10, a4: /// *(kete āñ)m(e) kartse nessi* ***śāñcapo*** *tesa n(ä)s(s)ai(t yamaṣle)* /// "… [For one] who has the wish to become beautiful, ***śāñcapo*** [is to be used]; over that (i.e., ***śāñcapo***) one should cast a spell …"[3]

iii. PK NS 2, b2–3: *(naṣ u)pacār pätāñäkte anapär* ***śāñcapo*** *nesset yal 20-1 ke ñomā ne (yāme)ñc cami yälya tkanā knāl cam ṣñi waṣtäṣ lutseñc-äṃ* "This is the [procedure] (*upacāra*): In front of the Buddha [image] one should cast a spell on ***śāñcapo*** 21 [times]. In whose name they do so, it (i.e., ***śāñcapo***) has to be strewn over the earth that is expected to be trodden by him; [then] they expel him from his own house …"

1.2. d) PK NS 2, a2–4: – – *kāts kuñcit dhanyamāṣ pippaläs : āragvat :* ***śāñcapo*** *• kosne (tā)ṣ puk täprenäk sasak kuṣ taṃpar tosäs puk ywār triwäṣäl ken (täm) śwātsyaṃ yoktsyaṃ pat eṣ säm unmatte mäskaträ* "… [1] *dhānyamāṣa* of sesame, long pepper (*pippalī*), *Cassia fistula* (*āragvadha*), ***śāñcapo***. As much as everything is [available], as much indeed a single [person] pours it in …-wise. One should mix together all these [condiments]. To whom one gives that in food or drink, this one becomes insane (*unmatta*) …"

1.2. e) i. W 10, b2–3 (ed. Filliozat 1948, 68): […] *se laiko tucepi yetsentse* • || *(ma)ñcäṣṭä • śaparalodṛ • prapuṇḍarikä (•) [r](i)m(mā •* ***śā)ñcapo*** *• – – – (śa)kkar spaitu* […] "… this embrocation[4] is for yellow skin. Indian madder (*mañjiṣṭhā*), a kind of

[1] For the new interpretation of TochB *koṣkīye* as "(fire-)pit," see Bernard and Chen 2022, 1–31.

[2] See also the French translation by Filliozat (1948, 102): "[Si] il y a pour quelqu'un le désir de faire amitié avec le roi, [des] fagot[s] de bûches de tronc de cassie sont à faire, [des] Dalbergia Sisoo sont à incanter sept fois, [les] oblation[s de tout cela] sont à faire dans le feu; le roi à quitter devient sollicitable."

[3] See also the French translation by Filliozat (1948, 55): "… être salutaire, Dalbergia sisu, par cela …" The restoration of *kete āñme* was first proposed by Sieg (1954, 70).

[4] Filliozat (1948, 82) translated TochB *laiko* as "onguent," but Sieg (1954, 73) analyzed it as a noun of the *palsko*-type (so Del Tomba 2023, 197) derived from the TochB verb *likᵃ*- "to wash" (hence "Waschung, Bad;" Sieg *ibid.*). But to the best of our knowledge, bath is not prescribed in the Āyurvedic tradition as a pharmaceutical preparation. Furthermore, it is perplexing that Filliozat (1948, 119) glossed *laiko* with Skt. *leha*, which means "electuary" rather than "unguent." Perhaps *leha* is there a typo for Skt. *lepa* "unguent, ointment"? Skt. *lepa* is otherwise translated by TochB *laupe* or *lauwalñe* (< *laupalñe*); see Filliozat 1948, 120 and Pinault 1988, 114. In our opinion, Sieg's etymological connection with *likᵃ*- is well taken, but the meaning of *laiko* can be postulated in a slightly different way, i.e., "embrocation"

Sumplocos racemosa (*śabaralodhra*), the rhizome of *Nymphaea lotus* (*prapauṇḍarīka*), neem,[1] ***śāñcapo***, ..., sugar dust, ..."[2]

ii. W 37, a4–5 (ed. Filliozat 1948, 77): *śakkar devadāru* • ***śāñcapo*** *kuñcit* • *traiwoṣṣai maikisa ṣpärkaṣälle* • *platkāre mäśсakene se laiko – .ai .e (nakṣäṃ)* "Sugar, deodar, ***śāñcapo***, sesame, to be diluted with the essence[3] of the three ingredients (*traivṛta*);[4] in case of a rash(?) or jaundice(?), this embrocation removes ..."[5]

To sum up, a number of characteristics of the substance to which TochAB *śāñcapo* refers can be deduced from the textual evidence classified above: First, it is a leguminous plant, from which oil can be extracted (cf. §1.2. a). Second, it can be crushed, along with other plants, to make a powder for apotropaic and medical purposes (cf. §1.2. b). Third, it can be used in rituals, either put into the fire as an oblation (*homa*) or strewn on the ground as some kind of contact objects; and their ritual efficacy is guaranteed by a magical spell cast over them a certain number of times (cf. §1.2. c). Fourth, it is mentioned among a number of condiments to be mixed together and added to food and

(Skt. *pūraṇa*), whose use is well attested in the Āyurvedic tradition. In that case, TochB *likᵃ*- "to wash" may also be understood in the sense of "to embrocate, foment," i.e., "to moisten and rub with liquid."

[1] The substance to which TochB *rimmā* refers is obscure. It is possible to read it as a scribal error for TochB *rimmākka*, which is otherwise attested as a flowering plant (*rimmā[k]kaṣṣa pyāpyo*; W 9, b1 [ed. Filliozat 1948, 68]). But it is difficult to identify its meaning. Our tentative hypothesis is to derive it from Skt. *nimba*- "neem/*Azadirachta indica*" through a Middle Indic intermediary: cf. Prakrit *ṇiṃba*- > *liṃba*- (CDIAL 413, §7245; PSM 726a). For the sound changes *l*- > *r*- and *-mb*- > *-mm*-, compare Skt. *ālambana*- "foundation, base" > **ālammana*- > Pāli *ārammaṇa*- (Lüders 1954, 36f., §33 with n. 2).

[2] See also the French translation by Filliozat (1948, 82): "... cet onguent est ce qui est de ce ... (= appartient à ce ...). ‖ Garance, Symplocos rac., racine de lotus blanc, ..., Dalbergia sisu, ..." Filliozat had erroneously analyzed *tucepi* (gen. sg. m. of *tute* "yellow") as *tu cepi*, which was corrected by Sieg (1954, 73).

[3] TochB *maiki* is semantically unclear. Elsewhere the word seems to refer to a medical preparation made of chicken (*kräṅkaiñai maiki*-; W 14, a5, b1). Since chicken is not ubiquitous in Āyurvedic recipes, it is conceivable to identify the preparation as "chicken-broth" (*viṣkirarasa*), as suggested by Sieg (1954, 74). The same preparation is otherwise rendered in Tocharian B as *kräṅkaññe yot*- (W 39, b3), which is used to make an unguent (*laupe*). It is not clear to us whether there is any significant difference between *maiki* and *yot*, while both words seem to fall within the semantic field of Skt. *rasa* "essence, nectar; soup, broth; and so on."

[4] On TochB *traiwo*, see Filliozat 1948, 146 and Carling 2003, 51 (*pace* Adams 2013, 341, s.v. *traiwo*: "mixture"): The three ingredients are thick sour milk (*dadhi*), sour rice or barley (*tuṣodaka*), and sour cream or whey (*mastu*). The Tocharian form could have derived from a Middle Indic counterpart of Skt. *traivṛta* (possibly Gāndhārī **trevu[d]a* > **trevo*). In addition, Skt. *traivṛta* is also a derivative from Skt. *trivṛt[ā]* "*Ipomoea Turpethum*" (PW s.v.), a medical herb which is widely used in the Āyurvedic tradition. If TochB *traiwo* inherited the polysemy of its Indic source, it might also refer to a preparation made of *Ipomoea Turpethum*, which is known in Late Khotanese as *traula* (< **travula* < **trevuḍ/da* > **trevura* > Sogdian *tr'ywr* "turpeth").

[5] See also the French translation by Filliozat (1948, 87): "Sucre, déodar, Dalbergia sisu, sésame, à diluer avec ... de combinaison des trois, ... Cet ouguent détruit ..."

drink, the consumer of which will go insane (cf. §1.2. d). Fifth, it is mentioned among a number of substances to be diluted with a certain solvent so as to make an embrocation for treating skin diseases (cf. §1.2. e).

2.1 TochAB *śāñcapo* ≠ Skt. *śiṃśapā-*

It remains to be examined whether the characteristics summarized above can be attributed to Skt. *śiṃśapā-* "sissoo." Renate Syed has systematically surveyed the occurrences of this word in extant Sanskrit literature in her dissertation *Die Flora Altindiens in Literatur und Kunst* (Syed 1992, 572–577). The observations below are mainly based on Syed's collection of primary sources.

2.1.1. a) In the *Carakasaṃhitā* and the *Suśrutasaṃhitā*, sissoo is mentioned among a number of trees, from whose heartwood (*sāra*) medicated spirituous liquor is to be prepared.[1] The plant is apparently not leguminous. In one case, we are informed about the medical use of the oil extracted from the heartwood of sissoo among other trees as a remedy for leprosy and so on.[2] The oil of sissoo is light brown, viscous, non-drying, and can be used as a lubricant for heavy machinery (Orwa et al. 2010).

2.1.1. b) The idea that the wood of sissoo is the material for a part of a carriage is very archaic and dates back to the *Ṛgveda*.[3] In his *Arthaśāstra*, Kauṭilya (50–125 AD; Olivelle 2013, 29) categorised sissoo as a "hard wood" (*sāradāru*),[4] which is by definition hard to

---

[1] CarS 1.25.49: *śāla-priyaka-aśvakarṇa-candana-syandana-khadira-kadara-saptaparṇa-arjuna-asana-arimeda-tinduka-kiṇihī-śamī-śukti-śiṃśapā-śirīṣa-vañjula-dhanvana-madhūkaiḥ sārāsavā viṃśatir bhavanti* "Sal, priyaka, flowering murdah, sandalwood, spandana, acacia, mimosa, devil's tree, arjuna, Indian laurel, sweet acacia, Indian ebony, chaff-flower, śamī, tamarind, sissoo, siris, rattan, dhanvana, and mahua—these are [trees] with [whose heartwood] the twenty wines [made from] heartwood [are manufactured];" SuŚr 4.10.8: *atha surā vakṣyāmaḥ śiṃśapā-khadirayoḥ sāram ādāyotpāṭya cottamāraṇī-brāhmī-kośavatīs tat sarvam ekataḥ kaṣāyakalpena vipācyodakam ādadīta maṇḍodakārthaṃ kiṇvapiṣṭam abhiṣuṇuyāc ca yathoktam* "Then we will speak of [various kinds of medicated] spirituous liquor: one should take the heartwood of sissoo and acacia, pluck *Asparagus Racemosus*, *Herpestis monieria* (or *Hydrocotyle asiatica*), and *Cucumis acutangulus* (or *sulcatus*), boil everything all together down to almost an infusion, take the liquid [as a decoction], and, for the sake of yeast, distill [it into] flour of the drug [producing vinous fermentation], as is prescribed."

[2] SuŚr 4.31.5: *sarala-pītadāru-śiṃśapāguru-sāra-snehā dadru-kuṣṭha-kiṭibheṣu* "The expressed oils [prepared from] the heartwood of chir pine, deodar, sissoo, and aloes wood [are to be applied] in cases of cutaneous eruption, leprosy, and keloid tumour."

[3] RV III 53.19: *abhí vyayasva khadirásya sā́ram ójo dhehi spandané śiṃśápāyām | ákṣa vīḷo vīḷita vīḷáyasva mā́ yā́mād asmā́d áva jīhipo naḥ ||* "Hülle dich in des *Khadhira*(-Holzes) Härte, Kraft setze ins *Spandana*(-Holz), ins *Śiṃśapā*(-Holz)! Du Achse, fest, festgemacht, sei fest! Laß uns nicht von unserm Dahinziehen abkommen!" (tr. Witzel 2013, 90); "Engird yourself in the hardwood of the acacia tree; place strength in the *śiṃśapā*(-wood) in its recoil. O Axle, you who are firm and were made firm, stay firm. Don't make us leave off from this journey." (tr. Jamison and Brereton 2014, 539).

[4] *Arthaśāstra* 2.17.4 (ed. Kangle 1960, 67): *kupyavargaḥ śāka-tiniśa-dhanvana-arjuna-madhūka-tilaka-sāla-śiṃśapā-arimeda-rājādana-śirīṣa-khadira-sarala-tāla-sarja-aśvakarṇa-somavalka-kuśāmra-*

crush. This categorisation is in line with the references to sissoo as a kind of timber that can be used for the making of furniture, e.g. couches,[1] handlooms,[2] etc.

2.1.1. c) The application of sissoo in a ritual of fertility for barren women is known from the *Kauśikasūtra* of the *Atharvaveda*.[3] In that case, the branches of sissoo are not to be put into the fire or strewn on the ground; there is no mention of their consecration with a magical spell either.[4] The specific ritual takes place on the bank of a river, and is different from the so-called *homa* rites, i.e., burnt oblations made to deities or for specific purposes.

2.1.1. d) To the best of our knowledge, there is no evidence that any preparation from sissoo can be added to food and drink, and no clear connection between sissoo and insanity is known. Nonetheless, sissoo seems to have a vague connection to death and zombie in the *Vetālapañcaviṃśatika*, where an eerie image of a corpse hanging from the tree of sissoo is depicted.[5]

---

priyaka-dhavādiḥ sāradāruvargaḥ "The category of forest produce consists of the following: Teak, tiniśa, dhanvana, arjuna, madhūka, tilaka, sal, sissoo, acacia, mimusops, siris, cutch, chir pine, palmyra palm, Indian copal, flowering murdah, white cutch, kuśāmra, priyaka, dhava, and the like constitute the category of hard woods." (tr. Olivelle 2013, 141).

[1] Varāhamihira's (6th cent. AD) *Bṛhatsaṃhitā* 79.12 (ed. Kern 1865, 400): *yaḥ kevalaśiṃśapayā vinirmito bahuvidhaṃ sa vṛddhikaraḥ* "The [couch (*paryaṅka*)], which is exclusively made of the wood of sissoo, promotes prosperity in manifold ways." 79.15 (ed. Kern 1865, 401): *anyena samāyuktā na tindukī śiṃśapā ca śubhaphaladā* "Coupled with another wood, neither Indian ebony nor sissoo is yielding auspicious results."

[2] *Pañcatantra* 5.7 (ed. Kosegarten 1848, 249f.): *kasmiṃścid adhiṣṭhāne Mantharako nāma kaulikaḥ / tasya kadācit paṭakarmāṇi kurvataḥ sarvāṇi paṭakarmakarakāṣṭhāni bhagnāni / tataḥ sa kuṭhāram ādāya kāṣṭhārthaṃ paribhraman samudrataṭaṃ prāpa / tatra ca mahāntaṃ śiṃśapāpādapaṃ dṛṣṭvā cintitavān / mahān ayaṃ vṛkṣo dṛśyate / tad anena kartitena prabhūtāni paṭakarmopakaraṇāni bhaviṣyanti* "In a certain city, there [lived] a weaver named Mantharaka. Incidentally, when he was weaving cloths, the woodwork of his handloom was all broken. Then he took an axe and, wandering about for timber, reached the seashore. There he saw a huge sissoo tree and thought: This tree looks large! Thus, [if] this [tree] has been cut down, by means of it, plenty of handlooms (lit. weaving instruments) will be manufactured."

[3] KauśS 4.10[34].1: *asyai śiṃśapāśākhāsūdakānte śāntā adhiśiro avasiñcati* "[Während die Frau] auf Zweigen der Dalbergia sisu (*śiṃśapā*) am Ufer eines Stromes [sitzt], giesst er ihr [Wasser, in welches er] die zu *res faustae* gebräuchlichen [Kräuter gethan und das er mit diesem Liede eingesegnet hat,] übers Haupt" (tr. Caland 1900, 111).

[4] There is in fact a mantra from the Śaunakīya recension of the *Atharvaveda*, i.e., AVŚ 1.32.1a (*idáṃ janāso* ...), the recitation of which accompanies the ritual act prescribed in the *Kauśikasūtra*. For the parallel in the Paippalāda recension, i.e., AVP 1.23.1a, see Franceschini 2007, 385. But this mantra serves to consecrate the water sprinkled over the woman's head, according to Caland *ibid*., rather than the branches of sissoo, on which the woman sits.

[5] Śivadāsa's *Vetālapañcaviṃśatikā* (ed. Uhle 1914, 6): *yoginoktam bho rājan yojanārdhe mahāśmaśānam asti tatra śiṅśipāvṛkṣe* (lege *śiṃśapā-*) *mṛtakam avalambitam āste* "The conjurer said: Your Majesty! Half a league away there is a large charnel ground. There a corpse is hanging from a sissoo tree." This sets the

2.1.1. e) The oil of sissoo, as mentioned above, is applied to skin diseases such as leprosy etc., but the plant itself is not. Even in the case of its oil, there is no indication that it is to be diluted with other ingredients and used as an embrocation or the like.

2.1.2 To sum up, although sissoo yields oil that can be used to cure skin diseases (cf. §2.1.1. a), there is some significant difference between sissoo (Skt. *śiṃśapā-*) and the substance to which TochAB *śāñcapo* refers: First, the wood of sissoo is hard and difficult to crush, and as such mostly used in carpentry rather than in medicine and witchcraft (cf. §2.1.1. b). Second, the ritual use of sissoo seems to be in a different context from that of the *homa* rites or the like (cf. §2.1.1. c). Third, there is no preparation made of sissoo that can be considered a condiment such as sesame, long pepper, etc., whose addition to food and drink would not raise any eyebrow (cf. §2.1.1. d). Fourth, no embrocation is known to stem from sissoo or its oil (cf. §2.1.1. e). Viewed in this light, the received identification of TochAB *śāñcapo* as the word for sissoo seems to be unwarranted.

2.2 TochAB *śāñcapo* = Skt. *sarṣapa-*

If the evidence surveyed above suffices to disprove the received *Bedeutungsansatz*, the meaning of the Tocharian word must be reconsidered. In the following, we argue that TochAB *śāñcapo* is likely to mean "mustard (seed)," and that its Indic counterpart is Skt. *sarṣapa-* "id." No Tocharian word for "mustard (seed)" has been identified so far, which is a bit odd, since references to mustard seeds are ubiquitous in medical and ritual works of Indian origin. The assumption that all the occurrences of the Tocharian word for mustard (seed) fall into the lacunae and thus get lost by accident is not impossible, but not quite plausible, given that mustard seeds are much more frequently mentioned in Buddhist and Āyurvedic literature than sissoo. Rather, one should reckon with the possibility, if not probability, that the word for mustard (seed) does occur in the extant Tocharian fragments, but has been hitherto misrecognized as a different word.

2.2.1. a) Indian Āyurvedic literature testifies to mustard seeds (*sarṣapa/siddhārthaka*) being used in the same way as the substance to which TochAB *śāñcapo* refers. Mustard

scene for the corpse's persistent return to the tree and the king's Sisyphean labour of fetching the corpse from the tree over and over again, which serves as the *Rahmenerzählung* for this collection of stories. For a recasting of the same plot see Somadeva's (11th cent. AD) *Kathāsaritsāgara* 75.50cd–51 (eds. Durgāprasād et al. 1889, 406): *gatvā tamasi taṃ prāpa kathaṃcic chiṃśapātaruṃ // tasya skandhe citādhūmadagdhasya kravyagandhinaḥ / so 'paśyal lambamānaṃ taṃ bhūtasyeva śavaṃ taroḥ //* "In the darkness he went and reached the sissoo tree with some difficulty. The tree was scorched with the smoke rising from a funeral pile [and] smelt of carrion, he saw the corpse hanging on the trunk of the tree like on the shoulder of a demon."

oil (*sarṣapataila*) serves to fry the flesh of birds,[1] as an anthelmintic unguent (*kṛmighna*),[2] as an embrocation against tinnitus,[3] and as a drinkable antidote to elephantiasis or phlegmatic cough.[4]

2.2.1. b) Mustard seeds can be ground or crushed, sometimes mixed with other substances, to prepare paste (*kalka*) or poultice (*pradeha*), which serves various functions.[5] More often than not, mustard seeds are listed together with the same substances as those which are juxtaposed above with what is designated by TochAB *śāñcapo* (cf. §1.2. b [i]): α. the three spices (*tryūṣaṇa/trikaṭuka*), i.e., black pepper (*kolaka*), long pepper (*pippalī*), and ginger (*śṛṅgavera*); β. the three myrobalans (*triphalā*),[6] i.e., the fruits of *Tertminalia chebula* (*harītakī*), *Tantras bellerica*, and *Phyllanthus emblica*; γ. *Asa foetida* (*hiṅgu*); δ. sweet flag/*Acorus calamus* (*ṣaḍgranthā/vacā*); and ε. fruits of *Pongamia glabra* (*karañja/śārṅgeṣṭā*).[7] Many of those substances are spicy in flavour, and thus have

---

[1] CarS 1.26.84: *hāridrakaḥ sarṣapatailabhṛṣṭo viruddhaḥ pittaṃ cātikopayati* "the flesh of a yellowish-green pigeon, [if] fried in mustard oil, becomes incompatible, and riles the bilious humour;" SuŚr 6.41.36: *gṛdhrāṃś ca dadyād* [...] *sasaindhavān sarṣapatailabhṛṣṭān* "[the physician] should give (i.e., prescribe) the flesh of vultures etc., marinated with rock salt [and] fried in mustard oil;" Vāgbh 4.5.9ab: *bhṛṣṭāḥ sarṣapatailena sarpiṣā vā yathāyatham* "[the flesh of a bird of prey etc.] are fried in mustard oil or clarified butter in a proper manner."

[2] CarS 6.7.126ab: *eḍagaja-kuṣṭha-saindhava-sauvīraka-sarṣapaiḥ kṛmighnaiś ca* "[parasitic infections etc. become alleviated] by means of anthelmintic [substances such as] *Cassia tora* or *alata*, *Costus speciosus* or *arabicus*, rock salt, jujube, and mustard seeds;" SuŚr 1.45.117ab: *kṛmighnaṃ sārṣapaṃ tailaṃ kaṇḍūkuṣṭhāpahaṃ laghu* "anthelmintic mustard oil is quickly curing the leprosy [and] itch."

[3] SuŚr 6.21.54ab: *karṇakṣveḍe hitaṃ tailaṃ sārṣapaṃ caiva pūraṇam* "in case of tinnitus, mustard oil is beneficial as an embrocation;" Bower 533cd: *karṇakṣveḍe karṇanāde kaṭutailena pūrayet* "in case of tinnitus [or] ringing in the ear, one should fill [the ear] with pungent oil (i.e., oil of white mustard)."

[4] SuŚr 4.19.60: *pibet sarṣapatailaṃ vā ślīpadānāṃ nivṛttaye* "or, [as an alternative, the patient] should drink mustard oil for the cure of [various kinds of] elephantiasis;" Bower 465: *pāyayet sārṣapaṃ tailaṃ kausuṃbham athavā bhiṣak / paṃcakolakasiddhaṃ vā pibet kāse kaphātmake* "either [the physician] should give to drink mustard oil dyed with safflower as a remedy, or [the patient] should drink [mustard oil] prepared with the five spices (i.e., long pepper, its root, *Piper chaba*, plumbago, and dry ginger) in case of phlegmatic cough."

[5] See Ram Manohar et al. 2009, 400ff.

[6] On the three myrobalans, see Chen 2021, 1–78.

[7] SuŚr 4.40.61: *trikaṭuka-vacā-sarṣapa-harītakī-kalkam āloḍya* "having dissolved the paste of the three spices, sweet flag, mustard seeds, and *Tertminalia chebula* [in oil etc.] ...;" Vāgbh 6.5.38–39: [...] -*kvāthe 'rdhapalikaiḥ pacet // tryūṣaṇa-triphalā-hiṅgu-ṣaḍgranthā-miśi-sarṣapaiḥ* [...] "one should cook in the decoction [an ointment] with the three spices, the three myrobalans, *Asa foetida*, sweet flag, seeds of *Anethum sowa*, and mustard seeds, [weighing] half a *pala* (≈ 18.88 grams; Olivelle 2013, 459) ..." For shortened versions of the list see CarS 6.26.13: *piṇyāka-sauvarcala-hiṅgubhir vā sarṣapa-tryūṣaṇa-yāvaśūkaiḥ* "[prepare a suppository] with sesamum oil cake, sochal salt, and *Asa foetida*, or with mustard seeds, the three spices, and alkaline salt prepared from the ashes of burnt barley-straw;" Vāgbh 6.5.28: *hiṅgu-sarṣapa-ṣaḍgranthā-vyoṣair ardhapalonmitaiḥ* "[thick sour milk] with *Asa foetida*, mustard seeds, sweet flag, and the [three] spices, as much as half a *pala*, [is prescribed as an offering to deities]." With fruits of *Pongamia glabra*, see SuŚr 4.5.37 = Vāgbh 4.21.52: *kuryād dihyāc ca mūtrāḍhyaiḥ karañjaphala-*

a purgative or laxative effect. On the other hand, the use of mustard seeds alongside with rock salt (*saindhava*) among other substances is well attested (cf. §1.2. b [ii]). The preparations made from their admixture function as ointments (*lepana*) or emetics (*vamana*).[1]

2.2.1. c) Mustard seeds are one of the favourite substances used in Tantric rituals, and their ritual efficacy probably underlies the epithet of white mustard, namely Skt. *siddhārtha(ka)*, lit. "leading to the goal, efficacious" (PW s.v.). A sample of the ritual uses of mustard seeds is found in the *Amoghapāśakalparāja*, an encyclopaedic compendium of Tantric Buddhist rites. According to this compendium, mustard seeds are cast into fire as one of the sacrificial oblations,[2] or scattered in the four directions of the compass, performing an exorcistic or apotropaic function (cf. §1.2. c [i]).[3] By way of an empowerment, mustard seeds are often consecrated, in a ritual context, with a mantra (*abhimantrita*), which is to be recited for a certain number of times.[4] This is perfectly in line with the

sarṣapaiḥ "one should make [a plaster] with fruits of *Pongamia glabra* and mustard seeds, richly endowed with cow's urine, and apply [it to the affected part];" SuŚr 4.23.12: *sarṣapa-suvarcalā-saindhava-śārṅgeṣṭābhiś ca pradehaḥ kāryaḥ* "with mustard seeds, sochal salt, rock salt, and fruits of *Pongamia glabra*, a plaster is to be made."

[1] SuŚr 4.20.37: *lepanaṃ ca vacā-rodhra-saindhavaiḥ sarṣapānvitaiḥ* "and the application of ointments [prepared] with sweet flag, *Symplocos racemosa*, and rock salt, joined by mustard seeds [is also recommended];" Vāgbh 6.9.25: *vamet kṛṣṇā-yaṣṭī-sarṣapa-saindhavaiḥ* "[the patient] should vomit using black pepper, licorice, mustard seeds, and rock salt." Although we are not yet able to pinpoint similar occurrences in any Āyurvedic recipes dealing with abscess, it is only natural to conceive of an ointment prepared with mustard seeds, rock salt, etc. to be used as a cure against diseases of that nature. Note that the rendition of TochB *ampoño* as "abscess" is provisional at best, and that the word is likely to be of Late Khotanese origin and might simply mean "rottenness, infection" (Dragoni 2021, 307f.; 2023, 35f.). Its Old Khotanese cognate, i.e., *haṃbūta-*, is attested in the sense of "fester," which should be treated with "ointment" (Khot. *ālīva* ← Skt. *ālepa*); see *Book of Zambasta* 5.16 (Emmerick 1968, 98 & 99).

[2] The casting of mustard seeds into fire is testified to by quite a few Buddhist tantric texts in Chinese translation. It seems to have originally served an apotropaic function, and have later become fused with the *homa*-rites. See Strickmann 1996, 63, 141, and 339.

[3] See the following passage (eds. Kimura et al. 2000, 60 [= 313]): *rājavṛkṣa-samidhānāṃ kuryāc chatapuṣpa-śatāvarī-pattaṅga-candana-sarṣapa-yava-ghṛtāktānām ekaviṃśati āhutīs trisandhyaṃ divasāni sapta mahārājā vaśī-bhavati sāntaḥpuraparivāraḥ* / [...] "One should make twenty-one oblations of fuel-sticks of the *Cassia fistula* wood, besmeared with clarified butter, [with the addition of] seeds of *Anethum sowa*, *Asparagus racemosus*, red sandalwood, sandalwood, mustard seeds, and grains of barley —three times daily (i.e., at dawn, noon, and eventide) for seven days; [then] a great king, together with women of his harem and his retinue, becomes subject [to one's charm]." The emendations and the English translation of this passage are after Bernard and Chen 2022, 7. An Iranian parallel to this ritual practice seems to have existed. Henning (1965, 39 = 1977, II 607) took note of an Ahrimanian tradition, according to which mustard "seeds are thrown into the fire to excite fat black smoke."

[4] See *Mañjuśriyamūlakalpa* (ed. Gaṇapati 1920–1925), vol. 1, 39.22–23: *⁺śvetasarṣapam aṣṭābhimantritaṃ kṛtvā yamāntakakrodharājenābhimantrya śarāvasampuṭe sthāpayet* "having made [a seed of] white mustard sacred using a mantra [recited] eight times, and consecrated [it] with [the mantra of]

way the substance to which TochAB *śāñcapo* refers is dealt with (cf. §§1.2. c [i]–[iii]), an act for which a technical term is coined in Tocharian (i.e., TochA *nesset ya[p]-/yām-*, TochB *nässait yām-* "to make/cast a spell [over]").[1] Thus empowered, mustard seeds are sometimes hurled at the target that will then be possessed by their magical power.[2] Viewed in this light, it may be conceivable that a person who walks over an empowered mustard seed will be expelled from his original abode (cf. §1.2. c [iii]). Although no close parallel to this witchcraft practice is known from extant Indic sources, the context tallies well with the ritual efficacy of mustard seed in exorcism, etc.

2.2.1. d) Mustard seeds, usually ground into a fine powder, are commonly used as a condiment to add flavour to food and drink. We are not yet able to identify any textual evidence for the use of mustard seeds to make one's mind unsound. However, the seeds, leaves, and oil of mustard are commonly used as part of the cures for insanity (*unmāda*).[3]

Yamāntaka, the Lord of Wrath, one should place [it] in the hollow of an earthenware vessel;" vol. 3, 675.6–7: *gaurasarṣapāṇāṃ saptābhimantritānāṃ saṅgrāme prakire<t> / śāntir bhavati* "when seeds of white mustard are made sacred by a mantra [recited] seven times, one should scatter them in a battle, and there will be peace;" 710.26–27: *śvetasarṣapaṃ saptābhimantritaṃ yasya śirasi dadāti sa* ⁺*vaśī-bhavati* "he, whom one gives on [his] head a seed of white mustard made sacred by a mantra [recited] seven times, becomes subject to [one's charm];" 715.25–26: *udaka-bhasma-sarṣapānyatamam aṣṭa-sahasrābhimantritaṃ kṛtvā caturdiśaṃ kṣipet / maṇḍalabandhaḥ kṛto bhavati* "having made sacred any mustard seed in water and ash with a mantra [recited] eight-thousand times, one should throw it in the four directions (i.e., on all sides), [and] the demarcation of a [ritual] circle will be done." This practice also finds parallel in Chinese tantric texts; see Strickmann 1996, 199, 200, and 219.

[1] The etymology of TochA *nesset* and TochB *nässait* (v.l. *nessait, niset*) remains obscure. A.J. van Windekens proposed to connect the second component (i.e., TochA *-set*, TochB *-sait*) with Old Icelandic *seiðr* "spell, charm, incantation" or with words of Uralic origin such as Finnish *soitta-* "to play (an instrument);" see van Windekens 1944, 34; 1976, 318. The former can be traced back to Proto-Germanic **saida-* "magic, charm" (Kroonen 2013, 421). Alternatively, see Malzahn (2010, 64, n. 21): "maybe a loan from Skt. *niṣedha* 'repulsion.' " Malzahn's hypothesis does not account for the germinate *-ss-*. Tracing the lexeme back to the same root, G.-J. Pinault (*apud* Pan 2021, 106, n. 173) does not regard it as an Indic loanword, but as an inherited Indo-European *nomen actionis* (**nəssaitə* < **nis-soi̯dʰ-u* "fending off, repulse"); in that case, the TochA form is likely to be a borrowing from its TochB counterpart.

[2] See Bhavabhaṭṭa *ad Catuṣpīthatantra* 3.3.12 (ed. Szántó 2012, II 166): *amunā mantreṇa sarṣapān abhijapya* [...] *taiḥ sādhyaṃ hanyāt. tata āviṣṭo bhavati* "with the said mantra one should empower mustard seeds ... and hurl them at the target. Then [the target] becomes possessed." (cf. Szántó 2012, I 384). See also *Catuṣpīthatantra* 3.3.19cd (ed. Szántó 2012, II 169): *sarṣapena tu yogīnāṃ* | *adaityābaliyuktitam* ‖ "The yogin [should use] mustard seeds in conjunction with the *adaityābali*" (tr. Szántó 2012, I 388); Bhavabhaṭṭa *ad* 3.3.19: *tena pūrvasevāsiddhena mantreṇa sarṣapān abhimantrya* [...] *sādhyaṃ hanyāt. tata āviṣṭaḥ syāt* "With the mantra perfected by the preliminary service one should consecrate mustard seeds ... and hurl [them] at the target. Then [the target] would be possessed." (cf. Szántó 2012, I 388).

[3] See Ram Manohar et al. 2009, 400ff.

2.2.1. e) The medical use of mustard seeds to prepare embrocation and the like is unknown to us. That being said, mustard seeds constitute one of the ingredients that induce emesis, cleanse the cranial cavity, etc. Such procedures are instrumental in healing diseases such as pallor and jaundice (*pāṇḍuroga*).[1]

2.2.2 To sum up, there are a certain number of commonalities shared between mustard seeds (*sarṣapa/siddhārthaka*) and the substance to which TochAB *śāñcapo* refers: First, mustard is a leguminous plant, and mustard oil is used for various purposes (cf. §2.2.1. a). Second, crushed mustard seeds are used for various medical preparations and in conjunction with more or less the same substances as those mentioned above in the case of TochAB *śāñcapo* (cf. §2.2.1. b). Third, the ritual use of mustard seeds is well attested, and the ways that they are used in a ritual context are in line with what is known from the extant Tocharian sources (cf. §2.2.1. c). Admittedly, the match is not perfect (cf. §§2.2.1. d & e), but is strong enough to make us consider a new interpretation of TochAB *śāñcapo* as "mustard (seed)."

3.1 Morphological Remarks

If the new interpretation proposed above is approximately correct, the etymology of TochAB *śāñcapo* must be reconsidered. Since a borrowing from Tocharian B to Tocharian A is quite plausible, our remarks below focus on the TochB word. Before delving into the etymological discussion, we consider it apposite to make a few morphological remarks. TochB *śāñcapo* is attested with *-o* as the stem-final vowel both in the nominative singular and in the genitive singular (*śāñcapotse*), and thus is likely to belong to the so-called *palsko*-type rather than the *arṣāklo*-type. The two classes of nominal declension differ from each other in the stem, on which all non-nom.sg. forms, e.g., the genitive singular, the plural, and the derived forms, are built. While, as for the *arṣāklo*-type, the stem in *-o* is limited to the nom.sg. and all the other forms are built on another stem in *-a* (nom.sg. *arṣāklo* "snake," non-nom.sg. stem *arṣākla-*), the nouns exemplifying the *palsko*-type exhibit no formal differentiation between the nom.sg. and the non-nom.sg. stem (nom.sg. *palsko* "mind," non-nom.sg. stem *palsko-*).[2]

To the same class of nominal declension belongs also TochB *pito* "price, cost," a word which ostensibly has a bizarre paradigm combining the *palsko*-type, the *arṣāklo*-type, and the *okso*-type. Alessandro Del Tomba (2019, 112–116) has demonstrated that all the occurrences of what are purportedly forms built on non-*palsko*-stems (i.e., *pīta-* and *pitai-*) can be interpreted otherwise, and that nothing speaks against the

[1] See Ram Manohar et al. 2009, 401.

[2] On the *arṣāklo*-type and the *palsko*-type and their diachronic evolution, see most recently Del Tomba 2023, 153–172, and 196–209.

categorization of TochB *pito* as a regular example of the *palsko*-type.[1] This assigns TochB *pito*, along with TochB *śāñcapo*, to a small group of nouns belonging to this declensional class, which, unlike most members of the *palsko*-type, are without cognate verbs in Tocharian.[2] Whereas some of the nouns without cognate verbs can be hypothetically linked to verb roots attested in other Indo-European languages, there are some exceptional cases in which the nouns cannot be traced back to the Proto-Indo-European type in **-eh₂* or to old thematic neuter plurals. In the case of TochB *pito*, an Iranian origin has long been postulated, and the *communis opinio* tends to consider it a loanword derived from Pre-Khotanese **pīθa-*, the antecedent of Khot. *pīha-* "price."[3]

TochB *śāñcapo* does not seem to have any cognate verb in Tocharian, and shows no etymological association with any Indo-European verb root. Therefore, it is conceivable that the word was borrowed into Tocharian in a manner similar to, if not exactly the same as TochB *pito*. Viewed in this light, the presumption of an Iranian origin may not be far-fetched, insofar as TochB *śāñcapo* shares some formal characteristics with other loanwords from Iranian (e.g. initial stress). Both TochB *śāñcapo* "mustard (seed)" and TochB *tvāṅkaro* "ginger" are trisyllabic and stressed on the first syllable (C_1áNC_2aC_3o), while the two substances designated by these words are quite similar in character. Previous scholars traced the latter word back to the Pre-Khotanese antecedent of Late Khot. *ttūṃgara(a)*- "ginger."[4] It is not until recently that Dragoni (2021, 305) points out that "[t]here is indeed no need to consider T[och]B *tvāṅkaro* as a Pre-Khotanese loanword," for the Tocharian word may well have been borrowed from an unattested Old Khot. **tvā́ṃgaraa-* or *tváṃgaraa-* (> Late Khot. *ttūṃgára*[*a*]-).[5] Despite the fact that TochB *tvāṅkaro* belongs to the *arṣāklo*-type rather than the *palsko*-type, the formal affinity between the two words might be indicative of a certain relationship between the source languages from which they were borrowed. That is to say, TochB *śāñcapo* could have derived from a language related to Khotanese.

[1] See also Del Tomba 2023, 203f.

[2] For the treatment of the other members of this group, especially those which can be diachronically explained as deverbal, see Del Tomba 2023, 205–209.

[3] See Bailey 1967, 196f. and 1979, 242; who, however, merely quoted the Tocharian word without specifying its relationship to the Iranian cognates. To our knowledge, van Windekens 1979, 28, §63 first proposed the hypothesis of an Iranian loanword. See also Tremblay 2005, 428; and most recently Dragoni 2023, 142–145. (← acc.sg. **pīθu*).

[4] See Bailey 1937, 913; Tremblay 2005, 428. Late Khot. *ttūṃgára(a)*- was borrowed into Old Tibetan by the 9th century CE and reduced to a disyllabic word: **toŋgára* > **li-dóŋ(g)ara* > Old Tibetan *li dong (g)ra* "dried ginger," with the voicing of the initial consonant triggered by the compounding with the toponym *li* "Khotan;" see Emmerick 1985, 313. A loanword with voiceless initial, i.e., *ṭoŋgára* "ginger," is preserved in modern Purik-Tibetan, which, in its turn, is the source of *tuŋgára* "id." in Brokskat, a Shina dialect (the Tibetan antecedent of Tamang *tungra* "id." remains obscure); see Bielmeier 2012, 22–27.

[5] See also Dragoni 2023, 125–127.

3.2 Etymological Discussions

The word for "mustard (seed)" is a productive *Wanderwort* attested in not a few ancient languages, the relationship between which is not fully clarified: Apart from Skt. *sarṣapa-* (< **sanšapa-*)[1] and Greek σίνᾱπι (→ Latin *sināpi[s]*, Arabic *ṣināb*, etc.),[2] a handful of cognates are found in Middle Iranian languages, such as Parthian *šyfš-d'n*, Sogdian *šywšp-δn*, and Middle Persian *span-dān* (EWAia II 712, s.v. *sarṣapa-*). The second component of the latter forms are descended from Old Iranian **dānā-* "cereal grain, seed" (NIL 125). All the Middle Iranian cognates seem to go back to a single etymon **sinšapa-*,[3] and the only exception is Khot. *śśaśvāna-*, which will be discussed a few lines below.

Walter B. Henning investigated the etymology of the word for "mustard (seed)" in detail, and offered a hypothetical reconstruction of the state of affairs: "The following hypothesis may serve to cut across all such difficulties: the word for "mustard" was approximately ***s¹eṇs²ap*** and belonged to a non-Indo-European language, whence it was adopted by Iranians and Indo-Aryans, severally, at a remote date, at the time of their immigration, and inducted into the phonological systems of their languages; thus, e.g., the brief *e*, alien to either group, came to be replaced variously by *i* or *a*." (Henning 1965, 45 = 1977, II 613). If Henning's hypothesis is anything to go by, and if TochB *śāñcapo* can be added to the same family of cognates, the Tocharians apparently adopted the word from a language, in which the diagnostic vowel **-ĕ-* turns into *-a-* rather than *-i-*. In other words, TochB *śāñcapo* was borrowed from the **s**a**nšapa*-group rather than the **s**i**nšapa*-group. This would narrow down the candidates for the source language to two: either Indic (Skt. *s**a**rṣapa-*) or (Pre-)Khotanese (Khot. *śś**a**śvāna-*). With all these observations in mind (cf. §3.1), we are tempted to regard (Pre-)Khotanese as the more likely candidate among the two.

Given that Khot. *śśaśvāna-* shows a developed and compounded form, the source of TochB *śāñcapo* is, in all likelihood, to be sought in an anterior stage of this language. Federico Dragoni (2023, 173f.) suggests a scenario to derive TochB *śāñcapo* from a hypothetical Pre-Khotanese[4] form **śaNźapa-*, a hypothesis to which we subscribe in the

[1] For the sound change between *-r-* and *-n-*, see also Skt. *karpūra-* < **kampūra-* "camphor," which may also be due to a contamination from the root **karp-* "strong-smelling plant" (Bernard 2020, 51, §8.3.2.3). The consonant *-r-* was prone to assimilation in Middle Indic (e.g. Pāli *sāsapa-*, Prakrit *sāsava-*; PSM 895a), but is well attested in the modern Indic cognates which almost exclusively presuppose a pre-form **sarṣ-* (or **śarṣ-*; CDIAL 767, §§13281 & 13282).

[2] See Beekes 2010, II 1333.

[3] See Henning 1965, 43f. = 1977, II 611f.; who also reconstructed Avestan **siušapa-* (with *-uš-* < **-ns-*) to account for the strange *-w-* of Sogdian *šywšp-*.

[4] In his discussion, Dragoni (op. cit.) distinguishes between Pre-Khotanese and Proto-Tumshuqese-Khotanese. While considering this distinction to be well taken, we beg to differ from Dragoni's system in the present case, since no Tumshuqese cognate of Khot. *śśaśvāna-* has been identified yet. Our use

present paper. His arguments are twofold: First, whatever the second component of Khot. *śśaśvāna-* originally was,[1] the first component should be *śśaśva°* /*śaźwa°*/. In such a form, the cluster *-śv-* /*-źw-*/ arose within Pre- or Old Khotanese through the weakening and syncope of the medial unstressed syllable (i.e., **śáNźapa-* > **śáNźäwa-* > **śaNźwa-*), and resulted in the subsequent loss of the preceding nasal (i.e., **śaNźwa-* > *śaźwa°*). Second, the reconstructed proto-form **śáNźapa-* has the initial *ś-* by assimilation from **sanšapa-*, which, as mentioned above, underlies Skt. *sarṣapa-*. It is probably this proto-form that found its way into Tocharian through the de-fricativisation of the fricative **-ś-* (← **-ź-*), which became the corresponding palatal stop *-c-* in a postnasal position (i.e., **śá**Nź**apa-* → TochB **śá**nś**apo* > *śā**ñc**apo*). This sound change **-nś-* > *-ñc-* is an inner-TochB development which is parallel to the *t*-epenthesis in the cluster *-ns-* (> *-nts-*) as well as to the "irregular" palatalisation of the cluster *-ṅk-* (> **-ñś-* > *-ñc-*; Ringe 1996, 115).

The aforesaid theory about the origin of the Tocharian word for "mustard (seed)," it is hoped, sheds new light on the long-lasting interaction between Tocharian and (Pre-)Khotanese, a language which the honorand of the present volume cherished as her own. To her memory, we dedicate this humble contribution, which, as we are well aware, is disproportionately small relative to the honorand's own achievements, "[a]s a grain of mustard appears before Mount Sumeru, a single drop of water in conne[ct]ion with the great ocean."[2] May the spicy etymology, inadequate as it may be, help to keep alive the remembrance of this extraordinary scholar.

Abbreviations

AVP — LeRoy C. Barret, ed. "The Kashmirian Atharva Veda: Book One." *Journal of the American Oriental Society* 26 (1905): 197–295.

AVŚ — Rudolph Roth and William D. Whitney, eds. *Atharva Veda Sanhita: Zweite verbesserte Auflage besorgt von Max Lindenau*. Berlin: Ferd. Dümmlers Verlag, 1924.

Bower — A.F. Rudolf Hoernle, ed. *The Bower Manuscript: Facsimile Leaves, Nāgarī Transcript, Romanised Transliteration and English Translation with Notes, and Sanskrit and English Indexes*. Calcutta: Archaeological Survey of India, 1893–1912.

---

of the term "Pre-Khotanese" is broadly conceived, covering both Proto-Tumshuqese-Khotanese and Pre-Khotanese in Dragoni's chronology.

[1] The second component *°āna-* was traditionally understood as the descendant of Old Iranian **dānā-* (after the loss of the initial *d-* in the *Kompositionsfuge*) in accord with the other Middle Iranian cognates; see Henning 1965, 35 = 1977, II 603. This explanation is difficult given the gender of Khot. *śśaśvāna-*, which seems to be attested in Old Khotanese as a masculine *a*-stem rather than a feminine *ā*-stem; see Dragoni 2023, 174. For the up-to-date state of the art, see Peyrot, Dragoni, and Bernard 2022, 408. No matter what the exact origin of the element *°āna-* is, it must be secondary in view of the aforementioned Sogd. *šywšp-δn* and Parth. *šyfš-d'n*, which presuppose the shorter forms *šywšp°* and *šyfš°*, respectively.

[2] *Book of Zambasta* 2.118: *kho ggarä Sumīrä śśaśvānä kaśte pata mahāsamudrä śśo kanä utca baña*; see Emmerick 1968, 30–31. For the simile of mustard seed in general, see Emmerick 1967, 22–25.

CarS Priyavrat V. Sharma, ed. *Caraka-Saṃhitā: Agniveśa's Treatise Refined and Annotated by Caraka and Redacted by Dṛḍhabala*, 4 vols. Jaikrishnadas Āyurveda Series 36. Varanasi & Delhi: Chaukhambha Orientalia, 1981–1994.

CDIAL R.L. Turner, ed. *A Comparative Dictionary of the Indo-Aryan Languages*. London: Oxford University Press, 1966.

CEToM *A Comprehensive Edition of Tocharian Manuscripts* <https://cetom.univie.ac.at/?home>. Vienna, 2011–.

EWAia Manfred Mayrhofer, ed. *Etymologisches Wörterbuch des Altindoarischen*, 3 vols. Heidelberg: Universitätsverlag C. Winter, 1992–2001.

KauśS Maurice Bloomfield, ed. *The Kāuçika-Sūtra of the Atharva-Veda with Extracts from the Commentaries of Dārila and Keçava*. New Haven, CT: American Oriental Society, 1890.

NIL Dagmar S. Wodtko, Britta Irslinger, and Carolin Schneider, eds. *Nomina im Indogermanischen Lexikon*. Heidelberg: Universitätsverlag C. Winter, 2008.

PSM Pandit Hargovind Das T. Sheth, ed. *Pāia-Sadda-Mahaṇṇavo: A Comprehensive Prakrit-Hindi Dictionary*. Delhi: Motilal Banarsidass, 1928.

PW Otto von Böhtlingk and Rudolph Roth, ed. *Sanskrit-Wörterbuch*, 7 vols. St. Petersburg, 1855–1875.

RV Barend A. van Nooten and Gary B. Holland, eds. *Rig Veda: A Metrically Restored Text*. London: Oxford University Press. Harvard Oriental Series 50. Cambridge, MA: Department of Sanskrit and Indian Studies, Harvard University, 1994.

SuŚr Jādavjī Trikamjī and Nārāyaṇa Rāma Ācārya, eds. *The Suśrutasaṃhitā of Suśruta with the Nibandhasaṃgraha Commentary of Śrī Ḍalhaṇācārya and the Nyāyancandrikā Pañjikā of Śrī Gayadāsācārya*. Jaikrishnadas Āyurveda Series 34. Varanasi: Chaukhambha Orientalia, 1980.

Vāgbh Anna Moreśvara Kunte and Navare Kṛṣṇaśāstrī, eds. *Aṣṭāṅgahṛdayam Composed by Vāgbhaṭa with the Commentaries of Aruṇadatta and Hemādri*. Jaikrishnadas Āyurveda Series 52. Varanasi: Chaukhambha Orientalia, 1982.

References

Abedi 2020 Milad Abedi. "On the Later Phase of Elamite-Iranian Language Contact." In: Romain Garnier, ed., *Loanwords and Substrata: Proceedings of the Colloquium Held in Limoges (5th–7th June, 2018)*, Innsbrucker Beiträge zur Sprachwissenschaft 164, 1–25. Innsbruck: Institut für Sprachwissenschaft der Universität Innsbruck.

Acharya 2016 Diwakar Acharya. "Three Fragmentary Folios of a 9th-Century Manuscript of an Early Bhūtatantra Taught by Mahāmaheśvara." In: Dominic Goodall & Harunaga Isaacson, eds., *Tantric Studies: Fruits of a Franco-German Project on Early Tantra*, Collection Indologie 131 / Early Tantra Series 4, 157–179. Pondicherry: Institut français de Pondichéry, École française d'Extrême-Orient.

Adams 2013 Douglas Q. Adams, ed. *A Dictionary of Tocharian B: Revised and Greatly Enlarged*. Leiden Studies in Indo-European 10. Amsterdam & New York: Rodopi.

Anderson and Giles
2012 Robert T. Anderson and Terry Giles. *The Samaritan Pentateuch: An Introduction to Its Origin, History, and Significance for Biblical Studies*. Atlanta: Society of Biblical Literature.

Bailey 1937 Harold W. Bailey. "Ttaugara." *Bulletin of the School of Oriental Studies* 8/4: 883–921.

1967 *Indo-Scythian Studies, Being Khotanese Texts Volume VI: Prolexis to the Book of Zambasta.* Cambridge: Cambridge University Press.

1979 ed. *Dictionary of Khotan Saka.* Cambridge: Cambridge University Press.

Beck 2005 Lily Y. Beck, tr. *De materia medica by Pedanius Dioscorides*. Hildesheim: Olms-Weidmann.

Beekes 2010 Robert Beekes. *Etymological Dictionary of Greek*, 2 vols. Leiden Indo-European Etymological Dictionary Series 10. Leiden & Boston: Brill.

Bernard 2020 Chams B. Bernard. "Some Plants and Animal Names in Gavruni." In: Romain Garnier, ed., *Loanwords and Substrata: Proceedings of the Colloquium Held in Limoges (5th–7th June, 2018)*, Innsbrucker Beiträge zur Sprachwissenschaft 164, 27–61. Innsbruck: Institut für Sprachwissenschaft der Universität Innsbruck.

Bernard and Chen

2022 Chams B. Bernard and Ruixuan Chen. "A Fall into the Pit: Remarks on Tocharian B *koṣko, koṣkīye*." *Indo-Iranian Journal* 65/1: 1–31.

Bielmeier 2012 Roland Bielmeier. "Ginger: A Khotanese Loanword in Modern Purik-Tibetan." In: Cristina Scherrer-Schaub, ed., *Old Tibetan Studies Dedicated to the Memory of R.E. Emmerick*, Brill's Tibetan Studies Library 10/14, 21–27. Leiden & Boston: Brill.

Caland 1900 Willem Caland. *Altindisches Zauberritual: Probe einer Uebersetzung der wichtigsten Theile des Kauśika Sūtra*. Amsterdam: Verhandelingen der Koninklijke Akademie van Wetenschappen.

Carling 2003 Gerd Carling. "Fragments bilingues du *Yogaśataka*: Révision commentée de l'édition de Jean Filliozat." *Tocharian and Indo-European Studies* 10: 37–68.

2007 "The Vocabulary of Tocharian Medical Manuscripts." *Asian Medicine* 3: 323–333.

Casson 1989 Lionel Casson. *The Periplus Maris Erythraei: Text with Introduction, Translation, and Commentary*. Princeton: Princeton University Press.

Chavannes 1897 Édouard Chavannes, tr. *Les Mémoires Historiques de Se-ma Ts'ien, traduits et annotés. Tome II: Chapitres V–XII.* Paris: Éditions Ernest Leroux.

Chen 2021 Chen Ming. "'Method from Persia': Study on the Origins of the 'Three Myrobalan Decoction.'" *Hualin International Journal of Buddhist Studies* 4/2: 1–78.

Degener 1989 Almuth Degener. *Khotanese Suffixe*. Stuttgart: Franz Steiner Verlag.

Del Tomba 2019 Alessandro Del Tomba. "Problemi paleografici e linguistici in tocario: Figure etimologiche e *hapax legomena*." *FormaMente* 14/2: 107–122.

2023 *The Tocharian Gender System: A Diachronic Study in Nominal Morphology*. Leiden & Boston: Brill.

Dragoni 2021 Federico Dragoni. "Materia Medica Tocharo-Hvatanica." *Bulletin of the School of Oriental and African Studies* 84/2: 295–319.

2023 *Watañi lāntaṃ: Khotanese and Tumshuqese Loanwords in Tocharian*. Wiesbaden: Dr. Ludwig Reichert Verlag.

Durgāprasād et al.
1889 Paṇḍit Durgāprasād and Kāśīnāth Pāṇḍurang Parab, eds. *The Kathāsaritsāgara of Somadevabhaṭṭa*. Bombay: Nirṇaya Sagar.

Elfenbein 1990 Josef Elfenbein, ed. *An Anthology of Classical and Modern Balochi Literature*, 2 vols. Wiesbaden: Otto Harrassowitz.

Emmerick 1967 Ronald E. Emmerick. "The Mustard *Upamā*," *The Journal of the Royal Asiatic Society of Great Britain and Ireland* 99/1: 22–25

1968 *The Book of Zambasta: A Khotanese Poem on Buddhism*. London Oriental Series 21. London: Oxford University Press.

Filliozat 1948 Jean Filliozat. *Fragments de textes Koutchéens de médecine et de magie*. Paris: Librairie d'Amérique et d'Orient Adrien-Maisonneuve.

Franceschini
2007 Marco Franceschini, ed. *An Updated Vedic Concordance: Maurice Bloomfield's A Vedic Concordance Enhanced with New Material Taken from Seven Vedic Texts*. Harvard Oriental Series 66. Cambridge, MA: Department of Sanskrit and Indian Studies, Harvard University.

Gaṇapati
1920–1925 Gaṇapati Śāstrī. *The Ārya-Mañjuśrīmūlakalpa*, 3 vols. Trivandrum: Superintendent Government Press.

Gershevitch 1957 Ilya Gershevitch. "Sissoo at Susa (OPers. *yakā-* = *Dalbergia sissoo* Roxb.)." *Bulletin of the School of Oriental and African Studies* 19/2: 317–320.

Henning 1965 Walter Bruno Henning. "A Grain of Mustard." *Annali dell'Istituto Universitario Orientale di Napoli: Sezione Linguistica* 6: 29–47.

1977 *Selected Papers II*. Acta Iranica 15. Leiden: E. J. Brill.

Hinz 1950 Walter Hinz. "The Elamite Version of the Record of Darius's Palace at Susa." *Journal of Near Eastern Studies* 9/1: 1–7.

Jamison and Brereton
2014 Stephanie W. Jamison and Joel P. Brereton. *The Rigveda: The Earliest Religious Poetry of India*. Oxford & New York: Oxford University Press.

Kangle 1960 R.P. Kangle, ed. *The Kauṭilīya Arthaśāstra, Part I: A Critical Edition with a Glossary*. Bombay: University of Bombay.

Kern 1865 Hendrik Kern, ed. *The Bṛhat Sañhitá of Varáha-Mihira*. Bibliotheca Indica 48. Calcutta: Baptist Mission Press.

Kimura et al.
2000 Kimura Hideaki 木村秀明, Ōtsuka Nobuo 大塚伸夫, and Suzuki Kōshin 鈴木晃信 , eds. "Transcribed Sanskrit Text of the *Amoghapāśakalparāja*: Part III." *Annual of the Institute for Comprehensive Studies of Buddhism Taishō University / Taishō daigaku Sōgō bukkyō kenkyūjo nenpō* 大正大学綜合佛教研究所年報 22: 1–64(= 372–309).

Kosegarten 1848 Johann Gottfried Ludwig Kosegarten, ed. *Pantschatantrum sive quinquepartitum de moribus exponens*. Bonn: Koenig.

Kroonen 2013 Guus Kroonen. *Etymological Dictionary of Proto-Germanic*. Leiden Indo-European Etymological Dictionary Series 11. Leiden & Boston: Brill.

Löw 1881 Immanuel Löw. *Aramæische Pflanzennamen*. Leipzig: Verlag von Wilhelm Engelmann.

Lüders 1954 Heinrich Lüders. *Beobachtungen über die Sprache des buddhistischen Urkanons*. Berlin: Akademie Verlag.

MacKenzie 1971 David N. MacKenzie, ed. *A Concise Pahlavi Dictionary*. London: Oxford University Press.

Malzahn 2010 Melanie Malzahn. *The Tocharian Verbal System*. Leiden & Boston: Brill.

Morgenstierne

1956 Georg Morgenstierne. *Indo-Iranian Frontier Languages, III: The Pashai Language*. Oslo: H. Aschehoug & Co.

2003 ed. *A New Etymological Vocabulary of Pashto*. Beiträge zur Iranistik 23. Wiesbaden: Dr. Ludwig Reichert Verlag.

Olivelle 2013 Patrick Olivelle. *King, Governance, and Law in Ancient India: Kauṭilya's Arthaśāstra*. Oxford & New York: Oxford University Press.

Orwa et al. 2010 C. Orwa, A. Mutua, R. Kindt, R. Jamnadass, and A. Simons, eds. *Agroforestry Database: A Tree Reference and Selection Guide* <http://apps.worldagroforestry.org/treedb2/>. Kenya.

Pan 2021 Tao Pan. *Untersuchungen zu Lexikon und Metrik des Tocharischen*. PhD dissertation. Munich.

Partridge 2006 Eric Partridge, ed. *Origins: A Short Etymological Dictionary of Modern English*. London & New York: Routledge.

Pearson 1996 M.N. Pearson, ed. *Spices in the Indian Ocean World*. London & New York: Routledge.

Peyrot, Dragoni, and Bernard

2022 Michaël Peyrot, Federico Dragoni, and Chams Bernard. "The Spread of Iron in Central Asia: On the Etymology of the Word for 'Iron' in Iranian and Tocharian." *Bulletin of the School of Oriental and African Studies* 85/3: 403–422.

Peyrot, Pinault, and Wilkens

2019 Michaël Peyrot, Georges-Jean Pinault, and Jens Wilkens. "Vernaculars of the Silk Road: A Tocharian B-Old Uyghur Bilingual." *Journal Asiatique* 307/1: 65–90.

Pinault 1988 Georges-Jean Pinault. "Le *Pratītyasamutpāda* en Koutchéen." *Tocharian and Indo-European Studies* 2: 96–165.

Pulleyblank 1991 Edwin G. Pulleyblank, ed. *Lexicon of Reconstructed Pronunciation in Early Middle Chinese, Late Middle Chinese, and Early Mandarin*. Vancouver: University of British Columbia Press.

Ram Manohar et al.

2009 P. Ram Manohar, Pushpan Reshmi, and S. Rohmi. "Mustard and Its Uses in *Ayurveda*." *Indian Journal of Traditional Knowledge* 8/3: 400–404.

Ringe 1996 Don Ringe, Jr. *On the Chronology of Sound Changes in Tocharian, Volume 1: From Proto-Indo-European to Proto-Tocharian*. New Haven, CT: American Oriental Society.

Rossi 1979 Adriano V. Rossi. *Iranian Lexical Elements in Brāhūī*. Naples: Istituto Universitario Orientale.

Sanderson 2001 Alexis Sanderson. "History through Textual Criticism in the Study of Śaivism, the Pāñcarātra and the Buddhist Yoginītantras." In: François Grimal, ed., *Les sources et le temps / Sources and Time: A Colloquium, Pondicherry 11–13 January 1997*, Publications du département d'Indologie 91, 1–47. Pondicherry: Institut français de Pondichéry, École française d'Extrême-Orient.

Sieg 1955 Emil Sieg. "Die medizinischen und tantrischen Texte der Pariser Sammlung in Tocharisch B." *Zeitschrift für vergleichende Sprachforschung* 72/1–2: 63–83.

Schwentner 1955 Ernst Schwentner. "Toch. B *sal* 'schmutzig.'" *Zeitschrift für vergleichende Sprachforschung* 73/1–2: 117.

Strickmann 1996 Michel Strickmann. *Mantras et mandarins: Le bouddhisme tantrique en Chine*. Paris: Gallimard.

Syed 1992 Renate Syed. *Die Flora Altindiens in Literatur und Kunst*. PhD dissertation. Munich.

Szántó 2012 Péter-Dániel Szántó. *Selected Chapters from the Catuṣpīṭhatantra*, 2 vols. PhD dissertation. Oxford.

Tremblay 2005 Xavier Tremblay. "Irano-Tocharica et Tocharo-Iranica." *Bulletin of the School of Oriental and African Studies* 68/3: 421–449.

Uhle 1881 Heinrich Uhle, ed. *Die Vetālapañcaviṁśatikā des Śivadāsa und eines Ungenannten mit kritischem Commentar*. Leipzig: Brockhaus.

van Windekens

1944 Albert J. van Windekens. *Morphologie comparée du tokharien*. Louvain: Muséon.

1976 *Le tokharien confronté avec les autres langues indo-européennes. Vol. I: La phonétique et le vocabulaire*. Travaux publiés par le Centre International de Dialectologie Générale de l'Université Catholique Néerlandaise de Louvain 11. Louvain: Centre International de Dialectologie Générale.

1979 *Le tokharien confronté avec les autres langues indo-européennes. Vol. II, 1: La morphologie nominale*. Travaux publiés par le Centre International de Dialectologie Générale de l'Université Catholique Néerlandaise de Louvain 12. Louvain: Centre International de Dialectologie Générale.

von Hinüber

2001 Oskar von Hinüber. *Das ältere Mittelindisch im Überblick, 2., erweiterte Auflage*. Vienna: Verlag der Österreichischen Akademie der Wissenschaften.

Wellmann 1907 Max Wellmann, ed. *Pedanii Dioscuridis De materia medica libri quinque: Volumen I quo continentur libri I et II*. Berlin: Weidmann.

Wilkens 2021 Jens Wilkens, ed. *Handwörterbuch des Altuigurischen: Altuigurisch – Deutsch – Türkisch*. Göttingen: Universitätsverlag Göttingen.

Witzel 2013 Michael Witzel, Toshifumi Gotō and Salvatore Scarlata. *Rig-Veda, das heilige Wissen: Dritter bis fünfter Liederkreis*. Frankfurt a. M.: Verlag der Weltreligionen.

Wolska-Conus
1973 Wanda Wolska-Conus, tr. *Cosmas Indicopleustès, Topographie chrétienne*, vol. III. Paris: Les Éditions du Cerf.

Yamada 1971 Yamada Nobuo. "Four Notes on Several Names for Weights and Measures in Uighur Documents." In: Lajos Ligeti, ed., *Studia Turcica*, Bibliotheca Orientalis Hungarica 17, 491–498. Budapest: Akadémiai Kiadó.

Yoshida 2003 Yoshida Yutaka. "Review of Nicholas Sims-Williams, *Bactrian Documents from Northern Afghanistan I*." *Bulletin of the Asia Institute* 14: 154–159.

2007 "Notes on the Khotanese Secular Documents of the 8th–9th Centuries." In: Maria Macuch & Werner Sundermann, eds., *Iranian Languages and Texts from Iran and Turan: Ronald E. Emmerick Memorial Volume*, Iranica 13, 463–472. Wiesbaden: Harrassowitz.

The Niya Conjuncts*

A Catalogue of Kharoṣṭhī Conjunct Consonants Unique to the Niya Corpus

Andrew GLASS

Abstract: This paper focuses on identifying the distinct forms of Kharoṣṭhī consonant conjunct signs attested in the Gāndhārī documents discovered at Niya and other sites along the Southern Silk Road. The work complements Rapson's paleographic studies which were based on 764 documents of this type known before 1929. The present study extends Rapson's work by providing a thorough accounting of the distinctive conjunct consonant signs in this important collection of Kharoṣṭhī documents, now totaling 901 documents. For the purposes of this study, only paleographic conjuncts are investigated rather than the orthographic representation of conjunct sounds or Gāndhārī reflexes of OIA consonant conjuncts. The author has checked the available images of the Niya corpus and provided the most extensive illustrated inventory of conjunct signs in the Kharoṣṭhī script. The paper concludes with some additional observations on the formation types of the Niya conjuncts and documents improvements to readings that resulted from this study.

Keywords: Niya; Kharoṣṭhī; conjunct consonant; palaeography

In this paper I document the forms of the Kharoṣṭhī consonant conjunct signs attested in the Gāndhārī documents discovered at Niya and other sites in the oasis states along the Southern Silk Road. The script of these documents has already been described in detail—including the conjuncts—in Rapson's appendix to Boyer, Rapson, Senart, and Noble's *Kharoṣṭhī Inscriptions* (1920–1929). But, while Rapson's work continues to be a valuable study of the writing system of these materials, the documentation and understanding of the Kharoṣṭhī script has progressed considerably over the past century, in particular, my earlier study, *Kharoṣṭhī Manuscript Palaeography* (Glass 2000). Moreover, we now have at our disposal digital tools that make it far easier to investigate the details

---

Andrew GLASS, Independent Scholar, United States of America.

* I will be forever grateful to Prof. Duan Qing for—and will always remember—the unique visit to the Niya ruins that she arranged in December 2014. This visit followed a valuable and fascinating short conference focused on readings of some recently discovered Kharoṣṭhī documents from Central Asia. The conference and visit coincided with work Dr. Stefan Baums, and I had, at that point, embarked on to update the seminal work of Boyer, Rapson, Senart, and Noble *Kharoṣṭhī Inscriptions Discovered by Sir Aurel Stein in Chinese Turkestan* (1920–1929) in connection with our work on our *Dictionary of Gāndhārī* (GD, Baums and Glass 2002a). So it was, with real pleasure, that I joined the activities in 2014; and then, with real honour and appreciation, that I accepted the invitation to contribute to this volume. Alas, what was intended as a festschrift celebrating the work and achievements of Prof. Duan has now become a memorial volume for a life well lived. So it is with real sorrow and respect that I offer this posthumous token for Prof. Duan's leadership in the field and in the desert.

of specific forms via high-definition digital images; and also, broader patterns via statistical analysis of the entire corpus. However, this additional depth and breadth requires much time to do in full and we have no more of that today than Rapson will have had a century ago; so, I do not attempt to update or supersede Rapson's Palaeography, but rather supplement it where new insights can be gained.

Rapson's study was based on his close reading of the 764 documents of this type which had been discovered by Aurel Stein on three expeditions to Central Asia in 1900–1901, 1906–1908, and 1913–1916. Since then, 137 additional documents of this type have been published. Unfortunately, Boyer, Rapson, Senart, and Noble's publication appeared with only a selection of images of the materials. Additional photographs of some of the documents appeared in Stein's own expedition reports, but the available documentation for independent palaeographic study was woefully incomplete. The International Dunhuang Project made significant contributions to filling gaps in the visual record by making high-quality digital images of the materials in the British Library collection and publishing them online (https://idp.bl.uk/). Even so, the documentation of this collection is still incomplete as many of the Kharoṣṭhī documents in the Stein Collection are not kept at the British Library and were not included among the published plates.

As a core constituent of work on their Gāndhārī Dictionary (2002a), Baums and Glass have been compiling a corpus of published Gāndhārī documents (2002b). This corpus comprises digital text editions fully linked to the dictionary headwords and, where available, images of the texts and objects concerned. In addition to supporting the lexicographic work, this linked database can be used to analyse other aspects of Gāndhārī, particularly, palaeography. One of the distinctive characteristics of the script of the Niya documents is the frequent use of conjunct consonants, which in many cases are not found in documents from other regions where Kharoṣṭhī script was used. As such, these signs represent local innovations to represent the sounds used in the local languages, and do so using established patterns in the script grammar of Kharoṣṭhī.

This article will investigate this distinctive innovation of Niya Kharoṣṭhī using the available images of the central Asian documents of the Southern Silk Road. Note that this study focuses on the palaeographic conjuncts, and not the orthographic representation of conjunct sounds, nor Gāndhārī reflexes of OIA consonant conjuncts, which I will leave for a future study.

1 Attested conjunct consonants

The first step of the analysis is to identify the full list of conjunct consonants that occur in the documents from sites on the Southern Silk Road (Niya, Loulan, Endere, Hotan). This is easily done by querying the database for transcriptions comprising two or more consonants among the documents from these sites. This yields a list of 188 distinct conjunct akṣaras.

kḍha, kta, ktva, kma, kya, kra, kla, kva, kṣa, kṣya, ksa, ḱga, ḱra, khma, khva, gcma, gta, gtsa, gna, gya, gra, gva, gsa, ghra, cga, ctva, cma, cya, cra, cva, chya, jga, jña, jya, ñga, ñca, ñya, ṭhra, ḍḍha, ḍya, ḍhga, ḍhra, tka, tkva, tga, tgha, tna, tpa, tma, tya, tra, trya, tva, tsa, tsga, tsma, dma, dya, dra, drya, dva, dhya, dhva, nga, nḍha, nta, nna, nma, nya, pga, pca, pña, pṭa, pḍha, pta, pna, pma, pya, pra, pla, pṣa, psa, bdha, bra, bhta, bhya, bhra, mka, mga, mca, mña, mḍha, mta, mtsa, mna, mma, mya, mla, mśa, mṣa, mṣya, msa, ysa, rka, rga, rca, rja, rña, rḍha, rta, rtsa, rtha, rda, rdha, rna, rpa, rba, rbha, rma, rmma, rya, rra, rla, rla, rva, rvra, rśa, rśya, rṣa, rsa, rsta, rza, lka, lkha, lga, lca, lta, ltsa, lda, lna, lpa, lpva, lbha, lma, lya, lva, lsa, lýa, lýya, vya, vra, śta, śpa, śya, śra, śva, ṣka, ṣga, ṣṭa, ṣṭha, ṣḍha, ṣta, ṣtsa, ṣpa, ṣma, ṣya, ṣra, ṣla, ṣva, ṣṣṕa, ṣṕa, sga, sḍha, sta, stra, stha, spa, sma, sya, sra, sva, ssa, sṕa, zdha, zba, zma, hma, hya

It can reasonably be said that the forms transcribed as *kṣa, sta* and *stha* should be excluded from this list as they are basic signs of the script rather than being true conjuncts; however, let us not get side-traced by this topic which is dealt with elsewhere (Glass 2000, 115, 119; Brough 1962, 72–73, 75–77) as we will eliminate them from the study in the next step anyway. Our goal, here, is to focus on the conjunct forms that are unique to the documents of Niya and related sites on the Southern Silk Road, so we will subtract from the above list forms which occur in "standard" Kharoṣṭhī, which I will take to mean the script as attested in the inscriptions, manuscripts, and coin legends of Gandhara and its environs. Here are the 133 conjunct forms of "standard" Kharoṣṭhī:

kta, kya, kra, kva, kṣa, kṣma, kṣya, kṣva, khkṣa, khti, khya, khra, khsa, gga, ggya, gra, gva, gha, ghra, cya, chya, jña, jra, jva, ṭra, ṭhra, ṭhva, ḍra, ḍha, ṇya, tge, tma, tya, tra, tva, tsa, thya, thra, dya, dra, dva, dhdha, dhya, dhra, dhrya, dhva, nta, nma, nya, nri, nva, pta, pya, pra, pśa, phra, phśpa, phsa, bra, bhya, bhra, bhva, mga, mma, mya, mra, mha, rka, rkha, rga, rgha, rca, rja, rñe, rḍha, rṇa, rta, rtha, rda, rdha, rna, rpa, rbha, rma, rya, ryya, rla, rva, rśa, rṣa, rsa, rza, lpa, lya, lýi, vthi, vya, vra, vhra, vhrya, śpa, śpri, śma, śya, śra, śva, ṣka, ṣkri, ṣṭi, ṣṭha, ṣṇi, ṣthu, ṣna, ṣpa, ṣma, ṣya, ṣra, ṣva, sta, stra, stha, sna, spa, spra, sphu, sma, smri, sya, sra, srva, sva, hma, hya

Similarly, I have not included the nine conjunct forms that are unique to the Khotan Dharmapada manuscript: *khkṣa, gga, jva, tḡa, tga, mma, mra, rṇa, śma*—preferring to leave the question of these conjuncts and whether the Khotan Dharmapada manuscript was written in Khotan or imported from Gandhāra for another time.

This leaves 102 conjunct akṣaras which are unique to central Asian documents or otherwise only occur in documents that come from the Southern-Silk-Road sites. Note that I have chosen not to exclude forms that are attested at Niya if they also occur in texts from sites on the Northern Silk Road (Dunhuang, Kizil, Kucha, Toyuq), but I have not included forms from the Northern Silk Road not found in the materials from the Southern-Silk-Road sites. For convenience, I refer to this set as the "Niya conjuncts."

My investigation consisted of reviewing all documented forms of these conjuncts, either directly from the available images or in Rapson's table (Boyer, Rapson, Senart, and Noble 1920–1929, plate XIV), where it can be assumed that Rapson's reproductions are faithful to the source documents. This brings the number of verified conjuncts down to just fifty-eight. The following list enumerates all 102 Niya conjuncts with verified forms in bold. To focus on conjunct formation, these akṣaras are referenced in their basic form without vowel diacritics.

kḍha, **ktva**, **kma**, **kla**, **ksa**, **ḱga**, **khma**, **khva**, **gcma**, **gta**, **gtsa**, **gna**, gsa, **cga**, **ctva**, **cma**, **cra**, **cva**, jga, **jya**, **ñga**, ñca, ñya, ḍya, ḍhga, ḍhra, tka, tkva, **tga**, tgha, tna, tpa, trya, tsga, **tsma**, **drya**, **nga**, nḍha, nna, **pga**, **pca**, **pña**, pṭa, pḍha, **pna**, pma, **pla**, **pṣa**, **psa**, **bdha**, **bhta**, mka, **mga**, mca, mḍha, mta, mtsa, mma, **mla**, mśa, **mṣa**, mṣya, **msa**, ysa, rña, **rtsa**, rba, rmma, rra, rla, **rvra**, rśya, **rsta**, **lka**, lkha, lga, **lca**, **lta**, **ltsa**, lda, **lna**, **lpa**, lbha, **lma**, **lva**, **lýa**, lýya, śta, **ṣga**, **ṣḍha**, **ṣta**, **ṣtsa**, **ṣla**, ṣṣṕa, **ṣṕa**, sga, **sḍha**, ssa, **sṕa**, zdha, **zba**, **zma**

In the table that follows, I have illustrated all fifty-eight verified Niya conjuncts illustrating their forms from the best available source as well as the illustration in Rapson's chart (cited according to the integer value given in his chart). As noted above, Rapson's forms are in a *few* cases the only available witness (*cma, ñg̱a, drya*). To help interpretation, I have rendered each form using a modern standardized Kharoṣṭhī font designed for typesetting the script (Segoe UI Historic). For each conjunct I note the details of the illustrated attestation and provide references to the *Dictionary of Gāndhārī* (GD, Baums and Glass 2002a) where one may easily look up additional attestations. Where known, the etymology of the illustrated form has been given based on GD. In most cases, the etymology is unclear and therefore omitted. Sometimes, additional commentary on the form is provided as a note.

I distinguish four types of conjuncts:

- Ligature—specialized forms that have no graphic resemblance to their presumed component parts, e.g., *sta* 𐨯𐨿𐨟.
  The ligature forms are well attested in Gandhari generally, hence the only forms included in this catalog are tripartite: *gtsa, tsma, rtsa, ltsa, ṣtsa.*
- Reduction—one of the consonants (usually a semi-vowel) takes a reduced form that diacritically marks or extends from the other consonant, e.g., *rta* 𐨪𐨿𐨟.
  The seventeen forms involving reduction are: *ktva, kla, khva, ctva, cra, cva, jya, drya, pla, rtsa, rvra, rla, rsta, lpa, lva, lýa, ṣla.*
- Cursive stack—a vertical stack in which two consonants are cursively connected and share a single stroke. The two components are readily identifiable based on their standalone forms, e.g., *kma* 𐨐𐨿𐨨.
  The seven cursive stack forms are: *kma, khma, cma, tsma, bhta, lma, ṣpa.*
- Stack—a vertical stack comprising two discrete consonants. The two components are readily identifiable based on their standalone forms, e.g., *ṣta* 𐨮𐨿𐨟.
  This is the most common type, with thirty-six examples: *kḍha, ktva, ksa, ḱg̱a, g̱cma, gta, gtsa, g̱na, cga, ctva, ñg̱a, tg̱a, ng̱a, pg̱a, pca, pña, pna, pṣa, psa, bdha, mg̱a, mla, mṣa, msa, lka, lca, lta, ltsa, lna, ṣg̱a, ṣḍha, ṣta, ṣtsa, sḍha, zba, zma*

Tri-partite conjuncts do occur and can be analysed using two of the above types.

These types represent a slight revision of my previous enumeration (Glass 2000, 114–115). Not included in this study are the forms with superscript horizontal that generally correspond to OIA conjunct forms, e.g., *s̄a* for OIA *sna* (Salomon 2000, 78). For details on these forms generally see Glass 2000, 136, and in Niya documents in particular, see Rapson in Boyer, Rapson and Senart 1920–1929, 320–321.

Conjunct	Details	Rapson	Illustration	Font
kḏha	*[Lýa]***k[ḏha]** CKD 701 rl4 GD sv. Lýakḍha Total attestations: 1 Type: Stack	—		
ktva	***bhuktvā*** CKD 523 r3 GD sv. bhuṃjadi Total attestations: 1 Skt. *bhuktvā* Type: Stack + reduction	 No. 170		
kma	*lýo***kma***na* CKD 318 uo6 GD sv. lýokmana, Sukmana Total attestations: 4 Type: Cursive stack	 No. 171		
kla	*a***kla***tsa* CKD 330 o2 GD sv. aṃklatsa, klaseṃciya, Klaseṃna, klaseṃna-dhaṃma, Cakla, vulutsukla, Ṣekla Total attestations: 34 Tocharian B *aknātsa*; Tocharian A *aknats* Type: Reduction Note: here and following, the horizontal stroke is now interpreted as a post-consonantal *la* rather than the *ra'* of Rapson's time (Glass 2000, 124; Glass, Baums, and Salomon 2002: 10).	 No. 173 *kra'* [Sic]		

ksa	*Yoksenaṣa CKD 762 rK2* GD sv. Yoksena Total attestations: 1 Type: Stack	–	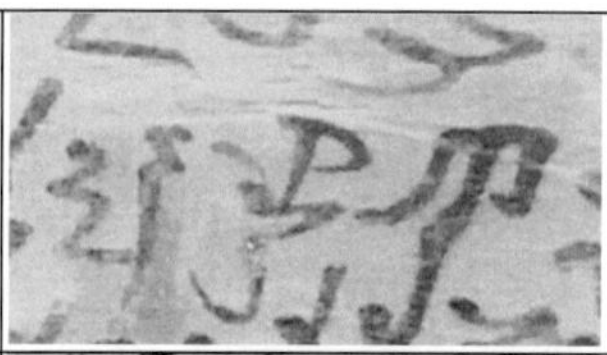	
ḱga	*Rici**ḱga**ṣa* CKD 590 uo8 GD sv. Ricga Total attestations: 2 Type: Stack	–		
khma	tra**khma** CKD 324 o5 GD sv. drakhma Total attestations: 3 Greek δραχμή Type: Cursive stack Note: the cursive connection in the illustrated example seems to be a secondary formation, suggesting that the scribe intended to link the *ma* to the base of the *kha* but did not actually do so at first.	–		
khva	**khva**ni CKD 505 o3 GD sv. kuhani, Khvarnarse Total attestations: 12 Tibetan *khu ñe, skun khar, sku mkhar* Type: Reduction	 No. 175	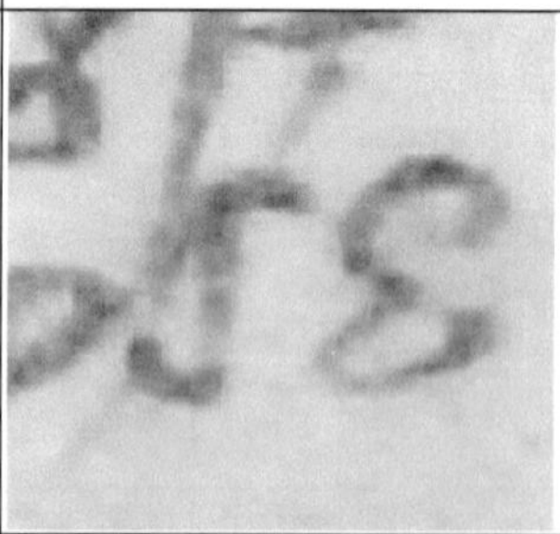	
g̱cma	Lu**g̱cma**naṣa CKD 701 rD1 GD sv. Lugcmana Total attestations: 1 Type: Stack + stack Note: normally written as a cursive stack, this example clearly shows the distinct stroke used for the *-ma*.	–	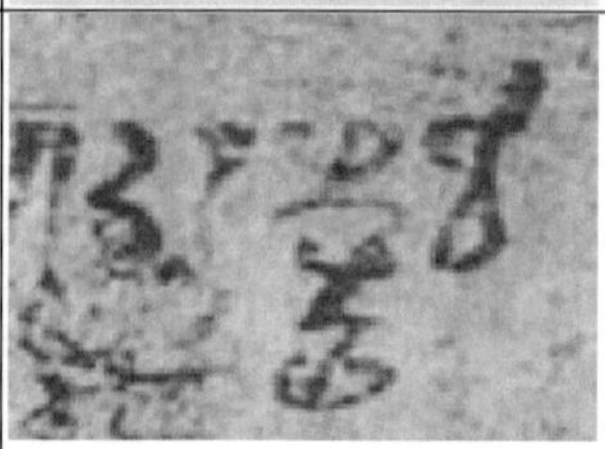	

gta	parimu**gta** CKD 702 o5 GD sv. parimuta Total attestations: 4 Skt. *parimukta* Type: Stack	–	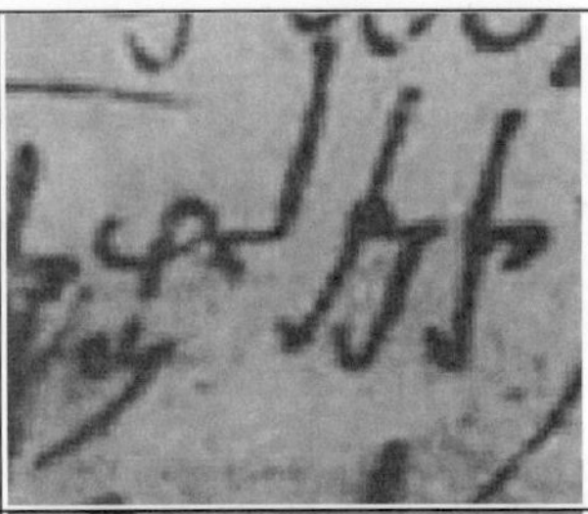	
gtsa	Śaṃ**gtsi**ya CKD 318 uo3, GD sv. Śaṃgtsi Total attestations: 2 Type: Stack + ligature	 No. 177	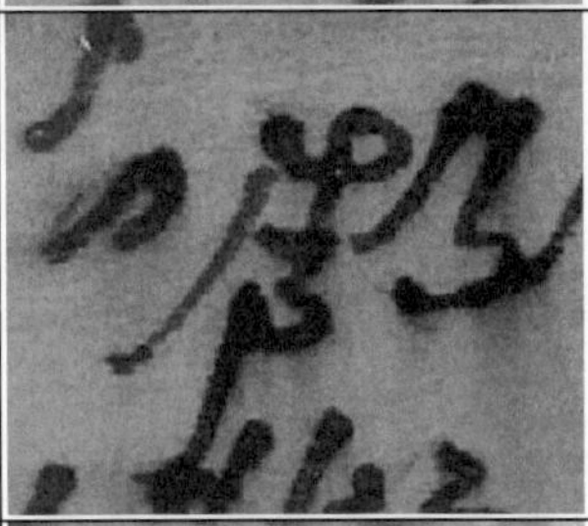	
g̱na	Si**g̱na**yaṣa CKD 422 o7 GD sv. Sig̱aya, Sug̱ata, Sug̱uta, sug̱uma Total attestations: 7 Type: Stack	–	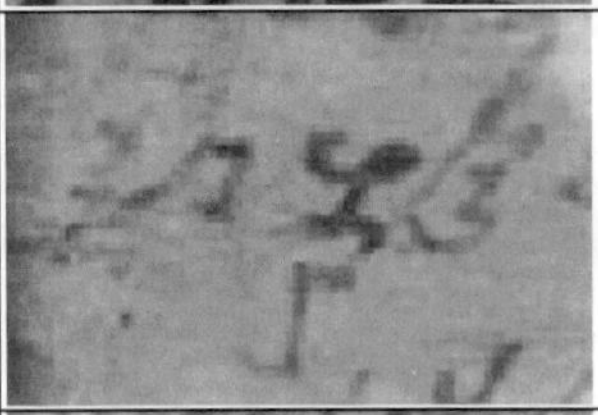	
cg̱a	**Cg̱**oya CKD 701 rD8 GD sv. Aṃcge, Kaṃcge, Kaṃcgoa, Korecga, Krucga, Cgito, Cgote, Cgoya, Taṃcga, Taṃcge, Taṃcgo, Taṃcgota, Tsaṃcgeya, Pacgo, Paṃcge, Picga, Piltacga, Ponicga, Micga, Micge, Miṃcga, Mogecga, Mocge, Moticga, Yipicga, Racge, Ricga, Lacgea, Soṃcge, Svaṃcga Total attestations: 21 Type: Stack	–	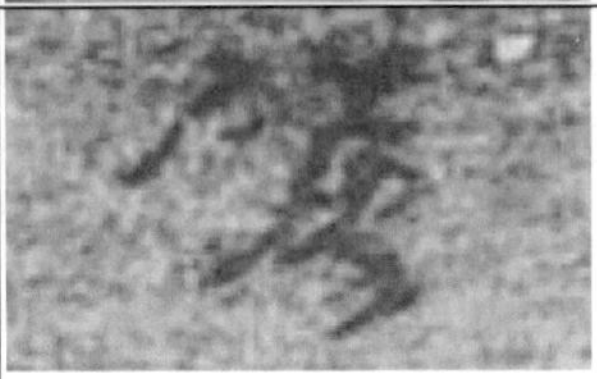	
ctva	Kra[**ctva**]yaṣa CKD 342 oA4 GD sv. Kractvaya Total attestations: 1 Type: Stack + reduction	–	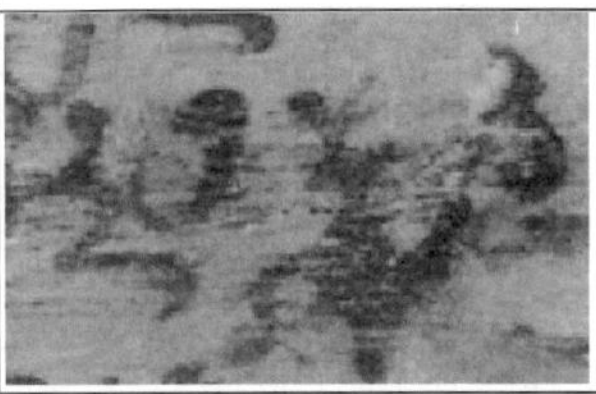	
cma	No clear image GD sv. Cmaka Total attestations: 7 Type: Cursive stack	 No. 183	–	

cra	**Cra**maena CKD 400 o2 GD sv. Cramaena, curorma Total attestations: 2 Type: Reduction	–	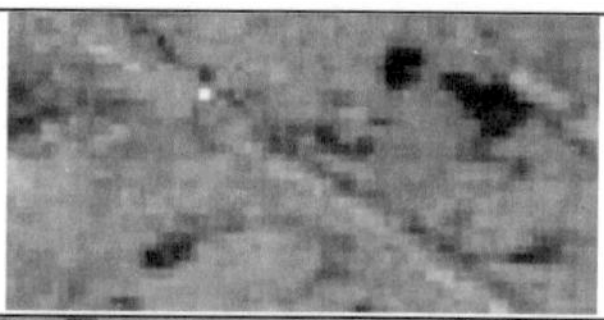	
cva	**cva**y̱alayina CKD 314 o2 GD sv. cvavalayina Total attestations: 5 Type: Reduction	 No. 184	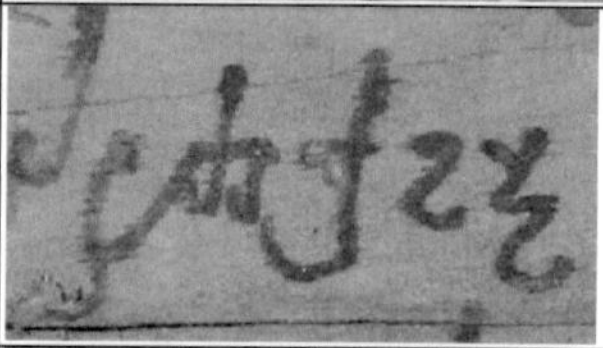	
jya	bahira**jya**de CKD 714 o5 GD sv. bahiraja, raja Total attestations: 9 Skt. *bahiḥ rājya* Type: Reduction	–		
ñg̱a	Ma**ñg̱e**ya CKD 587, uo2 GD sv. Mañgeya Total attestations: 2 Type: Stack	 No. 187	–	
tg̱a	Pi**tg̱a** CKD 774 uoA2 GD sv. atga, Arkatga, Arkaṃtga, Krarkatga, Caṃtgala, Cipitga, Civiṃtga, Namatga, Namatgaka, Pagutga, Pitga, Pisratga, potga, Pratga, Platga, Mopatga, Rahulatga, letga, lautgaiṃci, Lpatga, Lẏipatga, Lẏimitga, Vukiṃtga, Ṣitga, ṣitgapotge Total attestations: 86 Type: Stack	–	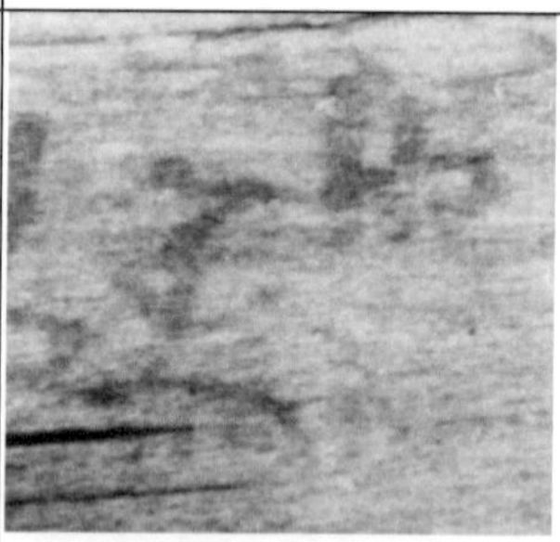	
tsma	Tsmayena CKD 552 r4 GD sv. Tsmaya Total attestations: 22 Type: Ligature + cursive stack	 No. 193	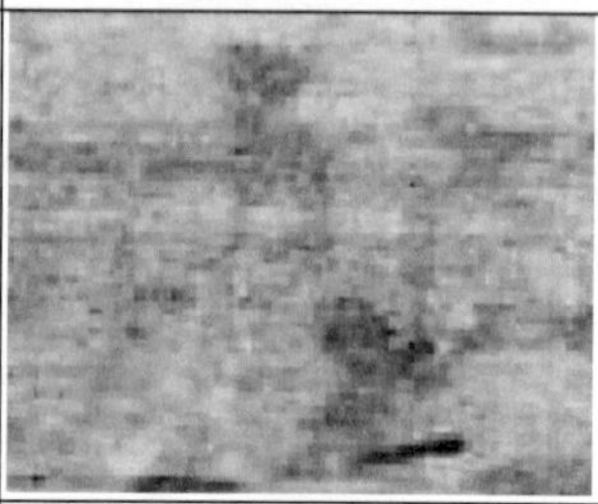	
drya	Dryakṣiya CKD 685 oA1 GD sv. Dryakṣi Total attestations: 6 Type: Reduction + reduction	 No. 195	–	

ṉga	Śaṃ**nga** CKD 560.1 G5 GD sv. Śaṃnga Total attestations: 32 Type: Stack	 No. 199 *ṉge*	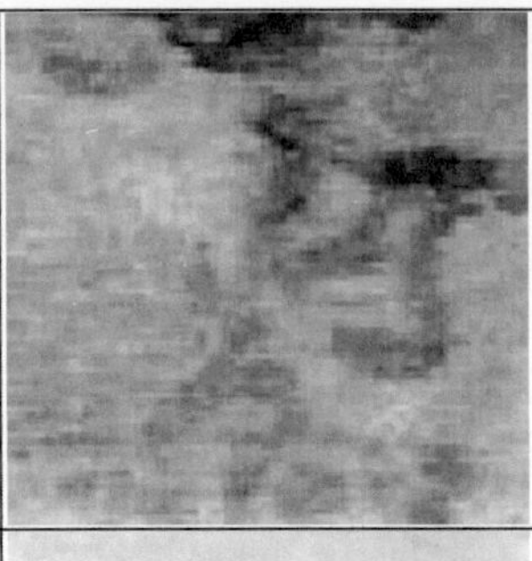	
pg̱a	Le**pg̱a** CKD 511 g GD sv. Lepg̱a Total attestations: 15 Type: Stack	–	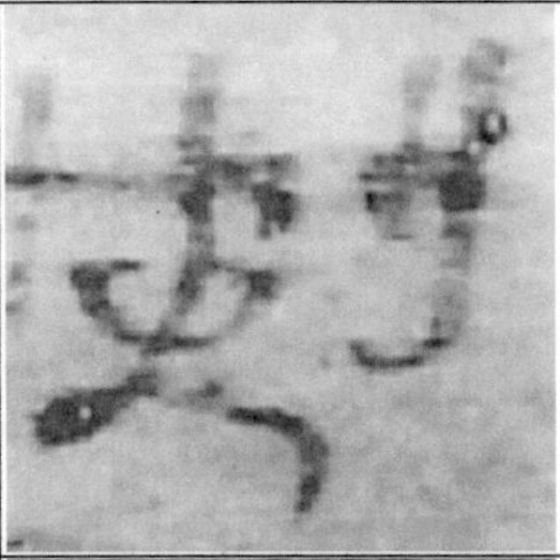	
pca	Sag̱a**pca**ae CKD 552.1 B3 GD sv. Sag̱apcaa Total attestations: 1 Type: Stack	–	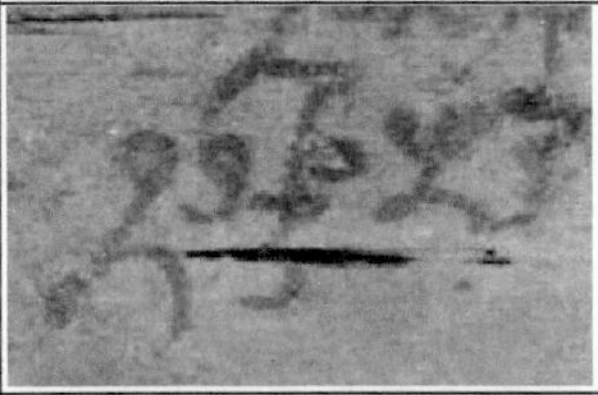	
pña	A**pñi**ya CKD 215 o2 GD sv. Apgi Total attestations: 17 Type: Stack	–		
pna	Ci**pna**ya CKD 754 oA1 GD sv. Cipnaya Total attestations: 5 Type: Stack	–	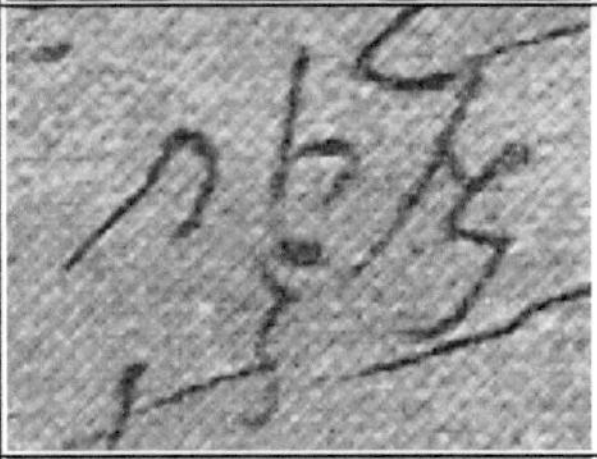	
pla	Pleyaṣa CKD 546 o4 GD sv. Pleya Total attestations: 3 Type: Reduction Note: see kla.	 No. 205 *pre'* [Sic]	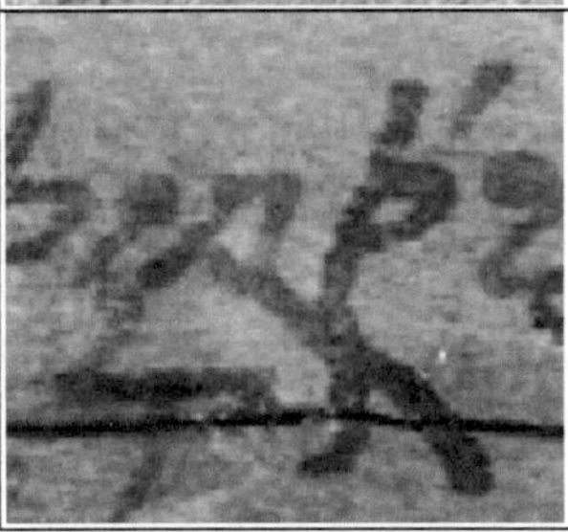	

pṣa	Ki**pṣa**ya CKD 701.1 E9 GD sv. Kipṣaya Total attestations: 2 Type: Stack	—		
psa	a**psu** CKD 290 oB3 GD sv. apsu Total attestations: 45 Type: Stack	—		
bdha	śa**bdha**ñananaṃ CKD 514 o2 GD sv. chadañana Total attestations: 1 Skt. *śabdajñāna* Type: Stack	—	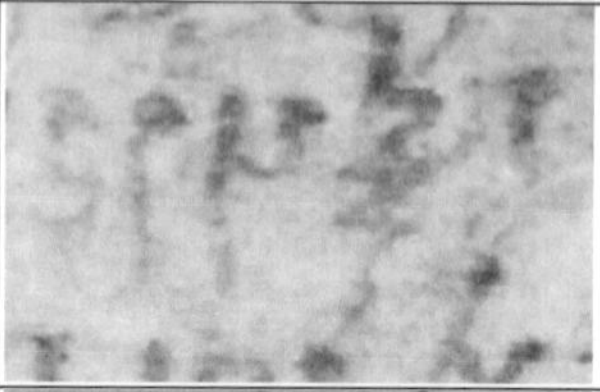	
bhta	ara**bhti**davya CKD 565 rA3 GD sv. aravhidava Total attestations: 1 Skt. *ārabhitavya* Type: Cursive stack Note: in the illustrated example the stem of *bha* curves artificially to connect the top of *ta*.	—		
mga	Lyi**mge**yena CKD 399 o2 GD sv. Ciṃge, Cimgaya, Cimge, Namge, Puramge, Laṃgo, Lẏimge, Samgo Total attestations: 3 Type: Stack	 No. 208	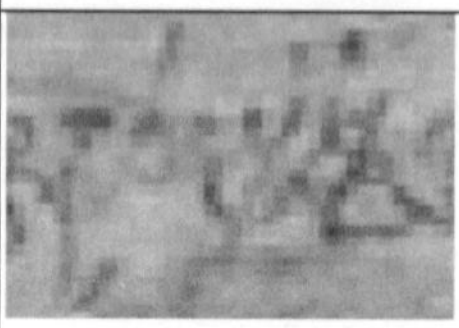	
mla	Ka**mla**na CKD 754 oA5 GD sv. Kamlana, Comle, Namla Total attestations: 3 Type: Stack	—		

mṣa	Saṃ**mṣa**na CKD 513.1 C6 GD sv. Camṣana, Namṣana, Samṣana Total attestations: 8 Type: Stack	 No. 210 *mṣo*		
msa	Ata**msi**yae CKD 702 o2 GD sv. Atamsiya Total attestations: 2 Type: Stack	–	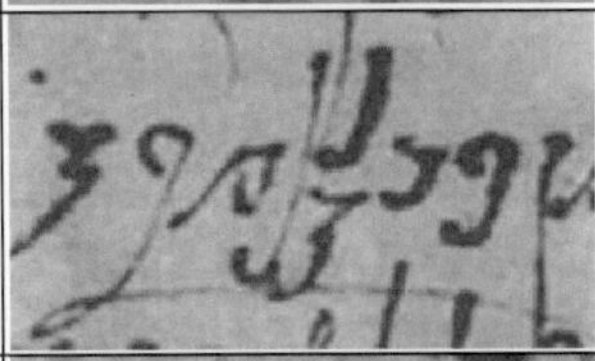	
rtsa	Pa**rtsa**yaṣa CKD 701 rE10 GD sv. Kartsa, Cartse, Partsaya, Pirtsu, Portsaya, Raṃśartsa, Vurtsita Total attestations: 5 Type: Reduction + ligature		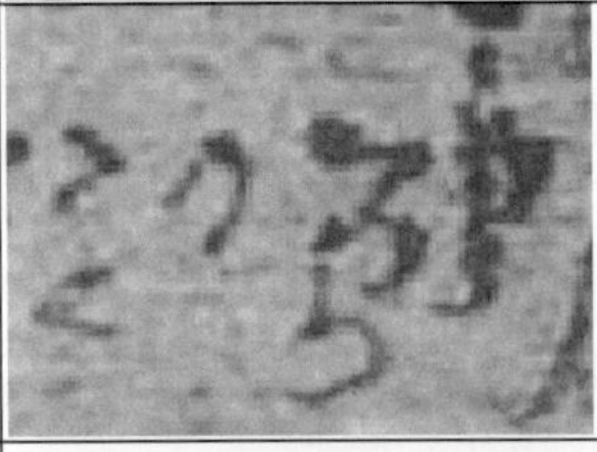	
rvra	puna**r** vrajaṃti CKD 523 r1 Total attestations: 1 Type: Reduction + reduction Note: this form only occurs due to the Sanskritic orthography with word boundary internal to the conjunct.	 No. 216		
rla	du**rlā**pa CKD 565 A4 GD sv. drulavha Total attestations: 1 Skt. *durlabha* Type: Reduction Note: the vowel length mark extends from the end of the post consonantal r sign.		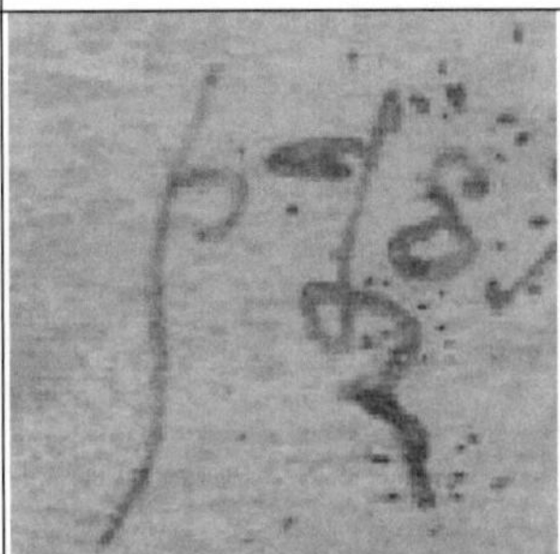	
rsta	Tsagi**rsta** CKD 419 cr2 GD sv. Tsagirsta Total attestations: 1 Type: Reduction	–	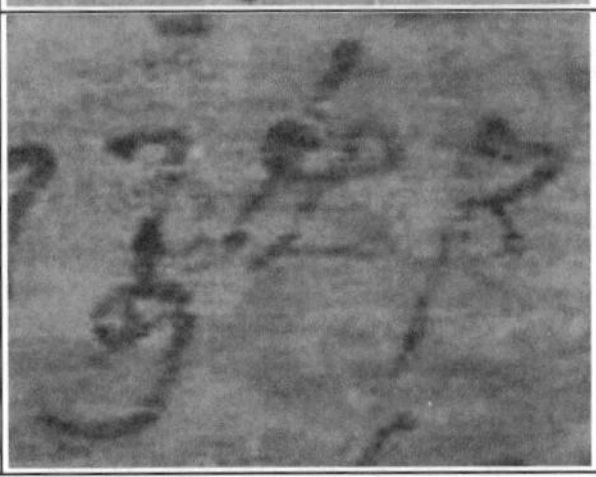	

lka	**Rilka** CKD 701 rE3 GD sv. Rilka Total attestations: 1 Type: Stack	—	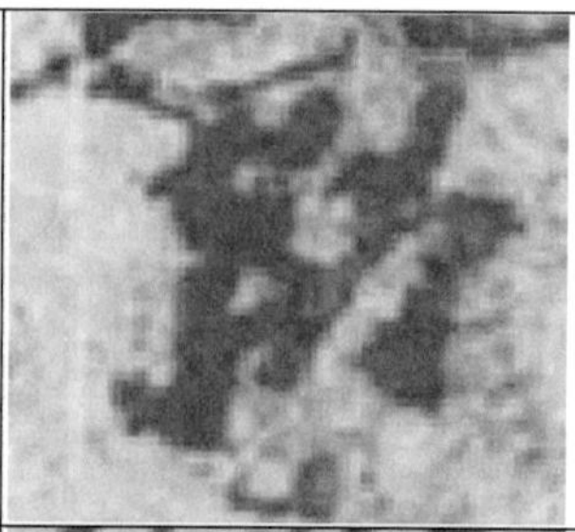	
lca	Oṃgi**lca** CKD 701 rC3 GD sv. Oṃgilca Total attestations: 1 Type: Stack	—	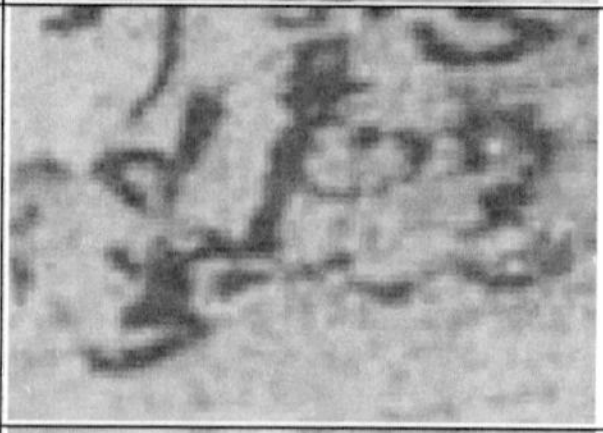	
lta	ko**lta**rṣa CKD 210.1 rD2 GD sv. koltarṣa, Piltacga, Maltaya Total attestations: 6 Type: Stack	—	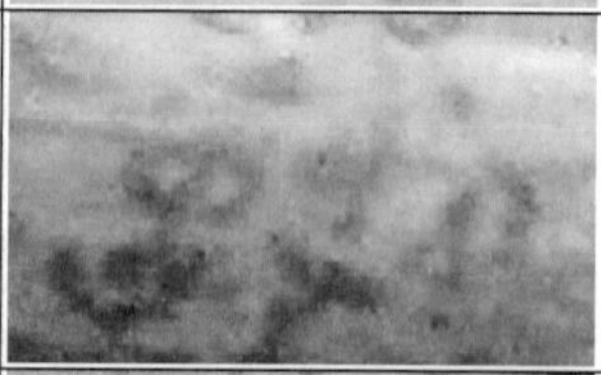	
ltsa	agi**ltsa** CKD 422 o6 GD sv. agiltsa, Kultsu, Kultsuta, Pultsaya, Maltsage, Maltsaya, Maltsige, Maltsu, Maltsuta Total attestations: 12 Type: Stack + ligature	—	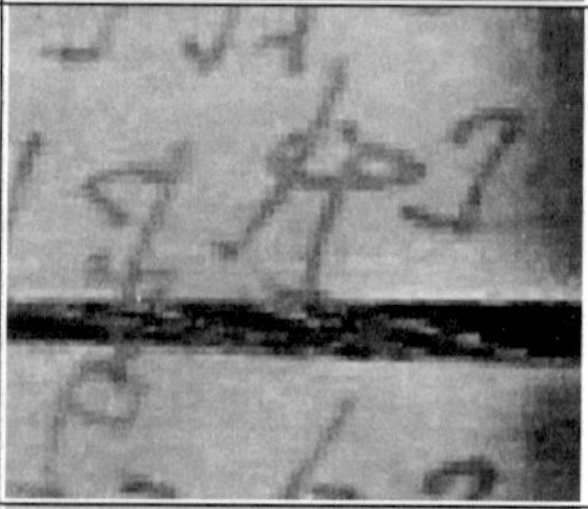	
lna	Pu**lna**bhayae CKD 897 1 GD sv. Pulna, Pulnaṃto, Pulnaṃbhaya Total attestations: 1 Type: Stack	—		
lpa	a**lpa** CKD 248 o3 GD sv. apa, japida, japidava, Lpatca, śilpa, śilpiga Total attestations: 12 Skt. *alpa* Type: Reduction	 No. 220 *lpi*		
lma	Ca**lma**dana CKD 296 uo2 GD sv. Kulmoya, Calmadana, Calmadana, Calmadanamiṣi, Calmadaneṃci, Calmasa, jalma, Petaavanakilme, Yaveavaneṃci, Vegakilmi, vegakilmedharma Total attestations: 51 Type: Cursive stack	 No. 222 *lme*		

lva	Salvaṣena CKD 533 oB2 GD sv. Tsugelva, Paluvisa, saṃlva, Saluva, Saluveta, Salvasena, Salve Total attestations: 8 Type: Reduction	 No. 224 *lve*		
lýa	ṣilýoka CKD 312 uo2 GD sv. Aralýi, Alalýi, Alýakama, Alýaya, Alýasena, Kalanadhaṃma, Kalýana, Kalýanadhaṃma, Kalýikoa, Kalýige, Kalýita, Kalýisa, Kalýotsa, Kilýagi, Kilýama, kilýigaṃci, Kolýaya, Kolýara, Kolýige, Kolýina, Kolýisa, gilýaṃya, gilýaṃyapaśu, gunakalana, ghidabali, Calýe, Tsulýita, pakebali, Palýi, Pisali, Pulýa, bali, baliuṭa, balidhaṃma, balipaśu, Malýige, Malýina, Malýimage, Molýina, lihida, Lýaka, Lýakḍha, Lýi, Lýiṃsu, Lýiga, Lýipa, Lýipaṃgaa, Lýipatga, Lýipana, Lýipanena, Lýipama, Lýipava, Lýipita, Lýipiṃtsaa, Lýipe, Lýipedana, Lýipo, Lýipga, Lýipta, Lýiptata, Lýimavatiya, Lýimiṃrke, Lýimitga, Lýimina, Lýimira, Lýimirkaka, Lýimirta, Lýimirna, Lýimisoa, Lýimo, Lýimge, Lýimsu, Lýira, Lýivaṃma, Lýivrasma, lýokmana, Lýyaṣe, vala, śeṣabali, ṣilýoga, ṣilýogalihidaga, ṣilýogahastaleha, ṣulýagaṃdha, Ṣulýita, Ṣvalýaya, Ṣṗalýaya, saṃkaledi, Spalýaya Total attestations: 701 Tocharian A *ṣlyok,* Skt. *śloka*. Type: Reduction Note: this sign is now transcribed as *lýa* rather than lṗi as in Rapson (Glass 2000: 126–7; Burrow 1937: 11; Boyer, Rapson, and Senart 1920–9: 318–9).	 No. 221		

ṣga	A**ṣga**ra CKD 604 o2 GD sv. Aṣgara, Ṣgaśi Total attestations: 34 Type: Stack	 No. 231		
ṣḍha	Pru**ṣḍha**ya CKD 533 oA2 GD sv. agiṣḍha, Aṣḍhaya, aṣḍhila, Kalaṣḍha, paṣḍha, Pruṣḍhaya, Pruṣḍhoa, Maṣḍha, Maṣḍhige, Maṣḍhega, muṣḍhaṣi, Moṣḍhaya, vaṣḍhiga, vaṣḍhigayina, Vuṣḍhaya, Śraṣḍha Total attestations: 32 Type: Stack	 No. 234 *ṣḍhi*	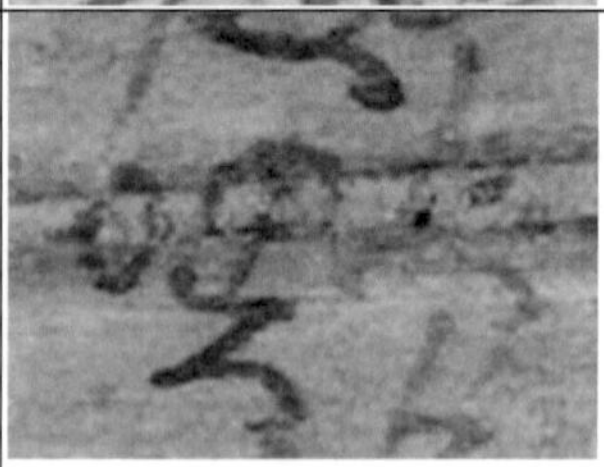	
ṣta	suve**ṣta** CKD 432 uo3 GD sv. suveṭha Total attestations: 7 Type: Stack	 No. 231	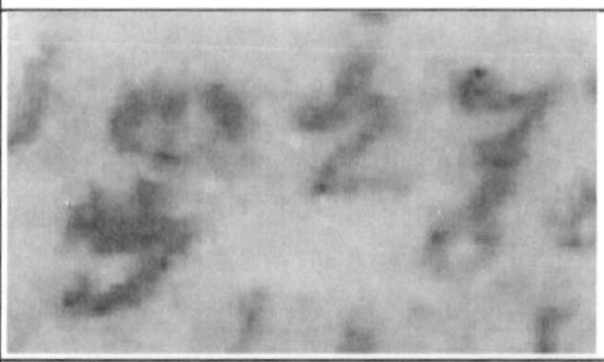	
ṣtsa	Rama**ṣtso** CKD 582 cr6 GD sv. Ramaṣtso Total attestations: 2 Type: Stack + ligature	—	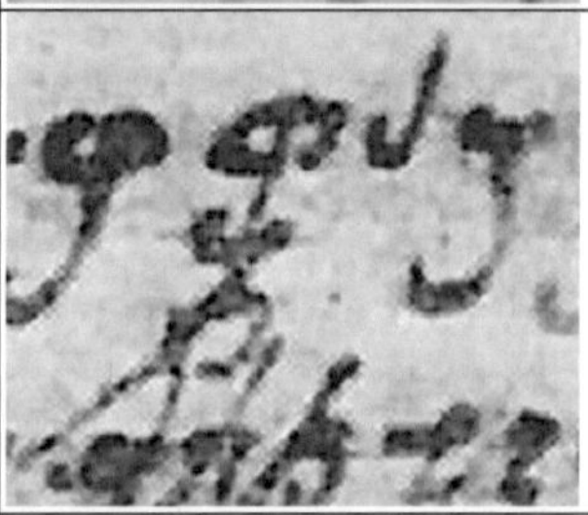	
ṣla	Tsuge**ṣla** CKD 505 o1 GD sv. Tsugeṣla Total attestations: 11 Type: Reduction Note: the interpretation of this conjunct is supported by the form *Tsugeṣila* CKD 297 uo2. See also note on *kla*, above.	 No. 236	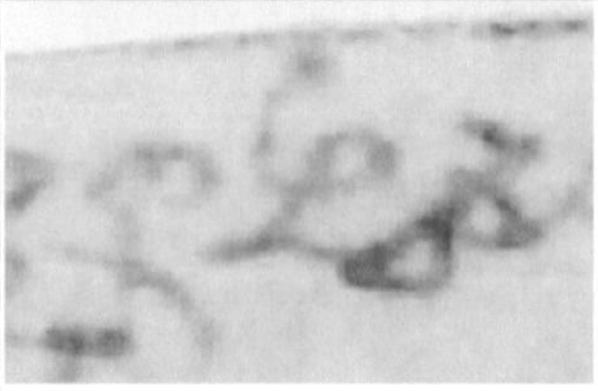	
ṣpa	Ari**ṣpa** CKD 581 cr1 GD sv. Ariṣpa Total attestations: 4 Type: Cursive stack	 No. 238		

sḏha	Bhas**ḏhe**na CKD 551 r1 GD sv. Bhaṣdha Total attestations: 3 Type: Stack	—	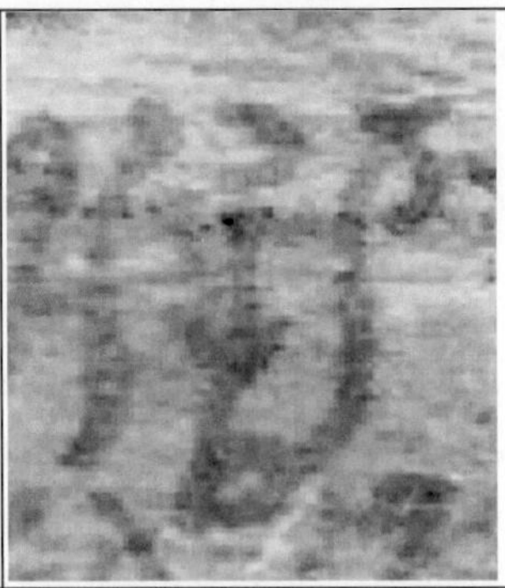	
zba	co**zbo** CKD 017 uo1 GD sv. cozbo, cozboṢamasenagoṭha-dara, mahacozbo Total attestations: 597 Tumshuqese at Maralbashi *cazba*, Avestan *čazdahvant* Type: Stack	 No. 185		
zma	Naṃmara**zma** CKD 376 o1 GD sv. uzmayuga, Namarasma, Naṃmarazma, Buzmoyiga, Livarazma Total attestations: 10 Type: Stack	 No. 186 *zmo*		

2 Observations

Preconsonantal l — It was already noted by Rapson (Boyer, Rapson, and Senart 1920–1929, 316) that the preconsonantal form of *l* is normally the full form written in a stack, but in the case of *lpa*, it takes a special reduced form, as an x shape written over the stem of *pa*. It is quite surprising to have a reduced form occur in only this case, while the full form is well-attested in stacks otherwise. This reason may be a desire to avoid confusion with the similar form *lýa*.

Superscript vowel positioning — The positioning of the superscript vowels in the stacked conjuncts is interesting. One might have expected the vowel diacritics to appear at the top of the stack, where these vowel signs are generally written, however, the general practice is to associate the vowel with its immediately preceding consonant, transecting the top portion of it as with *-i-* (e.g., *gtsi*, see *gtsa*), or extending to the left or right as with *-e-*. The position of *-e-* seems to be quite fluid, appearing to the left or right of the stack based on the available space, compare *kse* (see *ksa*) and *ñge* (see *ñga*). This treatment of -e- was noted already by Rapson (Boyer, Rapson, and Senart 1920–1929, 298).

3 Corrections to previous readings

As a result of this analysis the following readings have been updated.

- *Śaṃgkoya* → *Śaṃgtsiya* CKD 318 uo3 (https://gandhari.org/corpus/ckd0318). This reading was a hapax, but upon inspection is clearly the same name with the same spelling as *Śaṃgtsiya* which also occurs in CKD 532 co1, uo1.
- *Śaṃ.dha/Śaṃṅḍha/Śaṃṭṭa* → *Śaṃnga* CKD 560 oG5 (https://gandhari.org/corpus/ckd0560). The problematic akṣara had been variously interpreted, but the form is almost certainly to be read as the much better attested syllable *nga*.
- *Lepga* → *Lepga* CKD 511 g (https://gandhari.org/corpus/ckd0511). The attested form has the cauda foot on *ga*.
- *Lpaṅga* → *Lpatca* CKD 415 cr3 (https://gandhari.org/corpus/ckd0415). The form certainly has *-c-* rather than *-g-*.
- *amña* → *aṃña* CKD 146 oB2 (https://gandhari.org/corpus/ckd0146), CKD 225 r1 (https://gandhari.org/corpus/ckd0225); *pravamnaga* → *pravaṃnaga* CKD 571 r5 (https://gandhari.org/corpus/ckd0571); *deyamnae* → *deyaṃnae* CKD 897 3 (https://gandhari.org/corpus/ckd0897). The anusvara dot has been dropped in the printed editions (Boyer et al. 1920–9; Jiang 2020).
- *Tsugeṣra* → *Tsugeṣla* CKD 505 o1 (https://gandhari.org/corpus/ckd0505). The reading has the post-consonantal form for *la*. The form of the name with *-la* is well attested, see Baums and Glass 2002a sv. Tsugeṣla.
- *Dmusvaṃta* → *Drusvaṃta* CKD 375 o2, o3, r1 (https://gandhari.org/corpus/ckd0375). The akṣara *dru* occurs three times in this document. The hook form of the vowel sign *u* has been confused with the right arm of a subjoined *-m-*. Boyer et al. recognized the possibility of reading *dru* in a footnote (1920-1929, 135). This interpretation is to be preferred.
- *sulpvi* → *? ?* CKD 423 r1 (http://gandhari.org/corpus/ckd0423). The reading and interpretation of this section is unclear. Boyer, Rapson, and Senart provided an alternate reading in a footnote "*na ci ra*" (1920–1929, 151). Burrow did not explain this form (1937) or attempt to translate (1940). The available image is unclear. Given that the conjunct *lpvi* is otherwise unattested in the language, there is no reason to give this interpretation much weight at this time.

References

Baums and Glass

2002a Baums, Stefan and Andrew Glass. *A Dictionary of Gāndhārī.* https://gandhari.org/dictionary

2002b *Catalog of Gāndhārī Texts.* https://gandhari.org/catalog

Boyer, Rapson, Senart, and Noble

1920–1929 Boyer, A. M, E. J. Rapson, E. Senart, and P. S. Noble. *Kharoṣṭhī Inscriptions Discovered by Sir Aurel Stein in Chinese Turkestan*. Oxford: Clarendon Press.

Brough 1962 Brough, John. *The Gāndhārī Dharmapada.* London Oriental Series, Volume 7. London: Oxford University Press.

Burrow 1937 Burrow, T. *The Language of the Kharoṣṭhi Documents from Chinese Turkestan.* Cambridge: University Press.

1940 *A Translation of the Kharoṣṭhi Documents from Chinese Turkestan.* James G. Forlong Fund, vol. XX. London: The Royal Asiatic Society.

Glass 2000 Glass, Andrew. "A Preliminary Study of Kharoṣṭhī Manuscript Paleography." MA Thesis. University of Washington.

Glass, Baums, and Salomon

2002 Glass, Andrew, Stefan Baums, and Richard Salomon. "Proposal to Encode Kharoṣṭhī in Plane 1 of ISO/IEC 10646." The Unicode Consortium Document Registry L2/02-203. https://unicode.org/L2/L2002/02203-kharoshthi.pdf Accessed 2022-12-22.

Jiang 2020 Jiang Yixiu 姜一秀. "The Xinjiang Region Museum Collection: An Interpretation of a Kharoṣṭhī Letter." In: *Non-Han Literature along the Silk Road* edited by Xiao Li, 133–147. Singapore: Springer.

Salomon 2000 Salomon, Richard. *A Gāndhārī Version of the Rhinoceros Sūtra: British Library Kharoṣṭhī Fragment 5B.* Gandhāran Buddhist Texts, Volume 1. Seattle: University of Washington Press.

Looking for the Right Descent*

Viṣṇu's Incarnation as Rāma and the Bodhisattva's Departure from Heaven

Max DEEG

Abstract: This paper discusses the similarity of the episodes in heaven prior to the descent of the Buddha in different Buddha biographies, and the incarnation of Viṣṇu as Rāma in the *Rāmāyaṇa*. It is suggested that the *Rāmāyaṇa* may have adapted certain motifs of the narrative of the Buddha's descent from Tuṣita-Heaven when Rāma became regarded as a (partial) incarnation of Viṣṇu and a respective episode of the god's descent to the earth had to be inserted into an older form of the epic.

Keywords: *avatāra*; Viṣṇu; Rāma; *bodhisattva*; Buddha; *Rāmāyaṇa*

The last two decades or so have seen a rise in scholarship on the connection between the *Rāmāyaṇa* and Buddhist narratives.[1] While the larger Indian epic, the *Mahābhārata*, has played a role in this comparative discourse of Brahminical and Buddhist (and Jain) narratives as well, the *Rāmāyaṇa* has many more direct points of connection with the (extended[2]) Buddha biography.[3] Parallels between the Rāma story and the Viśvantara-jātaka have been seen in the fact that both focus on the exile of the crown-prince protagonist and the reestablishment of his rightful claim to the throne;[4] in this case it is the penultimate existence of the Buddha/*bodhisattva* then which has an obvious

---

Max DEEG, Cardiff University.

* I remember my first encounter with Professor Duan on the occasion of my first visit to Peking University—in fact, the first visit to mainland China at all—when she acted as my chaperone and brought me to many places in the city. During these tours our discussions (in German) were by no means restricted to Buddhism but turned to all kinds of Indological themes, including the Veda, Pāṇini and things I do not remember. It therefore seems more than appropriate to commemorate a scholar like Professor Duan by choosing a topic that goes beyond the boundaries of one field of the many that she was interested in and did research on. So here I will focus on the interaction between the Brahminical and the Buddhist tradition, and more specifically on the interrelation between the Brahminical epics—particularly the *Rāmāyaṇa*—and the biography of the Buddha.
It is my pleasure to thank my Cardiff University colleague Laxshmi Greaves for correcting my English and for saving me of some inaccuracies and mistakes.

[1] Hiltebeitel 2006, 247–254; Olivelle 2008, xxii–xxiv; Deeg 2022b. Parallels were, of course, already detected and discussed before: see, for instance, Johnston 1936 (Introduction) and Gawroński 1919. See also the overview and discussion in Eltschinger 2018, 311–314.

[2] In the sense of including some previous birth stories (*jātaka*).

[3] For a brief overview see Hiltebeitel 2006, 229–235. See also Appleton 2017, 94–100.

[4] For an attempt to put this parallel—and others—into a wider historical context and perspective see Deeg 2022b.

similarity with the story of Rāma (Gombrich 1985; Hiltebeitel 2006, 248). Both the epic and the biography of the Buddha[1], ascribe to their main agents, Viṣṇu-Rāma and the *bodhisattva*-Buddha, a descendance from the solar dynastic lineage of the Ikṣvāku (Johnston 1936, xvii–xviii, xlvii–l), which Aśvaghoṣa in his *Buddhacarita* is particularly keen to emphasize. The two narratives also share, I would claim, a similar attitude towards the central term *dharma*; while, as Alf Hiltebeitel has observed, "in the *Mahābhārata dharma* is always up for question, in the *Rāmāyaṇa* it is viewed from a standard of one who embodies it to perfection," (Hiltebeitel 2006, 232) the latter could also be claimed for the Buddha as an "embodiment" of the (Buddhist) *dharma*[2].

In this article I will discuss what I consider another narrative parallel between the *Rāmāyaṇa* and the Buddha's biography, the (re)incarnation or birth of both "heroes," Rāma and the *bodhisattva*. Epic scholars have emphasized the singularity of the birth/incarnation story of Viṣṇu-Rāma in the *Rāmāyaṇa*'s *Bālakāṇḍa* (Brockington 1998, 379–380; Scharf 2003, 5): "The basic purpose for the addition of the *Bālakāṇḍa* is to provide a curious audience with information on Rāma's birth, youthful exploits and marriage, while at the same time giving Rāma the enhanced status that was by then being assigned to him." (Brockington 1998, 380)

There is some agreement that the incarnation of Viṣṇu as Rāma is a relatively late development in the first of two later-added or -developed chapters of the epic, the *Bālakāṇḍa* and the Uttarakāṇḍa, the latter showing more features of Rāma's divinity than the first (Brockington 1984, 212–213). In such a context, the influence of the Buddhist narrative of the Buddha's conception on the epic narrative can well be imagined, since it is particularly the concept of (re)incarnation which was missing in earlier developmental stages of the *Rāmāyaṇa* in which Rāma had not fully achieved his divine status yet and which had to be brought into some narrative form and added to or inserted into the first chapter. Although the narrative context and the function of the incarnation differs in the case of each protagonist (the Buddha-*bodhisattva* and Viṣṇu-Rāma), there are enough intriguing similarities and parallels to justify investigating the two narratives and their relationship in some detail.

Since the Buddhist situation—with various Buddha biographies containing different versions of the same episode—is more complex, I will start with the narrative of Viṣṇu's incarnation as Rāma in the Bālakaṇḍa of the Vālmīki *Rāmāyaṇa*. The respective passage in the epic contains a few peculiar features, some of which, I think,

[1] By "biography of the Buddha" I do not mean any specific text but rather a string of narratives that were developing and changing and which "manifested" themselves in the individual Buddha biographies (like the *Lalitavistara*, *Mahāvastu*, etc.).

[2] See Olivelle 2008, xxiv. More recently, Vincent Eltschinger has argued that the description of Kapilavastu and the *bodhisattva*'s father Śuddhodana as a "righteous king" (*dharmarāja*) was influenced by the epic (Eltschinger 2018).

bare a similarity with the episode of the *bodhisattva*'s preparation for his birth on earth. Viṣṇu is asked by the gods to fulfil his task of killing the demon Rāvaṇa and therefore to be born as a human on earth (Rām.1.14.16ff.):

> 16. Just then glorious Viṣṇu arrived, and joining Brahmā, he stood there intent upon the work at hand. 17. All of the gods prostrated themselves and praised him. Then they spoke, "In our desire of the welfare of the worlds, we shall set a task for you, Viṣṇu. 18. Lord, King Daśaratha, lord of Ayodhyā, is righteous, generous, and equal in power to the great seers. Viṣṇu, you must divide yourself into four parts and be born as the sons of his three wives, who are like Modesty, Majesty, and Fame. 19. And when you have become a man, Viṣṇu, you must kill Rāvaṇa in battle, that mighty thorn in the side of the world; for he is vulnerable to the gods. 20. "This foolish *rākṣasa*, Rāvaṇa, in the insolence of his power, is oppressing the gods, perfected beings, and great seers. 21. "Pluck out this thorn in the side of holy men and ascetics—this haughty Rāvaṇa, swollen with arrogance and might—for he is the bitter enemy of Indra, lord of the thirty gods, a terror to ascetics, and a source of lamentation to the world."[1] The end of the fourteenth *sarga* of the *Bālakāṇḍa* of the *Śrī Rāmāyaṇa*. (Sarga 15)
> 1. After the principal gods had set this task for Viṣṇu Nārāyaṇa, he courteously put a question to them, even though he knew the answer. 2. "O gods, is there some means of slaying the lord of the *rākṣasas* that I might adopt to kill that thorn in the side of the seers?" 3. Addressed in this fashion, all the gods replied to the eternal Viṣṇu, "You must take on human form and kill Rāvaṇa in battle. 4. "For, foe-conquering hero, he once performed severe and prolonged austerities whereby he won the favor of Brahma, who made the world and whom the world worships. 5. "The lord was so pleased with the *rākṣasa* that he granted him the boon of having nothing to fear from all the various kinds of beings except man. 6. "At the time the boon was granted, he left men out of his reckoning. Therefore, destroyer of foes, we foresee that his death must come at the hands of men." 7. When the self-controlled Viṣṇu had heard these words of the gods, he chose king Daśaratha to be his father. 8. Now at that very moment, that splendid king, destroyer of his enemies, in hopes of getting a son, was performing a sacrifice to produce a son, for he had none.[2]

---

[1] This description of Rāvaṇa recalls the Buddhist Māra who tries to lure the ascetic *bodhisattva* away from enlightenment. The parallels between the two figures are, I think, interesting enough to dedicate further research to them.

[2] Translation Goldman 1984, 153–155. Text quoted after the electronic version GRETIL and checked against the critical edition Bhatt 1960, 107–111: *16. etasminn antare Viṣṇur upayāto mahādyutiḥ / Brahmaṇā ca samāgamya tatra tasthau samāhitaḥ. // 17. tam abruvan surāḥ sarve samabhiṣṭūya saṃnatāḥ: / "tvāṃ niyokṣyāmahe Viṣṇo lokānāṃ hitakāmpayā. // 18. rājño Daśarathasya tvam Ayodhyādhipater vibho / dharmajñasya vadānasya maharṣisamatejasaḥ / tasya bhāryāsu tisṛṣu hrīśrīkīrtyupamāsu ca / Viṣṇo putra-tvam āgaccha kṛtvātmānaṃ caturvidham. // 19. tatra tvaṃ mānuṣo bhūtvā pravṛddhaṃ lokakaṇṭakam / avadhyaṃ daivatair Viṣṇo samare jahi Rāvaṇam. // 20. sa hi devān sagandharvān siddhāṃś ca ṛṣisattamān / rākṣaso Rāvaṇo mūrkho vīryotsekena bādhate // 21. tam uddhataṃ Rāvaṇam ṛddhatejasaṃ pravṛddhadarpaṃ tridaśeśvaradvipam / virāvaṇaṃ sādhutapasvikaṇṭakaṃ tapasvināṃ uddhara taṃ bhayāvaham. // iti*

Not much discussion has been dedicated to this pre-incarnation episode in heaven. In his discussion of the narrative, Horst Brinkhaus has made the following remark: "... Viṣṇu is explicitly directed by the other gods to assume a human shape in order to subdue the demon Rāvaṇa. Viṣṇu appears here as an unpretentious god among others, and he exactly follows the suggestions or even directions of the gods."(Brinkhaus 1992, 104) Looking at the story from the standpoint of the assumed Buddhist parallel, however, Viṣṇu may not be as "unpretentious" as Brinkhaus supposed: he acts precisely according to his "predestiny"—if a god has one—which is clearly expressed by his self-choice of his father Daśaratha, an action again very similar to the *bodhisattva*'s action in heaven (see below).

As far as I know, the incarnation process as described in the *Rāmāyaṇa* is singular for any Hindu god, even for the other incarnations of Viṣṇu in the Purāṇas, including the Rāma *avatāra*[1]: Viṣṇu is asked by the other gods to fulfil a task on earth—to be born as Rāma and to defeat the demon Rāvaṇa—and from heaven he chooses as his father (*pitaraṃ rocayāmāsa*),[2] King Daśaratha of Ayodhyā. He pretends to be ignorant about the task and goal of his incarnation. Although in a Hindu context, this narrative of the incarnation of a god is unique, with the described features it clearly recalls another "(re)incarnation" story, that of the *bodhisattva*'s last birth or existence as Siddhārtha before his enlightenment in the Buddha's biographies.[3]

Śrīrāmāyaṇe Bālakāṇḍe caturdaśaḥ sargaḥ || 14 || [15] 1. tato Nārāyaṇo Viṣṇur niyuktaḥ surasattamaiḥ | jānann api surān evaṃ ślakṣṇaṃ vacanam abravīt: || 2. "upāyaḥ ko vadhe tasya rākṣasādhipateḥ surāḥ | yam ahaṃ taṃ samāsthāya nihanyām ṛṣikaṇṭhakam?" || 3. evam uktāḥ surāḥ sarve pratyūcur Viṣṇum avyayam: | "mānuṣīṃ tanum āsthāya Rāvaṇaṃ jahi samyuge. || 4. sa hi tepe tapas tīvraṃ dīrghakālam arindam | yena tuṣṭo abhavad Brahmā lokakṛl lokapūjitaḥ. || 5. saṃtuṣṭaḥ pradadau tasmai rākṣasāya varaṃ prabhuḥ | nānāvidhebhyo bhūtebhyo bhayaṃ nānyatra mānupāt. || 6. avajñātāḥ purā tena varadānena mānavāḥ | tasmāt tasya vadho dṛṣṭo mānuṣebhyaḥ paraṃtapa." || 7. ity etad vacanaṃ śrutvā surāṇāṃ Viṣṇur ātmavān | pitaraṃ rocayāmāsa tadā Daśarathaṃ nṛpam. || 8. sa cāpy aputro nṛpatis tasmin kāle mahādyutiḥ | ayajat putriyām iṣṭiṃ putrepsur arisūdanaḥ. ||

[1] For an overview on Rāma in the Purāṇas see Brockington 2012. Freiberger 2019 deals with the different aspects of Viṣṇu's reincarnation as the Buddha.

[2] The choice of the verb—instead, for instance, of √*vṛ*- or similar roots—is interesting: the causative of √*ruc*- (Böhtlingk and Roth 1868–1871, 376, s.v. *rocayati*) literally means "to let (sth.) shine" which somehow seems to involve the act of looking (around) as in the case of the *bodhisattva*'s selection of his circumstances of birth. It is interesting that the *Rāmāyaṇa* uses a verb which is etymologically related to the basis of the word used for the inspections or considerations of the *bodhisattva* (*lokana*: Mayrhofer 1976, 75–76, s.v. *rócate*, and 112f., s.v. *lókate, ā-locayati*; see below).

[3] In the early biographies of the "founder" of Jainism, Mahāvīra, there is not episode in heaven before birth, but the focus is on the transfer of the fetus from the womb of a Brahmin woman to the womb of the *kṣatriya* woman Trisalā: see Āyāraṅga/Ācāraṅga 2.15.2–6 (text Jacobi 1882, 121–122; translation Jacobi 1884, 189–191); this is elaborated on more in Kalpasūtra 2.2–30 (text Jacobi 1879, 33–41; translation Jacobi 1884, 218–229). According to both texts, it is god Śakra who has the embryo removed and transplanted into the "right" womb while Mahāvīra stays inactive although he is ascribed the knowledge of his descent and his transplantation.

The Buddhist source which has been compared most often with the *Rāmāyaṇa* (and the *Mahābhārata*) is Aśvaghoṣa's *Buddhacarita*. And indeed, the direct and indirect references to the epics are frequent enough to allow Alf Hiltebeitel to call the *Buddhacarita* "the first known close and critical reading of the Brahmanical Sanskrit epics." (Hiltebeitel 2006) Already Johnston pointed out that Aśvaghoṣa, a native of Saketa/Ayodhyā, and therefore certainly familiar with the version of the *Rāmāyaṇa* extant at the time, probably did not know the *Bālakāṇḍa* (Johnston 1936, xlix). The fact that the Buddhist poet does not include the episode of the *bodhisattva* selecting his circumstances of birth may indirectly support this view. While there is comparison of the miraculous birth of the *bodhisattva* from the right hip of his mother Māyā with the birth of well-known Brahminical royal figures (*Buddhacarita* 1.10)[1], Aśvaghoṣa, despite his frequent references to the *Rāmāyaṇa*, does not refer to Rāma's birth and does not elaborate on the *bodhisattva*'s stay in heaven at all[2]. He rather brusquely and briefly refers to the conception in the form of a white elephant and then continues with the birth story. With all the necessary caution, one may conclude that Aśvaghoṣa did not know the episode of Viṣṇu's incarnation as Rāma, or that he did not want to acknowledge it as a Brahminical claim of their hero's direct divine "status."

In his other poem *Saundarananda*, however, Aśvaghoṣa briefly refers to the episode of the departure from Tuṣita Heaven (2.46–48):

> 46. Now at that time the inhabitants of Heaven, being lovers of righteousness and desirous of seeing its practice, passed over the regions of the world. 47. As they whose very natures were informed with righteousness wandered over the world to enquire about its righteousness, they saw that king whose nature was righteous in such a high degree. 48. Then the Bodhisattva, descending to earth from among the Tuṣita gods, decided to become incarnate in the family of that monarch.[3]

Here, Aśvaghoṣa obviously refers to a version of the story which had the gods look for the right place for the *bodhisattva*'s descent, and one may be allowed to suppose that they advise the *bodhisattva* to be born in that very place. What is interesting is that first

---

[1] Olivelle 2008, 4–5: *ūror yathaurvasya Pṛthoś ca hastān Māndhātur Indrapratimasya mūrdhnaḥ, Kakṣīvataś caiva bhūjāṃsadeśāt tathāvidhaṃ tasya babhūva janman.* ("As Aurva from the thigh, as Pṛthu from the hand, as Māndhātṛ from the head, he who was Indra's peer, as Kakṣīvat from the armpit, so was his birth." Olivelle's translation, with orthographic adjustments). See also Olivelle 2008, xxxi.

[2] While the first verses of the Sanskrit are missing, the Chinese translation, the Fosuoxing-zan 佛所行贊 (T 4, no. 192, 1a8–1b1; translation Willemen 2009, 3–4), is complete and reflects the complete omission of the episode in heaven.

[3] Johnston 1928, 14: *46. Atha tasmin tathā kāle dharmakāmā divaukasaḥ / vicerur diśi lokasya dharmacaryā didṛkṣavaḥ // 47. Dharmātmānaś carantas te dharmajijñāsayā jagat / dadṛśus taṃ viśeṣeṇa dharmātmānaṃ narādhipam // 48. Devebhyas tuṣitebhyo 'tha bodhisattvaḥ kṣitiṃ vrajan / upapattiṃ praṇidadhe kule tasya mahīpateḥ //*. Translation Johnston 1932, 12.

the gods are looking for the right royal family into which the *bodhisattva* should be born, and then the *bodhisattva* decides to be born in that family (*upapattiṃ praṇidadhe*). So, the sequence of decision-making is exactly the same as in the case of the *Rāmāyaṇa*: first the gods point out the right father and set the task for him, and then omniscient Viṣṇu, pretending that he does not know and needs the god's advice, decides to be born as Daśaratha's son.

While the scene in the Tuṣita Heaven is missing in Aśvaghoṣa's *Buddhacarita*[1], most of the other versions of the Buddha's biography refer to it, some in quite some detail. The art historical evidence—in some cases with uncertainty over whether the *bodhisattva* Śākyamuni or the *bodhisattva* Maitreya is depicted (Luczanits 2010, 59–61; Schlingloff 2013, 304–307)—shows that the episode was known at a quite an early stage of the development of the Buddha's biography.

The point of comparison is before the departure from heaven. In the case of the Buddha this is marked by the so-called "considerations" or "examinations" (*vilokana*, *(vy)avalokana*, *guan* 觀)[2]. The commentary to the Prajñāpāramitā-sūtra ascribed to Nāgārjuna and translated by Kumārajīva, the *Da zhidu lun* 大智度論, thematizes four of these considerations (T 25, no. 1509, 89c10–11):

> With the four [examining] views [the *bodhisattva*] looks at the world: first, [he] looks for the [right] time; second, [he] looks for the [right] land; third, [he] looks for the [right] caste; fourth, [he] looks for the right birthplace.[3]

Two different versions of the decision-making process of where the *bodhisattva* is to be born can be discerned: one in which the gods encourage and assist the *bodhisattva* in his decision under which circumstances to be born, and one in which they try to convince the *bodhisattva* not to be reborn but to stay in heaven.

For the comparison of the episode with the incarnation of Viṣṇu as Rāma in the *Rāmāyaṇa*, the second version which is only found in the Mūlasarvāstivāda-vinaya[4] can be neglected because it is probably a later "Sonderentwicklung" (singular development): here the gods, troubled by the pending departure of the *bodhisattva*, try to convince him to stay in heaven with them instead of descending to earth.

---

[1] Only the conception in the form of a white elephant is mentioned: Olivelle 2008, 3. For an attempt at a reconstruction of the first verses missing in the Skt. version of the poem from the Chinese and Tibetan translations see Johnston 1936, 1–4.

[2] The number of these considerations is not uniform: see Lamotte 1944, 268.

[3] 以四種觀人間：一者、觀時，二者、觀土地，三者、觀種姓，四者、觀生處。See also the translation by Lamotte 1944, 268.

[4] Text Gnoli 1977, 37–39. Recently, Vincent Eltschinger has analysed the narrative of the *bodhisattva*'s selecting his incarnation in the Buddha biography in the Vinaya of the Mūlasarvāstivādin: Eltschinger 2019, 297–298. A similar narrative is found in the *Guoqu xianzai yinguo jing* 過去現在因果經 (T 3, vol. 189, 623a24–624a19), translated by Qiunabatuoluo 求那跋陀羅/Guṇabhadra.

In the other versions of the episode the gods are involved in the decision-making process to be born and where to be born in one way or another. In chapter 3 of the *Lalitavistara*, for instance, first the gods and *bodhisattvas* of the Tuṣita-Heaven examine the different regions and noble families of Jambudvīpa (Magadha, Kośala, Vatsa, Vaiśālī, Ujayanī, Mathurā, Hastināpura[1], Mithila) and find shortcomings with all of them; when they ask the *bodhisattva* he decides on king Śuddhodana as his father, Māyā as his mother and the Śākyas as his clan[2].

According to the Mahāvastu, some of the important protagonists in the Buddha's biography, king Bimbisāra of Magadha and king Udayana of Kauśambī, ask the *bodhisattva* to be reborn in their realm or region, but he finally decides to be born as the son of the Śākya king Śuddhodana[3].

In the commentarial introduction to the Pāli Jātaka, the Nidānakathā, it is the *bodhisattva* himself who has the five considerations (*pañcamahāvilokana*)[4] after the gods have asked him to be born on earth:

> [The gods] begged of him: "Sire, when you were fulfilling the Ten Perfections, you did not do so with a view to attain the state of a Sakka or a Māra, a Brahmā or a Universal Monarch; but you have fulfilled them with the intention of gaining Ominscience in order to save mankind. Now, Sire, the moment has come for your Buddhahood. Sir, it is now the time for your Buddhahood." Then the Great Being, even before giving an assurance to the deities, looked for the five Great Considerations which consist of the time, the country, the district, the family, and the mother and her age-limit.[5]

[1] Here the text notes that the Pāṇḍavas of Hastināpura are not eligible as the family of the Buddha because of their confused divine genealogy (in the *Mahābhārata*).

[2] Text Lefmann 1902, 20–29; translation Foucaux 1884, 21–29. See also the Chinese translations *Puyao jing* 普曜經, (T 3, no. 186, 485a25–486c9), ascribed to Zhu Fahu 竺法護/Dharmarakṣa, and *Fangguang dazhuangyan jing* 方廣大莊嚴經 (T 3, no. 187, 541c15–543c23), translated by Dipoheluo 地婆訶羅 /Divākara.

[3] Text Senart 1890, 2; Marciniak 2020, 2–3; translation Jones 1952, 2–3. Interestingly, the text which is relatively close to the Mahāvastu and usually very detailed, the *Fo benxing ji jing* 佛本行集經, translated by Zhe'najueduo 闍那崛多/Dhyānagupta—for the Indic name of the translator, normally reconstructed as Jñānagupta or Jinagupta, see Deeg 2022a—does describe the lamentation of the gods when they recognize that the *bodhisattva* is about to leave heaven, but not the selection of the birth place, father and mother, etc. (T 3, no. 190, 676c24–682c21). The *bodhisattva* simply descends from heaven and enters his mother's womb. The *bodhisattva* does, however, realize the right time of his descent by five signs of loss of immortality: the flowers on his head are withering; he is sweating under his armpits; his clothes are getting dirty; his body is losing its brilliance; he does not feel joy when sitting on his heavenly seat (676c21–24).

[4] Text Fausbøll 1962, 48–50; translation Jayawickrama 2002, 64–66.

[5] Fausbøll 1962, 48: *"mārisā, tumhehi dasapāramiyo pūrentehi na Sakkasampattiṃ na Māra-Brahma-Cakkavattisampattiṃ patthentehi pūritā lokanittharaṇatthāya pana sabbaññuttaṃ patthentehi pūritā, so vo dāni kālo mārisa Buddhattāya, samaho māriso Buddhattāya" 'ti yāciṃsu. Atha Mahāsatto devatānaṃ paṭiññaṃ adatvā va kāladīpadesakulajanettiāyuparicchedavasena pañcamahāvilokanaṃ nāma vilokesi.* Translation Jayawickrama 2002, 64.

The sequence is similar to that in the *Rāmāyaṇa*: first, the gods ask the protagonist to be born on earth, then the protagonist makes his choice.

There are, however, also versions in which the gods do not play a role at all. One of the oldest translations of a Buddha biography into Chinese, for example, the *Xiuxing benqi jing* 修行本起經, translated by Zhu Dali 竺大力 and Kang Mengxiang 康孟詳 (fl. 194–210) just has the *bodhisattva* choose his future parents himself without any intervention or even mentioning of the gods (T 3, no. 184, 463a26–463b7):

> When the right time had arrived to descend [on earth] and to become a Buddha, [the *bodhisattva*] looked around from [his place] up in Tuṣita Heaven, started with the four kinds of [examining] views[1], looked for a place, looked for a father and a mother, [looked for] a kingdom in which to be born, who was appropriate to be taught and converted, and who was the first to be led across [to the other shore]? "Śuddhodana has been the one to whom I have been born for generations." The Koliya-*kṣatriya* had two daughters [who] took a bath in a pond in the backyard [of the palace]; the *bodhisattva* raised [his] hand [and pointed at one of them with his] fingers [saying]: "This is the mother to whom I have been born time after time, [so I] will now go [to her] to be born [again]." At that time, there were five hundred ascetics (*brahmacārin*) who all had the five supernatural powers and were flying across the palace, [but they] could not pass and said in surprise: "With our supernatural powers [we normally can] go through stone walls—for what reasons are we not able to pass now?" The master of the ascetics said: "Do you see these two girls? One girl will bear a great man with thirty-two marks, [and] the other girl will bear a man with thirty marks—it is this mighty supernatural power which is the cause of you loosing [your] magical skills." At that time, the sound [of his words] was heard all over the realm.[2]

In the context of the Buddha's birth, already Windisch has observed the similarity with the general Indian concept of the *gandharva* and the situation of the *bodhisattva* in Tuṣita Heaven[3]: like the *gandharva*, the *bodhisattva* in heaven is in an intermediate state (*antarabhāva*) between his penultimate existence as prince Viśvantara and his last existence before *parinirvāṇa* as Siddhārtha Gautama. Like a *gandharva*, he chooses the place where and the womb from which he will be born. While this connection makes sense in the case of the *bodhisattva*, who, up to this point, is still a living being with a

[1] For the four views see above.

[2] 期運之至，當下作佛，於兜術天上，興四種觀，觀視土地，觀視父母，生何國中，教化之宜，先當度誰？"白净王者，是吾累世所生之父。"拘利刹帝有二女，時在後園池中沐浴，菩薩舉手指言："是吾世世所生母也，當往就生。"時有五百梵志，皆有五神通，飛過宮城，不能得度，驚而相謂："吾等神足，石壁皆過，因何等故，今不得度？"梵志師言："汝見此二女不？一女當生三十二相大人；一女當生三十相人。是其威神，令吾等失神足。"是時，音聲普聞天下。

[3] Windisch 1908, 28–29, et al.; for a discussion of the wider historical and conceptial development of the *gandharva* from the earliest (Vedic) period to the Buddhist concept of *gandharva* and rebirth see Haas 2004.

remnant of karmic substance, the idea had to be given up in case of the reincarnation of a full-fledged god like Viṣṇu who cannot be subject to the regular process of rebirth[1] — yet Viṣṇu behaves exactly like the *bodhisattva* or a *gandharva*, "choosing" the place of his reincarnation.

One of the striking features of both narratives, that of the *avatāraṇa* of Viṣṇu in the *Rāmāyaṇa* and that of the *bodhisattva*'s descent to the world—and, in fact, of his whole biography—is the contradiction between the assumed omniscience of the protagonists and the process of reaching a decision as to where and how to be born[2]. The *bodhisattva*, in the case of his descent when inside of his mother's womb and after having been born, reflects ignorance of the most elementary immanent conditions when, for instance, venturing out on the three departures during which he encounters sickness, age, and death (Silk 2003, 867–868). Strictly speaking, the *bodhisattva*, by conducting several inspections in choosing where to be born reflects a partial ignorance since he still has to consider different places and families before he makes the—obviously right—decision.

Generally speaking, in the case of Viṣṇu this tension between ignorance feigned out of politeness and his assumed divine omniscience is even more striking than the similar tension in the case of the *bodhisattva*, because a god like him is or, at least, should be omniscient. The "author" who inserted the episode was well aware of this, since the text emphasises that Viṣṇu asked the gods about their plans and complied with their wishes out of courtesy although he already knew (*jānan*)[3].

It appears as if the "author(s)" of the *Bālakāṇḍa* responsible for drafting the episode of Viṣṇu's incarnation used a version of the *bodhisattva*'s descent to the earth as a model for the episode of Viṣṇu's descent to and birth on earth. The elements adapted from the Buddha biography are the request of the gods to be born on earth and take on the predestined task, the protagonist's choice of his place and family of birth, and the tension between an assumed omniscience and the need to make a decision or choice which is not exactly what one would expect from an omniscient god. According to the logic of divine incarnation—instead of the Buddhist concept of reincarnation—and the pre-existing narrative of King Daśaratha's childlessness and the ongoing sacrifices to obtain male offspring, certain features of the incarnation process had to be modified:

---

[1] See Windisch 1908, 33–35 & 98 where he points out, in opposition to Senart's (1907, 24) suggestion that the idea of the descent of the different Buddhas is influenced by the *avatāra* concept of Viṣṇu, that the repeated incarnation of a *bodhisattva*/Buddha is different from the reincarnation of one individual god like Viṣṇu.

[2] This paradox of the juxtaposition of the omniscience of the *bodhisattva* in the Buddha biography has been pointed out and discussed by Jonathan Silk (2003).

[3] This is exactly the verb form (*jānann eva*) used in the *Lalitavistara* when during the excursions the *bodhisattva* asks the charioteer about the meaning of their encounters with the sick, old and dead man: Silk 2003, 873–874.

instead of the *bodhisattva*'s conception in the form of a white elephant, Viṣṇu's successful conception is fostered by the son-providing porridge (Rām.1.15.17: *pāyasa(ṃ) devanirmitta(m) prajākara(ṃ)*) prepared by the gods and given to Daśaratha for his wives by the divine powerful deity arising from the sacrificial fire (Rām.1.15.9ff.; translation Goldman 1984: 155ff.). After such a powerful demonstration of divine intervention in Daśaratha's efforts to beget the male heirs needed, the "authors" of the *Bālakāṇḍa* switch back to a very straight-forward narrative mode and neither the pregnancy of the queens nor a miraculous birth is recounted in the epic. The text quite bluntly states (Rām.1.17.6):

> Kausalyā gave birth to an illustrious son named Rāma, the delight of the Ikṣvākus. He bore the signs of divinity, for he was one-half of Viṣṇu[1].[2]

But it is exactly because of this "normality" of Rāma's birth that the miraculous and divine episode in heaven stands out as special—and the only clear parallel is indeed found in the biography of the Buddha.

References

Appleton 2017 Naomi Appleton. *Shared Characters in Jain, Buddhist and Hindu Narrative: Gods, Kings and Other Heroes*. London, New York: Routledge.

Bhatt 1960 G.H. Bhatt. *The Vālmīki-Rāmāyaṇa, Critical Edition. Volume I: The Bālakāṇḍa, the First Book of the Vālmīki Rāmāyaṇa, the National Epic of India*. Baroda: Oriental Institute.

Böhtlingk and Roth 1868–1871 Otto Böhtlingk and Rudolph Roth. *Sanskrit-Wörterbuch. Sechster Theil (ya-va)*. Sankt Petersburg: Kaiserliche Akademie der Wissenschaften (Japanese reprint, Tokyo: Meicho-Fukyū-Kai, 1976).

Brinkhaus 1992 Horst Brinkhaus. "Early Developmental Stages of the Viṣṇuprādurbhāva Lists." *Wiener Zeitschrift für die Kunde Südasiens* 36 (Supplement: Proceedings of the VIIIth World Sanskrit Conference, Vienna 1990): 101–110.

Brockington 1984 John, L. Brockington. *Righteous Rāma: The Evolution of an Epic*. Delhi, et al.: Oxford University Press.

1998 *The Sanskrit Epics*, Handbook of Oriental Studies II.12. Leiden, Boston, Köln: Brill.

2012 "The *Rāmāyaṇa* in the Purāṇas." In: François Voegeli, et al., eds. *Devadattīyam: Johannes Bronkhorst Felicitation Volume*, 703–730. Bern: Peter Lang.

Brodbeck 2019 Simon Brodbeck. *Krishna's Lineage: The Harivaṃsha of Vyāsa's Mahābhārata*. New York: Oxford University Press.

Deeg 2022a Max Deeg. "An Unromantic Approach: Dhyānagupta's (aka Jñānagupta) Fo-benxing-ji-jing." In: Ines Konczak-Nagel, Satomi Hiyama and Astrid Klein, eds., *Connecting the Art, Literature, and Religion of South and Central Asia: Studies in Honour of Monika Zin*, 61–71. New Delhi: DEV Publishers & Distributors.

[1] The other two quarters of Viṣṇu went to Sumitrā's sons Lakṣmaṇa and Śatrughna.

[2] Translation Goldman 1984, 159. Text quoted after the electronic version GRETIL: 6. *Kausalyājanayad Rāmaṃ divyalakṣaṇasaṃyutam | Viṣṇor ardhaṃ mahābhāgaṃ putram Ikṣvākunandanam ||*

2022b "The Buddha in the 'Wild West': The Localisation of Jātakas in Gandhāra and the *Rāmāyaṇa*." *Religions of South Asia* 16/2–3: 202–248

Eltschinger 2018 Vincent Eltschinger. "Aśvaghoṣa on Kings and Kingship." *Indo-Iranian Journal* 61: 311–352.

2019 "Why Did the Buddha Come to Earth? Monastic Lineage, Interreligious Polemics, and Philosophy." In: Dan Arnold, Cécile Ducher and Pierre-Julien Harter, eds., *Reasons and Lives in Buddhist Traditions: Studies in Honor of Matthew Kapstein*, 293–206. Somerville, MA: Wisdom Publications.

Fausbøll 1962 Viggo Fausbøll. *The Jātaka, Together With Its Commentary, Being Tales of the Anterior Births of Gotama Buddha*. Vol.1. London: Pali Text Society.

Foucaux 1884 Philippe Édouard Foucaux. *Le Lalita Vistara, Développement des Jeux: contenant l'histoire du Bouddha Çakya-Mouni depuis sa naissance jusqu'à sa prédication, traduit du Sanscrit en Français. Première partie: traduction française*, Annales du Musée Guimet 6. Paris: Ernest Leroux.

Freiberger 2019 Oliver Freiberger. "Der Buddha als Avatāra: Zur Analyse von Grenzen zwischen Religionen." In: Max Deeg, Oliver Freiberger and Christoph Kleine, eds., *Religionsbegegnung in der asiatischen Religionsgeschichte: Kritische Reflexionen über ein etabliertes Konzept*, 55–73. Göttingen: Vandenhoeck & Ruprecht.

Gawroński 1919 Andrzej Gawroński. *Studies About the Sanskrit Buddhist Literature*. Krakow: Nakładem Akademji Umiejętności.

Goldmann 1984 Robert P. Goldmann. *The Rāmāyaṇa of Vālmīki: An Epic of Ancient India, Volume I: Bālakāṇḍa*. Princeton: Princeton University Press.

Gombrich 1985 Richard Gombrich. "The Vessantara Jātaka, the *Rāmāyaṇa*, and the Dasaratha Jātaka." *Journal of the American Oriental Society* 105/3: 427–437.

Gnoli 1977 Raniero Gnoli. *The Gilgit Manuscript of the Saṅghabhedavastu (Being the 17th and Last Section of the Vinaya of the Mūlasarvāstivādin)*, Part 1, Serie Orientale Roma XLIX 1. Roma: Is.M.E.O.

Haas 2004 Cornelia Haas. *Wie man den Veda lesen kann: Gandharva und die »Zwischenzustände« im Ṛgveda und im Kommentar des Sāyaṇa. Wege der Interpretation eines archaischen Textes*. Göttingen: Vandenhoeck & Ruprecht.

Hiltebeitel 2006 Alf Hiltebeitel. "Aśvaghoṣa's *Buddhacarita*: The First Known Close and Critical Reading of the Brahmanical Sanskrit Epics." *Journal of Indian Philosophy* 34: 229–286.

Jacobi 1879 Hermann Jacobi. *The Kalpasûtra of Bhadrabâhu, edited with an Introduction, Notes and a Prâkṛit-Saṃskṛit Glossary*, Abhandlungen für die Kunde des Morgenlandes VII.1. Leipzig: F.A. Brockhaus.

1882 *The Âyâraṃga Sutta of the Çvetâmbara Jains. Part I.–Text*. London: The Pali Text Society.

1884 *Gaina Sûtras Translated from Prâkrit. Part I: The Âkârâṅga Sûtra, The Kalpa Sûtra*, Sacred Books of the East, Vol.XXII. Oxford: The Clarendon Press.

Jayawickrama

2002 N.A. Jayawickrama. *The Story of Gotama Buddha: The Nidāna-kathā of the Jātakaṭṭhakathā*. Oxford: The Pali Text Society.

Johnston 1928 E.H. Johnston. *The Saundarananda of Aśvaghoṣa, Critically Edited with Notes*. London: Oxford University Press.

	1932	*The Saundarananda, Or Nanda the Fair, Translated from the Original Sanskrit of Aśvaghoṣa*. London: Oxford University Press.
	1936	*The Buddhacarita, or The Acts of the Buddha, Part II: Cantos i to xiv translated from the original Sanskrit, supplemented by the Tibetan version, together with an introduction and notes*. Calcutta: Baptist Mission Press.
Jones	1952	J.J. Jones. *The Mahāvastu (Translated from Buddhist Sanskrit)*, Vol. 2. London: Luzac & Company, Ltd.
Lamotte	1944	Étienne Lamotte. *Le Traité de la Grande Vertu de Sagesse de Nāgārjuna (Mahāprajñāpāramitāśāstra), Tôme I: Châpitres I-XV, Première Partie (Traduction Annotée)*. Louvain/Leuven: Institut Orientaliste/Instituut voor Oriëntalistik.
Lefmann	1902	Salomon Lefmann. *Lalita-Vistara: Leben und Lehre des Çâkya-Buddha. Textausgabe mit Varianten-, Metren- und Wörterverzeichnissen. Erster Teil: Text*. Halle a.d.S.: Verlag der Buchhandlung des Waisenhauses.
Luczanits	2010	Christian Luczanits. "Prior to Birth: The Tuṣita episodes in Indian Buddhist literature and art." In: Christoph Cueppers, Max Deeg, Hubert Durt, eds., *The Birth of the Buddha. Proceedings of the International Conference Held in Lumbini, Nepal, October 2004*, 41–91. Lumbinī: Lumbinī International Research Institute.
Marciniak	2020	Katarzina Marciniak. *The Mahāvastu: A New Edition, Volume 2*. Tokyo: The International Research Institute of Advanced Buddhology, Soka University.
Mayrhofer	1976	Manfred Mayrhofer. *Kurzgefaßtes etymologisches Wörterbuch des Altindischen/A Concise Etymological Sanskrit Dictionary. Band III: Y–H, Nachträge und Berichtigungen*. Heidelberg: Carl Winter Universitätsverlag.
Olivelle	2008	Patrick Olivelle. *The Life of the Buddha by Ashvaghosha*, Clay Sanskrit Library. New York: New York University Press & JJC Foundation.
Scharf	2003	Peter Scharf. *Rāmopakhyāna: The Story of Rāma in the Mahābhārata: An Independent Study Reader in Sanskrit*. London, New York: Routledge Curzon.
Schlingloff	2013	Dieter Schlingloff. *Ajanta: Handbook of the Paintings 1. Narrative Paintings, Volume I: Interpretation*. Delhi: Aryan Books International.
Senart	1890	Émile Senart. *Le Mahāvastu*, vol. 2. Paris: Imprimerie Nationale.
	1907	*Origines bouddhiques*. Paris: Ernest Leroux.
Silk	2003	Jonathan A. Silk. "The Fruits of Paradox: On the Religious Architecture of the Buddha's Life Story." *Journal of the American Academy of Religion* 71/4: 863–881.
Willemen	2009	Charles Willemen. *Buddhacarita: In Praise of Buddha's Acts*, Taishō Volume 4, Number 192. Berkeley: Bukkyō Dendō Kyōkai.
Windisch	1908	Ernst Windisch. *Buddhas Geburt und die Lehre von der Seelenwanderung*. Leipzig: B.G. Teubner.

A Composite Manuscript from Qizil (SHT 191) and the *Tridaṇḍamālā**

Jens-Uwe HARTMANN

Abstract: The *Tridaṇḍamālā* is most probably a collection of texts used for recitation during specific ritual events. It contains forty canonical sūtras, embedded in verse sections. Many, if not all, of these verses are quotations, and some of them preserve the Sanskrit original of verses in Aśvaghoṣa's *Buddhacarita* that were previously known only in Tibetan translation. Now, it turns out that verses preserved in the *Tridaṇḍamālā* are also found in Sanskrit manuscripts from the Northern Silk Road. One of them, SHT 191, shares three passages with the *Tridaṇḍamālā*, which are presented here.

Keywords: Aśvaghoṣa; *Buddhacarita*; *Tridaṇḍamālā*; SHT 191

1 Introduction

When I recall my last meeting with Professor Duan Qing, visions arise of an extremely dynamic, energetic, and target-oriented person, devoted to fostering the academic study of manuscripts, and preferably those from the region that we usually refer to as the ancient Silk Road. In 2017, on a trip to Budapest, Duan and her entourage made a detour to Munich in order to study a collection of Central Asian manuscripts. I took her to the Museum Fünf Kontinente (Museum Five Continents), formerly known as the Staatliches Museum für Völkerkunde, where we were granted access to the Francke-Körber-Sammlung, a collection of finds from Central Asia, among them 442 manuscript fragments, acquired in Khotan in 1914 by August Hermann Francke and Hans Körber (Richtsfeld 2010–2011a, b). The collection contains fragments of Sanskrit manuscripts (210),[1] but also some in Chinese (41), Tibetan (24), Uighur (2), Sogdian (1), and a significant number of manuscripts in Khotanese (74),[2] and naturally it was these, in which Duan was especially interested. We were shown the originals, and I vividly remember how Duan and her team immediately delved into the fragments. As a result, we started thinking about the publication of the collection, and I wish that we had been more active in pursuing this goal. However, Duan Qing's untimely passing will now provide an additional motivation for making the collection better accessible.

Jens-Uwe HARTMANN, Ludwig Maximilian University of Munich.

* It is my pleasant duty to thank Mitsuyo Demoto-Hahn (Marburg) and Péter-Dániel Szántó (Budapest) for excellent comments leading to valuable improvements, especially in the translation of section 3.1, and Henry Albery (Tokyo) for correcting my English.

[1] They are presently being described by Klaus Wille and will appear as volume 13 of the series *Sanskrithandschriften aus den Turfanfunden*. Most of the Sanskrit fragments belong to Prajñāpāramitā texts, among them *Aṣṭasāhasrikā Prajñāpāramitā*, *Vajracchedikā*, and the less well-known *Pañcapāramitānirdeśasūtra*, and to the *Saddharmapuṇḍarīkasūtra*.

[2] Especially from the Khotanese *Karmavibhaṅga* and *Saṃghāṭasūtra*.

2 The Multiple-text Manuscript SHT 191

As a tribute to her constant support for research on Central Asian manuscripts and her own numerous contributions to advancing this field of study, I present here the results of some recent research conducted on one manuscript in the possession of the German Turfan Collection in Berlin. It carries the current catalogue number SHT 191. According to its description in the first catalogue volume of the *Sanskrithandschriften aus den Turfanfunden* (Waldschmidt 1965, 107), it was found in Qizil and brought back by the third of the so-called Prussian Turfan Expeditions which visited the Tarim basin from December 1905 until May 1907. It was described as a *Sammelhandschrift mit Buddhastotras, Lehrversen, Versen erzählenden Inhalts, Versen über das Geben*, "a composite manuscript that contains a variety of different texts, among them Buddhastotras, doctrinal verses, narrative verses, and verses about giving." The seventeen fragments of the manuscript had been published by Dieter Schlingloff under the old "Lüders number"[1] K 1233 in his study of the Stotra texts in the Turfan collection (Schlingloff 1955, 34–40, numbers 23–50). According to Schlingloff and the catalogue volume, the manuscript combined the following texts:

- a1–c) a Buddhastotra, a praise of the Buddha's awakening, in Vasantatilakā meter; folios 31–33 with various verse numbers preserved (15 on folio 31; 21, 23, 26 and 28 on folio 32; 30, 31, 33–36 on folio 33);
- d) verses[2] in Mattamayūrī; folio 47 with verse numbers 16 and 17;
- e–f) verses with changing meters (Upajāti, Vasantatilakā, Āryā) and at least two numberings;
- g) narratives in verse with verse numbers 21 and 22 on the recto side; on the verso side the story of King Kṛkin and his daughters with verse numbers 3, 4 and 7;
- h) verses about giving with three different numberings (twice up to five, the last is impossible to decide, see below);
- i) two Buddhastotras with 5 verses each;
- k–o) verses with undetermined contents.

All the fragments exclusively contained verses, but neither Lüders nor Schlingloff could trace any to known poetical works. Thus, the question remained open as to whether some of the verses had been imported from India or if all of them had been written by local Sanskrit scholars in Central Asia. Since the manuscript was made from

[1] Heinrich Lüders had arranged the fragments according to their content, a somewhat cumbersome classification scheme, which led to the splitting up of manuscripts that contained texts of different genres. This system was abandoned in favour of running numbers in the catalogue volumes.

[2] Verses d–f are described as Lehrverse ("doctrinal verses") in the catalogue volume; they are too fragmentary to forward any reliable classification.

paper and written in a form of Central Asian Brāhmī, it was doubtlessly a local product, and this did not help much in answering the question of its origin. Equally unclear were the purpose and function of the manuscript, with the only clue lying in Schlingloff's characterization of one folio, reproduced under numbers 37–38 in his edition, as containing *Verse über das Geben*, "verses about giving." This is reminiscent of *Schenkungsformulare*, donation formulas, a genre of ritual texts apparently used by monks when receiving a donor who intends to make or has made a significant donation. No small number of such texts are known from Central Asia and some of them have been studied, not least for the historical information they contain.[1] However, none of the "verses about giving" occurred in any of the formulae, and therefore the relation remained vague.

As is so often the case, a new source is needed to gain new insights, and by happy coincidence, such a source recently became accessible. Since 2018, Kazunobu Matsuda and I have been working on the Sanskrit manuscript of the *Tridaṇḍamālā* (TDM). This is apparently a ritual text consisting of forty chapters, each of which seems to provide a recitation requisite for a specific purpose. We have already introduced and described this text on various occasions,[2] and therefore a summary of the relevant points should here suffice. Each of its forty chapters consists of three parts: a verse section, followed by a canonical sūtra, and another verse section. The verse sections are of differing length, but are always more or less closely related to the contents of the sūtra. No sources are given for either the verses or the sūtras. So far, their application seems clear in the case of only two chapters; namely, chapter 11 with the *Anityatāsūtra*, which may have been used at the funeral of a dead monk, and chapter 25, which contains the *Pravāraṇasūtra* as the canonical text and, judging from the accompanying verses, most probably served a function on the occasion of the Pravāraṇā ceremony.

The verse sections surprised us for their including a great number of verses that are associated with the name of Aśvaghoṣa. Primarily, these are quotations from the *Buddhacarita* (Bc) and the *Saundarananda* but are by no means confined to them (Hartmann and Matsuda forthcoming). Especially noteworthy is the fact that a fair number of the *Buddhacarita* verses come from the second half of this poem, which is not preserved in Sanskrit. Thus far, we have identified 181 and a half verses of the Bc in the TDM, 136 of which belong to its latter half. In other words, more than two thirds of the quotations recover Sanskrit text of the Bc which was previously unknown. These findings in turn opened up new possibilities with regard to the Central Asian manuscripts, initiating a search of the texts, which, following a number of positive matches, became standard procedure. The *codex unicus* of the *Tridaṇḍamālā* is a fairly late manuscript (possibly 11th century) preserved in Xizang, and the overall doctrinal

[1] For instance, Lüders 1922 and 1930.

[2] Hartmann forthcoming; Matsuda 2019.

orientation of the Sanskrit manuscripts in Xizang does not immediately indicate an intimate connection to the canonical literature of the (Mūla-)Sarvāstivādins, as is the case for those retrieved from the Buddhist cave monasteries along the northern route of the Silk Road. However, the relationship between the TDM and the Buddhist literature from Central Asia could hardly be any closer. This affinity begins with the sūtra quotations in the TDM, which correspond precisely to versions of the same sūtras transmitted in Central Asia,[1] and it is as such, quite clear that the compilers of the TDM had a (Mūla-)Sarvāstivādin version of the Sūtrapiṭaka at their disposal. When we further take into account that the Tridaṇḍaka seems to be a ritual format that was developed in Mūlasarvāstivādin circles and is referred to on several occasions in their Vinaya,[2] the canonical orientation of the TDM becomes less surprising.

3 Identification of Three Texts Contained in SHT 191

To return to the composite manuscript SHT 191, there are three points of connection between this manuscript and the verses quoted in the TDM. Two are directly related to Aśvaghoṣa and therefore unambiguous with regard to their origin, while the source of the third is still unknown and its context raises interesting questions.

1) SHT 191h[3] (no. 38 in Schlingloff 1955): lines 2–6 of the verso side contain remnants of Bc 18.62–66.
2) SHT 191k+m (nos. 41/42 and 45/46 in Schlingloff 1955): the two fragments belong to the same folio. It preserves the remains of verses 19d–32a of Aśvaghoṣa's *Śokavinodana*.
3) SHT 191g (no. 35 in Schlingloff 1955): lines 1–5 of the recto side correspond to TDM fol. 55v2–4.

3.1 *Buddhacarita* 18.62–66

The five verses in Upajāti meter could be identified with the help of the first section in chapter 16 of the TDM. The core text of this chapter is the *Sumanā-rājakumārī-sūtra*, which is quoted in full in section 2. This sūtra is devoted to Sumanā, the sister of King Prasenajit, who asks the Buddha about two imaginary disciples, both being equal with regard to faith, virtue and insight, but one being an almsgiver and the other not. The Blessed One explains that there are indeed notable differences in all possible states below arhat-ship; only then the differences finally disappear. Up to here, the Sanskrit text preserved in the TDM and the Pali parallel in the *Aṅguttaranikāya* (AN III 32–33)

---

[1] A published example is the *Āryikā-sūtra*, first edited from a Central Asian manuscript fragment and then reedited once the quotation in the TDM became accessible, cf. Hartmann 2017 and 2022; another example is the still unpublished *Pravāraṇa-sūtra*.

[2] Schopen 1992, 32–34, note 62 (= Schopen 1997, 231–233); see also the additional footnote in Schopen 2010, 118, note 35 (= Schopen 2014, 69–70); Hartmann forthcoming.

[3] Excellent images of all the fragments are available at Digitales Turfan-Archiv: http://turfan.bbaw.de/dta/.

are largely in agreement. The Pali text ends with a number of verses, but the Sanskrit continues with a description of the five advantages (*anuśaṃsa*) of giving, followed by three verses, and then an additional instruction on the five aspects which accompany a donation of food (*bhojana*) to a recipient (*pratigrāhaka*). These are health (*āyus*), beauty (*varṇa*), strength (*bala*), happiness (*sukha*) and *pratibhāna*, here probably "eloquence," since the envisaged recipients are most likely monks who are expected to teach the dharma.

It is easy to imagine that the canonical text was recited in the context of a donation to the order, especially a feeding of the monks or nuns. The verse sections before and after the sūtra quotation are usually connected to the topic of the sūtra and serve to underline or reinforce the message, as it were. The first section of chapter 16 contains thirty verses altogether, among them the seventeen verses Bc 18.62–78, which are quoted consecutively on folios 32v5–33v2. They represent the Buddha's speech after the rich merchant Anāthapiṇḍada announced his intention to donate a monastery to the Buddha. They therefore perfectly fit any occasion in which a gift is promised or announced to the order and strongly support the understanding of SHT 191h as a donation formula. This is further confirmed by the fact that the same verses are quoted in two other manuscripts form Central Asia. The first, SHT 141/2,[1] belongs to the German Turfan Collection, and the second, the Tocharian bilingual fragment PK NS 14 (Couvreur 1970, 179–180), to the Pelliot Collection in Paris. Both have already been identified as part of donation formulas. The Pelliot fragment preserves only remains of verses 18.62–64, but in SHT 141/2 another text follows after Bc 18.66 and makes it clear that here only five verses are quoted from the Bc. Most likely it is the same case in SHT 191h, especially since the preceding passage on lines r1–v2 also consists of two sets of five verses with verse 66 ending on the next folio, which is not preserved, and therefore the matter in SHT 191h cannot be finally decided. The five Bc verses will be edited below in comparison with all sources and their Tibetan translation.

Symbols Used in the Edition

[ ]	damaged *akṣara*(s)
+	one destroyed *akṣara*
..	one illegible *akṣara*
.	illegible part of an *akṣara*
< >	editorial insertion
« »	interlinear insertion
///	beginning or end of an fragment when broken
*	*virāma*
○	space left blank for the string hole

[1] Lüders 1930, 5 (Blatt 4, r3–v3) and 11, note 2, with a reference to SHT 191h. Lüders still had complete folios at his disposal and therefore could read more; cf. SHT X, 287–288, catalogue nos. 4158 and 4161, which contain many small fragments, among them also some belonging to Blatt 4.

SHT 191h Verso[1]

2 /// [ki]ñcit* || || nirvvāhyate yad bhavanāt pradīptā[t t]. .t. [s]y. [kā] .y. [k]u[r]u[t].
3 /// śnute saḥ 1 ataś ca jānanti viśālasatvās tyaktuṃ ca samyag viṣayāṃ
4 /// na bhayād dadāti 2 kāle ca pātre ca vimoktum artthaṃ śauryā[c c]a mānāc ca ta
5 /// dadat priyatvaṃ jagati prayāti .ā .. ti kīrttiṃ paramaṃ yaśaś ca d[ā]ta
6 /// [m e]ti tathaiva .. [k]e na do + + + + .. dāruṇebhyaḥ kṛtāni pu

Edition of the Quotation in the TDM[2] with SHT 141/2,[3] SHT 191h, PK NS 14, and the Tibetan Translation[4]

nirvāhyate yad bhavanāt pradīptāt tat ta(33a1)sya kāryaṃ kurute na dagdham |
kālāgninaivaṃ jagati pradīpte dadāti yo yat tad upāśnute saḥ || <Bc 18.62>

SHT 141 fol. 4r3 /// ni[r]v[ā]hyate yad bhavanāt pradīptat tat tasya kāryaṃ kurute na dagdham* kālāgninaivaṃ jagati pradī(r4)*pte* [da]dāti yo ya○t tad upāśnute saḥ 1

SHT 191h v2: /// [ki]ñcit* || || nirvvāhyate yad bhavanāt pradīptā[t t]. .t. [s]y. [kā] .y. [k]u[r]u[t]. (v3) /// śnute saḥ 1

PK NS 14 b1: ni[r]v[ā]hyate yad bhava[nā] .[r]. /// (b2) pte dadāti y[o] ya[t] tad u[p]. ///

| gang zhig khyim ni tshig las phyi rol 'thon byed pa |
| de yi don de 'tshig par byed pa ma yin te |
| de bzhin dus kyi me yis 'gro ba tshig pa na |
| gang gis gang zhig sbyin pa de yis de nyer 'thob | 18.62

"Whatever is taken out of a burning house, fulfills its purpose, (but) not the burnt; similarly when the world is burnt up by the fire at the end of time, a man gains whatever he gives away."[5]

ataś ca jānanti viśālasatvā dātuṃ ca samyag viṣayāṃś ca bhoktum |
klības tu loke kṣayadoṣadarśī naivopabhuṅkte na bhayād dadāti || <Bc 18.63>

SHT 141 fol. 4r4: ataś ca jānanti viśālasatvās tyaktuñ ca sa(r5)*myag viṣa*[y]āṃś ca bhoktum* klības tu loke kṣayadoṣadarśī naivopabhujkte[6] na bhayād dadāti 2

SHT 191h v3: ataś ca jānanti viśālasatvās tyaktuṃ ca samyag viṣayāṃ (v4) /// na bhayād dadāti 2

[1] For an image see Digitales Turfan-Archiv (http://turfan.bbaw.de/dta/), SHT 191h.

[2] For images of the manuscript see Hartmann forthcoming, note 6. They are also available from the Niedersächsische Staats- und Universitätsbibliothek in Göttingen, where digital copies of Rāhula Sāmkṛtyāyana's photographs are kept (hsd@sub.uni-goettingen.de).

[3] When Lüders edited the folio, it was nearly complete. *Akṣaras* still read by Lüders, but lost today, are marked in italics.

[4] D no. 4156, *skyes rabs*, Ge, 67b5–68a1; P no. 5656, *mdo 'grel*, Nge, 81b8–82a5.

[5] Cf. Johnston 1937, 59; Johnston's translation from the Tibetan is amazingly good, and therefore it is retained whenever possible. Here, however, pāda b in Tibetan seems to miss the sense.

[6] Lüders, note 5: "Lies *-opabhuṅkte*."

PK NS 14 b3: yāṃś ca [bho] .[tu]ṃ klī ○ /// (b4): [2]

TDM: dātuñ; °bhuṃkte

| de phyir rnam spangs sems dpa' rnams kyis sbyin par dang |
| yul rnams yang dag longs spyod par ni shes pa nyid |
| bkren pa 'jig rten dag na zad pa'i skyon mthoṅ bas |
| nye bar longs spyod ma yin 'jigs las sbyin ma yin | 18.63

"Therefore the broad-minded know (how) to give and to enjoy in the right way the objects of sense. But the coward in the world, seeing the danger of exhaustion (of his wealth), out of fear neither enjoys nor gives away."

kāle ca pātre ca niyoktum arthaṃ śauryāc ca mānāc ca tathaiva yoddhum |
jānāti sattvādhika eva nānyaḥ sattvaṃ (33a2) dadāty eva hi yudhyate ca || <Bc 18.64>

SHT 141 fol. 4r5: kāle (r6) *ca pātre ca vim*[ok]. [m]. r.ṃ śauryāc ca mānāc ca tathaiva yoddhum* jānāti satvādhika eva nānyaḥ satvaṃ (r7) *dadāty eva ca yuddhyate ca 3*

SHT 191h v4: kāle ca pātre ca vimoktum artthaṃ śauryā[c c]a mānāc ca ta ///

PK NS 14 b4: kāle ca pātre [c]a .. /// (b5) eva nānyaḥ .. ///

TDM: satvādhika; satvaṃ

| dus su smod la don ni rnam par gtong ba dang |
| dpal dang nga rgyal las ni de bzhin g.yul 'gyed par |
| sems dpa' lhag pa nyid kyis shes te gzhan gyis min |
| sems dpa' yis ni sbyin pa nyid dang g.yul 'gyed do | 18.64

a: correct smod to snod for pātra?

b: dpal D : dpa' P

"Only the man who is eminent in resolution, but no other man, knows (how) to spend wealth at the right time and for a proper recipient, and (how) to fight with heroism and pride; resolution alone gives and fights."

dadat priyatvaṃ jagati prayāti prāpnoti kīrtiṃ paramaṃ yaśaś ca |
dātāsti kaś cety avagamya sadbhiḥ saṃmānyate cāpy abhigamyate ca || <Bc 18.65>

SHT 141 fol. 4r7: dadat priyatvaṃ [j]agati [pr]*ayāti* [p]*r*āp[n]o[t]i *kīr*tiṃ *paramāṃ*[1] *yaśa*[ś]. .. (v1) *dātāsti kaś cety avagamya sadbh*iḥ saṃmānyate [c]āpy ani[gamyat]*e*[2] [ca] 4

SHT 191h v5: /// dadat priyatvaṃ jagati prayāti .ā .. ti kīrttiṃ paramaṃ yaśaś ca d[ā]ta ///

TDM: jaga«ti»; kīrttim*; sammānyate

| sbyin byed dga' ba nyid du 'gro la 'gro ba ste |
| snyan pa dang ni dam par grags pa rab tu 'thob |

[1] Lüders, note 6, refers to the better reading *paramaṃ* in SHT 191h.

[2] Lüders, note 7: "Lies *abhigamyate*."

| sbyin pa po yod gang zhes dam pa rnams sbyin nas |
| yang dag bkur ba dang ni mngon du 'gro bar byed | 18.65

"Giving, he becomes beloved in the world, and he obtains fame and a good name. When they perceive that he is quite a giver,[1] good men honour him and associate with him."

viśvāsyatām eti tathaiva loke na doṣam āpnoty api dāruṇebhyaḥ |
kṛtāni puṇyāni mayeti tuṣṭo na trāsam abhyeti ca mṛtyukāle || <Bc 18.66>

SHT 141 fol. 4v1: *viśvāsyatām eti ta[th](ai)[va]* (v2) *loke na doṣa*m *āpnoty a*pi dāruṇebhyaḥ kṛtāni puṇyāni mayeti tuṣṭo na trāsam abhyeti (v3) *ca mṛt*[y]u[kāl]*e* 5 ||
SHT 191h v6: /// [m e]ti tathaiva .. [k]e na do + + + + .. dāruṇebhyaḥ kṛtāni pu ///
TDM: «na» trāsam

| de bzhin 'jig rten dag na blo gtad nyid 'gyur zhing |
| mi bzad pa rnams las kyang nyes pa 'thob ma yin |
| bsod nams rnams ni bdag gis byas zhes tshim pa ste |
| 'chi ba'i dus su skrag par mngon par 'gro ma yin | 18.66

"Thus he becomes trustworthy in the world, and he also does not obtain hatred[2] from the dreadful. Contented in the thought "I have done meritorious acts," he is not affrighted in the hour of death."

3.2 The *Śokavinodana* Ascribed to Aśvaghoṣa

The TDM was discovered together with a second text, a *parikathā*, which is being studied by Péter-Dániel Szántó. He provisionally names it **Saddharmaparikathā* and considers it a preacher's manual that details how to provide sermons for the laity (Szántó 2021). Chapter 11 of this manual deals with the subject of *śokavinodana*, the "consolation of grief," and when Szántó looked into the 14th chapter of the TDM, he found two sets of twenty stanzas, which treat exactly such a consolation. Next, he looked into the Tanjur section of the Tibetan Buddhist canon and found the translation of a work entitled *Śokavinodana*, which consists of forty stanzas and was, according to its colophon, composed by *ācārya* Aśvaghoṣa (Tib. *slob dpon rta dbyangs*). A comparison of the Tibetan text with the Sanskrit stanzas immediately revealed that the two texts were identical. He shared his discovery with us, and this resulted in two more identifications, namely that of SHT 191k+m as a folio of the *Śokavinodana* and that of the *Jieyou jing* 解憂經 (T 804) not only as containing the *Śokavinodana*, but as a text closely corresponding to the 14th chapter of the TDM. In SHT 191, only two fragments of a single folio from the

[1] The exact connotation of kaś ca is unclear; Péter-Dániel Szántó wonders if it is to be taken as *dātā* + *āstikaś ca*. Tibetan *sbyin pa po yod gang zhes* is no help, and the Tibetan *sbyin nas* for *avagamya* must be a mistake.

[2] Szántó suggests taking *doṣa* in the Buddhist Hybrid Sanskrit sense of *dveṣa*, which is not, however, confirmed by Tibetan *nyes pa*.

section which once covered the *Śokavinodana* have come down to us. They are sufficient enough, however, to prove that the manuscript originally must have contained the full text and not only a few verses as a quotation. Sanskrit manuscripts from Central Asia usually add verse numbers, and the preserved numbers 19, 23 and 31 show that the order corresponds exactly to the Sanskrit text included in the TDM. Originally, the folio must once have contained at least the verses 18 to 32, and the *Śokavinodana* must have comprised about three folios of the manuscript. It is a remarkable text, full of expressive imagery, and anonymous quotes from its forty Anuṣṭubh verses are found in a wide range of Sanskrit works outside Buddhist literature. A first introduction to the text has appeared,[1] and an edition with a complete list of citations will be published by Péter-Dániel Szántó, Kazunobu Matsuda, and myself, hopefully in the near future.

3.3 Āryā Stanzas Shared by SHT 191 and the *Tridaṇḍamālā*

The fragment SHT 191g is a highly interesting case. In lines 1–5 of its recto side it contains the remains of six Āryā verses. Lines 2 and 3 preserve the verse numbers 21 and 22, which exactly correspond to the sequence in the TDM, although in late manuscripts such as that of the TDM, verse numbers are never written. Section three of chapter 22 of the TDM consists of 25 Āryā stanzas, followed by the usual two verses that end a chapter in a more or less formulaic way, a Śārdūlavikrīḍita and a Vasantatilakā stanza. SHT 191g seems to have contained exactly the same 25 Āryās, but not the two concluding verses. After them, the TDM starts with three verses of homage to Buddha, Dharma and Saṃgha, which invariably open the first section of a new chapter, while in SHT 191g a versified story about the seven daughters of King Kṛkin, generally known as the *Saptakumārikā-avadāna*, immediately follows the verses. The *Bhikṣuṇīvinaya* of the Mahāsāṃghika-Lokottaravādins contains a very similar version of this famous story, and Gustav Roth had already referred to SHT 191g in his edition of this Vinaya.[2] I owe the reference to my friend Klaus Wille whose reconstruction of this narrative passage in SHT 191g will appear in the section Ergänzungen und Korrekturen ("additions and corrections") of volume 13, which will conclude the SHT series. When we look at the evidence presented by SHT 191g, there is, first, a sequence of verses found also in the TDM, and, second, another sequence that is very similar to a set of verses preserved in the Vinaya of the Mahāsāṃghika-Lokottaravādins. This is remarkable, although at present difficult to assess. With regards to contents, there is an obvious relation: The verses corresponding to the TDM present general thoughts, accompanied by illustrations, on the constant separation of living beings due to death and rebirth, while the following story describes a visit of Kṛkin's seven daughters to a burial place (*śmaśāna*)

[1] Hartmann, Matsuda and Szántó 2022.

[2] Roth 1970, 115, notes 6–7; see also Dargyay 1978, 30–32.

and their awareness of the fact that the association with their father will not last.[1] Thus, the latter could have been meant as an illustration of the former.

Equally remarkable is the parallelism observed between the apparently identical 25 Āryā stanzas in the SHT fragment and the TDM, but again it is difficult to draw any sound conclusions. By now, there are two Central Asian manuscripts, which contain text very close to or even identical with a chapter of the TDM (see Concluding Remarks below), but SHT 191g is clearly a different case. A ritual function of at least parts of the manuscript is suggested by the folio which contains the Bc verses and potentially confirmed by the *Śokavinodana*, but that is all that can be said about a possible function at the present moment. Below I will present a revised edition of lines r1–5 and their parallel in the TDM.

SHT 191g Recto

1 /// + + + + + + yuvegavaśāt* tyaktvā punar anyo [ny]. + + + + + + + ///
2 /// + + + + [p]. vrajanti cānyo nyam utsṛjya 21 pūrvve janma[n]. + + + ///
3 /// + + + m. ṣyāmaḥ 22 niśi vihaganaṃ vṛkṣe pathi pathikānāṃ ca .. + ///
4 /// + + tyaktāḥ priyais subahuśaḥ priyān parityajya cāvaśo bahuṣaḥ lo ///
5 /// + śaraṇam asvantam anityam atibahubhayārttam* lokam avekṣya ya ///
6 /// [||] kṛkir āsīn narādhipaḥ babhūvopāsikā [s]arvvās tasyā .ī + + ///[2]

Combined Edition of the TDM (normal) and SHT 191g (italics):

nabhasi yathā meghānāṃ samāgamo bhavati vā(r1)*yuvegavaśāt* |
*tyaktvā punar anyony*aṃ cāmbudhārās te praṇaśyanti || <20>

"Like a conjunction of clouds in the sky occurs by the force of vehement winds, and abandoning each other, the 'water holders' (= clouds) vanish,"

anyonyasaṃgamaṃ prāṇināṃ tathā bhavati he(55v3)tusambhavāt |
hetuvigamāt punar a(r2)*pi vrajanti cānyonyam utsṛjya* || *21*

"So is the mutual coming together of living beings caused by reasons; when the reasons disappear, they leave each other and move on."

*pūrve janman*i dayitaṃ janaṃ parityajya vayam iha prāptāḥ |
asmāt tyaktvā svajanaṃ cānyatra punar ga(r3)*miṣyāmaḥ* || *22*

a: *pūrvve* TDM, SHT 191g
c: *svajanam** TDM

"After giving up a person cherished in a previous existence, we reach here; and from here, having abandoned one's own people, we will go again to another existence."

[1] Especially verse 2 of their answer to their father, see Roth 1970, 118, with translation in Dargyay 1978, 23.

[2] It is not clear if this line is already supposed to be metrical. The following verses are *śloka*s, but here *sarvvās* would create a severe metrical problem.

niśi vihagānāṃ vṛkṣe pathi pathikānāṃ ca samāgamo yadvat |
bhūtvā punar na bhavati priyasaṃyogas tathaivaṃ nṛṇām || <23>

a: *vihaganaṃ* SHT 191g

"As at night a meeting of the birds on a tree and of travellers on the road has occurred, but will not happen again, exactly like this is the connection of people with the beloved ones."

(r4)*tyaktaḥ priyaiḥ subahuśaḥ* (55v4) *priyān parityajya vāgato bahuśaḥ* |
*lo*ko 'yam anālokaḥ sumahati bhavasaṃkaṭe bhramati || <24>

a: *tyaktāḥ* SHT 191g; *priyais* SHT 191g
b: *priyāṃ* TDM; *cāvaśo for vāgato* SHT 191g

"Very often one has been deserted by the beloved, and often one has abandoned the beloved;[1] this gloomy world circulates in the vast dire straits of existence."

tasmād anātham a(r5)*śaraṇam asvantam unityam atibahubhayārtam* |
*lokam avekṣya ya*thāvan nirvvāṇe niścayaḥ kriyatām || <25>

b: *°bhayārttam** TDM, SHT 191g
d: *nirvvāṇe* TDM

"Therefore, perceiving the world without protection, without refuge, without taking a good end, transient, struck by exceeding dangers, the resolution for nirvana should be duly made!"

4 Concluding Remarks

By now, the *Tridaṇḍamālā* has proven to be an amazingly rich source for many purposes. Here I will address only the three most important ones. First, it recovers verses connected with Aśvaghoṣa of which the Sanskrit original was lost, and it affords us the possibility of reviewing the edited text of those verses which have come down to us. Second, it preserves the Sanskrit text of sūtras, which were either lost or known only from Central Asian fragments or Chinese and Tibetan translations. Third, it brings into view an astonishing net of intertextuality. This is especially unexpected with regard to the textual traditions transmitted along the Silk Road, since they are geographically distant from the supposed origin of the manuscript of the TDM, which was likely in north-eastern India. There are several other Sanskrit manuscripts from Central Asia, which, similar to SHT 191g, share verses with the TDM in the same order, most notably SHT 378,[2] or even seem to reproduce another version of the/a TDM. The most surprising case here are the two fragmentary folios SHT 4437 and 4438. They immediately follow each other and preserve remains of all three sections of chapter 19

[1] With the reading *vāgato* "having come together," or with *cāvaśo* "unwillingly."

[2] SHT IV, pp. 310–314; for a reedition of the fragments a–c see Hartmann and Matsuda 2023.

of the TDM: the last verse (no. 35) of the first section, the sūtra quotation in the second section, and the first eight Śārdūlavikrīḍita stanzas of the third section.[1] Another, no less surprising case is the Sanskrit-Uigur bilingual manuscript TT VIII D,[2] which contains the last verse of section 1 in chapter 5 of the TDM, a few excerpts of the sūtra in section 2, and the first nine Vasantatilakā stanzas of the following section 3. Both manuscripts reproduce the structure and the order of the respective chapters of the TDM. It is difficult not to assume that they served the same ritual purpose already described for the TDM, an assumption underlined in the case of SHT 4437 and 4438 (due to its many glosses in Tocharian A and B), and in the case of TD VIII D (for its bilingualism), with both phenomena pointing to local practitioners actually using the texts. Thus, it is very likely that these two manuscripts inform us not only about literary traditions but also about Buddhist practices observed in the ancient civilizations along the Silk Road; civilizations, which Duan Qing has contributed so much to exploring.

Abbreviations

AN	*Aṅguttara-Nikāya*, ed. Richard Morris, E. Hardy, 5 vols. London: Pali Text Society, 1885-1900.
AtüHs I	see Maue 1996.
Bc	see Johnston 1936.
SHT I–XII	*Sanskrithandschriften aus den Turfanfunden*, Teil 1–12, ed. Ernst Waldschmidt, Lore Sander, Klaus Wille, Wiesbaden, Stuttgart: Franz Steiner 1965–2017.
TDM	*Tridaṇḍamālā*.

References

Couvreur 1970 Walter Couvreur. "Boeddhistische Sanskritfragmenten in Koetsjische handschriftenverzamelingen," *Anamnhcic. Gedenkboek Prof. Dr. E. A. Leemans*. Brugge: De Tempel, 175–184.

Dargyay 1978 Lobsang Dargyay. *Die Legende von den Sieben Prinzessinnen (Saptakumārikā-Avadāna) in der poetischen Fassung von Guhyadatta/Gopadatta aufgrund der tibetischen Übersetzung herausgegeben, übersetzt und bearbeitet*. Wien: Arbeitskreis für tibetische und buddhistische Studien Universität Wien.

Gabain 1954 Annemarie von Gabain. *Türkische Turfan-Texte VIII, Texte in Brāhmīschrift*. Berlin: Akademie-Verlag.

Hartmann 2017 "King Prasenajit Bemoans the Death of His Grandmother: A Study of the Manuscript SHT 7185." *International Journal of Buddhist Thought & Culture* (Special Issue: Recent Results of Buddhist Manuscript Research) 27/1: 73–105.

[1] SHT XI, pp. 32–35. The remains of the sūtra start in line recto 1 of SHT 4437 and end in line recto 3 of SHT 4438; its only parallel is found in the Chinese translations of the *Saṃyuktāgama*, no. 592 in T 99 (157b18 ff.) and no. 185 in T 100 (440a2ff.). A revised edition will appear in SHT XIII.

[2] The folio was published several times; the last edition is Gabain 1954. It is catalogued as AtüHs I 18; for a reedition of this text and the corresponding part of the TDM see Hartmann and Maue 2022.

2022 "Trauer um die Großmutter und Trost vom Buddha: das *Āryikā-sūtra*." In: Ines Konczak-Nagel, Satomi Hiyama, Astrid Klein, eds., *Connecting the Art, Literature, and Religion of South and Central Asia: Studies in Honour of Monika Zin*, 153–160. New Delhi: Dev Publishers and Distributors.

Forthcoming "Forms of Intertextuality and Lost Sanskrit Verses of the Buddhacarita: the Tridaṇḍaka and the *Tridaṇḍamālā*." In: Dan Boucher, Shayne Clarke, eds., Fs. Schopen.

Hartmann and Matsuda

2023 Jens-Uwe Hartmann, Kazunobu Matsuda. "Possible Fragments of Aśvaghoṣa's Lost *Sūtrālaṃkāra* from the 'Manuscript Cave' in Šorčuq." In: Hiroko Matsuoka, Shinya Moriyama, and Tyler Neill, eds., *To the Heart of Truth. Felicitation Volume for Eli Franco on the Occasion of His Seventieth Birthday*, 111–130. Wien: Arbeitskreis für tibetische und buddhistische Studien Universität Wien.

Forthcoming "The Case of the Appearing Poet: New Light on Aśvaghoṣa and the *Tridaṇḍamālā*." In: Charles DiSimone, Nicholas Witkowski, eds., *Buddhakṣetrapariśodhana: A Festschrift for Paul Harrison*. Marburg: Indica et Tibetica.

Hartmann, Matsuda and Szántó

2022 Jens-Uwe Hartmann, Kazunobu Matsuda, and Péter-Dániel Szántó. "The Benefit of Cooperation: Recovering the *Śokavinodana* Ascribed to Aśvaghoṣa." In: Mahinda Deegalle, ed., *Dharmayātrā. Felicitation Volume in Honour of Ven. Tampalawela Dhammaratana*, 173–180. Paris: Nuvis Press.

Hartmann and Maue

2022 Jens-Uwe Hartmann and Dieter Maue. "Ein sanskrit-uigurisches Fragment der *Tridaṇḍamālā* in Brāhmī-Schrift: Reedition des Texts TT VIII D." *Acta Asiatica Varsoviensia* 35: 39–130.

Johnston 1936 E. H. Johnston. *The Buddhacarita or Acts of the Buddha*. Calcutta: Baptist Mission Press.

1937 "The Buddha's Mission and Last Journey: Buddhacarita, xv to xxviii." *Acta Orientalia* 15: 26–111, 231–292.

Lüders 1922 Heinrich Lüders. "Zur Geschichte und Geographie von Ostturkestan." *Sitzungsberichte der Preussischen Akademie der Wissenschaften*: 243–261 [= H. Lüders. 1940. *Philologica Indica, Ausgewählte kleine Schriften, Festgabe zum 70. Geburtstage*. Göttingen: Vandenhoeck & Ruprecht, 526–546].

1930 "Weitere Beiträge zur Geschichte und Geographie von Ostturkestan." *Sitzungsberichte der Preussischen Akademie der Wissenschaften*: 7–64 [= H. Lüders. 1940. *Philologica Indica, Ausgewählte kleine Schriften, Festgabe zum 70. Geburtstage*. Göttingen: Vandenhoeck & Ruprecht, 595–658].

Matsuda 2019 Kazunobu Matsuda. "三啓集 (*Tridaṇḍamālā*) における勝義空経とブッダチャリタ Sankeishū (*Tridaṇḍamālā*) ni okeru Shōgikū-kyō to Buddacharita. [The *Paramārthaśūnyatā-sūtra* and the *Buddhacarita* in the *Tridaṇḍamālā*]." *Indogaku bukkyōgaku kenkyū* 印度學佛教學研究 [*Journal of Indian and Buddhist Studies*] 68/1: 1–11.

Maue 1996 Dieter Maue. *Alttürkische Handschriften. Teil 1: Dokumente in Brāhmī und tibetischer Schrift*, Verzeichnis der orientalischen Handschriften in Deutschland XIII, 9. Stuttgart: Franz Steiner.

Richtsfeld

2010–2011a Bruno Richtsfeld. "August Hermann Franckes (1870–1930) Bearbeitung der Serindien- und Ladakh-Sammlung Francke/Körber im Völkerkundemuseum München aus dem Jahre 1928. Die Serindien-Sammlung des Staatlichen Museums für Völkerkunde München I." *Münchner Beiträge zur Völkerkunde* 14: 65–128.

2010–2011b "Der Briefwechsel Lucian Scherman – Albert von Le Coq und die Gründe für das Scheitern einer Serindien-Abteilung am Völkerkundemuseum München. Die Serindien-Sammlung des Staatlichen Museums für Völkerkunde München II." *Münchner Beiträge zur Völkerkunde* 14: 129–193.

Roth 1970 Gustav Roth. *Bhikṣuṇī-vinaya. Including Bhikṣuṇī-prakīrṇaka and a summary of the Bhikṣu-Prakīrṇaka of the Ārya-Mahāsāṃghika-Lokottaravādin*. Patna: K. P. Jayaswal Research Institute.

Schlingloff 1955 Dieter Schlingloff. *Buddhistische Stotras aus ostturkistanischen Sanskrittexten*, Berlin: Akademie-Verlag.

Schopen 1992 Gregory Schopen. "On Avoiding Ghosts and Social Censure: Monastic Funerals in the Mūlasarvāstivāda-Vinaya." *Journal of Indian Philosophy* 20: 1–39.

1997 *Bones, Stones, and Buddhist Monks. Collected Papers on the Archaeology, Epigraphy, and Texts of Monastic Buddhism in India*. Honolulu: University of Hawai'i Press.

2010 "On Incompetent Monks and Able Urbane Nuns in a Buddhist Monastic Code." *Journal of Indian Philosophy* 38: 107–131.

2014 *Buddhist Nuns, Monks, and Other Worldly Matters. Recent Papers on Monastic Buddhism in India*. Honolulu: University of Hawai'i Press.

Szántó 2021 Péter-Dániel Szántó. "Buddhist Homiletics on Grief (*Saddharmaparikathā, *ch. 11*)." *Indo-Iranian Journal* 64: 291–347.

Waldschmidt

1965 Ernst Waldschmidt. *Sanskrithandschriften aus den Turfanfunden*, Teil 1. Wiesbaden: Franz Steiner.

Tibetan Treatises on the Pronunciation/Recitation of Sanskrit and Sanskrit Mantras*

An Incomplete Bibliographic Survey

Leonard W.J. van der Kuijp

Abstract: The numerous Sanskrit texts that were translated in Tibetan often contained mantras, short, long, and quite long, that according to "the tradition" required that they be pronounced and articulated in the "correct" way. If not, so goes that same tradition, they would lose their salvific power and force. A number of Tibetan Sanskritists, both professional and amateur, wrote on the subject of what came to be called *sngags kyi bklag thabs* or *rgya skad / legs sbyar gyi bklag thabs*, which can be roughly translated as "the right way of the pronunciation of mantras" and the "right way of the pronunciation of Sanskrit." And the subject gradually grew into something tantamount to a literary genre in the Tibetan region. Unfortunately, on but very few occasions do we find that authors differentiate between the pronunciation of Sanskrit in Kashmir and what is now Bihar State or even between Tibetan as spoken in Gtsang and Dbus. This essay, incomplete as it is, aims to provide a first guide into this literature, much of which remains unexplored.

Keywords: Snar thang Lo tsā ba; *sngags kyi bklag thabs*; Sanskrit; *rgya skad*; *legs sbyar*; Slob dpon Bsod nams rtse mo

In an earlier paper, I briefly outlined the available corpus of Snar thang Lo tsā ba or Snar thang Paṇ chen Dge 'dun dpal bzang po's (ca. 1370–after 1439/1441) contributions to the language arts (*sgra rig*), which consist of grammar, poetics, lexicography, prosody, and dramaturgy.[1] The corpus is substantial. However, we know for sure that we are still missing his commentary on Śarvavarman's (?2nd c.) *Kātantra* / *Kalāpasūtra* grammar of Sanskrit to which he refers in his large work on Daṇḍin's (7th–8th c.) *Kāvyādarśa*, and it stands to reason that there may very well be additional writings on the language arts by this largely forgotten and elusive scholar that await excavation and publication.[2]

Leonard W.J. van der Kuijp, Harvard University.

* I offer this slight contribution to the memory of Duan Qing whom I first met some forty years ago in Hamburg where she was a doctoral student studying with Profs. R. Emmerick and L. Schmithausen, and with whom I shared a pizza on the Grindelallee, just around the corner from the Institut, together with my classmate and friend Burkhard Quessel.
It will be noticed that I have abbreviated the names of Tibetan authors to a recognizable minimum in the footnotes; these can be easily identified in the bibliography.

[1] See van der Kuijp [Forthcoming]a. Snar thang Lo tsā ba often seems to have referred to himself as Saṅghaśrī, the Sanskrit equivalent of the first portion of his name.

[2] Snar thang Lo tsā ba's continued obscurity is illustrated by his absence from Kapstein 2018, which is a very useful survey of the role played by Sanskrit and its study among Tibetan scholars from the fourteenth to the nineteenth centuries.

Judging from the available literature, and it is rather skimpy, it would appear that he had two main claims to fame in the fairly limited intellectual circles in which the study of the language arts was taken as a serious endeavor. The first is his brief tract, together with an auto-commentary, on the correct pronunciation/recitation of Sanskrit mantras, the titles of which are *Sngags kyi bklag thabs bsdus pa['i 'grel ba mthong ba don gsal]*.[1] The second is his commentary on the *Kāvyādarśa*. Given that his *Sngags kyi bklag*[2] *thabs bsdus pa*, *The Method of the Pronunciation of Mantras: A Synopsis*, and later works belonging to this genre have yet to be studied, it seems only apposite to do some additional bibliographic weeding and supplement P. Verhagen's valuable, incidental remarks, to which I have drawn attention whenever appropriate. To be sure, treatises that deal with the pronunciation of Sanskrit mantras (*sngags kyi bklag thabs*) are part and parcel of the ones that expressly discuss the pronunciation of Sanskrit as such (*rgya skad / legs sbyar gyi bklag thabs*). Thus, many of the works that are mentioned below also deal with the pronunciation of Sanskrit, period.

This essay and the sources on which it is based may *in toto* may serve as a prolegomenon to the future study of this rather special genre. Of course, given the fact that new Tibetan sources on every conceivable subject are recovered on a regular basis, not claim can be made at comprehensiveness. In addition, it is quite conceivable that I will have overlooked several treatises that were available in one form or another. This essay also has a precedent of sorts. On June 12, 2023, I gave a talk on the subject for the Center of Tibetan Studies of Sichuan University, Chengdu. At the end of my talk, a young Tibetan scholar from, I believe Qinghai, briefly showed me his recent, unpublished dissertation on the very same subject of this essay. Unfortunately, I was unable to learn his name or the title of his work which I was briefly able to inspect. But I remember that it left me quite impressed and gratified by its quality and comprehensiveness, and I hope that it will be published.

The versified *Sngags kyi bklag thabs bsdus pa* and the prose *Mthong ba don gsal* commentary were likely written in 1420; the latter is explicitly so dated. Snar thang Lo tsā ba cites only a few Indic sources in his *Mthong ba don gsal* and no Tibetan works. Since no biography of this interesting scholar has been published so far, indeed if there ever were one, we do not know whether he had ever journeyed to the Kathmandu Valley to study Sanskrit with the local pandits. There is nothing in his extant writings that even hints at this. However, there is one passage in his commentary on Daṇḍin where he refers to information that he had received from the famous Assamese scholar Vanaratna (1384–1468), and I examine the relevant passage in a forthcoming study of his quotations of Shong ston Lo tsā ba Rdo rje rgyal mtshan (ca.1225–ca.1285) translation

[1] See van der Kuijp [Forthcoming]a. Nos.11–12, and Snar thang [No date]a and b.

[2] For the verb *klog [pa]* and its derivatives, see Hill 2010, 2. Years ago, de Jong 1973 drew attention to *blags pa* and concluded that it is "a variant of *bklags pa*," the perfective of *klog [pa]*.

of the *Kāvyādarśa*. Often Sanskrit oriented, it should not be surprising that the study of grammar, lexicography, and prosody among the language arts was not an altogether popular endeavor even for the monastery-educated elite. And it apparently took quite some time before these two works became more "public," that is, when xylographs from the much later printing blocks that are/were housed, for example, in the printeries of Sku 'bum monastery and the Rnam rgyal seminary allowed for their wider dissemination.[1] Written by a reputable scholar of Sanskrit, as indicated by his titles *lo tsā ba* and *paṇ chen*, this goes some way to explain their continued authoritativeness and relative popularity. I write "relative popularity" because the actual size of an audience for xylographs or even manuscripts of works of this kind remains far from clear. In fact, it is more than likely that these did not have very much appeal, never mind whether the suggestions they contained for the correct pronunciations were ever consistently heeded. The fact that these and kindred works suggest that one should seek the help of a qualified master—a *slob dpon mkhas pa* as we read in Snar thang Lo tsā ba's auto-commentary—if one wants to get the pronunciation right is good advice even if it is difficult to find one who might be qualified to provide this kind of service. To give just one example. Anyone who has been around even the most learned lamas will have noticed the ubiquitous "bandzar guru" for "vajraguru" and "pema" for "padma" when, for example, they intone the mantra dedicated to Padmasambhava: *oṃ āḥ hūṃ vajraguru padma siddhi hūṃ /*. The equivalence of *'bad dzar* [= 'bandzar'] for *vajra* is often found in older Tibetan manuals and thus has a long history. Finally, aside from Snar thang Lo tsā ba citing a few well-known Indic texts in his auto-commentary, he does at one point refer the reader to an otherwise unknown treatise titled *Sngags kyi bklag thabs kyi tsa kra* (< Skt. *cakra*) for the pronunciation of what he calls the "very long" (*shin tu ring ba*) /ai/ and /au/.[2] Otherwise, he just makes rather unhelpful notices about errors or points made by earlier generations (*snga rabs rnams*) and some[one] (*kha cig*), an earlier master (*slob dpon snga ma*), and someone (*'ga' zhig*).[3] Yet, he tantalizingly observes at the end of his work that his work was a mere summary of what is like "the ocean of the method of pronunciation of mantras that were written by many translators, *paṇḍita*-s, and scholars of countless early generations" (*sngon rabs dpag tu med pa'i lo paṇ mkhas pa mang pos brtsams pa'i sngags kyi bklag thabs rgya mtsho*). One must wonder what this ocean may have looked like!

[1] The two texts are registered in the catalog of printing blocks in Sku 'bum Monastery's printery for which see Rig dga' 1993, 77. Printing blocks for the *Sngags kyi bklag thabs bsdus pa* are also registered in the collection of such blocks at the Rnam rgyal grwa tshang in Lhasa; see Anonymous 1970, 205.

[2] Snar thang [No date]b, 9a.

[3] Snar thang [No date]b, 10a–b, 13b, 14a.

A commentary on the *Sngags kyi bklag thabs bsdus pa* was written by one who signed himself as Bhu su ku.[1] This is a nickname and not a *bona fide* name in religion, and seems to have been taken from the story of a Śāntideva (8th or 10th c.) who is also called Bhusuku owing to his persistent meditative practice called *bhusuku*, which derives, as Saitō Akira stated most recently, from having done this practice while "eating" (*bhuj* < *bhu{ñjana/ktvā}*, "sleeping" (*su* < *su{pta}*), and "walking" (*ku*< *ku{ṭiṃ gataḥ}*.[2] However, Āryadeva II's (mid 9th–late 10th c.) *Cāryamelāpakapradīpa* defines *ku* more granularly as follows: "*ku* means one goes to the outhouse (*kuṭi*, *bshang sa*), with the aim of excreting feces and urine."[3] The expression *bhu su ku* is also occasionally used before an individual's name as an epithet. Moving on to the manuscript, its title page and first two pages are embellished by passages that are carefully calligraphed in a beautiful Rañjana script. Unfortunately, many passages in the body of the text are hardly legible or not quite fully illegible because the scribe of the manuscript, or a later reader, used not only black but also red or yellow ink to highlight certain passages and the latter has either faded considerably, fell victim to oxidization, or has stubbornly refused to be scanned! Thus, Snar thang Lo tsā ba's verse text and the numerous annotations are virtually illegible. According to the colophon, the author wrote it during the waxing-half of the eighth lunar month (*khrums stod*) of an iron-hen year while at an unspecified place. But this is not very helpful. His references to other authors and works are few and far between, and most of them are known and, again, are not altogether helpful when we attempt to provide a rough date for this work.[4] One of these references is to a certain Dpal dbang. The author uses the afterword to make a plea for the correct pronunciation of Sanskrit and the pitfalls for not doing so—of course this begs the question whether there ever was a "correct" pronunciation of the language and there is evidence that the Tibetans were aware of regional differences in pronunciation [see below]. He also bemoans the fact that so few make any effort in studying the way in which Sanskrit and the mantras written in it are to be pronounced. In this connection, he cites a work that he calls the *Smra ba'i sgron me* in which this lament is further amplified. It now turns out that the cited lines were taken from the *Legs sbyar smra ba'i sgron me* that was written by Dpal ldan dbang po'i sde (16th c.), a disciple of the much better known Zhwa lu Lo tsā ba Rin chen chos skyong bzang po (1441–1528).[5] Given that Bhu su ku cites Dpal dbang, an

---

[1] Bhu su ku [No Date].

[2] Saitō 2018, 163–162 and 2019, 391; see also de Jong 1975, 170, 176.

[3] Wedemeyer 2007, 323 [Sanskrit, 491; Tibetan, 650]. Tibetan *'gro ba* rendered Sanskrit optative *gacched*, and I translate the Tibetan.

[4] Bhu su ku [No Date], 7a cites the *Ka lā pa'i spyi don* which most probably is Zhwa lu Lo tsā ba's general survey of the *Kālapasūtra* which he probably completed in 1520; see van der Kuijp with Chen Yilan [Forthcoming]b.

[5] Dpal ldan [No Date]a, 8a–8b; he is of course identical to the Dpal dbang who was just mentioned.

abbreviation of the name Dpal ldan dbang po'i sde, we can now conclude with comforting certainty that the iron-hen year in which he wrote his work cannot have been earlier than 1561 and that it could even have been written in 1621 or 1681, or even later. Verhagen pointed out that a recension of Dpal dbang's work was included in the works on the pronunciation of mantras that was compiled by Dngul chu Chos kyi bzang po (1772–1851), alias Dharmabhadra, and that his nephew and disciple Dngul chu Dbyangs can grub pa'i rdo rje (1809–1887) had also referred to it.[1] Both contribute somewhat to the textual criticism of Dpal dbang's text to which I just referred. For it now transpires that this text is in fact a commentary on Dpal dbang's own verse text which is reproduced in full in Dngul chu Chos kyi bzang po's study of the subject.[2] Further, Chos kyi bzang po's commentary on his teacher Ngag dbang rdo rje's (1720–1803) *Sngags kyi yi ge'i klog tshul dngos bstan pa* cites two lines from Snar thang Lo tsā ba's *Sngags kyi bklag thabs bsdus pa*.[3] Dbyangs can grub pa'i rdo rje cites the concluding portion of Dpal dbang's treatise in which there occurs a line within a larger passage, a true *cri de coeur*, from the same that is cited by Bhu su ku.[4] The passage essentially bemoans the decline in interest in the domains of knowledge, and that this holds in particular for the language arts. And the author writes that many intone mantras without the slightest understanding of how they should be intoned, not to mention their complete lack of embarrassment (*ngo mtshar dang 'dzem pa cung zad kyang med pa*) at their own ignorance.[5] Dpal ldan dbang po'i sde most likely authored other works as well. But I have so far only found a manuscript of one other treatise by him. This is a short tract on Zhwa lu Lo tsā ba's study of the fifth *pāda* of the *Kātantra/Kalāpasūtra* on the *sandhi* rules for the *visarga* (*mtshams sbyor lnga pa*).[6]

Two additional studies of Snar thang Lo tsā ba's *Sngags kyi bklag thabs bsdus* are now available. The first is by a certain Blo bzang yar 'phel whose succinct commentary may have been written sometime in the early nineteenth century. For some reason, the

[1] See the excellent remarks in Verhagen 2001, 186–187, 195–196.

[2] Dngul chu Chos kyi bzang po [No date]a, 226–228.

[3] Dngul chu Chos kyi bzang po [No date]b, 241 *ad* Snar thang Lo tsā ba [No date]a, 2b.

[4] Dngul chu Dbyangs can grub pa'i rdo rje [No date], 570. He completed his work "on the good day of a completely full moon, the disc that gives off coolness, the third complete day [= fifteenth day] of the waxing half of the *snron* [= fifth] lunar month, the wood-dog year called *dngos po*" (*dngos po zhes pa shing khyi lo snron gyi zla ba'i dkar phyogs rdzogs pa gsum pa bsil sbyin gyi dkyil 'khor nya yongs su gang ba'i tshe dge bar*), that is, on June 29, 1874. He furthermore states that he owed his poetic/linguistic name, that is, Dbyangs can grub pa'i rdo rje, to his study of the thirty chapters of the *Sarasvatīvyākaraṇa* and most of the *Kalāpatantra*'s chapters.

[5] Dpal ldan [No date]a, 8a–8b and Bhu su ku [No date], 17a.

[6] Dpal ldan [No date]b; his teacher's name is included in its opening verse of homage: ***rin chen chos skyong*** *mkhyen pa'i snyan grags kyi / dga' ston 'jig rten 3 na skyong ba yi / mkhas pa'i mdzad pa* ***bzang pos*** *mkhas kun gyi / yid 'phrog 'jig rten mig der phyag bgyid do //*.

printing blocks for this commentary came to be included in the Dga' ldan chos 'khor gling edition of Dpal mang Dkon mchog rgyal mtshan's (1764–1853) collected works, and the xylograph of his work was thus published among them.[1] Dpal mang was an erstwhile abbot of Bla brang bkra shis 'khyil monastery and it appears that Blo bzang yar 'phel was also affiliated with this monastery. In the colophon, he modestly prefaces his name by *'du shes gsum pa rab 'byams* [*pa*], which means "the expert in the three notions [of eating, sleeping, and going {to the outhouse}]," where *'du shes gsum pa* is just another way of saying *bhu su ku*! Of Tibetan authors, he only cites by name Kun dga' snying po (1575–1634), alias Tāranātha, and his cognate treatise, on which see below.[2] A much more comprehensive commentary was written by Gser tog pa Blo bzang tshul khrims rgya mtsho (1845–1915) which bears no date and was possibly written after his 1896 study of the *Sum Rtags* treatises on the Tibetan language. To be sure this is mere surmise on my part since neither text cite one another, and his biography does not mention their composition. He does quote on numerous occasions the earlier work of Slob dpon Bsod nams rtse mo (1142–1182) as well as Sa skya Paṇḍita Kun dga' rgyal mtshan's (1182–1251) contributions to the theme at hand—see below—as well as an unidentified work by A rig Dge bshes chen po Byams pa dge legs rgyal mtshan 'od zer (1728–1803).[3] He also severally cites the *Sngags bklag thabs kun las btus pa* by Sku 'bum pa Shes rab dpal bzang (1550–1633), the fourth abbot of Sku 'bum monastery, and in the first instance places him in conversation with [A lag sha{n}] Bstan dar Lha rams pa (1759–after August 1, 1840), alias Ngag dbang bstan dar.[4] At issue is the reading of a passage in Snar thang Lo tsā ba's exposition of the pronunciation of Sanskrit retroflexes; he writes the following in his verse text:

> */ ṭa sogs log sde'i bklag tshul ni /*
> */ lce rtse rkan sbyar stibs kyis bsgyur /*[5]
>
> The manner of articulating the class of retroflexes such as /ṭa/ etc.
> Joining the tip of the tongue to the palate, ...?

---

[1] Blo bzang yar 'phel [No Date] and 1974. Both are identical, but the first is a better-quality xylograph copy.

[2] Blo bzang yar 'phel 1974, 8a, 9b.

[3] Gser tog pa 1915, 3a. Gser tog pa's treatise is contained in vol. 6 of the ten volumes of his collected works for which printing blocks were prepared in 1916—another volume was added later. Printing blocks were never carved for the additional three volumes of "sealed manuscripts" (*dka'* [read: *bka'*] *rgya can bris ma*); see Gser tog pa's biography, which is partly based on his auto-biography, in Blo bzang 1915, 133a. Blo bzang byang chub bstan pa'i sgron me, the author of the biography, prefaces his name by *'du gsum snyom las pa* where *snyom las pa* means "lazy" and *'du gsum* is no doubt an abbreviation of *'du shes gsum* for which see above.

[4] Gser tog pa 1915, 28a and Bstan dar Lha rams pa 2008, 648. Gser tog pa's 1903 history of Sku 'bum monastery only devotes a few lines to Shes rab dpal bzang but notes that he had written a "very fine summary inventory" (*dkar chag bsdus pa shin tu legs pa*) of the monastery which by his time had become quite rare; see Gser tog pa 1982, 52.

[5] Snar thang [No date]a, 2b and b, 10a.

There was a problem with the word *stibs*, which recurs in the auto-commentary, and you will no doubt have noticed that I did not venture to translate the phrase *stibs kyis bsgyur*. Gser tog pa notes that the word *stibs* is unclear apart from the fact the *Ngag sgron*, an abbreviation of the title of the famous lexicon Dpal khang Lo tsā ba Ngag dbang chos kyi rgya mtsho (16th c.), alias Dbyangs can snyems pa'i sde, compiled in 1538, has something similar, namely *ldab ldib*, which Khu nu Bstan 'dzin rgyal mtshan (1894–1977) glossed by *mi gsal ba*, "unclear," and *gsang po med pa*, "untruthful."[1] Shes rab bzang po had evidently read *ldig gis* , "trilling," instead of *stibs kyis* and when Bstan dar Lha rams pa defined *ldibs* by *lce mi bde ba*, "uncomfortable/unclear tongue," this led Gser tog pa to opt for *ldibs* rather than *stibs*, a rather unusual word that Bstan lha Ngag dbang tshul khrims (1930–) equates with *'khrigs pa* and *thibs pa*, both of which have the sense of "dense, unclear."[2]

Otherwise, much of Gser tog pa's exposition is owed to the work of Kun dga' snying po, on which see below. Lastly, he mentions his tutor Yongs 'dzin Ngag dbang chos grags twice as one who taught him the language arts, and who also functioned as his "confessor" (*gsang ston*) when he was ordained a monk in 1864.[3]

Snar thang Lo tsā ba's contemporary, Bo dong Paṇ chen Phyogs las rnam rgyal (1375/76–1451), also *appears* to have authored a *Legs sbyar kyi skad kyi bklag thabs* which was one of the more detailed treatments of the subject. It is available to us for inspection. But as Li Xiaonan, kindly pointed out to me this work is essentially a copy of Dpang Lo tsā ba Blo gros brtan pa's (1276–1342) *Tshogs gsum gsal ba*.[4] The latter is a comparative treatise on the grammar of Sanskrit and Tibetan which he composed at the behest of a certain Gzhon nu seng ge while they were at E chos 'byung monastery. This relatively short treatise is a highly original work that is structured around the format of "the three collections" (*tshogs gsum, trikāya*) that is so well-known from abhidharma sources, the three being the letter-phoneme/syllable (*yi ge*), the noun (*ming*), and the phrase (*tshig*).[5] And a substantial section of the text is devoted to the pronunciation of Sanskrit. Cognate texts are credited to'Jam dbyangs Shes rab rgya mtsho (?–1476), the third abbot

[1] Dpal khang 2004, 232 and the gloss in Khu nu 2004, 312. Dpal khang Lo tsā ba is also called the Karma 'phrin las pa II; the date of the first Karma 'phrin las pa I is 1456–1539, and he figures among Dpal khang Lo tsā ba's tutors (*yongs 'dzin*); see Dpal khang Lo tsā ba's poetic letter addressed to him in a marvelous collection of dozens such letters to many Central Tibetan notables, both clerics and officials, in Dpal khang [No Date], 16a–19b.

[2] Btsan lha 1997, 265.

[3] Gser tog pa 1915, 16a and 60a; and see also Blo bzang 1915, 72a.

[4] See van der Kuijp [Forthcoming]a, no. I2a, and Dpang Lo tsā ba [No date]a and Bo dong Paṇ chen 2019.

[5] For Dpang Lo tsā ba and this work, see Verhagen 2001, 75–79, and Index, and Verhagen 2021, 269–270 and 292–294. For the "three collections," see now also Choi 2020 and Li 2023.

of Ngor Evaṃ chos ldan monastery.[1] Another treatise belonging to the genre was authored by Byams gling Paṇ chen Bsod nams rnam rgyal ba'i sde (1400–1475). Rgya ston Lcags ri ba Byang chub rnam rgyal writes in his 1486 biography of Byams gling Paṇ chen that in 1474 the latter wrote a slight tract (*yig chung*) which he [roughly] titled *Legs sbyar bklag thabs*; the register of some two hundred and seven titles of Byams gling Paṇ chen's oeuvre in 'Jam dbyangs dga' ba'i blo gros legs pa chos 'byor's (1429–1503) shorter study of his life gives its full title as *Legs sbyar gyi yi ge klog pa la thog mar 'jug pa'i rim pa gsal ba ngag gi 'od zer*.[2] This is the same short, versified piece for which the title page reads *Legs sbyar bklag pa'i legs bshad ngag gi 'od zer*.[3] It bears no date and the scribe is identified as Bsod nams tshe brtan.

A junior contemporary of Snar thang Lo tsā ba and also a student of Nags kyi rin chen [Vanaratna], Rong ston Shākya rgyal mtshan (1367–1449), and Kun Mkhyen Blo brtan—is he the Sanskritist Blo gros brtan pa IV of Snye thang monastery? —a Paṇ chen Nam mkha' bstan pa completed a short treatise on the pronunciation of Sanskrit in 1437 [?or1497].[4]

It stands to reason that the question of how Sanskrit ought to be pronounced was a long-standing one in the Tibetan region, and it should therefore not be surprising that there were several notable precedents to the early fifteenth century tracts by Snar thang Lo tsā ba. It now appears that the cognate versified treatises by Slob dpon Bsod nams rtse mo and Dol po pa Shes rab rgyal mtshan (1291–1362) are among the earliest works of this genre. Titled *Yi ge'i bklag thabs byis pa bde blag tu 'jug pa*, the Slob dpon's work is *prima facie* dated April 3, 1167 or, more plausibly, March 22, 1179 (*phag lo rta'i tshe bcu gcig pa*).[5] He wrote this relatively short but surprisingly complex work in a place called Rked/sked slas and in Sa skya monastery at the behest of a Zhang ston; some recensions of this work add Phyar bu pa to Zhang ston, about whom I can say nothing. Its third and last chapter is explicitly titled: *Showing the Technique of Reading Sanskrit and Mantras out Loud* (*rgya gar gyi skad dang sngags kyi bklag thabs bstan pa*), and it is perhaps quite important for Central Tibetan historical phonology. It turns out that this work was quite influential and quotations from it appear in many treatises of the genre, albeit not in Snar thang Lo tsā ba's work! One of the many interesting points the Slob dpon makes in his treatise is the following in connection with Sanskrit */jña/*; he writes:

[1] We are alerted to this work in his capsule biography which Sangs rgyas phun tshogs (1649–1705), himself the monastery's twenty-fifth abbot, had written while at the monastery; see Sangs rgyas phun tshogs 2010, 126. The latter had stepped down from his abbatial seat in 1689 and departed for Sde dge in 1699 never to return; see the exceptional capsule biography of him in Heimbel 2014.

[2] Rgya ston [No Date], 68a and 'Jam dbyangs [No Date].

[3] Byams gling [No Date].

[4] Paṇ chen [No Date].

[5] Slob dpon 2007a and b; Verhagen 1995 and Dol po pa 2011.

/ dznya zhes bya ba'i yi ge la /
/ rgya gar 'gyar klog kha che gnya' /
/ bod kyis gnya' zhes bya bar klog /
/ kha che'i lugs su bklag na bde /[1]

The ligature *dznya*,
Is read /*'gya*/ in India, /*gnya'*/ in Kashmir.
Tibetans read it is as /*gnya'*/;
It is good were it read in the Kashmiri tradition.

Dpang Lo tsā ba clearly has this statement in mind when he declared:

/ dza la nya btags 'gya gnyar klog / klog lugs de gnyis rgya gar dbus pa dang kha che'i lugs so // zhes gsung te nges pa yod med the tshom za'o //[2]

The *nya* subscript under *dza* [/*dznya*/] is pronounced as /*'gya*/ and /*gnya'*/. It is said that these two ways of pronunciation are Central Indian and Kashmiri; whether that is certain or not is doubtful.

And Snar thang Lo tsā ba suggests with a slight variation that /*jña*/ was pronounced /*'gya*/ by the inhabitants of East India.[3]

The Slob dpon's work is also referred to and cited in a commentary on Yol c[h]ag or Yol Lo tsā ba Rdo rje dbang phyug's yet to be studied *Sgra'i bstan bcos rig pa bklag thabs*, alias *Dkar po gling*, that was written by a Zhang ston.[4] We learn from the colophon of his work that he was associated with Brag ram and Snar thang monasteries, I am inclined tentatively to identify him as the fifth abbot of the latter institution, so that his name in full is Zhang ston Chos kyi bla ma (1184–1232).[5] It is of course quite tempting to identify him as the person who had requested the Slob dpon for his work but what to my mind mitigates against this assumption is that this Zhang ston does not mention Sa skya monastery. In any event, Zhang ston cites his own *Lde mig mgo bcu pa* several times, a work that is otherwise completely unknown.[6] A manuscript of another commentary on the short *Dkar po gling* treatise that provides some important historical background is what appears to be Yol Lo tsā ba's auto-commentary.[7] This work is included in a twenty-folio collection of texts that is written in one hand, the title page of which reads: *Dkar gling gi 'grel pa* [*dbu bzhugs legs so*]. Aside from Yol Lo tsā ba's auto-commentary, the

[1] Slob dpon 2007a, 510; Slob dpon 2007, 502–503 contrasts Gtsang versus Dbus pronunciations—see Verhagen 1995, 963–965—and Slob dpon 2007a, 507–508 even refers to the pronunciation of Sanskrit in Uryan, that is, Uḍḍiyāna or Swat!

[2] Dpang Lo tsā ba [No Date], 6a and Bo dong Paṇ chen 2019, 55.

[3] Snar thang [No date]b, 10b.

[4] Zhang ston [No Date], 4b, 7b, 15a.

[5] For his biography, see Mchims 2015, 282–296.

[6] Zhang ston [No Date], 8a, 11a, 12a.

[7] Yol Lo tsā ba [No Date]. The colophon is found on fol. 18a of the manuscript.

collection includes a slightly annotated recension of Candragomin's (7th c.) *Varṇasūtra* [*Yi ge'i mdo*] as well as a short instruction on the six points of articulation (*gnas drug*). The very end, the colophon, of this collection presents a problem that I am unable to solve. It mentions Sa skya Paṇḍita and a Blo gros bstan [pa'i] rdo rje, and then notes that Shes rab rdo rje had written what appears to be a commentary on the *Dkar po gling* with the title *Rig klag 'grel pa gsal ba'i sgron*. I wonder if this means that the entire collection of three distinct texts should be conceived to be this commentary. Lastly, we should point out that the works of the Slob dpon and Yol Lo tsā ba are to some degree based on Smṛtijñānakīrti's (11th c.) *Vacanamukhāyudopama*, often referred to in Tibetan sources as the *Smra sgo*.

Not being recognized by the tradition as *bona fide* Sanskritists, neither the Slob dpon nor Dol po pa had a pedigree on which basis they could really lay claim to have expertise in the language and their biographies are indeed silent on with whom they might have studied Sanskrit. Some have recently suggested that Sa skya Paṇḍita, the Slob dpon's nephew, had written the brief *Sngags kyi klog thabs 'bras bu 'phyung ba'i me tog*, which evidently was a little treatise on the proper pronunciaton of [Sanskrit] mantras. It is [so far] only contained in the 1736 Sde dge edition of his oeuvre—this edition was edited by Zhu chen Tshul khrims rin chen (1697–1774)—and its title is absent from any of the earlier, extant title-catalogs of his writings that have now become available as well as from the considerable oeuvre of his descendant A mes zhabs Ngag dbang kun dga' bsod nams (1597–1659), who was one of the great bibliophiles and the twenty-eighth abbot of Sa skya. Well, no wonder! Now almost three decades ago, Verhagen had already shown that this brief study is nothing more than a compilation of extracts from the third chapter of the Slob dpon's treatise—it also includes a piece from its very beginning –, so that we can quickly lay to rest the idea that Sa skya Paṇḍita was its author, while retaining the notion that "one of the earliest examples of the genre" of manuals that deal with the pronunciation of mantras is an honor that belongs to his uncle.[1] Simply excerpting passages from the *Yi ge'i bklag thabs byis pa bde blag tu 'jug pa* does not make a bona fide author, but this is of course not to deny that Sa skya Paṇḍita had in fact written a study of his uncle's treatise at the age of twenty-two, a work that certainly was his own![2] On the other hand, he was the author of the *Sgra nye bar bsdus pa*, a series of pronouncements on the pronunciation of Sanskrit in general. An edition of this work together with glosses written by Lo tsā ba Byang chub rtse mo (1315–1379) was published under the title of *Legs sbyar klog tshul gyi bstan bcos rin chen phreng ba*.[3]

---

[1] Verhagen 1995, 945.

[2] Sa skya Paṇḍita 2007a.

[3] Sa skya Paṇḍita 2007b. The literature provides different dates for the Lo tsā ba. The present dates for him are taken from his biography which Zhwa lu Grags pa rgyal mtshan (1365–1448) completed in 1381 (doubtful!) or 1441; see Zhwa lu 2011, 4, 128.

A different manuscript of the Slob dpon's text with what are ostensibly his interlinear notes has also come to light. And it sheds new light on its transmission for the final part of its colophon states that the text with the notes was augmented on the basis of a manuscript of Gna' ro Bande Gshin rje grags and that Phyar ru pa ?wrote it out (*bgyis*).[1] It ends on a note by the late 'Phan po Nalendra scholar Tshul khrims rgyal mtshan (1933–2002) to the effect that Sa skya Paṇḍita appears to have been working with this version of the Slob dpon's text when writing his own study.

Turning to Dol po pa, his brief exposition has neither a date nor a place of composition. Yet, Kun dga' snying po, who figures most prominently in his doctrinal lines of transmission makes the point that he indeed knew what he was doing where Sanskrit was involved. And even if he does not mention Dol po pa's brief *Sngags klag thabs*, he does comment on his ability to read and understand Sanskrit on other occasions. For example, he writes in his large *circa* 1624 treatise on the process of visualization (*bskyed rim*) in the context of the meditative evocation (*sgrub thabs*) of the deity Kālacakra that Dol po pa had made corrections (*'gyur bcos*) to many crucial points (*gnad che sa mang por*) of Shong ston Lo tsā ba Rdo rje rgyal mtshan's (ca.1225–ca.1285) translation of the *Kālacakra* corpus.[2] He also states that apparently Tibetan exponents of the *Kālacakra* precepts had quite misunderstood the context of the phrase "*jñānapuja*[*anurāge*] etc." that we find in Yaśas' (10th–11th c.) *Laghukālacakratantra* IV: 100c [and/or Puṇḍarīka's (10th–11th c.) *Vimalaprabhā* commentary], and that only Dol po pa had correctly recognized it.[3] It is quite evident that while preparing to write his very large work, Kun dga' snying po had been able to marshal a sizable corpus of manuscripts and xylographs of the relevant literature and this allowed him often to make interesting text-critical remarks that occasionally even included a mention Indic and Nepalese traditions to which he had direct or indirect access. The documentation that informed his work lends a decent level of authority to his declamations about Dol po pa, but they still need further verification. Although Kun dga' snying po's own formal studies of Sanskrit as far as his autobiographical writings are concerned remain a bit of a mystery, he was not only translator of the *Sarasvatīvyākaraṇa* Sanskrit grammar and the author of a large commentary on that work, but he was also the author of a brief manual on the pronunciation of Sanskrit mantras that was quite influential. This

[1] Slob dpon 2007b, 274: *rje btsun nyid kyis mdzad pa'i mchan bu gna' ro bande gshin rje grags kyi phyag bris kyi dpe las 'phel ba / ithi / phyar ru pas bgyis so //*. A very close disciple of Rje btsun Grags pa rgyal mtshan (1147–1216), the Slob dpon's younger brother, Gshin rje grags is said to have requested Sa chen Kun dga' snying po (1082–1158), their father, for a commentary on the *Lam 'bras rdo rje tshig rkang*, and to have added notes to an unidentified work by Sa chen; for the latter, see A mes zhabs 2012b, 101.

[2] Kun dga' snying po 2008a, 15.

[3] Kun dga' snying po 2008a, 405; see Bstan, vol. 6, 156 and 818 and Dwivedi and Bahulkar 1994, 197.

versified work continued to enjoy some popularity and authority right down to the late nineteenth century.[1] Accompanied by illustrations, his erstwhile secretary Kun dga' bde legs wrote a commentary on this work.[2]

The great historian Dpa' bo II Gtsug lag phreng ba (1504–1566) also contributed to the genre when he wrote his versified study in 1527. He signed this little tract with his other, much less familiar name of Ma pham chos kyi rgyal po don yongs su grub pa, one that he also used in the colophon of his celebrated ecclesiastic history of Tibetan Buddhism.[3]

More than a hundred years later, A mes zhabs, Kun dga' snying po's junior contemporary, compiled a short treatise on the same subject which, he admits, in fact consisted of remarks from Dpang Lo tsā ba's *Tshogs gsum gsal ba* to which his nephew and disciple Lo tsā ba Byang chub rtse mo had written some annotations, the Slob dpon's *Yi ge'i bklag thabs*, and the main points of Snar thang Lo tsā ba's treatises.[4] He stresses that he avoided any personal in[ter]ventions when writing it. The treatise is dated a dog-year which of course is hardly helpful! Staying just a little longer in the seventeenth century, the 'Bri gung pa scholar Rig 'dzin Chos kyi grags pa (1597–1659) also composed a small, undated treatise on the subject.[5]

A hundred or so years later, Co ne Grags pa bshad sgrub (1675–1748) also wrote on the subject, and he did so with a summary that is titled *Sngags kyi bklag thabs mdor bsdus pa*, as we find in the colophon, rather than the *Sngags kyi bklag thabs smra ba'i rgyan* that we read in the table of contents and above this work's first page.[6] The similarity with the title of Snar thang Lo tsā ba's little tract is of course obvious. But that is where the resemblance stops. Snar thang Lo tsā ba cites no Tibetan author in his texts, but Grags pa bshad sgrub cites the relevant works by Snar thang Lo tsā ba, Dpang Lo tsā ba, and Kun dga' snying po. Admonishing his readership to know how to pronounce mantras, he writes:

> *'on kyang bod rnams kyis rgya gar gyi skad mi shes pas sngags ji lta ba bzhin klog mi shes kyang cung zad tsam ma sbyangs par sngags klog pa'i khung byas na'ang gang*

[1] Kun dga' snying po 2008b; printing blocks for this work were also housed in Bkra shis lhun po monastery's printery, for which see Anonymous 1970, 223. Verhagen 2001, 147–149 briefly studied this work. 'Phrin las rgyal mtshan 2015 is an edition which includes the works by Snar thang Lo tsā ba, Kun dga' snying po, and a longer study by the Bon po treasure-revealer Rig 'dzin Kun grol grags pa (1700–?1769). For some references to later treatments of the subject, see Verhagen 2001, 185–190.

[2] Kun dga' bde legs [No Date].

[3] Ma pham [No Date]—this minor work escaped the keen eyes of Bjerregaard and Dell 2022—and Dpa' bo II 1986, 1527.

[4] A mes zhabs 2012b.

[5] Rig 'dzin 1999.

[6] Co ne 2009.

min du bklag pas 'bras bu legs par 'grub par dka' ste / sa skya paṇ chen gyis

/ bod yul rmongs pas chos la ni /
/ chos sgra rgya min bod min klog /[1]

zhes dang

/ rgya min bod min sngags 'don gangs can pa /
/ phal cher ngal ba 'bras bur ma gyur tam /

zhes gsungs pas /[2]

However, although Tibetans do not know how exactly to pronounce mantras because they do not know Sanskrit, even if they made a grunting noise of pronouncing mantras without a smattering of training, it is difficult to realize a spiritual result by having pronounced what is not the case, since Sa skya Paṇ chen had said:

The befuddled of the Tibetan area pronounce 'religion'
In a religious language that is neither Indic nor Tibetan.

and

Tibetans who intone mantras that are neither Indic nor Tibetan,
Don't they mostly get weary as a result?

Another unstudied work that belongs to this genre was completed by the great Sanskrit scholar Si tu Paṇ chen Chos kyi 'byung gnas (1699–1774), alias Bstan pa'i nyin byed, in December 27, 1748 (*'byor ba'i lo mgo zla'i tshes brgyad pa*) while he stayed in Mtshur phu monastery, the home monastery of the Karma pa hierarchs.[3] We notice the colophon's use of *'byor ba* for *vibhava*, which is a nod to the terminology for the year that is often used by Mtshur phu tradition of the Tibetan calendar. The Sanskrit names of each of the years of the Indo-Tibetan sexagenary cycle of the calendar are only given in Vajrapāṇi's *Laghutantraṭīkā* on the *Cakrasamvaratantra* and this work was first translated into Tibetan by the team Śrībhūtiśānti [= Bhūtiśrīśānti?] and Cog gru Ting nge 'dzin bzang po (11th c.). They had evidently rendered *vibhava* by *'byor ba* and their translation was used in Karma pa III Rang byung rdo rje's (1284–1339) 1318 study of the first

[1] For the first citation, see Sa skya Paṇḍita 2007b, 191, where the lines read: */ bod yul rmongs pa'i chos lugs 'di / sgra skad* *dharmā /* *rgya min bod min klog /* *dar ma /*. This is the same text as in Sa skya Paṇḍita and Lo tsā ba Byang chub rtse mo 2015, where the subscribed glosses stem from the Lo tsā ba. I have not been able to identify the source for the second citation.

[2] Co ne 2009, 163.

[3] Si tu Paṇ chen 1990a and Verhagen 2001, 165–169; see also the notice in Si tu Paṇ chen 1968, 279, where we learn that it was written in compliance with the wish of Mi 'gyur rgyal mtshan (1717–?), the then current Klu sdings abbot of Ngor Evaṃ chos ldan monastery. The colophon also mentions that the "supreme leader of the 'Brug pa Bka' brgyud pa" had requested him for this work as well. I am unable to identify him at this time. Si tu Paṇ chen also briefly dealt with the correct pronunciation of Sanskrit in Si tu Paṇ chen 1990b, 324–325.

chapter of the *Laghukālacakratantra*.[1] Somewhat earlier, Shong ston [Lo tsā ba] Blo gros brtan pa's (late 13th c.) revision of the translation of the *Laghutantraṭīkā* resulted in the more ubiquitous *rnam byung* for *vibhava*. A manuscript of this translation may not have been available to the Karma pa and, hence, he used the older rendition. Si tu Paṇ chen's text contains numerous and often substantial glosses that were written by the author himself, as he informs us in the colophon. Finally, mention also needs to be made of his undated commentary on the one hundred-syllable Vajrasattva mantra, the *Yi ge brgya'i 'grel pa*, which also contains many guidelines on the pronunciation of Sanskrit.[2]

Titled *Legs par sbyar ba'i skad kyi klog thabs rnam gsal sgron ma*, Si tu Paṇ chen's contemporary Zhu chen Tshul khrims rin chen also completed a small, versified tract on the subject in 1750, which he composed at the behest of Rin chen mi 'gyur rgyal mtshan (1717–?), the thirty-seventh abbot of Ngor Evaṃ chos ldan monastery. He cites a few standard Indian sources as well as Dpang Lo tsā ba's *Tshogs sgum gsal ba* and what he has wrongly assumed to be Sa skya Paṇḍita's *Sngags kyi klog thabs 'bras bu 'phyung ba'i me tog*.[3] The text also includes a number of annotations in smaller characters, and in one it cites Sa skya Paṇḍita's commentary on the Slob dpon's treatise.[4] On a later occasion, he briefly returned to his work when a Ngag dbang shes rab had queried about the thirty-seven syllables that he mentioned in the text and in a gloss but had not made explicit. Zhu chen responded as follows[5]:

de'ang brda sprod pa'i mdo ka lā pa las /[6]

ka la sogs pa rnam gsal byed do /	[*kādīni vyañjananī*]	1.1.9
/ aḥ zhes rnam par gcad bya'o /	[*aḥ iti visarjanīyaḥ*]	1.1.16
/ ^{x}*ka/ẖka zhes pa lce rtsa can no /*	[^{x}*ka/ẖka iti jihvāmūlīyaḥ*]	1.1.17
/^{m}*pa/ẖpa pa zhes pa mchu can no /*	[^{m}*pa/ẖpa ity upadhmānīyaḥ*]	1.1.18
/ aṃ zhes pa rjes su nga ro'o /	[*aṃ ity anusvāraḥ*]	1.1.19

zhes 'byung ltar te / ka sde nas pa sde'i bar lnga tshan lnga ste nyi shu rtsa lnga / ya ra la va ste mthar gnas bzhi / sha ṣa sa ha ste dro ba'i yi ge bzhi'i bar te / so[a] *gsum dang / aḥ zhes pa'i rnam gcad kyi yi ge dang /* ^{x}*ka pa'i ḍa ma ru'i yi ge dang /* ^{m}*pa zhes pa mchu can gyi yi ge dang / aṃ zhes pa rje su nga ro'i yi ge zhes bya ba / ... rnam par gcad bya la sogs pa'i yi ge bzhi bsnan pas sum cu rtsa bsdun du 'gyur bar sgra 'grel rnams su bshad pa ltar smras pa lags so //*

---

[1] Karma pa III 2006, 525.

[2] Si tu Pan chen 1990c and Verhagen 2001, 163–165.

[3] Zhu chen 1972a, 327. The quoted lines are found in Slob dpon 2007, 509.

[4] Zhu chen 1972a, 328 and Sa skya Paṇḍita 2007a, 169

[5] Zhu chen 1972b, 480 and [No Date], 480 *ad* Zhu chen 1972a, 322 which reads: */ gsal byed / ka nas ha'i bar dang / sum cu bdun cu gnas /*.

[6] Liebich 1919, 15; Zhang 2014, 77, 79 and Bstan 109, 3–4.

[a] Zhu chen [No Date]: 480: *ta / spo*.

Well, as the grammatical sutra the *Kalāpa* stated:

> *ka* etc. are consonants.
> *aḥ* is the *visarjanīya* [= *visarga*].
> ^{x}*ka* involves the base of the tongue.
> ^{m}*pa* involves the lips.
> *aṃ* is the *anusvāra*.

That is, from the *ka*-group to the *pa*-group, five by five units, that is twenty-five consonants; *ya*, *ra*, *la*, *va* are the four semi-vowels (*mthar gnas*, *antaḥsthā*), up to the four spirants *sha* [*śa*], *ṣa*, *sa*, *ha*, thirty-three, plus the *visarjanīya* phoneme *aḥ*, the *ḍamaru* phoneme ^{x}*ka*, the labial phoneme ^{m}*pa*, and the *anusvāra* phoneme *aṃ*; ... by having added the four phonemes such as the *visarjanīya* etc., I said that there were thirty-seven consonants was stated in the commentaries on grammar.

Lastly, the collected works of the Jo nang pa scholar 'Ba mda' Thub bstan dge legs rgya mtsho (1844–1904) includes a title-page of a work that reads *Legs sbyar gyi sgra bklags tshul bshad pa blo gsal dga' bskyed tam bu ra'i sgra dbyangs*.[1] This one title obscures the fact that three distinct treatises on Sanskrit are included in it. The first bears this very title, the second has no title, and the third treatise includes a gloss on p. 20 which duplicates the title in the colophon: *'Phags yul gyi brda ?sprod legs sbyar gyi brjod pa gsal ba'i me long*.

And this wraps up our bibliographical inroad into a relatively unexplored genre of Tibetan literature. To be sure, Tibetan works of the kind that were discussed in the above are obviously not entirely irrelevant provisions for a religion that is so thoroughly infused with Indian Buddhist tantric concepts and in whose religious experience the proper enunciation of Sanskrit mantras plays a fundamental role, and where the purported spiritual efficacy of mantras resides *in theory* in their proper articulation, that is to say, no spiritual success (*dngos grub*, *siddha*) will accrue to the practitioner if mantras are incorrectly intoned. The Slob dpon writes accordingly in his work that:

> */ gang gis bklag thabs mi shes pa /*
> */ rigs sngags log par bzlas gyur na /*
> */ dad med rnams la don med 'gyur /*
> */ dad pa yod kyang dngos grub ring /*[2]
> Were one, not knowing the technique of reading aloud,
> To have wrongly recited mantras,

[1] 'Ba mda' 199?, 1–16, 16–20, 20–56. For his capsule biography, see Ngag dbang blo gros grags pa 1992, 412–424.

[2] Slob dpon 2007a, 505–506.

They would be meaningless for those who have no belief.
Even for those who have belief, spiritual realization would be far off.

The presumed auto-commentary adds laconically: "Therefore you must study!"[1] That said, there are also prevailing counterarguments to this. The Tibetan tradition obviously does not as a whole endorse this point of view and shows a lot of flexibility where the pronunciation/recitation of Sanskrit [or Prakrit] mantras are concerned. And quite understandably so. There was an awareness, however limited this may have been, of regional differences in the subcontinent of the phonological realization of Sanskrit [or Prakrit] syllables and words, apart from the fact that, unbeknownst to the majority [this also holds for non-Tibetans], some mantras are quite unintelligible and amount to phonological gibberish.[2] And not to put too fine a point on this, much depends also on the number of teeth one has in one's mouth or whatever other speech impediments one has to contend with. But, surprise, surprise, even their flawed pronunciation/recitation may ultimately have some interesting results, provided, as the Tibetan tradition would have it, one has enough faith.

Abbreviation

Bstan — *Bstan 'gyur dpe sdur ma*, Krung go'i bod kyi shes rig zhib 'jug lte gnas kyi bka' bstan dpe sdur khang, ed., vols. 120. Beijing: Krung go'i bod kyi shes rig dpe skrun khang, 1994–2008.

References

Tibetan Sources

A mes zhabs Ngag dbang kun dga' bsod nams

2012a *Dpal kyai rdo rje'i mngon par rtogs pa yan lag drug pa'i dka' gnas kyi don mdor bsdus bshad pa zab don bcud kyi snying po*. In: Si khron bod yig dpe rnying sgyur skyob 'tshol sgrig khang, ed., *Collected Works*, vol. 30, 92–110. Lhasa: Bod ljongs dpe rnying dpe skrun khang.

2012b *Legs sbyar klog tshul gyi bstan bcos blo gsal kun dga'*. In: Si khron bod yig dpe rnying sgyur skyob 'tshol sgrig khang, ed., *Collected Works*, vol. 9, 1–8. Lhasa: Bod ljongs dpe rnying dpe skrun khang.

Anonymous

1970 *Gangs can gyi ljongs su bka' dang bstan bcos sogs kyi glegs bam spar gzhi ji ltar yod pa rnams nas dkar chag spar thor phyogs tsam du bkod pa phan bde'i pad tshal 'byed pa'i nyin byed*. In: *Three Dkar chag's*, 169–243. New Delhi: Ngawang Gelek Demo.

Bhu su ku

[No date] *Sngags kyi bklag thabs bsdus pa'i ṭī ka brda sprod nges don smra ba'i mgrin rgyan* [*dbu med* manuscript]. bdrc.io, no. W8LS31161, fols. 18.

Blo bzang yar 'phel

[No Date] *Sngags klog thabs kyi tshig don bkral te bshad pa nor bu'i phreng ba*. In: *Brda sprod ma dpe phyogs bsdus*, vol. 29. bdrc.io, no. W3CN54, fols. 17.

[1] Slob dpon 2007b, 266.

[2] See the incisive and corrective comments in Staal 1993, 191 ff.

1974 *Ibid*. In: *Collected Works of Dkon mchog rgyal mtshan*, vol. 11, 140–173. New Delhi: Gyalten Gelek Namgyal.

Blo bzang byang chub bstan pa'i sgron me

1916 *Bstan pa'i gsal byed gser tog ho thog thu ta'i ching no min han khri chen chos kyi rgyal po skyes rabs rnam thar dad ldan padmo bzhad pa'i nyin byed*. In: *Collected Works of Gser tog pa* [Sku 'bum xylograph], vol. 11. bdrc.io, no. W29702, fols. 142.

Bo dong Paṇ chen Phyogs las rnam rgyal (1375/76–1451)

2019 *Legs sbyar kyi skad kyi bklag thabs*. In: Spong rong Zla ba and Padma chos sdings dgon, eds., *Collected Works*, vol. 1, 48–73. Lhasa: Bod ljongs bod yig dpe rnying dpe skrun khang.

Bstan dar lha rams pa

2008 *Gangs can gyi brda' gsar rnying las btsams pa'i brda' yig blo gsal mgrin rgyan*. In: Ser gtsug nang bstan dpe rnying 'tshol bsdu phyogs sgrig khang, ed., *Collected Works*. 622–679. Lhasa: Bod ljongs mi dmangs dpe skrun khang.

Btsan lha Ngag dbang tshul khrims

1997 *Brda dkrol gser gyi me long*. Beijing: Mi rigs dpe skrun khang.

Byams gling Paṇ chen Bsod nams rnam rgyal ba'i sde

[No Date] *Legs sbyar bklag pa'i legs bshad ngag gi 'od zer*. bdrc.io, no. WICZ1101, fols. 2 [PDF. 1109–1112].

'Ba mda' Thub bstan dge legs rgya mtsho

199? *Legs sbyar gyi sgra bklags tshul bshad pa blo gsal dga' bskyed tam bu ra'i sgra dbyangs*. In: *Collected Works*, vol. 22, 1–56. 'Dzam thang: No publisher's name. bdrc.io, no. W23899.

Co ne Grags pa bshad sgrub

2009 *Sngags kyi bklag thabs smra ba'i rgyan*. In: Dpal brtsegs bod yig dpe rnying zhib 'jug khang, ed., *Collected Works*, vol. 5/18, 155–165. Beijing: Krung go'i bod rig pa skrun khang.

Dngul chu Chos kyi bzang po

[No Date]a *Sngags kyi yi ge'i klog tshul dngos bstan*. [Dngul chu bla brang xylograph]. In: *Collected Works*, vol. 5. bdrc.io, no. W6493, 223–229.

[No Date]b *Sngags kyi yi ge'i klog tshul dngos bstan pa mdor bsdus kyi 'grel pa dper brjod dang bcas pa* [Dngul chu bla brang xylograph]. In: *Collected Works*, vol. 5. bdrc.io, no. W6493, 231–245.

Dngul chu Dbyangs can grub pa'i rdo rje

[No Date] *Gzungs sngags mkho che ba 'ga' zhig klog 'don bya tshul bshad legs sbyar smra ba'i nyin byed* [Dngul chu bla brang xylograph]. In: *Collected Works*, vol. 2. bdrc.io, no. W22334, 527–573.

Dol po pa Shes rab rgyal mtshan

2011 *Sngags klag thabs*. In: *Collected Works*, vol. 10, 355–357. Beijing: Krung go'i bod rig pa'i dpe skrun khang.

Dpal khang Lo tsā ba Ngag dbang chos kyi rgya mtsho

2004 *Bod kyi bdra'i bye brag gsal bar byed pa'i bstan bcos tshig le'ur byas pa mkhas pa'i ngag gi sgron ma*. In: Mkhan po Dam chos zla ba, ed., *Sgra dang sdeb sbyor*, 213–251. Lanzhou: Kan su'u mi rigs dpe skrun khang,

[No Date] *Gsung shog gi skor legs par bshad pa rin po che'i 'phreng ba*. bdrc.io no. W8LS37364, fols. 296.

Dpal ldan dbang po'i sde

[No Date]a *Legs sbyar smra ba'i rgyan*. In: *Brda sprod ma dpe phyogs bsdus*, vol. 13. bdrc.io, no. W3CN54, fols. 9.

[No Date]b *Mtshams sbyor gyi ṭī ka 'chad nyan rnam gsal*. In: *Brda sprod ma dpe phyogs bsdus*, vol. 34. bdrc.io, no. W3CN54, fols. 9.

Dpang Lo tsā ba Blo gros brtan pa

[No Date] *Tshogs gsum gsal ba* [Rtag brtan phun tshogs gling xylograph], fols. 18.

Dpa' bo II Gtsug lag phreng ba

1986 *Chos 'byung mkhas pa'i dga'ston*, Rdo rje rgyal po, ed., vol. smad. Beijing: Mi rigs dpe skrun khang.

2019 *Legs sbyar bklag thabs kyi rtsa ba blo gsal 'jug pa'i sgo 'phar*. In: *Collected Works*, vol. 4, 565–573. Lhasa: Bod ljongs bod yig dpe rnying dpe skrun khang.

Gser tog pa Blo bzang tshul khrims rgya mtsho

1916 *Sngags kyi bklag thabs btus pa'i mchan 'grel 'phags yul mkhas pa'i mgrin rgyan*. In: *Collected Works* [Sku 'bum xylograph], vol. 6. bdrc.io, no. W29702, fols. 60.

1982 *Sku 'bum byams pa gling gi gdan rabs don ldan chings pa'i dbyangs snyan*. Xining: Mtsho sngon mi rigs dpe skrun khang.

'Jam dbyangs dga' ba'i blo gros legs pa chos 'byor

[No Date] *Dpal byams pa gling pa chen po'i rnam par thar pa rin po che'i phreng ba*. Manuscript, fols. 38.

Karma pa III Rang byung rdo rje

2006 *Dpal dus kyi 'khor lo'i man ngag snang ba*. In: *Collected Works*, vol. 11, 511–577. Xining: Mtshur phu Mkhan po Lo yag bkra shis.

Khu nu Bstan 'dzin rgyal mtshan

2004 *Bod kyi brda sprod pa'i bstan bcos ngag sgron gyi 'grel pa tshig gsal*. In: Mkhan po Dam chos zla ba, ed., *Sgra dang sdeb sbyor*, 253–378. Lanzhou: Kan su'u mi rigs dpe skrun khang.

Kun dga' snying po

2008a *Dpal dus kyi 'khor lo'i sgrub thabs bskyed rim gyi rnam bshad dngos grub nyer 'tsho*. In: *Collected Works*, vol. 6. Beijing: Krung go'i bod rig pa dpe skrun khang.

2008b *Rgya skad du bris pa'i yi ge'i klog thabs 'phags yul mkhas pa'i lugs*. In: *Collected Works*, vol. 37, 643–647. Beijing: Krung go'i bod rig pa dpe skrun khang.

Kun dga' bde legs

[No Date] *Rgya skad bklag thabs kyi gzhung don dper brjod dang bcas pa bklags pas chog pa*. In: *Brda sprod ma dpe phyogs bsdus*, vol. 13. bdrc.io, no. W3CN54, fols. 15.

Ma pham chos kyi rgyal po don yongs su grub pa

[No Date] *Legs sbyar bklag thabs kyi rtsa ba blo gsal 'jug pa'i sgo 'phar*. bdrc.io, no. W3CN45, fols. 5.

Mchims Nam mkha' grags

2015 *Snar thang gi gdan rabs gser phreng*, Bu byung dbang 'dus, ed., Gangs can rig mdzod 77. Lhasa: Bod ljongs bod yig dpe rnying dpe skrun khang.

Ngag dbang blo gros grags pa

1992 *Jo nang chos ba'i sgron me*, Btsan lha Ngag dbang tshul khrims and Hre wan kri [佘万志], eds. Xining: Krung go'i bod kyi shes rig dpe skrun khang.

Paṇ chen Nam mkha' bstan pa

[No Date] *Legs sbyar sgra'i glag* [*sic!*] *thabs mkhas pa kha* rgyan. bdrc.io, no. W3CN45, fols. 10.

'Phrin las rgyal mtshan

2015 ed., *Sngags klog phyogs bsgrigs*. Beijing: Mi rigs dpe skrun khang.

Rgya ston Lcags ri ba Byang chub rnam rgyal

[No Date] *Dpal byams pa gling pa chen po'i rnam par thar pa ngo mtshar gyi phreng ba*. bdrc.io, no. W26621, fols. 95.

Rig dga' 1993 ed. "Sku 'bum byams pa gling gi par khang chen mor bzhugs pa'i dpe tho." *Rtser snyeg* 1: 75–78.

Rig 'dzin Chos kyi grags pa

1999 *Sngags kyi klog tshul dang yi ge'i khams kyi sdeb sbyor mdor bsdus don gsal phrin las kun 'grub*. In: *Collected Works*, vol. 15, 73–87. Kulhan: Drikung Kagyu Institute.

Sa skya Paṇḍita Kun dga' rgyal mtshan

2007a *Byis pa bde blag tu 'jug pa'i rnam bshad*. In: *Collected Works [dpe bsdur ma]*, Dpal brtsegs bod yig dpe rnying zhib 'jug khang, ed., vol. 3, 156–179. Beijing: Krung go'i bod rig pa dpe skrun khang.

2007b *Sgra nye bar bsdus pa*. In: *Collected Works [dpe bsdur ma]*, Dpal brtsegs bod yig dpe rnying zhib 'jug khang, ed., vol. 4, 190–192. Beijing: Krung go'i bod rig pa dpe skrun khang.

Sa skya Paṇḍita Kun dga' rgyal mtshan and Lo tsā ba Byang chub rtse mo

2015 *Sgra snye bar bsdus ba'i tshigs su bcad pa*. In: Sa skya'i dpe rnying bsdu sgrig khang, ed., *Brda sprod dpe rnying gces bsdus*, 106–108. Lhasa: Bod ljongs bod yig dpe rnying dpe skrun khang,

Sangs rgyas phun tshogs

2010 *Dpal ldan evaṃ chos ldan gyi gdan rabs nor bu'i phreng ba*. In: *E vaṃ bka' 'bum*, Dpal brtsegs bod yig dpe rnying zhib 'jug khang, ed., vol. 20/20, 118–178. Beijing: Krung go'i bod rig pa skrun khang.

Si tu Paṇ chen Chos kyi 'byung gnas

1968 *The Autobiography & Diaries of Si tu Paṇ chen* [Dpal spungs xylograph], reproduced by L. Chandra. New Delhi: International Academy of Indian Culture.

1990a *Legs par sbyar ba'i skad kyi klog thabs nyung ngu rnams par gsal ba*. In: *Collected Works* [Dpal spungs xylograph], vol. 10, 130–136. Sansal: Palpung sungrab nyamso khang.

1990b *Rgyal tshan sprul sku'i dri lan lung bzhin 'doms pa'i snyan tshig*. In: *Collected Works* [Dpal spungs xylograph], vol. 8, 316–341. Sansal: Palpung sungrab nyamso khang.

1990c *Yig brgya'i 'grel pa*. In: *Collected Works* [Dpal spungs xylograph], vol. 6, 625–634. Sansal: Palpung sungrab nyamso khang.

Shes rab rdo rje

[No Date] *Dkar gling gi 'grel pa [dbu bzhugs legs so]*. bdrc.io, no. W1KG14580, fols. 20.

Slob dpon Bsod nams rtse mo

2007a *Yi ge'i bklag thabs byis pa bde blag tu 'jug pa*. In: Dpal brtsegs bod yig dpe rnying zhib 'jug khang, ed., *Collected Works [dpe bsdur ma]*, vol. 3, 496–512. Beijing: Krung go'i bod rig pa dpe skrun khang.

2007b *Yi ge'i bklag thabs byis pa bde blag tu 'jug pa*. In: Dpal brtsegs bod yig dpe rnying zhib 'jug khang, ed., *Sa skya gong ma rnam lnga'i gsung 'bum kha skongs las dkar po gsum gyi gsung pod dang po*, 253–274. Beijing: Krung go'i bod rig pa dpe skrun khang.

Snar thang Lo tsā ba Dge 'dun dpal
[No Date]a *Sngags kyi bklag thabs bsdus pa*. bdrc.io, no. W1KG10582, fols. 3.
[No Date]b *Sngags kyi bklag thabs bsdus pa'i 'grel pa mthong ba don gsal*. bdrc.io, no. W1KG10582, fols. 16.

Yol [c{h}ag] Lo tsā ba Rdo rje dbang phyug
[No Date] *Sgra'i bstan bcos rig pa klag pa'i thabs zhes bya ba'i 'grel bshad gsal ba'i rin po che*. bdrc.io, no. W1KG14580, fols. 18.

Zhang ston Chos kyi bla ma
[No Date, No Title] In: *Brda sprod ma dpe phyogs bsdus*, vol. 12. bdrc.io, no. W3CN54, fols. 17.

Zhu chen Tshul khrims rin chen
1972a *Legs par sbyar ba'i skad kyi klog thabs rnam gsal sgron ma*. In: *Collected Works* [Sde dge xylograph], vol. 3, 321–329. New Delhi: Jamyang nor bu.
1972b *Dgos skabs chos kyi dka' gnas kyi dogs pa dris pa'i lan ldon me tog phreng ba*. In: *Collected Works* [retouched Sde dge xylograph], vol. 5, 495–535. New Delhi: Jamyang nor bu.
[No Date] *Dgos skabs chos kyi dka' gnas kyi dogs pa dris pa'i lan ldon me tog phreng ba*. In: *Collected Works* [Sde dge xylograph], vol. 5, 463–499. bdrc.oi, no. W1KG10853.

Other Sources

Bjerregaard and Dell
2022 Maria Bjerregaard and Dominik Dell. "The Second dPa' bo, gTsug lag phreng ba (1504–1566): Life and Works of the Great Sixteenth-Century Historian." *Revue d'Etudes Tibétaines* 63: 131–175.

Choi 2020 Choi Seongho. *The Buddhist Terms of Name set (nāmakāya), Phrase set (padakāya) and Phoneme set (vyañjanakāya)*. D.Phil. thesis, Ludwig-Maximilians-Universität.

Dwivedi and Bahulkar
1994 Vrajavallabh Dwivedi and S.S. Bahulkar, ed. *Vimalaprabhāṭīkā of Kalkin Śrīpuṇḍarīka on Śrīlaghukālacakratantrarāja by Śrīmañjuśrīyaśas*, vol. II. Sarnath: Central Institute of Higher Tibetan Studies.

Hill 2010 Nathan Hill. *A Lexicon of Tibetan Verb Stems as Reported by the Grammatical Tradition. Studia Tibetica, Quellen und Studien zur tibetischen Lexicographie*, Band V. München: Kommission zur Zentral- und Ostasiatische Studien, Bayerischen Akademie der Wissenschaften.

de Jong 1973 Jan W. de Jong. "Tibetan *blag pa* and *blags pa*." *Bulletin of the School of Oriental and African Studies* 36/2: 309–312.
1974 "La Légende de Śāntideva." *Indo-Iranian Journal* 16/3: 161–182.

Kapstein 2018 Matthew T. Kapstein. "Other People's Philology." In: Silvia D'Intino and Sheldon Pollock, eds., with the collaboration of Michaël Meyer, *L'espace du sens. Approches de la philologie indienne/The Space of Meaning. Approaches to Indian Philology*, Publications de l'Institut de civilization indienne, Fasc. 84, 465–494. Paris: College de France.

van der Kuijp
[Forthcoming]a Leonard W.J. van der Kuijp. "Some Bibliographic Remarks on the Contributions to the Language Arts by Two Early Fifteenth Century Tibetan Writers, Bo dong Paṇ chen and Snar thang Lo tsā ba." *Zangxue xuekan* 藏學學刊/བོད་རིག་པའི་དུས་དེབ/*Journal of Tibetology*.

[Forthcoming]b in collaboration with Chen Yilan. "Zhwa lu Lo tsā ba, Si tu Paṇ chen, and Daṇḍin's *Kāvyādarśa* / *Snyan ngag me long*: A Bibliographic Excursion." *Journal of Tibetan Literature*.

Li 2023 Li Xiaonan 李曉楠. "Fan Zang wenfa yanjiu 梵藏文法研究——以"名句文身"为綫索 [A Study of Sanskrit and Tibetan Grammar: On the Vicissitudes of Nāmakāyādi or Ming gi tshogs la sogs pa]." PhD thesis, Peking University.

Liebich 1919 Bruno Liebich. *Zur Einführung in die indische einheimsiche Sprachwissenschaft. 1. Das Kātantra*. Heidelberg: Carl Winter's Universitätsbuchhandlung.

Saitō 2018 Akira Saitō. "Facts or Fictions: Reconsidering Śāntideva's Names, Life, and Works." *Journal of the International College for Postgraduate Buddhist Studies* 22: 164–145.

2019 "Śāntideva." In: Jonathan Silk, ed., *Brill's Encyclopdia of Buddhism*, vol. II: *Lives*, 391–397. Leiden: Brill.

Staal 1993 Frits Staal. *Rules without Meaning. Ritual, Mantras and the Human Sciences*. New York: Peter Lang.

Verhagen

1995 Pieter C. Verhagen. "Studies in Tibetan indigenous grammar (2); Tibetan phonology and phonetics in the *Byis-pa-bde-blag-tu-'jug-pa* by Bsod-nams-rtse-mo (1142–1182)." *Asiatische Studien / Études asiatiques* 49/4: 943–968.

2001 *A History of Sanskrit Grammatical Literature in Tibet. Volume 2: Assimilation into Indigenous Scholarship*. Leiden: Brill.

2011 "Tibetan Expertise in Sanskrit Grammar (5): Two Blo gros brtan pas on *Vyākaraṇa*—So many Sthiramatis." *Revue d'Etudes Tibétaines* 57: 267–300.

Wedemeyer

2007 Christian K. Wedemeyer, ed. and tr. *Āryadeva's Lamp that Integrates Practices. Caryāmelāpakapradīpa. The Gradual Path of Vajrayāna Buddhism According to the Esoteric Community Noble Tradition*. New York: The American Institute of Buddhist Studies at Columbia University and Columbia University's Center for Buddhist Studies and Tibet House US.

Zhang 2014 Zhang Xueshan 張雪杉. "Jiadanduoluo yufa fanyi ji yanjiu 迦丹多羅語法翻譯及研究 [Kātantravyākaraṇa. Translation and Study]." PhD thesis. Peking University.

Kharoṣṭhī Out of Bounds*

Richard SALOMON

Abstract: The Kharoṣṭhī script was in wide use between about the third century BCE and the third century CE in its homeland in the northwestern frontier of the Indian world, and during the later phase also became established in northern Afghanistan and adjoining regions as well as in the kingdoms on the fringes of the Tarim Basin. Besides these established territories, inscriptions in Kharoṣṭhī are sporadically found further afield in various parts of northern India and western Afghanistan. But even beyond this extended range, Kharoṣṭhī inscriptions have sporadically been found far from the homeland, for example in northern India (e.g., at Bharhut and Kumrahar), in south India, in China (Luoyang and Chang'an), and even as far afield as Socotra (Yemen). Besides these and other certified instances of outliers, several other controversial claims for Kharoṣṭhī in eastern India and Southeast Asia are discussed and evaluated. It is argued that Kharoṣṭhī script was in some cases adopted for special technical or display functions in places where it was not the normal script, such as Bharhut, Kashmir, and south India. Finally, the reasons for the relatively limited spread and ultimate demise of the Kharoṣṭhī are discussed.

Keywords: Kharoṣṭhī; inscriptions; Gandhara; Indian numerals; Brāhmī; writing systems

0 Introduction: The Homeland and Spread of Kharoṣṭhī Script

It is well known that the Kharoṣṭhī script was the predominant script in the northwestern fringe of the Indian subcontinent and the adjoining regions of what has come to be called "Greater Gandhara" between about the third century BCE and the third century CE (Salomon 2008b). Kharoṣṭhī is richly attested in the form of inscriptions, manuscripts, and administrative documents, mostly of Buddhist content or reflecting a Buddhist environment.[1] In nearly all of these specimens Kharoṣṭhī is used to represent

---

Richard SALOMON, University of Washington.

* It is both a pleasure and an honor to dedicate to the memory of Professor Duan Qing this article, which I hope will be an appropriate tribute to her profuse and profound contributions to the study of cultural contacts and exchanges in South and Central Asia as well as in the Buddhist world at large. But I am indebted to Prof. Duan, not only for her important contributions to the fields of our mutual interest, but also and especially for the invitation she extended to me to participate in the tour of the Niya site which she arranged in December 2014. This was a once-in-a-lifetime opportunity and a rare experience for which I will always remain indebted to Professor Duan.

[1] Kharoṣṭhī is also abundantly attested in the coin legends of the Indo-Greek kings and their many successors in northern and western India, as well as in numerous seal inscriptions from this region; see, for example, Bopearachchi and Rahman 1995 and Rahman and Falk 2011 respectively. But these materials are not taken into consideration in this paper, as they are portable objects which do not provide reliable evidence as to their place of origin. (For example, coins of Menander and other Indo-Greek kings are reported to have been found as far afield as Wales; see, e.g., https://finds.org.uk/database/search/results/q/menander, accessed 20 Sept. 2021.)

the Gāndhārī language, except for a few examples in Sanskrit. The amount of Kharoṣṭhī material available has increased vastly over recent decades. For example, at the time of Sten Konow's then-definitive corpus of Kharoṣṭhī inscriptions, published in 1929 as volume II, part 1 of the *Corpus Inscriptionum Indicarum*, only about one hundred were known, whereas the on-line Corpus of Kharoṣṭhī Inscriptions (CKI; Baums and Glass ongoing) lists, as of this writing (20 September 2021), no fewer than 1175 examples. Similarly, until the early 1990's only one Kharoṣṭhī manuscript, the famous Khotan Dharmapada (Brough 1962), plus a few small scraps of others, were known; as of today, the *Catalog of Gāndhārī Texts: Manuscripts* (Baums and Glass ongoing) lists 431 manuscripts or fragmentary remains thereof on birch bark scrolls or palm leaf folios.[1]

But Kharoṣṭhī script was also used, to varying extents and in varying forms, in territories beyond, sometimes even far beyond its presumptive homeland in Gandhara. Here again, the picture has expanded since the time of Konow's corpus, in which he listed only four examples of inscriptions from "outside the Kharoshṭhī area" (Kumrahar, Pathyar, Kanhiara, and Karnal[2], 177–179). In recent decades, several Kharoṣṭhī inscriptions have been discovered in rather unexpected places, and it is these outliers, especially the newly discovered ones, which will be the principal focus of this paper.

The regions in which inscriptions and other documents in Kharoṣṭhī have been discovered can be roughly divided into (1) core regions, (2) wider spheres of influence, and (3) outlying areas.[3] The primary core region (1) of Kharoṣṭhī script is its presumptive homeland in Gandhara proper, that is, the Peshawar valley and the adjoining areas of modern northern Pakistan and eastern Afghanistan, where Kharoṣṭhī inscriptions are found in large numbers. From this region the use of Kharoṣṭhī spread in all directions over a wider range of more distantly adjoining territories (2), especially during the time of and under the influence of the Kuṣāṇa empire in the first to third centuries of the Common Era.

During this phase of expansion into the wider spheres of influence, Kharoṣṭhī spread especially readily in both directions along the Indus River valley. To the north, 166 Kharoṣṭhī graffiti inscriptions have been discovered at seven different sites along the upper Indus and the adjoining Hunza valleys.[4] A few other similar graffiti have in recent decades been found even further up the Indus in Ladakh; these will be discussed as "outliers" in §2.1.

[1] For an overview of the new manuscript materials, see the relevant articles by R. Salomon, M. Allon, C. Cox, and H. Falk and I. Strauch in Harrison and Hartmann 2014, 1–78.

[2] In this article I have as a matter of convenience presented modern place names in non-technical Roman transcription; thus, for example, Kumrahar rather than Kumrahār and Pathyar for Pāṭhyār.

[3] For more detailed discussions of the normal range of Kharoṣṭhī script see, for example, Mukherjee 1990b, 9–10 and Salomon 1998a, 42–46.

[4] See the entries in CKI for the Alam Bridge, Chilas, Helor Das, Hunza, Oshibat, Shatial, and Thalpan sites.

Toward the southwest along the Indus Valley and into adjoining territories, Kharoṣṭhī script is sporadically attested as far as Mohenjo-daro in Sindh, as well as to the west of the Indus Valley in Tor Dherai, Baluchistan. An important recent addition to the corpus is the bilingual inscription of King Dattayola, the last king of the Pārata dynasty, which had hitherto been known only coins from and references in Indian and western classical literature (Falk 2020–2021, 134–137). Here, as is not infrequently the case in such fringe areas, the inscription is bilingual and biscriptual, with the Kharoṣṭhī/Gāndhārī text placed above and the corresponding text Brāhmī and Sanskrit below it. The findspot of the inscription is unfortunately not reported, but since the territory of the Pāratarājas is known to have been around Loralai, the inscription most likely came from somewhere in that region of Baluchistan, not far from Tor Dherai. Since Dattayola is known from coin sequences to have been the last of the Pāratarājas, the inscription seems to be as late as about 300 CE (Falk 2020–2021, 135), making it one of the latest Kharoṣṭhī inscriptions from India.

To the west of Gandhara proper, inscriptions in Kharoṣṭhī have been found as far as Khawat (CKI no. 159) in the Wardak District of Afghanistan, 48 kilometers west of Kabul,[1] and at Dasht-e-Nawur (Dašt-e Nāwur; CKI no. 231) in Jaghatu District, Afghanistan, some 100 kilometers southwest of Kabul.[2] Here again Kharoṣṭhī is used in combination with other scripts, in this case in triscriptual/trilingual combination with Bactrian in a modified Greek alphabet and with a controversial script and only partially deciphered script (Fussman 1974, 33–34), which may be derivative of Kharoṣṭhī (Falk 2023) or of Aramaic (Bonmann et al. 2023). Several hundred small fragments of Buddhist manuscripts written in Kharoṣṭhī on palm leaves have also been found at a site, not firmly identified, at or near Bamiyan.[3]

Toward the northwest of Gandhara, during the Kuṣāṇa period and in connection with the spread of Buddhist institutions to Bactria, Sogdia, and other territories in and around the valley of the Oxus River, Kharoṣṭhī came into wide use in northern Afghanistan as well as in southern Uzbekistan and Tajikistan. Particularly important are some 250 inscriptions from Kara Tepe and Fayaz Tepe near Termez, Uzbekistan, which are authoritatively documented in Fussman 2011.

To the southeast, Kharoṣṭhī's sphere of influence extended to some degree into continental India, as manifested by the occasional occurrence of Kharoṣṭhī (as well as of biscriptual Kharoṣṭhī and Brāhmī; CKI no. 440) inscriptions in and around Mathura, as well as by two biscripts found at Pathyar and Kanhiara (CKI nos.167 and 168) in the Kangra Valley of Himachal Pradesh. Here once again we find Kharoṣṭhī in biscriptual combinations in its extended ranges of use which overlap with the territory of Brāhmī.

[1] So according to Falk 2008, 63.

[2] According to Fussman 1974, 3.

[3] Summarized in Salomon 2014, 6–8.

Finally, Kharoṣṭhī came to have a life of its own, so to speak, in the oasis cities of the Tarim Basin in the modern Xinjiang-Uighur Autonomous Region of the People's Republic of China.[1] Here it was adopted as the primary script in the kingdoms of Khotan and Kroraina/Shan-shan along the southern rim of the Takla Makan desert, where it continued in use well into the fourth century CE. This development is amply attested by as many as one thousand Kharoṣṭhī documents on wooden tablets, mostly secular and administrative in nature. Kharoṣṭhī was also in sporadic use, along with the better attested Brāhmī, in the oasis cities of the northern rim of the Takla Makan, both for manuscript texts (Salomon 1998b) and for secular documents. This material includes several manuscripts and inscribed wooden tablets in what seem to be later developments of Kharoṣṭhī script, commonly referred to as "Formal Kharoṣṭhī." These are still only partially understood, and may sometimes represent Tocharian and/or other languages rather than Gāndhārī.[2] In this derived form, Kharoṣṭhī continued to be used as late as the fifth or possibly the sixth century CE, well past the time of its demise in its homeland.

These extended regions I consider for the purposes of this article as part of the normal extended territory of Kharoṣṭhī in its time; that is, as part of category (2), wider spheres of influence, in the list above. In what follows, I will focus on group (3), the outliers[3]; that is, sporadic examples of texts in Kharoṣṭhī script—some of them just stray words or even a few syllables, others more substantial—which have been found, or in some cases alleged to have been found, in other regions of India and in various other parts of Asia and even beyond, including some places where its presence is quite unexpected, though never wholly unexplainable.

1 Kharoṣṭhī in the Indian Heartland

1.1 Chitradurga District, Karnataka

The earliest and best-known specimens of Kharoṣṭhī script outside of its normal range, and the only examples from the peninsular south, are in the signatures which were appended by the scribe Capaḍa to the end of the Aśokan minor rock edicts which he recorded at the closely adjoining sites of Brahmagiri, Jatinga-Ramesvara, and Siddapura in the Chitradurga District of Karnataka state. In the only completely surviving version,

[1] This material is presented in more detail in Salomon 2007 [2012], 182–186.

[2] This material is summarized in Salomon 2007 [2012], 185–186, and most recently in Dragoni et al. 2020, 340–343.

[3] The distinction between (2) "extended sphere of influence" and (3) "outliers" is admittedly to some extent arbitrary, and some of the items could have been assigned differently. For example, the Dasht-e Nawur inscription mentioned above could be categorized as an "outlier," and the Khalatse inscription discussed below as part of the "sphere of influence;" I found it difficult to formulate completely objective and consistent criteria to distinguish the two categories.

at Brahmagiri,[1] this reads *capaḍena likhite li[pi]kareṇa*, "Written by the scribe Capaḍa," where the first two words are written as normally in Brāhmī but the word "scribe" (*lipikareṇa*) is anomalously in Kharoṣṭhī (figure 1).

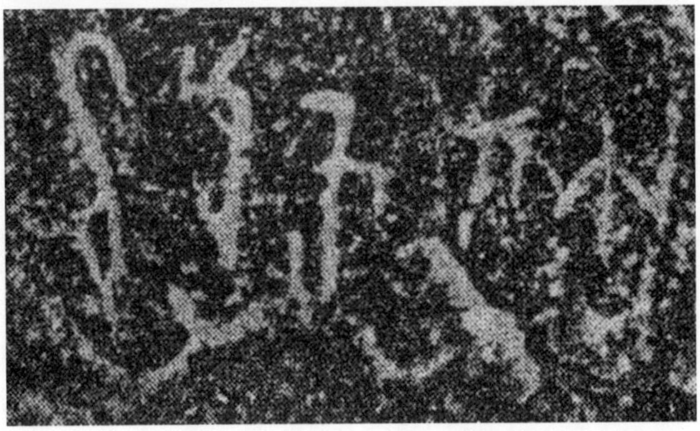

Figure 1: *lipikareṇa* written in Kharoṣṭhī at the end of the Brahmagiri minor rock edict of Aśoka
From Hultzsch 1925, plate facing p. 177

Bühler (1894–1895, 135) commented that "his winding up with *lipikareṇa* in Northern characters [i.e., Kharoṣṭhī] re-minds one of a trick of schoolboys, who sometimes sign their books in Greek or other foreign characters. The use of the Northern characters may further be taken to indicate that Paḍa [sic] once served in Northern India, where the Kharôshṭrî alphabet prevailed." Bühler's interpretation has generally prevailed up to modern times, and this instance of scribal display remains without a parallel, standing as a testimony to the uniquely cosmopolitan character of Aśoka's empire. But it does not indicate the spread of Kharoṣṭhī script in any meaningful way, since there is no other trace of it anywhere else in southern India.

1.2 Bharhut (Satna District, Uttar Pradesh)

Kharoṣṭhī is represented in the northeastern sector of central India, albeit in a very limited and special technical function, at the Śuṅga-period Buddhist stūpa at Bharhut in Satna District, Madhya Pradesh. Here it was noted by Alexander Cunningham (1879, 8 and pl. VIII) that several of the balusters between the crossbars on the toraṇa of the east gate have "*Árian* [i.e., Kharoṣṭhī] *letters* engraved on their bases or capitals." Cunningham read these *akṣaras* as "*p*, *s*, *a*, and *b*, of which the first three occur twice." In the accompanying plate VIII, reproduced here as figure 2, he drew in five of these seven syllables, representing them (from right to left) as *sa*, *a*, *ba*, *a*, and *pa*, thus

[1] At Jatinga-Ramesvara, only ...*ḍena [likhita]ṁ* ...*[pika]reṇa* survives, and at Siddapura, *capa* ...*[ṇa]*. All three readings are given according to Hultzsch 1925, 176–180.

including the two *a*-s but omitting the second occurrences of *pa* and *sa*. The plate does not clearly indicate which balusters the letters occur on.[1]

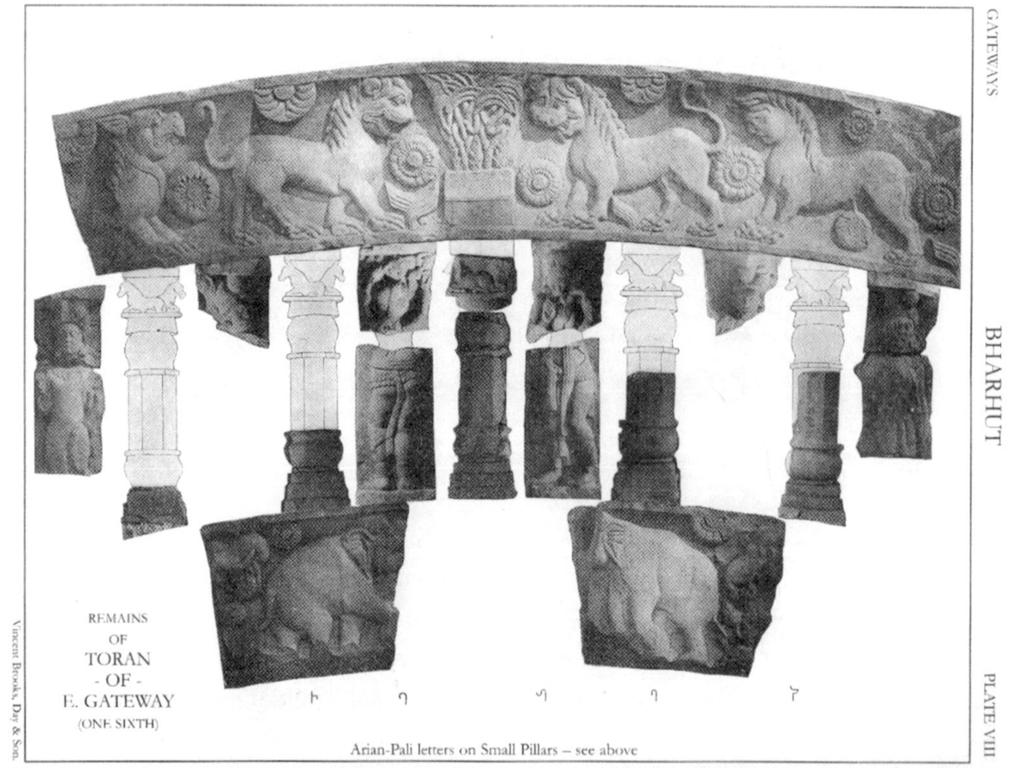

Figure 2: Reconstruction of the Bharhut toraṇa (east gate)
From Cunningham 1879, pl. VIII

In a footnote (p. 8, n. 2), Cunningham opines "I think it probable these letters may be numerals, the initials of the words *pânch* = 5, *sât* = 7, *âth* = 8, and *ba* = 2." If by this he meant to imply that the letters indicate something about the relative positions of the components on which they are engraved, he may have been on the right track; but he was completely wrong about the mode of indication that they embody. For it is now abundantly attested that Kharoṣṭhī syllables arranged in the order of the Arapacana alphabet (*a ra pa ca na la da ba ḍa ṣa va ta,* etc.) were widely used in Gandharan stūpa architecture to mark the intended locations of individual components such as balusters, decorative columns, or narrative panels, including some objects that are quite similar to

[1] It is unclear whether the positions of the letters copied at the bottom of pl. VIII were intended to indicate that they were on the balusters immediately above them in the plate (nos. 4, 5, 7, 8, and 10 from the left), or whether, as seems more likely, they were just spaced evenly across the bottom of the page without reference to the images above them.

the Bharhut balustrades in question here.[1] Thus it seems reasonable to suppose that the Kharoṣṭhī syllables were used here at Bharhut in a similar fashion, albeit out of their normal geographical range.

The eastern toraṇa originally had two rows of eleven balusters each, with alternating miniature pillars and standing figures. Since Cunningham was able to identify duplicates of three letters, namely—according to his readings—*pa*, *sa*, and *a*, this means that the location indicating system must have involved some duplication. But since he does not specify exactly where each letter occurs, the details of the system cannot be definitely reconstructed. Nevertheless, comparisons with better documented examples provide some possible explanations. Either the two separate rows of eleven balusters each were marked separately, or the location markers were applied according to the "matching system" (Salomon 2006, 185–186, 199), in which the same letter would be marked both on the separate component (the pillars and statues) and on the supporting element, that is, in this case, the toraṇa crossbars into which they were to be inserted. But it would seem from Cunningham's description ("letters engraved on their bases or capitals") that there we no indicator letters on the crossbars. Yet another possibility is that each baluster was marked on both the top and the bottom, but once again it is impossible to be sure due to the vagueness of Cunningham's descriptions.[2]

Cunningham's readings of the syllables are also open to doubt. *A* and *pa* are unproblematic, as they are exactly what we would expect to find in such a situation, being the first and third letters respectively of the Arapacana alphabet. *Ba*, as the eighth Arapacana letter, is possible, though I wonder whether what Cunningham read as *ba* was actually the similarly shaped *ra*, which is the third Arapacana syllable and which therefore like *a* and *pa* occurs very frequently in Arapacana location-marking sequences. I am even more doubtful about the letter read by Cunningham as *sa*, supposedly occurring twice; *sa* is the sixteenth letter of the Arapacana, which is quite unlikely to have occurred at all in this sequence, let alone twice. I therefore suspect that this was actually the somewhat similar *ca*, Arapacana letter number four.

---

[1] On this system, see Salomon 2006 and Koizumi 2008.

[2] Internet images of the reconstructed toraṇa in the Indian Museum show the lower row of eleven balusters complete and the upper row empty. This is inconsistent with the photograph shown in Cunningham's pl. VI, where both rows are shown as complete with partial reconstruction of several of the balusters. But a close comparison with the detail view of the lower row in pl. VIII shows that the reconstruction there differs in several respects from the one shown in pl. VI. The upshot of this is that we cannot be sure which, if any of the reconstructions is more accurate. If all of the balusters (and the crossbars) could be carefully re-examined for location letters, it would probably be possible to arrive at a more accurate reconstruction, such as was successfully done in the case of the Zar Dheri stupa (Koizumi 2016). But this would require a complete dismantling of the reconstructed toraṇa now standing in the Indian Museum in Kolkata, which is not likely to be feasible.

Cunningham assumed that the presence of Kharoshṭhī syllables on the balustrade scuptures meant that they were executed by artists from northwestern India, remarking (p. 8) that "if the same [northwestern] sculptors had been employed on the railings, we might confidently expect to find the same [Kharoṣṭhī] alphabetical letters used as private marks. But the fact is just the reverse, for the whole of the 27 marks found on any portions of the railing are *Indian* [i.e., Brāhmī] letters." Here, unfortunately, it is not at all clear what the "27 marks" he refers to are. This seems to imply that he found other location marks, but in Brāhmī script, on the railings of the stūpa, but I find in his work no further reference to or explanation of them. This is unfortunate, since these are potentially highly interesting because, in contrast to the far northwest where Kharoṣṭhī location letters are abundant, location letters of any kind in early monuments are scarcely attested in peninsular India, the only other well-known albeit poorly documented example being the Bodh Gaya pillars (Salomon 2006, 217).

But what primarily concerns us here is the presence of Kharoṣṭhī script at all in this region, so remote from its northwestern homeland. According to Cunningham (1879, 8), this is "a peculiarity which points unmistakably to the employment of Western artists, and which fully accounts for the superiority of their [i.e., the balusters'] execution." The notion that the presence of Kharoṣṭhī syllables on the Bharhut balusters is proof that they were the work of northwestern artists, and that this accounts for their allegedly superior quality, has been perpetuated by later authors, for example by John Marshall (1922, 567), who opines that "The only rational explanation of these phenomena is that some of the sculptors engaged on this railing came from the north-west of India, where, thanks to western teaching, the formative arts were then in a more advanced state, and that these sculptors were responsible for the better class of reliefs, the inferior work being done by the local artists of Central India."

This understanding of the development of Indian art, perhaps best described as quaint by modern standards, hardly constitutes a convincing explanation of the issue at hand. Moreover, the vague and incomplete documentation of both the Kharoṣṭhī and especially of the Brāhmī locator letters makes it difficult to evaluate the presence of Kharoṣṭhī at Bharhut.[1] For our purposes, the question is whether the Kharoṣṭhī/Arapacana locator letters constitute a one-off, incidental intrusion of Kharoṣṭhī script into the heartland, comparable to the signature of Capaḍa in the Aśokan inscriptions; or whether they indicate the involvement of artisans from the northwest at Bharhut, as

[1] I hope that in my critique of his work at Bharhut I have not been unfair to the memory of Alexander Cunningham, who is justly known as the "father of Indian archaeology." The failure to live up to modern standards of excavation and documentation and modern modes of interpretation are understandable and presumably excusable in view of the times and circumstances of his work, and especially of his epoch-making achievements. Like all of us, he was a creature of his own time and is best judged by its standards, not by ours.

assumed by Cunningham; or whether they perhaps mean something else. Although the assumption by Cunningham and other archaeologists and art historians of earlier generations that the Kharoṣṭhī letters indicate the involvement of northwestern artisans is not unreasonable, it is also conceivable that the Kharoṣṭhī/Arapacana letters came to be used along with the local Brāhmī characters outside of their usual territory as a sort of alternative or supplementary system, in the same way that Roman numerals survive today in complementary distribution with "Arabic" numbers for various technical or ceremonial purposes. Moreover, there is in fact at least one other context in which Kharoṣṭhī signs—in this case involving mostly the numerical rather than phonetic characters—have been used in a specific technical fashion in a region where the Kharoṣṭhī script was not otherwise in general use. I refer here to the use, now abundantly attested, of Kharoṣṭhī numerals on terracotta tiles in Kashmir, which will be discussed in detail below (§2.2).

1.3 Kumrahar (Patna District, Bihar)

We move now even further eastward into the heartland of north India, where in 1914, in the course of excavations at the site of Kumrahar in the modern city of Patna, Bihar, a terracotta plaque was discovered that bore the image of a Buddhist monument[1] and a short Kharoṣṭhī inscription (fig. 3).

Figure 3: The Kumrahar plaque
From Konow 1926, frontispiece

[1] There has been a long-standing disagreement over whether the monument in question was meant to represent the temple at Bodh Gaya, as originally proposed by D.B. Spooner (1915, 1916), or some other monument that once stood at Kumrahar or elsewhere (Smith 1916).

It was a matter of considerable surprise that a specimen of Kharoṣṭhī, however small, was found so far to the east of India; as Konow noted in his standard edition of the inscription (1929, 177–178; cf. CKI no. 166), "we have no indication of Kharoshṭhī having ever been used in Bihar," and this is still true. But it must be kept in mind that the inscription is on a portable object which could have been a souvenir brought from elsewhere by a pilgrim from the northwest. In fact, Falk (1991–1992, 269) has pointed out that there is evidence that "miniature stone and wood models of the [Bodh Gayā] temple were offered for sale to the pilgrims."

The reading of the inscription, engraved in very small characters, is highly problematic. Konow suggested, "With the utmost reserve"[1] (p. 178), *K[othumasa] Saṃghada[sa]sa kiti*, "The work of Saṃghadāsa, the Kauthuma." Mukherjee (1984–1985) proposes to read the name as *(Saṃ)ghadadasa*, without noting that Konow had already discussed this as a possible alternation reading. Mukherjee further says that there is on the plaque, besides the Kharoṣṭhī inscription, another one in Brāhmī that "has not been noticed by earlier scholars"[2] (p. 44), and he proposes to read this as *rajñ(o) ceti(ya)*, which "may mean 'the king's chaitya.'" From the published images available to me it is not possible to confirm the existence of this additional Brāhmī inscription, nor to confirm or improve upon Konow's reading of the Kharoṣṭhī one. It is doubtful whether even a direct examination of the original would produce a better result, since Konow himself examined it with his expert eye "in all kinds of light and shade" (1926, 181). The only hope for improvement would be digital photography by an imaging specialist, should the possibility arise. In any case, in view of the portability of the object on which the inscription is engraved, this inscription does not constitute proof that Kharoṣṭhī was ever in use as far east as Bihar.

1.4 Some Problematic Cases

1.4.1 Chunar (Mirzapur District, Uttar Pradesh): A Difficult Case

Field studies undertaken at the ancient quarry at Chunar[3] brought to light 59 inscriptions on the flat ends of cylindrical dressed stones that were apparently intended to be sections of pillars, but were never actually put to use. These were interpreted by B.N. Mukherjee and T.P. Verma (cited in Jayaswal 1998, 57, 100, 106–107) as representing

[1] Curiously, three years earlier (1926, 181) Konow had offered the same reading "with almost absolute certainty." It is difficult to account for the difference, but we may suspect that his initial enthusiasm at having arrived at a plausible reading was dampened upon a subsequent re-examination of the inscription "in the cold light of morning." Those who engage in similar work will be able to relate to the alternating excitements and disappointments that it inevitably involves.

[2] In 1990, 10, Mukherjee said that the Kumrahār plaque "bears a Kharoshṭī inscription and *perhaps* also a Brāhmī legend" (my emphasis).

[3] Pant and Jayaswal 1990, Pant and Jayaswal 1990–1991, Mukherjee 1990c, Mukherjee 1990–1991, Jayaswal 1998, Falk 2006, 154–157.

various scripts, including Brāhmī (5 examples), Kharoṣṭhī (13), "Kharoṣṭhī-Brāhmī" (7), Nagari, and Kaithi. But all or nearly all of these identifications are doubtful, as shown by Falk (2006, 156), who cites Verma's dating of the Nagari inscriptions to the eighteenth and nineteenth centuries in contrast to Mukherjee's eleventh and twelfth centuries, concluding that "Verma's view is certainly preferable, applying not only to the clear Nāgarī cases, but also to those of so-called Kharoṣṭhī, Brāhmī or mixed Kharoṣṭhī-Brāhmī inscriptions." Most of these inscriptions do in fact seem to be written in various recent or early pre-modern local scripts, apparently in casual, unpracticed, or idiosyncratic forms. Mukherjee's identifications of Kharoṣṭhī and Brāhmī are in nearly every case imaginative and forced, and fail to yield plausible readings. For example, inscription 59 was read by him as *Bodaṭ(h)ā śayada Ethe'asya*, which "we may meaningfully Sanskritise ... as *Vyastata-śayata-Eṭ(h)akasya*" and which "can be translated as 'of Eṭ(h)aka, who disorderly sleeps too much.'"[1] Regarding this interpretation, Mukherjee comments "According to the writer of the inscription, which records an instruction from a superior authority, the labourer concerned had the ill reputation of not doing his duty properly as he often fell asleep 'in a disordered manner' probably during the working hours when such an act was not permissible." Suffice it to say that the readings and interpretations of the other inscriptions are hardly more convincing.[2]

Figure 4: Chunar inscription no. 55
From Pant and Jayaswal 1990–1991, pl. 2

But there is one inscription which must give us pause before dismissing the Chunar material entirely. This is Jayaswal's inscription no. 55, reproduced here as figure 4, which Mukherjee read as *Ativaho shaha* (= *Ativaha-sahah*), "indicating the pillar ... bearing it as 'capable of excessive carrying.'"[3] Falk (2006, 156) says that it "should be

[1] Mukherjee 1990–1991, 56, and similarly in Mukherjee 1990c, 107; also cited in Pant and Jayaswal 1990–1991, 102.

[2] As to the supposed "mixed Kharoṣṭhī-Brāhmī" script, see below, §1.4.3.

[3] Mukherjee 1990–1991, 55 (no. 1) and pl. 2 ≈ Mukherjee 1990c, 104 and fig. 1.

read as *ativahaṣaha*," cautiously adding, "if it is Kharoṣṭhī at all." This one inscription does indeed—unlike all the others—look remarkably like Kharoṣṭhī script. Some of the characters, such as *a*, *ti*, and *ha* (twice) are quite similar to normal Kharoṣṭhī characters, while the others (*va*, *ṣa*) are at least reasonably close to the apparently corresponding forms. That the text, read in this way, does not yield an obvious or compelling sense (*pace* Mukherjee) does not rule out its identification as Kharoṣṭhī, since there are a great many short Kharoṣṭhī inscriptions from many different sites that presumably contain personal names that cannot be etymologically explained. But besides this exceptional case, there is only one other inscription at Chunar (Jayaswal's no. 14, p. 105 and pl. V) which has a few characters that resemble Kharoṣṭhī syllables (*a*, *ya*, and *la*), but this is pretty obviously not really a Kharoṣṭhī inscription, and the resemblances are presumably coincidental.

What, then, are we to make of the curious situation in which a single inscription that looks very much like Kharoṣṭhī was found in the context of a large number of other inscriptions that, claims to their antiquity notwithstanding, are probably more or less modern? Could this be the isolated remnant of much earlier stratum of remains at Chunar, or is it just a specimen of some other local script which happens to randomly resemble Kharoṣṭhī? Unfortunately, this case is particularly hard to judge, and we can only label it as a possible but quite doubtful instance of "Kharoṣṭhī out of bounds" in the heartland of northern India.

1.4.2 Two Doubtful Cases: Bodh Gaya and Sanchi

There are two other cases in which Kharoṣṭhī materials have been reported from important Buddhist sites in the Indian heartland. The first is a reference in Myer 1958, 286 to "an inscription in Kharoshthī characters around the upper edge" of a "Maurya-style stone found at the back of the temple" at Bodh Gayā. This apparently refers to what Cunningham (1892, pl. X, no. 11) labeled as the "outer Vajrâsan," but the inscription thereon is clearly in Brāhmī rather than Kharoṣṭhī. Thus, although the reference to Kharoṣṭhī is endorsed in Malandra 1988, 17, this seems to be based on a misunderstanding.

The same appears to be the case with the remark in Ghosh 1989, 295 that "In Stūpa 2 at Sanchi the occurrence of Kharoṣṭhī ... letters as against Brāhmī ... has been interpreted as signifying the employment of workers from the n.-w. who were also responsible for the carving of foreign art motifs and figures there." But I have been unable to find any other references to "Kharoṣṭhī letters" at Sanchi either elsewhere in Ghosh's encyclopedia or anywhere else, so that the close similarity of his remarks and interpretation to what has been said in various sources about the Kharoṣṭhī syllables at Bharhut (see §1.2) makes me suspect that the author has here confused the two sites. As far as I have been able to determine, there is no evidence for any Kharoṣṭhī writing at Sanchi.

1.4.3 "Kharoṣṭhī-Brāhmī": A False Case

In a special dedicated issue of the Indian Museum Bulletin (Mukherjee 1990b), B.N. Mukherjee published 64 inscriptions on earthernware vessels, seals, and various other objects found in West Bengal, mostly from the area of Chandraketugarh in South 24 Parganas District and Tamluk in Purba Medinipur District, which he interpreted as being in Kharoṣṭhī, Brāhmī, or a "mixed" Kharoṣṭhī-Brāhmī script. However, as clearly demonstrated in Falk 2013, 108, "there is not a single case of plain Kharoṣṭhī" among this material, and "the mixed [i.e., "Kharoṣṭhī-Brāhmī"] script never existed." Falk adds (p. 112), "The shapeless lines scratched carelessly on cheap pots and sherds are read by him usually from left to right, hopping from Brāhmī to Kharoṣṭhī and back, reading a text which is incomprehensible by itself, and which he turned into some sort of Indian dialect by ignoring every sound-law known and forcing semantics and syntax into unknown heights of fancy."[1] In reality, it is still the case, as stated by Kunja Gobind Goswami in 1948 (p. 12), that "it is not possible to connect the symbols with any of the early Indian letters," and the Chandraketugarh script must for the time being be classed among the several undeciphered scripts of India (Salomon 1983, 205–207)—unless, as proposed by Falk (2013, 111–113), this is actually a matter of "pseudo-script," that is, "graphs constructed on the idea of writing by someone who was not educated in scripts." However, this seems unlikely in view of the very large number of specimens of this writing that have been found—although, as pointed out by both Mukherjee (1990b, 41 n. 6) and Falk (2013, 107–108, 112, 114), some of these are modern forgeries produced for the art market.

In conclusion, the attestation of Kharoṣṭhī script in peninsular India beyond the Mathura region is extremely sparse. There are only three definite examples, and all of them are special cases: a single word written in Kharoṣṭhī at the end of three Brāhmī inscriptions in Karnataka as a display of the scribe's expertise; a few syllables used in a special technical function, as location markers, at Bharhut; and a short and only partially legible inscription on a portable object from Kumrahar in Bihar, which may been brought there from elsewhere. The other alleged instances are either highly doubtful (Chunar), undocumented, or wholly imaginary. The rarity of Kharoṣṭhī in the heartland of peninsular India is not hard to explain; Brāhmī script was already firmly entrenched in these regions and there was no scope or motivation for the adoption of what was presumably viewed as a foreign form of writing, except occasionally for

[1] For example, Mukherjee interprets his inscription no. 9 (1990b, 46) in "mixed script" as *Koriśajiḍha jeṭhaṇaṭasya, ḍhv(i)jade* [va]*r̥ishitane*, equated to Sanskrit (!) *Karrīśajita-jyeshṭha-natasya* (or *naṭasya) dvija-de*[va]*rishi-tane*, "of [the one who is-] the conqueror of the lord of the elephants [and] submissive to the elders (or the chief actor) ; for [*i.e.* issued praying for] the continuation (or propagation) of the Brahmins, gods and ascetics."

special and limited technical functions. But as we will see in the following sections, this was not necessarily the case in the farther reaches of the Indian cultural zone, and even in some regions beyond it, where Kharoṣṭhī did develop some footholds, albeit fleetingly.

2 Kharoṣṭhī in the Himalayan Fringe

2.1 Ladakh

A brief Kharoṣṭhī inscription at Khalatse (or Khaltse) on the upper Indus River in the Leh District of Ladakh (CKI no. 62), recording the name of the Kuṣāṇa king Vima Kadphises (*deva[pu]ta maharajasa uvimo kavthisasa*) and a date (the year 287), has been well known since its discovery in 1905 by A.H. Francke. Two other brief graffiti in Kharoṣṭhī (CKI nos. 1122–1123), along with a few Brāhmī inscriptions, were also noticed by him at the same place.

More recently, several further Kharoṣṭhī and Brāhmī graffiti have been found in neighboring regions of Ladakh, as described in Salomon, Devers, and Ldawa 2020–2021. These include a Kharoṣṭhī inscription recorded in triplicate at Kanutse, some 50 kilometers down the Indus from Khalatse, which has been tentatively read as *varṣako-raja-hasta*, "The signature of King Varṣaka" or "The signature of Varṣakorāja" (Salomon, Devers, and Ldawa 2020–2021, 96); but as is so often the case, the reading of these casual graffiti is uncertain and the etymological interpretation of the name that they record is not clear.[1] At Kharul, at the confluence of the Shingo and Suru Rivers some twenty kilometers south of the Indus, a stone was found that bore, besides one Brāhmī graffito, three stray Kharoṣṭhī syllables and two names in Kharoṣṭhī: *śrīdharma[sa]* and *spalasa* (ibid., 103–104). Here, unlike the previous case, the names are written carefully and are of familiar Buddhist and Indo-Iranian derivation.

The Kharoṣṭhī graffiti from Ladakh are evidently manifestations of an extension of the trade routes that are richly attested by the aforementioned (§0) inscriptions from the upper Indus River in Pakistan. They reflect an alternative to the main route which followed the Indus to the Hunza Valley and thence northward to the Khunjerab and other passes into the Tarim Basin, instead continuing along the Indus after its bend toward the southeast, whence travelers could cross over the Himalaya into Khotan and Yarkand (ibid., 106). It has been suggested (Skinner 2017, 63–64) that the inscription of Vima Kadphises was intended to demarcate the border of Kuṣāṇa territory or sphere of influence along this trade route, just as the Dasht-e Nawur inscription served to mark its western frontier.

[1] For an alternative interpretation of these inscriptions, see Harry Falk cited in Bruneau 2010, 1.209–10 and Bruneau 2011, 182.

2.2 Harwan and Other Sites in Kashmir

The Buddhist monastery site of Harwan in the Srinagar District of Kashmir has yielded at least two dozen decorative terracotta tiles that originally covered the floor and surrounding wall of one of the structures, with Kharoṣṭhī numbers that are presumed (Kak 1933, 109; Salomon 2006, 212 n. 40) to have indicated their intended position in the assembled structures. Kak illustrates over two dozen such numbered tiles, bearing numerals ranging from 3[1] to 53,[2] or possibly 65.[3] Several other specimens of numbered tiles from Harwan have made their way into various public and private collections and have been illustrated in various publications and on-line resources.[4]

For many years the tiled courtyard was thought to be unique to Harwan, but in recent decades at least a dozen more such artefacts have been discovered at various places in the valley of Kashmir.[5] According to available published reports—most of which are however inadequately detailed for our purposes[6]—at least four of these new sites have tiles with Kharoṣṭhī numbers: Ahan (Ahansar) in Kupwara District,[7] Matan in Anantnag District,[8] Darad Kut (Hutmur) in Anantnag District,[9] and most notably, Kanispur in Baramulla District.[10]

Some of the numerals on the Harwan tiles are written in the normal fashion, though sometimes arranged vertically rather than the usual horizontal direction, due to

[1] Three times; Kak's plates XXXII.27, XXXIII.28, and XXXVII.32.

[2] Kak, pl. XXXIV.30.

[3] Kak, pl. XXIX.20 (reading not clear).

[4] For example, Fisher 1982 and 1989, Paul 1986, Poster 1986, Bandey 1992; https://www.livehistoryindia.com/story/amazing-india/the-harwan-monastery-a-relic-of-kashmirs-buddhist-past, accessed Sept. 18, 2021; https://www.sahapedia.org/terracotta-art-kashmir-overview, accessed Sept. 18, 2021. The numerals attested on Harwan tiles known to me are: 3 (five times), 4 (twice), 5 (five times), 6 (twice), 7 (twice), 8 (four times), 10, 12 (three times), 13, 15 (twice), 16 (twice), 17 (six times), 19, 21 (twice), 22 (three times), 24, 25, 29, 32, 33, 34, 35, 41, 42, 51, 53, and (possibly) 65.

[5] Bandey 1992, 2, Mani 2008, 218, and Shah 2012–2013, 218 ("more than eleven sites").

[6] For example, with regard to the important Darad Kut site, Bandey reported in 1992 (22, n. 18) that "State Archaeology, Srinagar excavated three areas of the site during the summer of 1988, but remain to be reported yet." As far as I am aware this is still the case, with the welcome exception of Lone 2018–2019 (discussed below).

[7] Hassnain 1973, 50 and figs. iii–iv, showing the numbers 13 and 15; Bhan 1986, 44.

[8] Paul 1986, 268 n. 23 and fig. 2 (numbers not visible).

[9] Bandey 1992, 2, 15; Lone 2018–2019, 3–5.

[10] Mani 1999–2000, 12–13; Mani 2000, 11–12; Mani 2008, 218–220 and pls. 9–10. Mani (2008, 219) also refers to "a couple of tiles" in a private collection, said to have come from the area of Ganderbal, that represent "a late tradition ... but interestingly with Arabic script in place of Kharoshthi." One of these is illustrated in pl. 9 (on p. 38 of the separately numbered plates section at the end of the volume). The characters do seem to have a similarity to Arabic letters, but no sense has been made of them. The possibility of a modern forgery cannot be ruled out in this case.

exigencies of space for writing; see figure 5. But particularly interesting for our subject is that, as was first noted by Pran Gopal Paul,[1] several of the numerical sequences on the Harwan tiles, as well as on at least one tile from another site (Darad Kut), are written in an irregular fashion. For example, the numerals illustrated in Kak's plates XXIII.4, XXIV.5, and XLI.45 (reproduced here in fig. 6) are written from left to right instead of in the normal right-to-left order of Kharoṣṭhī.

Figure 5: Harwan tile, with numbers written vertically but in normal order: *20-20-1* = 41
Photograph courtesy of Museo Nazionale d'Arte Orientale "Giuseppe Tucci"

Figure 6: Harwan tile with numerals written in reverse order (i.e., left to right): *1-1-10* = 12
From Kak 1933, pl. XLI.45

[1] Paul 1986, 43–44; cf. also Bandey 1992, 6, 14–15.

Some other numerals are written upside down, for example the figure for *10* in the number *17* (i.e., *1-1-1-4-10* in the additive system of Kharoṣṭhī numerals[1]) in Kak's no. XXIII.4 (fig. 7).[2]

Figure 7: Harwan tile, with numeral *10* written upside-down: *10-4-3* = 17
From Kak 1933, pl. XXIII.4

In some other cases, one character is rotated 90 degrees counter-clockwise from its normal position relative to the other figures, for instance the *20* in Kak's no. XXV.8, shown here in figure 8.

Figure 8: Harwan tile, with numeral *20* rotated 90 degrees: *20-10-1-1* = 32
From Kak 1933, pl. XXV.8

[1] On the system of numerical notation in Kharoṣṭhī, see Salomon 1998a, 63–64.

[2] It is also possible to read this numeral with the tile turned top to bottom, as there are several other cases in which the position of the numeral is not oriented to the design on the tile. If read this way, the *10* is correctly oriented but the entire numerical sequence is backwards (right-to-left), as in the preceding example.

Several other Harwan numerals are irregular in various other ways. For example, on the tile shown in Fisher 1982, 37 = Poster 1986, 131, the numeral *21* is both upside-down with reference to the accompanying image and backwards, reading from right to left, *1-20* instead of *20-1*.

The inscribed tiles from Darad Kut are of interest in that the Kharoṣṭhī numerals are written on them in a different fashion from Harwan. At Harwan, the numerals are typically inscribed, somewhat surprisingly, in large characters and in prominent positions near the middle of the tile, as seen for example in figure 7. But at Darad Kut they are inscribed in very small figures near the edge of the tile, as one might expect with location signs that were intended to guide the builders in constructing the monuments, rather than to be seen by their viewers.[1] Lone (2018–2019, 4–5) describes four numbered tiles, with the numerals 24 ("probably"), 89, 92, and 102, of which only the last is visible in the accompanying images. In that case we find another surprising abnormality in the notational system, but a different kind of anomaly from those seen at Harwaṇ. Here the number *102*, which barely visible in Lone's figure 5 (p. 6) but clearly and accurately shown in the hand copy in the accompanying figure 5a, is represented by the sequence *20-20-20-20-20-1-1*, instead of the standard Kharoṣṭhī numeration *1-100-1-1*. The representation of one hundred by repeating the character for *20* five times instead of the normal Kharoṣṭhī character for *100* is to my knowledge unprecedented.[2]

But it is at Kanispur that we find the most interesting evidence. Mani (2008, 219) reports that "plain tiles with Kharoṣṭhī numerals" were discovered at site KNP-1, but unfortunately these are not illustrated or further discussed. At site KNP-2 Mani found some remnants of a "badly damaged pavement consisting of decorated terracotta tiles with a pattern of a large disc having several concentric circles,"[3] and reports (ibid.) that "These tiles also bear numerals in Kharoshthī and a few letters in Brāhmī." No further narrative details are provided, but the hand-drawn reconstruction of the circular floor in Mani 1999–2000, 13, fig. 9, reproduced here as figure 9, yields some intriguing hints.

[1] As noted in Salomon 2006, 181–182, the abundant location letters on Gandharan structures were always discreetly placed in inconspicuous locations such as the base fillet or back of narrative panels, where they would not be visible when the components were set in their final position.

[2] Bandey remarks (p. 15) concerning the Darad Kut/Hutmur tiles that "Fortunately for us the Hutmur tiles are *in-situ* as per the actual layment. Here this juxta-position of numerals is not found. The portions that have been exposed are as per the conventional system." The point is not exactly clear to me, but he seems to suggest that the positioning and direction of the Kharoṣṭhī numbers on the Darad Kut tiles are normal in contrast to the abnormal arrangements seen at Harwan.

[3] Mani 1999–2000, 12; see also Shah 2012–2013, 219.

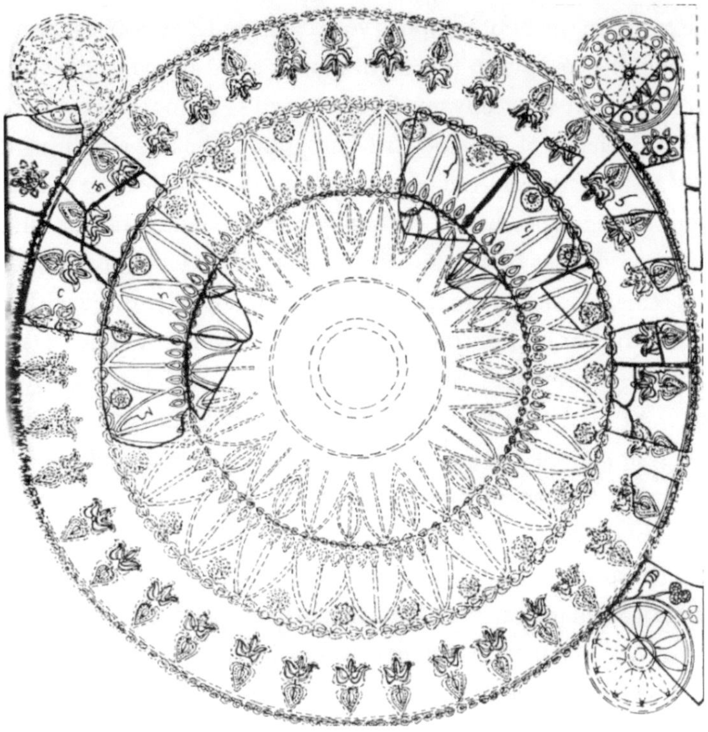

Figure 9: Reconstructed image of tiled floor at Kanispur 1
From Mani 1999–2000, 13, fig. 9

Here the author has copied eight inscribed characters, presumably location markers, on the surviving fragmentary tiles on the outer and next-to-outer rings. Among them, the upper of the two contiguous tiles in the upper left quadrant of the outer circle is marked with what looks something like a Brāhmī *na*, and the one below it could be seen as a Brāhmī *ga*. It is not clear whether these and the other marks on the circular floor are what Mani refers to as Brāhmī letters, but there is one important point which sheds a different light on the matter.

Figure 10: Kharoṣṭhī *ca* on a floor tile from Kanispur
From Mani 2008, 42, pl. 10

Plate 10 of Mani 2008, 42 [in the separately numbered plates section] provides a color photograph (reproduced here as fig. 10) of what is certainly, on the basis of the shape and the designs, the tile in the 3 o'clock position in the eye-copy of the reconstructed floor; but from this it becomes clear that the eight characters in the drawing have not been accurately copied. For the figure in the photograph is very clearly a Kharoṣṭhī *ca*, although it would not have been possible to discern this from Mani's hand-drawn reconstruction, where the letter is stretched out vertically and straightened so as to render it unrecognizable.

Moreover, if the letter at 3 o'clock is Kharoṣṭhī *ca*, the one adjoining it at 2 o'clock is pretty clearly a Kharoṣṭhī *na*. And if that is so, we must be dealing with an Arapacana marking system of the type that is so familiar from Gandhara and also attested at Bharhut, these two syllables being the fourth and fifth in the Arapacana sequence (*a ra pa* ***ca na*** ...). The remaining letters in the drawing cannot be identified with any certainty, no doubt because they are inaccurate renderings, and only the one detail photograph showing *ca* has been provided. But the four syllables in the next-to-outer ring at positions 8:30, 9:30, 1 and 2 o'clock as shown in the drawing could also be Kharoṣṭhī characters; for example, the first of these might be another *ca* and the last one *ba* (the eighth syllable in the Arapacana system). As noted above, the other two letters in the upper left section of the outer circle look more like Brāhmī, but this too is quite doubtful.

The upshot of all this is that at Harwan, Kanispur, and other sites in Kashmir, Kharoṣṭhī numerical characters, and in at least one case also almost certainly the Kharoṣṭhī Arapacana alphabetic sequence, were widely used as location markers.[1] This is relevant to our main topic—"Kharoṣṭhī out of bounds"—because, contrary to what has sometimes been assumed,[2] Kashmir, despite its proximity to the Kharoṣṭhī heartland, was apparently not part of the Kharoṣṭhī-writing area. In fact, the numerical and alphabetic notations on the tiles from Harwan and related Kashmiri sites seem to be the only real specimens of Kharoṣṭhī that have been found there.[3] Particularly

[1] Exactly how the location letters worked is unfortunately not clear due to inadequate documentation of all of the sites concerned. Mani (2008, 218) says with regard to the Harwan tiles "Each one of the tiles bears a number in Kharoshthi script ... and the order of the tiles in a series is in strict accordance with their consecutive numeral order." This however seems to be an assumption—albeit a reasonable one—rather than an archaeologically-based conclusion, since the Harwan site was apparently too disturbed to permit a reconstruction of the original positions of the tiles. Kak (1933, 109) similarly reports "That these tiles occupied exactly the position that they were laid in by ancient workmen is borne out by the fact that each one of them bears a number in Kharoshthi script, the order of the tiles in a series being in strict accordance with their consecutive numerical order." But this too seems to be more of assumption than an actual archaeological observation. At least from the information and illustrations provided by Kak it is impossible to determine exactly how the numerals were arranged in the actual (fragmentary and disturbed) remains. In only one of Kak's images (pl. XX) are we are shown three numbered floor tiles in their original position; their numbers, from right to left, are 22, 12, and 8, so that their sequence was presumably not horizontal linear order. In short, there is still much that remains to be clarified about the system of the Harwan tiles.

[2] For example, Rhie 1999, 1.340 refers to "some" Kharoṣṭhī inscriptions found in the "the Kashmir area." This is inaccurate, unless she refers to the Khalatse inscription of Vima Kadphises, from a region which is sometimes considered to be part of Kashmir in the wider sense.

[3] A possible marginal exception is the sealing of Jita-Iṣigata (CKI no. 366), which was "reported to have been found in Kashmir" (Salomon 1996 [1998], 244). But the report is only hearsay, and in any case since sealings are prone to travel, the findspot is not necessarily the place of origin.

interesting in this connection are the several abnormal features of the Kharoṣṭhī numerals in Kashmir, both in terms of misorientation, as in the several reversed, misaligned and upside-down characters attested at Harwan, and in terms of systemic abnormalities, as in the unusual way of representing *100* with 5 *20*-s at Darad Kut. It seems reasonable to assume that these numerical notations represent the work of persons who were not well acquainted with Kharoṣṭhī script in its normal functions and who were more familiar with a Brāhmī-derived system written from left to right, whence the frequent confusion about the sequence and orientation of the Kharoṣṭhī numerals.[1] In short, the use of Kharoṣṭhī in Kashmir for special purposes seems to be comparable to what we have already seen at Bharhut; evidently in both places Kharoṣṭhī numbers and/or letters (in the Arapacana sequence) were adopted as a secondary system for technical purposes such marking the intended position of construction components.[2]

3 Kharoṣṭhī in China

3.1 Luoyang

In 1925 or 1926, three fragments of a stone inscription were discovered in or near Luoyang in Henan Province of the People's Republic of China. Although the circumstances of its discovery are poorly documented, "we may reasonably conclude that the inscription was in fact found ' in the neighbourhood of Lo-yang ', or at least at some site not very far distant from Lo-yang" (Brough 1961, 525). The inscription was originally misinterpreted as Hebrew written in Palmyrene Aramaic script, but in 1961 it was correctly indentified as Kharoṣṭhī by W.B. Henning and published in the same year by John Brough (ibid., 517–518; CKI no. 193). The surviving fragments[3] preserve only part of the dating formula (unfortunately with the year missing), parts of the standard dedicatory formulae (... *caduradiśa ṣaghami* ... *ṣarvaṣa puyae bhavatu*, "... to the community

[1] The seemingly degenerate character of the Kharoṣṭhī in the Harwan tiles was taken by Paul (1986, 43–44) as indicative of a relatively late date for them, as late as the second half of fifth century or even later: "a determining factor for quite a late date of the script in our site, is the non-observance of the basic rule of Kharoṣṭhī [i.e., writing from right to left] against all conventions ... Such a complete reversal in the established system of the script ... would be unthinkable in a period when Kharoṣṭhī was flourishing." This may be true, but it does not affect the issue in question, which is the use of Kharoṣṭhī as a special, technical notational system, not the date of the artifacts. In any case, Bandey (1992, 15) disputes Paul's late dating of the Harwan and other inscribed tiles on the basis of the irregular disposition of the numerical figures: "This criteria [sic] should not ... make these tiles of later date."

[2] It is interesting in this connection that there is at least one example of a converse pattern. This is in the aforementioned (§0) biscript inscription of the Pārata king Dattayola, where (as noted in Falk 2020–2021, 135–137) the number 6 of the *tithi*-date in the Kharoṣṭhī version is noted with the Brāhmī unitary character for *6* instead of the normal Kharoṣṭhī sequence *4-1-1*. Evidently numerical or quasi-numerical characters (as in the case of the Bharhut and Kanispur Arapacana letters) were particularly prone to being used outside of their original or usual domain.

[3] Better images of the inscription than those published by Brough are now available in Kim 2023, 299-300 (figures 16.2, 16.3).

of the four directions ... May it be for the honor of all [beings]"), and the beginning of the main part of the inscription, reading *iyo vahara*, "this vihara." Although the purport of the inscription cannot be directly determined from these fragmentary remains, the curvature of the stones suggests that it was originally written around the edge of a well, and therefore that the inscription probably recorded the dedication of the well; for a dedicatory well inscription in Kharoṣṭhī on a similarly curved stone, datable to the second century CE, see Falk 2009, 33 (no. 5) and plates 3.2–3.4.[1]

This inscription is written in more or less normal Indian Kharoṣṭhī and Gāndhārī (though with a few anomalous peculiarities, such as *caduradiśa* instead of the usual *cadurdiśa*), and is probably datable to about the second century CE on paleographic and stylistic criteria (cf. Brough 1961, 527). It may also be assumed, in view of the form and weight of the stones, that the inscription was actually written in China, "far remote from any other examples of this script known in modern times" (Brough 1961, 523), rather than having been brought from India or elsewhere. Despite the rarity of Kharoṣṭhī in China—though it is no longer unique, as explained in the following section—its occurrence there is readily explained by the well-attested presence of foreign Buddhists, presumably including Gandharans and/or Iranians familiar with Kharoṣṭhī script, in Luoyang, the capital of the Later Han dynasty (ibid., 526–527).

3.2 Chang'an

In 1991, Lin Meicun 林梅村 published a Kharoṣṭhī inscription on the rear of the base of a gilt bronze statue of a seated Buddha, which was reportedly "found at a metal recycling plant in the northern suburbs of Sian [= Xi'an]."[2] The exact original findspot of the statue is uncertain (Kim 2011, 7 n. 6), but it was evidently somewhere in the district of modern Xi'an, the ancient Chang'an. The image is described and illustrated in Watt et al. 2004, 91 and 134, and in great detail in Rhie 1999 and 2002.[3]

The inscription is somewhat crudely written and thus difficult to read, so that interpretations differ. The text presented in CKI no. 170, *[lẏiva] sapana ha tasuca maregaputre kaṣ̄aka paḏima puj̄aya bhava[t]u*, represents the reading by Stefan Baums,

---

[1] The opening of the main part of the text of the Luoyang inscription, following the date, with *iyo vahara* ... (presumably = Skt. *ayaṃ vihāraḥ*) is not a typical beginning for a well dedication inscription, as shown by the many examples collected in Falk 2009 in which the date is typically followed either by the phrase "[This] well was excavated [by] ...]" (e.g., *khade kupe* in the Ara inscription, CKI no. 158), or by the name(s) of the donor(s) (e.g., *anaṃdaputreṇa saṃghamitreṇa kue karite*, "[This] well was caused to be made by Saṅghamitra, son of Ānanda," in the Paja inscription, CKI no. 56). But Falk does cite two examples of well inscriptions in which the location is given at the beginning; for example, the Peshawar Museum well inscription (CKI no. 61) has after the date *khuda[ci]ami ... kue khanavide ... viharami*. Thus there is every reason to believe that Brough's interpretation of the inscription as recording the dedication of a well is correct.

[2] Rhie 2002, part 2, figs. 21a–d, caption.

[3] Rhie 1999, 340–341; Rhi 2002, pt. 1, 325–334 and pt. 2, figs. 22a–d.

with several variant opinions including those of the original editor Lin noted in the footnotes. The prior part of the text evidently contains personal names, no doubt of the donor and his relatives and/or associates. But these, as is so often the case, are difficult to read and interpret, although at least one, *marega*, is familiar from other Kharoṣṭhī inscriptions (Lin 1991, 122). The last three words, *paḏima puȷaya bhava[t]u* (= Skt. *pratimā pujayai bhavatu*), "... the image; may it be for the honor," is an abridged variant of the standard conclusion to Kharoṣṭhī donative inscriptions (as in the Luoyang inscription discussed above). The omission of the designation of the honorees, presumably the usual "all beings" (*sarvasatvana* or the like), is probably due to lack of space and no doubt meant to be understood by the reader.

Minku Kim has recently pointed out (2023, 301) that in recent years the Chang'an Buddha has been featured in many exhibitions in China and elsewhere, and "has taken a consummate spot symbolizing an ancient analogue of how modern Chinese society conceives of the silk routes." Kim tentatively proposes to translate the entire inscription as "Lýiva, moneyed *tasuca*, son of Marega [causes to establish this image]. Let the established image be for the homage [of him]!" (p. 305). This attempt is however by no means free of uncertainties, and a complete understanding of the inscription still eludes us.

Despite some uncertainties about the details of its interpretation, the Chang'an inscription, like the one from Luoyang, is essentially a normal Kharoṣṭhī inscription which must have been recorded by members of a Gāndhārī-speaking immigrant Buddhist community of northwestern Indians and/or Central Asians. The image and its accompanying inscription have generally been dated to the later fourth century CE on stylistic grounds.[1] The script and language of the inscription are not particularly distinctive chronologically, but there is nothing about them that would rule out such a relatively late date. If this late dating is correct, this would be one of the latest Kharoṣṭhī inscriptions known, considerably later than the Luoyang inscription.

Although the discoveries of two Kharoṣṭhī inscriptions in China were regarded as great surprises when they first appeared, in retrospect they are not so strange in light of the abundant attestation of Gāndhārī-speaking/Kharoṣṭhī-writing Indians and Central Asian Buddhists in northern China during the early centuries of the Common Era. Indeed, perhaps the only surprise is more such inscriptions have not (yet?) been found. As remarked by Kim (2011, 8, n. 8), "just as in the case of Luoyang's Kharosthī-using monastery, there might be several more Buddhist communities of this nature outside of Luoyang and beyond." So it would not be too surprising if more such inscriptions are someday found in China; perhaps, as was the case with the Luoyang inscription for many years, they are already laying unnoticed in collections.

[1] Lin 1991, 124, 129; Rhie 2002, 333; Watt et al. 2004, 134.

4 Kharoṣṭhī across the Oceans

4.1 Hoq Cave, Socotra

The island of Socotra, part of modern Yemen, is located just east of the horn of Africa and south of the Arabian peninsula, and thus was a natural stopping point for mariners traveling between India and Africa or Arabia. This role is richly testified by the nearly two hundred short Indian-language inscriptions dating from around the second to the early fifth centuries CE which were found in the cave complex of Hoq on the northeast coast of the island, together with a handful of inscriptions in other languages (South Arabian, Axumite, Greek, and Palmyrene Aramaic). The Indic inscriptions, expertly presented in Strauch 2012a, are short graffiti mostly recording the names of sailors who entered the cave, which was apparently considered a sacred shrine, as pilgrims. A few of the inscriptions mention places of origin of the visitors, namely Bharukaccha (modern Broach) and Hastakavapra (modern Hathab), both in coastal Gujarat, a natural starting point for a sea journey to Africa. Of the nearly two hundred Indian texts, all but one are written in Brāhmī script and Sanskrit language (or some vernacular approximation thereof). The exception, no. 16:13 (Strauch 2012a, 205–206; shown here in fig. 11), is in Kharoṣṭhī script and Gāndhārī language, reading either *upalisa*, "Of Upāli," or, less likely, *upalasa*, "Of Upala" (Skt. *Utpala*).

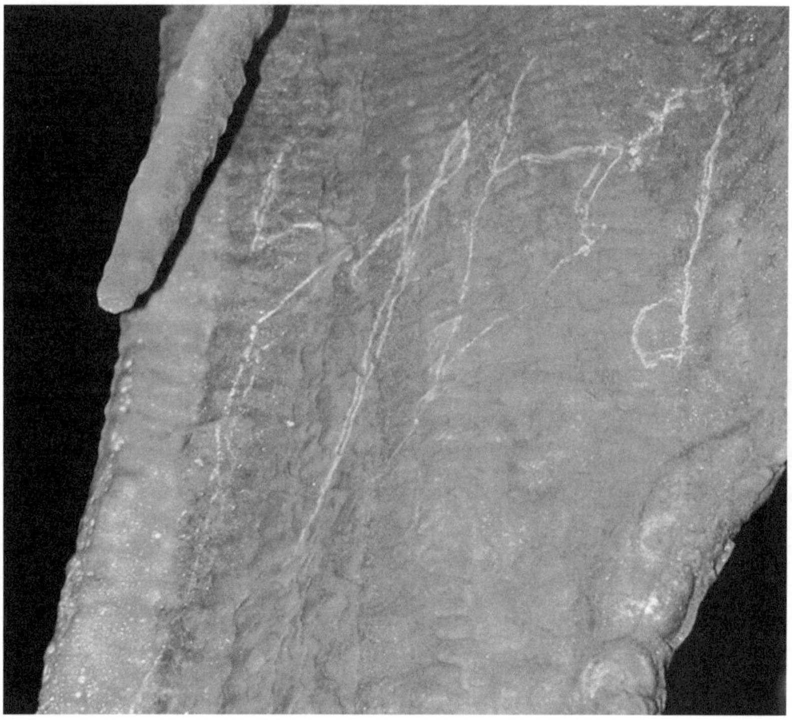

Figure 11: Kharoṣṭhī inscription from the Hoq cave, Socotra
Photograph courtesy of Ingo Strauch

As noted by Strauch (p. 206), the probable reading Upāli would suggest that the writer was a Buddhist, presumably a native of the Kharoṣṭhī-writing area in the northwest who had joined a maritime expedition from Gujarat. Thus the situation at Socotra is superficially comparable to that of Chunar (§1.4.1) in that it involves a single Kharoṣṭhī inscription in the midst of a large complex of other types of inscriptions. But at Chunar there are multiple uncertainties about the historical context of the surrounding materials, and thus serious doubt as to whether the single anomalous inscription is actually Kharoṣṭhī. In the case of the Hoq inscription, however, the context is clearly and abundantly established, so that its status as a genuine specimen of Kharoṣṭhī is beyond question. It thus constitutes the westernmost specimen of Kharoṣṭhī by far, some two thousand kilometers from the west coast of India. The reason for its presence there has also been convincingly explained by Strauch, so that the Hoq inscription is clearly a stray outlier and not in any sense indicative of the spread of the script to the west.[1]

4.2 Southeast Asia

The situation with regard to some alleged instances of Kharoṣṭhī inscriptions on portable objects found in maritime Southeast Asia is less clear. For example, the inscription on a sealing from U Thong in central Thailand, now in the Lopburi Museum, was interpreted by B.N. Mukherjee (1991, 86) as a mixture of Kharoṣṭhī and Brāhmī reading *Ḍhata'ava*, "the holder of (or adherent to) speed."[2] But as we have already seen (§1.4.3), this alleged hybrid script is a fantasy. The inscription on the seal is rude and illegible, probably merely pseudo-writing.

In Mukherjee 1990a, the author discussed a seal matrix from Oc-èo (An Giang Province, Vietnam) which has a clear legend in Brāhmī reading *apramādaṃ* ("Attention!"), as read by G. Coedès cited in Malleret 1960, 333. But Mukherjee claimed that there was also a second, previously unnoticed inscription below it in mixed Kharoṣṭhī-Brāhmī (including also an Aramaic *shin*!), which he read (pp. 100–101) as *Apumidaranaša* or *Aḍamiharan(a)š*, "King (or Lord) ... of the Artamihir (family)." The image accompanying Mukherjee's article is too unclear to make any determination, but in the original image in Malleret 1962, pl. LXI, no. 652 it is clear that there is nothing below the Brāhmī inscription but four apparently random straight lines in vertical or horizontal direction.

---

[1] A few inscriptions in south Indian Brāhmī or Tamil Brāhmī have been found further west, in Egypt (Salomon 1991, 1994), and recently a Sanskrit inscription in Brāhmī of the third century CE (not yet published) has been discovered at Berenike. But no specimen of Kharoṣṭhī has been found in Egypt, and it is unlikely—but not impossible—that Kharoṣṭhī was ever present among Indian traders in Egypt.

[2] The same image of the seal is shown in Ray 1996, 45 with the caption "Unbaked clay sealing with Kharoshthi legend," but is not further commented on in the accompanying text.

Another alleged instance of a Kharoṣṭhī inscription is on a small potsherd from the site of Sembiran on the north coast of Bali which was found together with numerous other uninscribed potsherds that were evidently of Indian origin. [1] Ardika and Bellwood report (1991, 225) that "At first the script was believed to be Brahmi ... However, according to Prof. B.N. Mukherjee of Calcutta University (pers. comm.), the script is Kharoshthi, although no definite translation is possible owing to the fragmentary nature of the inscription." The remnants of the characters scratched into the surface, as far as they are discernible in the accompanying figure 4 (reproduced here as fig. 12), seem to comprise three or four characters.

Figure 12: Kharoṣṭhī (?) inscription on a potsherd from Sembiran, Bali
From Ardika and Bellwood 1991, 225, fig. 4

The first relatively clear character (reading from the right) has a fair resemblance to Kharoṣṭhī *ta*, or possibly rather *ra*. The second looks like a *śra*, and the last, incomplete letter might be part of a *ṭh* (or the similar *ṭ́h*). None of these possibilities add up to any obvious name or other readings, but the sequence *śraṭh.* could conceivably be a defective writing for *śreṭha*, one of the several Gāndhārī equivalents of Sanskrit *śreṣṭha* or *śreṣṭhin*, "merchant." This word and its several variants are frequently found in Kharoṣṭhī inscriptions and documents as a proper name, for instance in a well dedication inscription of one *seṭha* (*seṭhasa danamukhe*; Falk 2009, 34) or as a professional designation "merchant, guildsman," as in *aghrasreṭhi-* "prominent merchant" in the Gāndhārī (London) Anavataptagāthā (Salomon 2008a, 211, 237). The presence of Indian guild merchants is well-attested epigraphically in Southeast Asia generally (Perret 2012, 22) and in Bali specifically (ibid., p. 23; Ardika 2013, 21–22), albeit from much later periods. It is also apparent on archaeological grounds that Sembiran was a harbor for international trade during the period of use of Kharoṣṭhī script.

Nevertheless, the argument for the Sembiran shard recording the presence of a Kharoṣṭhī-writing Indian merchant is slim at best, as both the suggested reading and the identification as Kharoṣṭhī are highly uncertain. Also suspicious is the circumstance that the Sembiran sherd was the sole inscribed sherd found in a site with hundreds or even thousands of Indian potsherds (Ardika and Bellwood 1991, 223). In conclusion, the evidence for the use of Kharoṣṭhī script in Southeast Asia is slim indeed, with only one very questionable specimen.

[1] Ardika and Bellwood 1991, 225–226; Ardika 2013, 24.

5 Kharoṣṭhī in Europe?

Harry Falk has recently proposed (in Falk, Miglbauer, and Pfahl 2023, 202–208) to identify the inscription on the ivory handle of an engraving tool (*Grabstichel*) which was found in 1918 in excavations of a Roman imperial site in Wels, upper Austria, as a specimen of Kharoṣṭhī. The inscription (fig. 13) consists of nine characters, all in the form of arcs or angles opening to the left. Were it not for the fact that the inscription is repeated in a virtually identical sequence on two sides of the handle, one would be tempted to discuss it as a specimen of pseudo-writing, given the minimal differentiation of the characters. Friedrich Carl Andreas (cited in Falk et al. 2023, 206) described the script "eine semitische Schrift in einem aramäischen Duktus" ("a Semitic script with an Aramaic ductus") and attempted to read it in terms of an Iranian language. It is true that the script is somewhat reminiscent of some of the highly cursive Iranian derivatives of Aramaic, but it has not been convincingly identified with any of them.

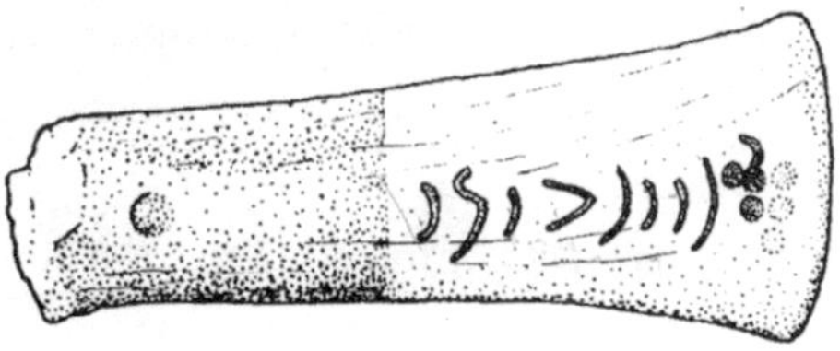

Figure 13: Alleged Kharoṣṭhī inscription on an ivory chisel handle found in Austria. From Falk et al. 2023, 204, fig. 4

Falk now proposes to understand the script as Kharoṣṭhī of the Niya or Central Asian variety and to read it as *manadadana ta daraa* (p. 206), taken as equivalent to Sanskrit *mānadadānam taṃ dārakaṃ*, and translates "Dieser Grabstichel ist ein Geschenk des Königs" ("This chisel is a gift of the king"; p. 208). However, this interpretation questionable in several respects. First of all, no other Kharoṣṭhī inscription of any remotely similar type, both in terms of content and physical form, has ever been found. Second, the interpretation depends on understanding *manada-/mānada-* as "king," equivalent to Sanskrit, allegedly "ein[en] häufig gebrauchten Titel für einen König" ("a frequently used title for a king"; p. 207), and *daraa* as equivalent to an unattested **dāraka*, "Stichel" (chisel) from the root *dar* "split, tear." As regards the script, it has some resemblance to a cursive variety of Kharoṣṭhī, but most of the nine characters only vaguely resemble Kharoṣṭhī letters; only the eighth letter is reasonably characteristic of Kharoṣṭhī *ra*. It therefore seems highly unlikely—perhaps impossible—that this is actually a specimen of Kharoṣṭhī in Europe.[1]

[1] Of course, even if this were a Kharoṣṭhī inscription, it would not provide evidence of the use of Kharoṣṭhī in Europe, as the ivory object is presumably an import from Asia.

6 Some Conclusions

The regions considered above—central and southern India, the Himalayan fringe of the Indian subcontinent, the Tarim Basin, China, and regions adjoining the Arabian and Indian Oceans—are places where economic, cultural, and/or political contacts with the northwest are well established or at least (in the case of the Indian Ocean) plausible. Thus it is *a priori* not too strange for Kharoṣṭhī to have been used in some functions or other there. But the quality of the actual attestation varies very considerably from place to place. In heartland of India, the attestation is marginal at best (e.g., Kumrahar, Bharhut) or doubtful (Chunar, Sanchi). In overseas regions, the only clear case is the Hoq site on Socotra, where a Kharoṣṭhī inscription, though unique at the site, is clearly legible and found in the context of hundreds of more or less contemporaneous Brāhmī inscriptions. But in Southeast Asia most of the claims made for Kharoṣṭhī are clearly mistaken, and there is only one case (Sembiran) which is conceivably, but not at all surely genuine.

Looking northward from the homeland of Kharoṣṭhī, however, we find a very different pattern. The script successfully established itself in the valleys to the north of Gandhara proper and was for several centuries in wide use in the Indianized oasis kingdoms around the Tarim Basin in Central Asia. The difference is not hard to explain: in spreading northward, Kharoṣṭhī infiltrated gradually into adjoining regions where no other relevant (i.e., Indic) script was in use, and it thus readily filled the vacuum. But to the south and east, Brāhmī and its several local varieties were already firmly implanted, and Kharoṣṭhī is accordingly attested there only in very limited and special situations, and never took root.

In the long run, of course, Kharoṣṭhī died out entirely. In the subcontinent it was displaced by scripts of the Brāhmī group and largely disappeared by the end of the third century CE (Salomon 2008b), and even though it had been firmly implanted in Central Asia and survived there for some two or perhaps three centuries longer, in the end it was replaced there too by Brāhmī-derived scripts. The reasons for the disappearance of Kharoṣṭhī were primarily historical and political; it thrived while the center of power in northern India was in its Gandharan homeland, especially under the Kuṣāṇa dynasty in the first to third centuries CE. But when in subsequent centuries dynasties of the Gangetic plain to the southeast become dominant, culminating in the rise of the pan-north Indian Guptas in the fourth century, the Brāhmī script group native to those regions came into universal use, and Kharoṣṭhī disappeared.

In short, Kharoṣṭhī's geography was its destiny. Contrary to what is sometimes claimed, its eventual death both in its homeland and in the other regions where it set foot was not due to any inherent defect such as the absence of vowel length distinction and lack of a full repertoire of consonantal conjuncts, which supposedly made it inadequate to represent Sanskrit. Actually, we have specimens of Sanskrit quite adequately written in Kharoṣṭhī (Salomon 1998b, 133–135; Salomon 2007 [2012], 185), mostly in Central Asia but occasionally even in Indian inscriptions. It is also clear from Kharoṣṭhī inscriptions and manuscripts of the later period, that is, from about the mid-second century CE, the Gāndhārī language was being gradually assimilated to Sanskrit, and new graphic devices such as characters for conjunct consonants peculiar to Sanskrit were readily developed as they were needed (Salomon 2001, 244–246).

Given the typically flexible relationship between language and script in India (where, for example, Sanskrit may be respresented by any of the major regional scripts), there is no objective reason why Kharoṣṭhī could not have become the main vehicle for Sanskrit, had the winds of history blown in different directions. Here I must respectfully disagree with Ingo Strauch, who thinks that "The gradual displacement of Kharoṣṭhī was ... the direct result of the gradual sanskritization of its cultural environment," so that it was eventually replaced by "a new script [i.e., Brāhmī] which was much better adapted to Sanskrit phonology and in this regard much superior to Kharoṣṭhī" (2012b, 163). For history teaches us that scripts, like languages, do not succeed or fail because of their inherent strengths and weaknesses. Any script can be adopted or adapted to write any language, and it is the vagaries of geography, history, and culture rather than the internal characteristics of the scripts that determine which ones survive and spread and which wither and die.[1] Kharoṣṭhī, for better or for worse, was destined to fall into the latter category. *Pace* Strauch, Brāhmī did not predominate because it was "better adapted" to Sanskrit; it predominated because of political developments that had nothing to with its inherent characteristics. After the decline of the Kuṣāṇa empire, Kharoṣṭhī had no political sponsor, as it were, and it gradually withered away and disappeared entirely, only to be rediscovered many centuries later.

Abbreviation

CKI — Corpus of Kharoṣṭhī Inscriptions (= *Catalog of Gāndhārī Texts: Inscriptions*, in Baums and Glass ongoing).

References

Ardika — 2013 — I. Wayan Ardika. "Sembiran: an Early Harbour in Bali." In: John N. Miksic and Goh Geoc Yian, eds., *Ancient Harbours in Southeast Asia: The archaeology of early harbours and evidence of inter-regional trade*, 21–27. Bangkok: SEAMO SPAFA Regional Centre for Archaeology and Fine Arts.

Ardika and Bellwood
1991 — I. Wayan Ardika and Peter Bellwood. "Sembiran: the beginnings of Indian contact with Bali." *Antiquity* 65, no. 247: 221–232.

[1] For example, it is only because of the power of the Roman empire and the consequent spread of Christianity that the Roman alphabet is used to write English, despite being phonetically quite poorly suited to it.

Bandey 1992 Aijaz A. Bandey. *Early Terracotta Art of Kashmir.* Srinagar: Centre of Central Asian Studies, University of Kashmir, Srinagar.

Baums and Glass
ongoing Stefan Baums and Andrew Glass. *Catalog of Gāndhārī Texts.* http://gandhari.org/catalog/.

Bhan 1986 J.L. Bhan. "Tile, a Vital Link." In: Ghulam Mohd. Buth, ed., *Central Asia and Western Himalaya: A Forgotten Link*, 43–50. Jodhpur: Scientific Publishers.

Bonmann et al.
2023 Svenja Bonmann, Jakob Halfmann, Natalie Korobzow, and Bobomullo Bobomulloev. "A Partial Decipherment of the Unknown Kushan Script." *Transactions of the Philological Society* 121: 293–329.

Bopearachchi and Rahman
1995 Osmund Bopearachchi and Aman ur Rahman. *Pre-Kushana Coins in Pakistan.* Karachi: Iftikhar Rasul, IRM Associates.

Brough 1961 John Brough. "A Kharoṣṭhī Inscription from China." *Bulletin of the School of Oriental and African Studies* 24: 517–530. Reprinted in: Minoru Hara and J.C. Wright, eds., *John Brough: Collected Papers*, 203–216. London: School of Oriental and African Studies, University of London, 1996.

1962 *The Gāndhārī Dharmapada*, London Oriental Series 7. London: Oxford University Press.

Bruneau 2010 Laurianne Bruneau. *Le Ladakh (État de Jammu et Cachemire, Inde) de l'Âge du Bronze à l'introduction du Bouddhisme: une étude de l'art rupestre*, 4 vols. PhD Thesis, Université Paris I Panthéon-Sorbonne.

2011 "Influence of the Indian Cultural Area in Ladakh in the 1st Millennium AD: The Rock Inscription Evidence." *Purātattva: Bulletin of the Indian Archaeological Society* 41: 179–190.

Bühler 1894–1895 G[eorg] Bühler. "The Siddapura Edicts of Asoka." *Epigraphia Indica* 3: 134–142.

Cunningham
1879 Alexander Cunningham. *The Stûpa of Bharhut: A Buddhist Monument Ornamented with Numerous Sculptures Illustrative of Buddhist Legend and History in the Third Century B.C.* London: Wm. H. Allen and Co.

1892 A[lexander] Cunningham. *Mahâbodhi or the Great Buddhist Temple under the Bodhi Tree at Buddha-Gaya.* London: W.H. Allen & Co.

Dragoni et al.
2020 Federico Dragoni, Niels Schoubben, and Michaël Peyrot. "The Formal Kharoṣṭhī script from the Northern Tarim Basin in Northwest China may write an Iranian language." *Acta Orientalia Hungarica* 73: 335–373.

Falk 1991–1992 Harry Falk. "Spurious Aśokan Records." *Annals of the Bhandarkar Oriental Research Institute* 72–73: 263–273.

2006 *Aśokan Sites and Artefacts: A Sourcebook with Bibliography*, Monographien zur Indischen Archäologie, Kunst und Philologie 18. Mainz am Rhein: Philipp von Zabern.

2008 "Another Reliquary Vase from Wardak and Consecrating Fire Rites in Gandhara." In: Claudine Bautze-Picron, ed., *Religion and Art. New Issues in Indian Iconography and Iconology. Proceedings of the 18th Conference of the European Association of South Asian Archaeologists, London, 2005*, vol. 1, 63–80. London: The British Association for South Asian Studies, The British Academy.

2009 "The Pious Donation of Wells in Gandhara." In: Gerd J.R. Mevissen and Arundhati Banerji, eds., *Prajñādhara: Essays on Asian Art, History, Epigraphy and Culture in Honour of Gouriswar Bhattacharya*, 23–36. New Delhi: Kaveri Books.

2013 "The Alleged Kharoṣṭhī-Brāhmī Mixed Script and Some New Seals from Bengal." *Zeitschrift für Indologie und Südasienstudien* 30: 105–124.

2020–2021 "Revision of Kharoṣṭhī Inscriptions in the Light of New Material." *Bulletin of the Asia Institute* 30: 113–142.

2023 "Wema Takhtu, the Graveyard Near Almosi, and the End of an 'Unknown' Script." *Annual Report of the International Research Institute for Advanced Buddhology* 26: 253–264.

Falk, Miglbauer, and Pfahl

2023 Harry Falk, Renata Miglbauer, and Stefan F. Pfahl. "Die westlichste Kharoṣṭhī-Inschrift: Ein Elfenbeigriff aus Wels. Mit einem Anhang zu fernöstlichen Funden des 1. bis 2. Jahrhunderts n. Chr. im Römischen Reich." *Archaeologisches Korrespondenzblatt* 53: 199–228.

Fisher 1982 Robert E. Fisher. "The Enigma of Harwan." *Art International* 25/9–10 (November–December): 33–44.

1989 "The Enigma of Harwan." In: Pratapaditya Pal, ed., *Art and Architecture of Ancient Kashmir*. Bombay: Marg Publications, 1–16. [Text mostly identical to Fisher 1982, but with different illustrations.]

Fussman 1974 Gérard Fussman. "Documents épigraphiques kouchans." *Bulletin de l'École française d'Extrême-Orient* 61: 1–66.

2011 *Monuments bouddhiques de Termez / Termez Buddhist Monuments, I : Catalogue des inscriptions sur poteries*, Publications de l'institut de civilisation indienne, fascicule 79.1–2. Paris: Édition-Diffusion de Boccard.

Ghosh 1989 A. Ghosh. *An Encyclopaedia of Indian Archaeology. Volume 1: Subjects*. New Delhi: Munshiram Manoharlal.

Goswami 1948 Kunja Gobinda Goswami. *Excavations at Bangarh (1938–41)*. Calcutta: Calcutta University.

Harrison and Hartmann

2014 Paul Harrison and Jens-Uwe Hartmann, eds. *From Birch-Bark to Digital Data: Recent Advances in Buddhist Manuscript Research. Papers Presented at the Conference Indic Buddhist Manuscripts: The State of the Field. Stanford, June 15–19 2009*. Österreichische Akademie der Wissenschaften, philosophisch-historische Klasse, Denkschriften 460 / Beiträge zur Kultur- und Geistesgeschichte Asiens 80. Vienna: Österreichische Akademie der Wissenschaften.

Hassnain 1973 F.M. Hassnain. *Buddhist Kashmir*. New Delhi: Light & Life Publishers.

Hultzsch 1925 Eugen Hultzsch. *Inscriptions of Aśoka. New Edition*. Corpus Inscriptionum Indicarum, vol. I. Oxford: Clarendon Press for the Government of India.

Jayaswal 1998 Vidula Jayaswal. *From Stone Quarry to Sculpturing Workshop: A Report on the Archaeological Investigations around Chunar, Varanasi, and Sarnath*. Delhi: Agam Kala Prakashan.

Kak 1933 Ram Chandra Kak. *Ancient Monuments of Kashmir*. London: The India Society.

Kim 2011 Minku Kim. *The Genesis of Image Worship: Epigraphic Evidence for Early Buddhist Art in China*. PhD dissertation, University of California, Los Angeles.

2023 "The Xi'an Kharoṣṭhī Inscription. A New Translation." In: Anke Hein, Rowan Flad, and Brian K. Miller, eds., *Ritual and Economy in East Asia: Archaeological Perspectives*, 297–312. Los Angeles: Cotsen Institute of Archaeology Press.

Koizumi 2008 Koizumi Yoshihide. "Die Funde von Zar Dheri." In: Christian Luczanits, ed., *Gandhara: das Buddhistische Erbe Pakistans. Legenden, Klöster und Paradies*, 308–313. Bonn: Kunst- und Ausstellungshalle der Bundesrepublic Deutschland/Mainz: Philipp von Zabern.

Konow 1926 Sten Konow. "The Inscription on the so-called Bodh-Gaya Plaque." *Journal of the Bihar and Orissa Research Society* 12: 179–182.

1929 Sten Konow. *Kharoshṭhī Inscriptions with the Exception of Those of Aśoka*, Corpus Inscriptionum Indicarum, vol. II, part I. Calcutta: Government of India, Central Publication Branch.

Lin 1991 Lin, Meicun 林梅村. "A Kharoṣṭhī Inscription from Chang'an." In: Li Zheng 李錚 and Jiang Zhongxin 蔣忠新, eds., *Ji Xianlin jiaoshou bashi huadan jinian lunwenji* 季羨林教授八十華誕紀念論文集, 119–131. Nanchang 南昌: Jiangxi renmin chubanshe 江西人民出版社.

Lone 2018–2019 Lone, Abdul Rashid. "The Archaeology of Early Historic DaradKut (Huthmura), Anantnag District, Kashmir." *Central India Journal of Historical and Archaeological Research* 7/8, no. 26/27: 1–7.

Malandra 1988 Geri H. Malandra. "The Mahabodhi Temple." *Marg* 40: 9–28.

Malleret 1960 Louis Malleret. *L'archéologie du delta du Mékong*, vol. 2: *La Civilisation Matérielle d'Oc-èo*. Publications de l'École française d'Extrême-orient 43.2. Paris: École française d'Extrême-orient.

1962 *L'archéologie du delta du Mékong*, vol. 3: *La culture de Fou-nan*. Publications de l'École française d'Extrême-orient 43.3. Paris: École française d'Extrême-orient.

Mani 1999–2000 B.R. Mani. "Excavations at Kanispur : 1998–99 (District Baramulla, Kashmir)." *Prāgdhārā: Journal of the U.P. State Archaeological Department* 10: 1–21.

2000 "Excavation News from Kashmir." *Circle of Inner Asian Art Newsletter* 12 (December): 10–13.

2008 "Concentric Circles: Kushan Structural Riddle in Kashmir." *Purātattva: Bulletin of the Indian Archaeological Society* 38: 217–221.

Marshall 1922 J.R. Marshall. "The Monuments of Ancient India." In: E.J. Rapson, ed., *The Cambridge History of India*, vol. I: *Ancient India*, 555–588. Cambridge: Cambridge University Press.

Mukherjee

1984–1985 B.N. Mukherjee. "Inscribed 'Mahabodhi Temple' Plaque from Kumrahar." *Journal of the Indian Society of Oriental Art* 14: 43–46.

1990a "A Kharoshṭī-Brāhmī Seal-matrix from Oc-Eo (S.E. Asia)." *Journal of the Asiatic Society* 32: 99–102. (Originally published in *Monthly Bulletin of the Asiatic Society* 19, June 1990: 1–4.)

1990b *Kharoshṭī and Kharoshṭī Brāhmī Inscriptions in West Bengal (India)*, Indian Museum Bulletin 25. Calcutta: Indian Museum.

1990c "Kharoshṭī Inscriptions from Chunar (U.P.)." *Journal of the Asiatic Society* 32: 103–108. (Originally published in *Monthly Bulletin of the Asiatic Society* 19, September 1990: 1–9.)

1990–1991 "Some Recently Noticed Kharoshṭī Epigraphs in U.P." *Prāgdhārā: Journal of the U.P. State Archaeological Organisation* 1: 53–57.

1991 "A Sealing in the Lopburi Museum (Thailand)." *Journal of the Asiatic Society* 33: 85–86. (Originally published in *Monthly Bulletin of the Asiatic Society* 19, December 1990: 1–2.)

Myer 1958 Prudence R. Myer. "The Great Temple at Bodh-Gayā." *The Art Bulletin* 40: 277–298.

Pant and Jayaswal

1990 P.C. Pant and Vidula Jayaswal. "Chunar Stone Quarries: Raw Material for Sculpture and Architecture." *Marg* 42: 59–61.

1990–1991 "Ancient Stone Quarries of Chunar : An Appraisal." *Prāgdhārā: Journal of the U.P. State Archaeological Organisation* 1: 49–52.

Paul 1986 Pran Gopal Paul. *Early Sculpture of Kashmir (Before the Middle of the Eighth Century A.D.): An Approach to the Art History and Epigraphy of the Jhelum Valley and its Peripheral Regions*. Leiden: Sneldruk Enschede.

Perret 2012 Daniel Perret. "Réflexions sur la présence sud-asiatique dans le monde insulindien (XIe–XIVe siècle)." *Aséanie. Sciences humains en Asia du Sud-Est* 29 (June): 11–27.

Poster 1986 Amy G. Poster. *From Indian Earth: 4,000 Years of Terracotta Art*. Brooklyn NY: The Brooklyn Museum.

Rahman and Falk

2011 Aman ur Rahman and Harry Falk. *Seals, Sealings and Tokens from Gandhāra*, Monographien zur Indischen Archäologie, Kunst und Philologie 21. Wiesbaden: Reichert.

Ray 1996 Himanshu Prabha Ray. "Early Trans-oceanic Contacts Between South and Southeast Asia." In: Nanda Chutiwongs et al., *Ancient Trades and Cultural Contacts in Southeast Asia*, 43–56. Bangkok: The Office of the National Culture Commission.

Rhie 1999 Marylin Rhie. *Early Buddhist Art of China and Central Asia*, vol 1: *Later Han, Three Kingdoms and Western Chin in China and Bactria to Shan-shan in Central Asia*, Handbuch der Orientalistik/Handbook of Oriental Studies, section 4, vol. 12. Leiden: Brill.

2002 *Early Buddhist Art of China and Central Asia*, vol. 2, parts 1–2: *The Eastern Chin and Sixteen Kingdoms Period in China and Tumshuk, Kucha and Karashahr in Central Asia*, Handbuch der Orientalistik/Handbook of Oriental Studies, section 4, vol. 12/2. Leiden: Brill.

Salomon 1983 Richard Salomon. "Undeciphered Scripts of South Asia." In: Jayanta Chakrabarty and D.C. Bhattacharyya, eds., *Aspects of Indian Art and Culture: S.K. Saraswati Commemoration Volume*, 201–212. Calcutta: Ṛddhi-India.

1991 "Epigraphic Remains of Indian Traders in Egypt." *Journal of the American Oriental Society* 111: 731–736.

1994 "Epigraphic Remains of Indian Traders in Egypt." *International Journal of Dravidian Linguistics* 23: 7–16.

1996 [1998] "Five Kharoṣṭhī Inscriptions." *Bulletin of the Asia Institute* n.s. 10: 233–246.

1998a *Indian Epigraphy. A Guide to the Study of Inscriptions in Sanskrit, Prakrit, and the Other Indo-Aryan Languages*. South Asia Research Series. New York: Oxford University Press.

1998b "Kharoṣṭhī Manuscript Fragments in the Pelliot Collection, Bibliothèque Nationale de France." *Bulletin d'études indiennes* 16: 123–160.

2001 "'Gāndhārī Hybrid Sanskrit': New Sources for the Study of the Sanskritization of Buddhist Literature." *Indo-Iranian Journal* 44: 241–252.

2006 "Kharoṣṭhī Syllables Used as Location Markers in Gandhāran *Stūpa* Architecture." In: Pierfrancesco Callieri, ed., *Architetti, Capomastri, Artigiani: L'organizzazione dei cantieri e della produzione artistica nell'asia ellenistica. Studi offerti a Domenico Faccenna nel suo ottantesimo compleanno*, Serie Orientale Rome 100, 181–224. Rome: Istituto Italiano per l'Africa e l'Oriente.

2007 [2012] "Gāndhārī in the Worlds of India, Iran, and Central Asia." *Bulletin of the Asia Institute* n.s. 21: 179–192.

2008a *Two Gāndhārī Manuscripts of the Songs of Lake Anavatapta (Anavatapta-gāthā): British Library Kharoṣṭhī Fragment 1 and Senior Scroll 14*. Gandhāran Buddhist Texts 5. Seattle: University of Washington Press.

2008b "Whatever Happened to Kharoṣṭhī? The Fate of a Forgotten Indic Script." In: John Baines, John Bennet, and Stephen Houston, eds., *The Disappearance of Writing Systems: Perspectives on Literacy and Communication*, 139–155. London: Equinox Publishing.

2014 "Gāndhārī Manuscripts in the British Library, Schøyen, and Other Collections." In: Harrison and Hartmann 2014, 1–17.

Salomon, Devers, and Ldawa
2020–2021 Richard Salomon, Quentin Devers, and Tashi Ldawa. "Kharoṣṭhī and Brāhmī Inscriptions from Ladakh." *Bulletin of the Asia Institute* 30: 93–111 + pls. 4–16.

Shah 2012–2013 Mohamad Ajmal Shah. "Early Historic Archaeology in Kashmir: An Appraisal of the Kushan Period." *Bulletin of the Deccan College Post-Graduate and Research Institute* 72/3: 213–224.

Skinner 2017 Michael Skinner. *Marks of Empire: Extracting a Narrative from the Corpus of Kuṣāṇa Inscriptions*. PhD dissertation, University of Washington.

Smith 1916 Vincent Smith. "The Bodh Gaya Plaque." *Journal of the Bihar and Orissa Research Society* 2: 375–378.

Spooner 1915 D.B. Spooner. "The Bodh Gaya Plaque." *Journal of the Bihar and Orissa Research Society* 1: 1–4.

	1916	"Reply to Mr. Vincent Smith's Note." *Journal of the Bihar and Orissa Research Society* 2: 378–383.
Strauch	2012a	Ingo Strauch. *Foreign Sailors on Socotra: The Inscriptions and Drawings from the Cave Hoq*, Vergleichende Studien zu Antike und Orient 3. Bremen: Hempen Verlag.
	2012b	"The Character of the Indian Kharoṣṭhī Script and the 'Sanskrit Revolution': A Writing System between Identity and Assimilation." In: Alex de Voogt and Joachim Friedrich Quack, eds., *The Idea of Writing: Writing across Borders*, 131–168. Leiden: Brill.
Watt et al.	2004	James C.Y. Watt with An Jiayao, Angela F. Howard, Boris I. Marshak, Su Bai, and Zhao Feng. *China: Dawn of a Golden Age, 200–750 AD*. New York: Metropolitan Museum of Art/New Haven: Yale University Press.

Further Texts in the Old Khotanese "Metre C"*

Nicholas SIMS-WILLIAMS

Abstract: The Old Khotanese *Book of Zambasta* is a long poem on Mahāyāna Buddhism. It is composed in three metres, of which I have given a new analysis in a recent book. As a pendant to that book, this article contains four additional passages in "metre C." One forms part of the *Saṃghāṭa-sūtra*, while another is a previously unidentified fragment of the *Book of Zambasta*. The other two cannot be definitely identified, but both have been suspected of being sections of the *Book of Zambasta* which are missing in the principal manuscript. All four texts are presented with a detailed metrical analysis and accompanied by an English translation and a brief commentary.

Keywords: Khotanese language, Old Khotanese poetry, metre, *Book of Zambasta*, *Saṃghāṭa-sūtra*.

As was discovered long ago by Ernst Leumann, Old Khotanese poetry makes use of three metres, which he named—conveniently if not elegantly—A, B and C. In a recent book,[1] I have presented a new analysis of all three metres as they are attested in the most substantial Khotanese poem which has come down to us, the *Book of Zambasta* (henceforth: "Z").

Of the three metres, C is by far the least common. In Z, it is characteristically used to indicate a poem spoken by a new speaker, e.g. the "verses" (*ggāha*) emitted by the gong in the "Tale of Bhadra," Z2.105–122, the verses (again *ggāha*) or "melody" (*nvāgä*) addressed to the earth in Z24.208–214, or the verses (*āljsanyau* "songs") addressed by the gods to the Buddha in Z24.244–248. Sometimes, however, metre C seems to be used merely for the sake of variety, without any more specific motivation, e.g. Z12.90–125. It can also be used for whole chapters, as in Z3, 7, 8, 17+18,[2] 20 and 21. Metre C is attested in about 450 verses of Z and hardly anywhere else. As I hope to have shown elsewhere, a group of fragments belonging to the National Library of China and containing some verses in metre C are almost certainly remnants of folios 221–222 of the principal manuscript ("Z_1") of the *Book of Zambasta*,[3] while a pair of fragments in the British Library help in restoring the damaged text of Z18.28–39 (Text 1 below). Some other manuscripts with verses in metre C (Texts 2 and 3 below) have also been suspected of containing parts of the *Book of Zambasta* which are missing in the main manuscript. So far as I am aware, the only poem in this metre which certainly does not belong to the

Nicholas SIMS-WILLIAMS, SOAS University of London.

* I am glad to have the opportunity to dedicate this paper to the memory of Professor Duan Qing, the founder of Khotanese studies in China and an unforgettable friend.

[1] Sims-Williams 2022.

[2] Z17 and 18 are now recognized as a single chapter, see Maggi and Martini 2014.

[3] Sims-Williams 2023b.

Book of Zambasta is a sequence of verses in the *Saṃghāṭa-sūtra* (Text 4 below), where metre C is used to translate both *śloka*s and verses in *triṣṭubh/jagatī* metre.

In my study of the metre of the *Book of Zambasta* I attempted to show that the metrical system was essentially moraic (as Ernst Leumann and others have also argued) but that it is also characterized by a compulsory ictus on specific syllables in the cadences. In the case of metre C, each hemistich attests one of the following patterns of morae:[1]

7 || 5 + 5/6 ||
9 || 3 + 5/6 ||
10 || 2 + 5/6 ||

Thus, each hemistich begins with a cadence of (usually) 7, (rarely) 9 or (even more rarely) 10 morae, followed by a non-cadential segment which, with the preceding cadence, makes up a total of 12 morae. The hemistich ends with a cadence of (usually) 5 or (somewhat less often) 6 morae. These cadences, including the position of the ictus, are more precisely described in the following table:

5-mora cadence	μμμ|'LL
6-mora cadence	μμμμ'LL, μμμμ'H
7-mora cadence	μμμμ'HL, μμμμ'LLL
9-mora cadence, Type 1	μμμμ'Hμμμ, μμμμ'LLμμμ
10-mora cadence, Type 1	μμμμ'HHμμ, μμμμ'LLHμμ
9-mora cadence, Type 2	μμμ'HLμμμ, μμμ'LLLμμμ
10-mora cadence, Type 2	μμμ'HLHμμ, μμμ'LLLHμμ

My book on the metre of the *Book of Zambasta* was deliberately restricted to a single text. The purpose of this paper is to assemble the remaining texts in metre C in order to complete the dossier and to ascertain whether they display any metrical features not found in Z. The commentaries to the texts below therefore concentrate on metrical issues.

[1] Note the following conventions: H = heavy syllable, L = light syllable, <u>L</u> = heavy syllable with metrical lightening, μ = one mora (i.e. one light syllable or half a heavy syllable), ' = metrical ictus, || = end of cadence, | = compulsory word (or compound) boundary, + = compulsory syllable boundary, ! = metrical irregularity. The hyphen in a formula such as -LHL (below, text 3, verse 107ab) marks a segment which is short by one mora (see Sims-Williams 2022, 66–7). Wherever possible, the length of the ambiguous letters *e* and *o* is marked: *ĕ ŏ*, *ē ō*. Superscript letters, as in *biśūn*^{i}*ya*, represent sounds pronounced but not written; subscript letters, as in *ha*$_{r}$*biśśä*, represent letters which are disregarded in the scansion. The grave accent, e.g. *ì*, *aù*, marks a long vowel or diphthong which is metrically shortened. Underlining as in *<u>bra</u>manä* draws attention to an assumed metrical lightening which is not obvious from other markings such as *ì*, *aù* or subscript letters.

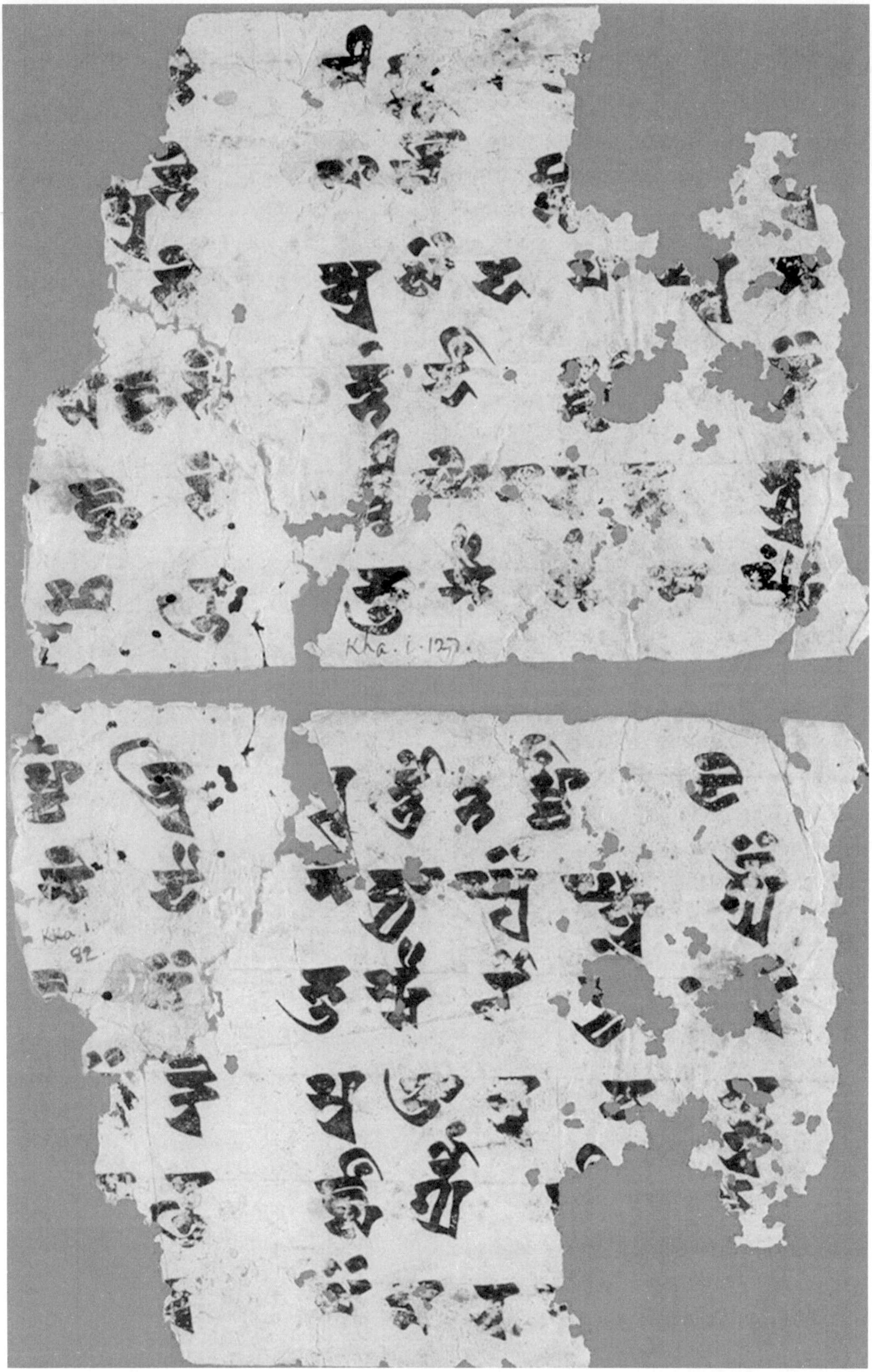

Fig. 1–2. IOL Khot 18/9 + 22/3, recto (= Z18.28–33) and verso (= Z18.34–39)
Montage by the author. Photos published by permission of the British Library.

Text 1

The very small fragment Kha. i.82a6 = IOL Khot 18/9 was identified by Skjærvø (2002, 202) as a variant to Z18.31–37, containing words from the end of the b *pāda*s (the second column of the manuscript). Recently I discovered that this fragment can be joined to the larger fragment Kha. i.127a1 = IOL Khot 22/3, first edited by Bailey (1963, 146), re-edited and translated by Skjærvø (2002: 213); see the montage in figs. 1–2. In addition to a few more *akṣara*s from the end of the second column, this larger fragment contains a substantial part of the third column, providing most of the text of the c *pāda*s of Z18.28–39,[1] which is missing in the principal manuscript Z_1. So far as can be seen, the text of these *pāda*s, consisting of 7-mora cadences, is metrically regular.

For the sake of simplicity, I give below a composite text of the relevant verses. The *akṣara*s from the end of *pāda* b and beginning of *pāda* c which are wholly or partially preserved both in the British Library fragments and in Z_1 are indicated with bold type.

Text

18.28 aṃgguli'mālä dvī byūrru hvaṃdä 'jsa**tě** biśśu rŏ *va* [. . .] [. . . . .]
HLL'HL || HHL HL|'LL || LLLL['μμμ ||] [. . . . .]

18.29 padumä narī ggaukāli ṣṣamani '**tsutě** harbiśśu '[×] × [. . . . .]
LLLLH! || HHL LLL|'LL || HLL'HL || [. . . . .]

18.30 cu ttärä pha'rāka värūlai śśāya 'jsa**tě** asäda ha'yūna [. . . . .]
LLLL'HL || LHH HL|'LL || LLLL'HL || [. . . . .]

18.31 sīśě pra'caina pharu ra$_{k}$ṣaysa rā**mä** '**jsatě** **tta**ṃdī 'śśūrä [. . . . .]
HLL'HL || LLLLL HL|'LL || HH|'HL || [. . . . .]

18.32 anārra 'rrundě bārggavī rāmä '**jsatě** . śśiyě vara 'ttatvu [. . . . .]
LHL'HL || HLH HL|'LL || LLLL'HL || [. . . . .]

18.33 asädä ha'yūnä ggārīva yīndä '**pha**ru ku nai ně 'balysä [. . . . .]
LLLL'HL || HHL HL|'LL || LHL'HL || [. . . . .]

18.34 ttäna ṣṣu pa'śśāñi asädi h^{u}vě' nai jsa '**hvañu** sūttrŏ tta 'hvīdě [. . . . .]
LLLL'HL || LLLLL HL|'LL || HLL'HL || [. . . . .]

18.35[2] nä ttärä pu'vā'ñi haryāsä śśaysdä **ně** '**dai** n*ě* vyāghrrä 'ysurgyä [. . . . .]
LLLL'HL || HHL HLL'H || LHL'HL || [. . . . .]

18.36[3] [× .]ai 'ttäna hvandi paḍā ṣṭānä ha'j[u]vä ku ṣṣai rrŏ 'byau*rě* [. . . . .]
[H]H|'LLHL || LH HLL'LL || LHL'HL || [. . . . .]

[1] In reality, Z17.61–72, cf. n. 3 above.

[2] On the unusual writing of *ysurgyä* see Skjærvø (2002, 213, note a).

[3] The partially preserved second *akṣara* of the verse was read as *pai* "foot" by Emmerick, following Vorob'ëv-Desjatovskij and Vorob'ëva-Desjatovskaja (1965, 120), but the consonant is far from clear on the latters' facsimile (p. 106). — There is a point as space-filler between the two *akṣara*s of *byaure*.

18.37	ku narŏ ma'raṇä hīśtä	haspäsāñu '**käḍĕ** .	puñānu 'vaska	[. . . . .]
	LLLL'LLHL ‖	HL HL|'LL ‖	LHL'HL ‖	[. . . . .]
18.38[1]	ku nĕ nĕ yĕ 'jsīḍä .	saṃtsēra jsātĕ bu'**ḍarŏ**	jsīrgyau '*j*[s]īḍ*ĕ*	[. . . . .]
	LLLL'HL ‖	HHL HLL'LL ‖	HH|'HL ‖	[. . . . .]
18.39	kyĕ ātma 'saittä	suhä surai nätya 'hä**ra**	*ṣ*ä maraṇ[u . . .]	[. . . . .]
	LHL'HL ‖	LLLH HL|'LL ‖	LLL[L'μμμ ‖]	[. . . . .]

Translation

[28]Aṅgulimāla slew twenty thousand men, also all ... [29]Gokāla the ascetic went to the Paduma hell, the whole ... [30]Since Virūḍhaka slew so many Śākyas, evil friends ... [31]On account of Sītā, Rāma slew many *rākṣasa*s, so great a hero ... [32]Rāma, the descendant of Bhṛgu, slew blameless kings. Of one there in truth ... [33]An evil friend causes many troubles, since the Buddha does not ... him. [34]Therefore an evil man is to be abandoned. One should not speak with him. In the *sūtra* is is said thus ... [35]Neither a black snake, nor fire, nor an angry tiger is so greatly to be feared (as) ... [36]... therefore in the first place a wise man, while ... still exist, [37]should greatly exert himself, until death comes, for the sake of merits ... [38]If one has not deceived (people, one) proceeds further in *saṃsāra*; (if one) has deceived (them) with deceptions ... [39]He to whom the self appears (to exist), (as well as) pure pleasure (and) permanent things—he ... death ...

Notes

28–36. In Z_1 these verses are contained in folio 293. For a commentary on this folio, including useful notes on the personal names and stories referred to, see Emmerick 1966, 166–167.

36–37. The genitive *hvandi ... haj[u]vä* "a wise man" in verse 36 may be the agent of the necessitative participle *haspäsāñu* "must strive" in the following verse.

Text 2

The fragment IOL Khot 141/6, which has been edited by Bailey (1963, 55) and by Skjærvø (2002, 323–324), contains the right-hand end of a *pothi* leaf with the ends of six verses on each side. These verses are numbered 55–66, which may be abbreviated for 155–166, 255–266, etc. As pointed out by M. Leumann (1967, 374), this fragment very likely belongs to a manuscript of the *Book of Zambasta*. In addition to features of language and phraseology and the four-column layout characteristic of Z, he cited the use of the rare metre C (not A as inadvertently stated by Skjærvø) as a support for this identification. On the supposition that the fragment might belong to Z_1, Leumann suggested a possible

[1] In place of *buḍaro*, IOL Khot 22/3 has the variant spelling with final *-u*.

identification as folio 325 containing Z21.155–166.[1] That cannot be correct, as it is now known that Z21 ends at verse 117;[2] moreover, the paper and writing of IOL Khot 141/6 do not seem to me to be those of Z_1. However, if this fragment belongs to a different manuscript of Z, it might fit as Z21.55–66. Z21 is wholly in metre C and the content of this fragment does not appear incompatible with that of the known folios of this chapter. So far as the metre is concerned, the fragmentary text contains no surprises.

Text and translation

55 [. . . . .] [. . . . .] [. . hä]ra 'dyārĕ trāmĕ ttätĕ ṣkaugyĕ 'biśśĕ 55
[. . . . .] [. . . . .] μμLL'HL ‖ HLLL HL|'LL ‖
... things appear, such (are) all these *saṃskāra*s.

56 [. . . . .] [. . . . .] [. . .] pha'rāka biśūn^{i}ya saindä 'hära 56
[. . . . .] [. . . . .] μμμL'HL ‖ LHLL HL|'LL ‖
... many ..., things of all kinds appear (to exist).

57 [. . . . .] [. . . . .] [. . .] ja'ḍīna uaiṣṣa ttätä saindä 'biśśä 57
[. . . . .] [. . . . .] μμμL'HL ‖ HLLL HL|'LL ‖
... through folly, all these appear awake.

58 [. . . . .] [. . . . .] [. . . .] '*sai*ndä cu ttätä hära sai[n]d[ä 'ja]ḍi 58
[. . . . .] [. . . . .] μμμμ'HL ‖ LLLLL HL|'LL ‖
... they appear ..., because to the fool these things appear (to exist).

59 [. . . . .] [. . . . .] [. . . a]$_{ys}$'mūna ṣkaugyĕ kṣiṃjī*nd*ä 'jaḍa 59
[. . . . .] [. . . . .] μμμL'HL ‖ HLH HL|'LL ‖
... in (their) mind fools long for the *saṃskāra*s.

60 [. . . . .] [. . . . .] [. . . . . . .]sä cu ṣei' saṃtsārä [. .]
[. . . . .] [. . . . .] μμμμ'μμL ‖ LHH HL|'LL ‖
... for this (is) *saṃsāra* ...

61 [. . . . .] [. . . . .] [. . . . . . .]ṣṭä ttätä ha$_{r}$biśśä *d*[ain]d[ä . .]
[. . . . .] [. . . . .] μμμμ'HL ‖ LLLLL HL|'LL ‖
... they see all these ...

62 [. . . . .] [. . . . .] [. . . . . . .]rĕ khŏ yĕ hūñä daiyä 'hära
[. . . . .] [. . . . .] μμμμ'μμL ‖ LLHL HL|'LL ‖
... as one sees things in a dream.

[1] Leumann refers to the chapter as "E22," using the older numbering of his father's edition (Leumann 1933–1936).

[2] See Maggi 1998, 287–288; 2017, 275.

63 [. . . . .] [. . . . .] [. . . .] '*byō*rĕ samu khŏ ātāśä '[bi]śśä 63

[. . . . .] [. . . . .] μμμμ'HL ‖ LLLH HL|'LL ‖

... they [do not] exist, they (are) all just like space.

64 [. . . . .] [. . . . .] [. . .] u$_{ys}$'nōra ṣkaugyĕ hīvyārĕ 'biśśĕ 64

[. . . . .] [. . . . .] μμμL̲'HL ‖ HLH HL|'LL ‖

... beings appropriate all the *saṃskāra*s.

65 [. . . . .] [. . . . .] [. . .] u'tāra hvāha ggaṃbhīra 'natä 65

[. . . . .] [. . . . .] μμμL'HL ‖ HLH HL|'LL ‖

... exalted, wide, profound, deep.

66 [. . . . .] [. . . . .] [ttä]na mamä 'vaysña uhŏ jsa āspāta 'samu 66

[. . . . .] [. . . . .] LLLL'HL ‖ LLLH HL|'LL ‖

... therefore my refuge now (is) only with you.

Notes

55. As noted by Leumann 1967, 374, the same cadence is found in Z20.71b: *ṣkauṃgyĕ biśśĕ.*

57. Cf. Z4.82: "Just as whatever things appear in a dream do not really exist, so whatever (things) appear (while one is) awake (*cu saindä tta ju uaiṣṣa*) do not really exist."

59. Leumann, *loc. cit.*, refers to the identical cadence in Z3.135b: *kṣiṃ]jindä gyaḍa*.

61. *d[ain]d[ä]* "they see." Thus Skjærvø (marking the initial *d* as uncertain). Bailey has *[sain]d[ä]* "they appear."

63. If Skjærvø's tentative reading *byōre* is correct, it is probably 3 pl. pres. middle of *byau-* "to exist." Bailey read *]vyāre*, marking the *v* as uncertain. This could be restored to *hì]$_{v}$yārĕ* L̲HL, cf. *hīvyārĕ* "they appropriate" in the next verse.

Text 3

This folio from the St Petersburg collection, now apparently lost, was published by Leumann (1920, 168–169). It bears 10 verses, five on each side, which are numbered 6–15. Since the folio itself is numbered 12, Leumann plausibly deduced that they are in fact 106–115, which, if the recto side of folio 1 was left blank so that the text began on the verso with verses 1–5, would be the expected contents of folio 12. More speculative, but not impossible, is Leumann's further suggestion that the manuscript in question may have been a copy of the *Book of Zambasta* and that these verses are Z1.106–115, which are missing in Z$_1$. Leumann's strange idea that the text is a hymn to Avalokiteśvara is clearly incorrect, however. This was based solely on verses 106–107, which refer to a brahmin making a vow in the presence of the Buddha Ratnagarbha, as Avalokiteśvara is also said to have done. In reality, it seems to me that the text is addressed to the Buddha Śākyamuni and alludes to a series of *jātaka*s, several of which are identifiable (see commentary below); see however M. Leumann in Leumann 1933–1936, xvi, n. 1.

So far as the metre is concerned, the most notable feature of this text is the comparatively large proportion of hemistichs which begin with a 9-mora cadence (rather than the more common 7-mora cadence): 110a, 111a, 111c, 113a, 113c, 114a and 115c. All of these belong to what I have called "type 1," with ictus on the 5th mora, except for *ku aysu 'h^{u}vē' mä vaysña* LLL'LLLHL in 111a, which belongs to "type 2," with ictus on the 4th mora. Although some of these 9-mora cadences are quite rare, they are all attested at least a couple of times in Z, as can be seen from the tables in Sims-Williams 2022, 56 and 58.

Text

106ab	samudrra'rēṇä	baña ratnaggarbh*ä* hva'tai	
	LHL'HL ‖	LLHL	HLL'H ‖
106cd	anāhu 'ysēru	ysamaśśa$_{n}$dau ttrāyŏ 'aysu	
	LHL'HL ‖	LL̲H	HL|'LL ‖
107ab	thu vätī 'ttāma	samudrrarēṇä b̲r̲a̲'manä	
	LLH|'HL ‖	-LHL	HLL̲'LL ‖
107cd	nĕ <nĕ> ju yĕ 'hōstä	tvī ha$_{n}$darä mulśdä 'karä 7	
	LLLL'HL ‖	HL̲LL	HL|'LL ‖
108ab	ka tä rrŏ ṣa 'īyä	ttĕrä päta'jsa mulysdä 'pharu	
	LLLL'HL ‖	LLLLL	HL|'LL ‖
108cd	ananta 'mästä	vaysña muhŏ vīrä 'yanu	
	LHL'HL ‖	HLLL	HL|'LL ‖
109ab	murāsä 'ṣṭānä	b$_{ä}^{ei}$' näta'tīru yä'ḍei	
	LHL'HL ‖	-HLL	HLL'H ‖
109cd	mamä rrŏ va'hāña	klaiśìnō mästu 'bätu' 9	
	LLLL'HL ‖	HL̲H	HL|'LL ‖
110ab	*ku*nālä 'murä ṣṭānä	khŏ vā kṛṅgä vä'tī	
	LHL'LLHL ‖	LH	HLL'H ‖
110cd	bustī 'śśaṭhṭhĕ	yōlĕ cu strì*y$_{y}$au jsa* 'bi*śśä* 10	
	HH|'HL ‖	HLLL̲	HL|'LL ‖
111ab	ku aysu 'h^{u}vĕ' mä vaysña	khŏ hanä kārrä 'mutä	
	LLL'LLLHL ‖	LLL	HL|'LL ‖
111cd	ttĕrä ṇä *nĕ 'b^{u}vĕ balysa	ttäna *mä mulśdu 'yanu* 11	
	LLLL'LLHL ‖	LLL	HL|'LL ‖
112ab	bāysä pa'dīyä	varä ttataraṣṣīkä vä'tī	
	HLL'HL ‖	LLLLL	HLL'H ‖

112cd buys^{u}vai 'ttīyä bāljsak$_{y}$au bāysu 'biśśu 2
LLH|'HL || HLH HL|'LL ||

113ab klaiśa bu'ysō karma kyě muhŏ vaysña 'biśśu
HLL'HHL || LLL HL|'LL ||

113cd ttrāmu pa'dīyāndä khŏ dei huṣkě 'ttarrě 13
HLL'HHL || LH HL|'LL ||

114ab ātī 'vālāhä laṃggi kīntha 'aśśä
HH|'HHL || HL HL|'LL ||

114cd ttrāmu tä 'sāṭä ātaśśätä bēndŏ 'biśśä 4
HLL'HL || HLLL HL|'LL ||

115ab khŏ *pīrä* 'bēndŏ vanda pharu pūra 'jaḍa
LHL'HL || HLLL HL|'LL ||

115cd nvāstai 'sūlīya rakṣays$_{y}$ō jsa 'biśśu 15
HH|'HHL || HL HL|'LL ||

Translation

[106](As) Samudrareṇu you said in the presence of Ratnagarbha: "May I save the protectorless, pitiable earth!" [107]You were then the brahmin Samudrareṇu. No-one else at all was capable of your mercifulness. [108]If you have so much mercy, mighty, very much, endless, great, take (pity) on me now. [109]As a peacock you made poison do the work of nectar: for me too make the great poison of the *kleśa*s disappear. [110]As a *kuṇāla* bird you were (watchful) as a cock, you perceived the wiles, all the deceits which (are) from women. [111]Since I am a man now, as if blind, deaf (and) dumb, I do not perceive them, Buddha: therefore have pity on me. [112]The forest was aflame. There you were a young partridge. Then you extinguished with your wings the whole (burning) forest. [113]Extinguish the *kleśa*s, the *karma*s which have now burned me up completely just as fire (burns) dry grass. [114]You came (as) the horse Vālāha to the city of Laṅkā. The whole caravan *clung to you [115]just as many foolish little children to (their) father. You delivered the merchants completely from the demons.

Notes

106. As noted by Leumann, the earth is described as *anāha- ysēra-* "protectorless, pitiable" several times in Z24.

107. The lightening of the first syllable of *bramanä* (for *braṃmanä* "brahmin") in the 6-mora cadence *samudrra]rēṇä bra'manä* HLL'LL was already noted by Leumann. It is a further example of what I have named the "*handara*-effect."[1]

[1] See Sims-Williams 2022, 46–47, especially 47 n. 92.

The insertion of a second *nĕ* to give a regular 7-mora cadence *nĕ nĕ ju yĕ 'hōstä* LLLL'HL was proposed by Leumann. The sequence *nĕ nĕ ju* or *nä nä ju* "absolutely not" occurs nine times at the beginning of a hemistich in Z.

109. Cf. Z5.11ab: *ttäna ggumērāñätĕ klaiśīnō bei' nei'tayīru ṇä yīndä* "By it he removes the poison of *kleśa*. It does the work of nectar for them."[1]

110. The *Kuṇāla-jātaka* is no. 536 in Cowell 1905, 219–245.

For the lightening of the first syllable of *strìy$_{y}$au jsa* $\underline{\text{L}}$'HL (for *strīyyau jsa* H'HL) cf. *strìyai* in Z13.76b (Sims-Williams 2022, 70 n. 141). Leumann scans this hemistich differently, i.e. (in my notation):

bustī śśa$_{ṭh}$ṭhĕ yōlĕ	cu strīy$_{y}$au jsa biśśä
HH|$\underline{\text{L}}$LHL ||	LH HL|LL ||

In my view, this cannot be correct, as *śśaṭhṭhĕ* must be stressed on the first syllable like all words of the shape HL. The case of *$\underline{\textit{śśa}}$'ṭh$_{y}$au* $\underline{\text{L}}$H in Z19.77c, to which Leumann refers, is not comparable, since the heavy ending *-yau* attracts the stress, allowing the lightening of the preceding syllable.

111. I have taken *ṇä* as the 3 pl. enclitic pronoun *nä* "them" (referring back to the "wiles" and "deceits" of verse 110), which is sometimes written with *ṇ* after *r*,[2] and emended Leumann's *te* to **ne* "not."[3] Leumann understood "I do not comprehend you," taking *ṇä* as the negative and *te* as the 2nd person singular enclitic pronoun "you." This is grammatically dubious and makes little sense in the context.

112. On this verse see Emmerick 1985, 42–43 (with a further improvement regarding the meaning of *bāljsaka-* "wing" in Emmerick and Skjærvø 1997, 114). The "Partridge-*jātaka*" is no. 40 in the Khotanese *Jātakastava* (Dresden 1955, 439–440, see also *ibid.*, 451, for further references).

113. Cf. Z20.64d: *samu khŏ dai huṣkä ttarrĕ* (already noted by Leumann).

114–115. The *Valāhassa-jātaka* is no. 196 in Cowell 1895, 89–91. Cf. also *jātaka* no. 4 in Dresden 1955, 425, 447.

From the context, *ātaśśätä* in 114d seems to be an otherwise unknown verbal form (3rd person singular masculine intransitive perfect) with a meaning such as "climbed" or "clung." According to the Pali version, some of the merchants climbed on the horse and some held on to his tail. As Mauro Maggi has kindly suggested to me, *ātaśś-* "to *cling"

[1] Thus translated in Emmerick 1968, 99. I take the opportunity to note that this hemistich is wrongly scanned in Sims-Williams 2022, 154. As correctly stated *ibid.*, 63 (§5.1), *bei' neì'ta[yīru* appears where a 2-mora segment is expected and should be scanned HLL! rather than -HLL.

[2] See Leumann 1933–1936, 449a.

[3] Since the manuscript has not been located, it is impossible to distinguish between the two possibilities of a scribal error or a misreading.

could be cognate with Khotanese *kaśś-* "to be attached," *kaṣṭa-* and *pacaṣṭa-* "attached," Ossetic Digoron *nixäsun*, Iron *nyxäsyn* "to cling" (cf. Bailey 1979, 57a). Leumann read *ātaśśätä* as two words, apparently taking *āta* as "they came" and *śśätä* as an otherwise unattested word for "first."

On *sūlīya* "merchants" in 115c see Bailey 1981, 16; 1982, 23; Emmerick and Skjærvø 1987, 148–149.

Text 4

A series of verses in metre C is preserved in §99 of the *Saṃghāṭa-sūtra*, where they are presented as continuous text, without any division into verse lines. The parallel passage in the underlying Sanskrit text can now be consulted in the edition by von Hinüber (2021, 39–42; cf. also the English summary of the contents, *ibid.*, lxvii–lxviii). For a diplomatic edition of the Khotanese see Canevascini 1993, 44–47 (text and translation), 139–140 (notes). The text of this passage is based on the three manuscripts in which it is partially preserved:

(i) A folio from Canevascini's "MS 6" (IOL Khot 170/1+2+3, formerly Khot(IO) 159.1+2+3) contains verses 1–13. Transcribed in Bailey 1956, 139–140; Canevascini 1993, 182–183; Skjærvø 2002, 380.

(ii) Three consecutive folios of Canevascini's "MS 17" (SI P/53, folios 8, 13 and 9) contain parts of this sequence of verses, beginning with the last words of verse 12. Transcribed in Canevascini 1993, 228–229 and (with translation) in Emmerick and Vorob'ëva-Desjatovskaja 1995, 53–55, 60–61 and 55.

(iii) The last line of a fragment belonging to Canevascini's "MS 24" (IOL Khot 141/3 + 174/3, formerly H. 144 NS 55 + H. 151.17) contains part of the first verse, with some insignificant spelling variants. These fragments are transcribed in Leumann 1920, 22 (part only, also reproduced in Konow 1932, 88–89); Bailey 1963, 76 and 106 (the two fragments, not yet joined); Canevascini 1993, 250; and Skjærvø 2002, 323.

The numbering of the Khotanese verses in the text below has been supplied by me as a matter of convenience. In the manuscripts a few verse numbers are attested but, as noted by Canevascini (1993, xvii), these do not appear to refer to the Khotanese but to the underlying Sanskrit verses. The Khotanese verses which I have numbered 1–13 correspond to verses 20–27 in von Hinüber's Sanskrit text, which are *śloka*s. To judge from the numbers 4, 5, 6 at the end of Khotanese verses 8, 10 and 12, one may assume that these *śloka*s were numbered 1–7 in the Sanskrit text used by the translator. The following Sanskrit verses 28–34 are in *triṣṭubh/jagatī* metre.[1] The Khotanese text of this passage is very poorly preserved, so that the precise number of verses and their metrical

[1] See von Hinüber 2021, lxviii.

structure are not clear. However, the Khotanese verse corresponding to the last Sanskrit verse of this sequence is numbered "5," which is probably an abbreviation for "15."[1] On the basis that the number of Khotanese verses in the preceding (*śloka*) sequence is approximately twice that of the underlying Sanskrit verses, I have hypothetically given the verse in question the number 30. The following Khotanese verses 31–40 correspond to a further Sanskrit sequence of *śloka*s, verses 35–41 in von Hinüber's edition. At this point the use of metre C comes to an end. The continuation (not included below) consists of an introductory line of prose and four verses in metre B translating the last two Sanskrit verses 42–43.

The metre of the Khotanese verses is briefly discussed by Canevascini (1993, xvii). He follows Emmerick's metrical theory,[2] which allows a great deal of variation in the number of morae, especially at the beginning of the hemistichs. Consequently, his restorations of the lacunae, which he describes as "tentative," sometimes need to be adjusted in order to give a text which conforms to the metrical system as I understand it. The text which is actually preserved is generally unproblematic from a metrical point of view. A notable feature is the frequency of 7-mora cadences which end with 'LLL instead of the more usual 'HL: 1c *hä'mätä mä*, 3a *'biśě ju*, 5c *'b*^{u}*vě sě*, 7c *'nar*^{i}*ya*, 10a *a*$_{ta}$*nanta'nar*^{i}*ya*,[3] 33a *'hvaḍä śtä*, 33c/35a *'hvatě sě*, 35c *'jsataì mä*,[4] 37c *'asädu*. Such endings are quite regular in principle (see Table 2 in Sims-Williams 2022, 50) and several of them are in fact attested in the *Book of Zambasta*. However, it is remarkable that this short text contains almost as many examples as are found in all the 450 verses of Z in metre C.

Text

1ab	*y*[ä]ḍ[ai]mä 'mästa	dīrě käḍäyāně 'aysu	
	LHL'HL ‖	HLLL	HL|'LL ‖
1cd	trāmä hä'mätä mä	khŏ ju sūta dīra 'stuna .	
	HLL'LLL ‖	LLHL	HL|'LL ‖
2ab	ně ně mara 'ysāně	ysamaśa$_{ṃ}$d^{i}ya lōvä 'baña .	
	LLLL'HL ‖	LLLLL	HL|'LL ‖
2cd	ně ně *mam*ä 'ysānä	paralōva aśtä 'karä .	
	LLLL'HL ‖	LLHL	HL|'LL ‖
3ab	haṃdarŏ 'biśě ju	mamä ysānä niśtä 'karä	
	HLL'LLL ‖	LLHL	HL|'LL ‖

[1] Thus Emmerick and Vorob'ëva-Desjatovskaja 1995, 60; already considered as a possibility in Canevascini 1993, 139, note 15.

[2] A brief statement of this can be found in Emmerick 1968, 437–440.

[3] The last two could alternatively be read with final 'HL (*'narya*, *a*$_{ta}$*nanta'narya*).

[4] Not quite certain, see commentary below.

3cd nätca *ju ně* 'aysu gvārna {. . .} lōvä 'baña .
LLLL'LLHL ‖ μμμ HL|'LL ‖

4ab *ysu*rrě jsa yä'ḍaimä dīra käḍä*g*[ā]ně 'aysu
LLLL'HL ‖ HLLL HL|'LL ‖

4cd ttäna hā 'tsīmä na*r*[^{i}y]ŏ *k*äḍě dī*rŏ* 'gatŏ .
LLH|'HL ‖ LLLLL HL|'LL ‖

5ab haṃ*da*ru 'ysa[ṃ]thu mamä mästa bēra 'dukha .
HLL'HL ‖ LLHL HL|'LL ‖

5cd ku ttu n[ě] ju $_{\text{ně}}$ 'b^{u}vě sě ku *ṣṭa mä* hīsāñu 'mam[ä] .
LLLL'LLL ‖ LLLH HL|'LL ‖

6ab gyastai 'py$_{\text{ū}}$v[ā] *'r*[ě] tt^{i}y[ě] hva'[n]d[ä] cv*ī* ttä 'dukha .
HH|'HL ‖ LLHL HL|'LL ‖

6cd brēmätä 'bēttě käḍägāně *käḍ*äna 'hamu
HLL'HL ‖ LLHL LLL|'LL ‖

7ab {. . .} a'nāspētä ṣä paralōvä 'mamä
μμμL'HHL ‖ LLL HL|'LL ‖

7cd ōṣku mä 'nar^{i}ya mamä tsuñō bēra 'dukha .
HLL'LLL ‖ LLLH HL|'LL ‖

8ab jaḍä h^{u}vě['] 'tsīmä dukha barämä vīyaně 'stŏrě
LLLL'HL ‖ LLLLL HLL'LL ‖

8cd ka ně mä ně 'ttrāyākä ně ārūvŏ 'karä 4
LLLL'HHL ‖ LH HL|'LL ‖

9ab dukhäna pa'śīmä puṣŏ jì*v*[ätu ttäna cu 'a]ysu
LLLL'HL ‖ LLLLL LLL|'LL ‖

9cd mātaru 'p$_{\text{ät}}$aru jsatä mä ttätä mä paṃjsa 'yäḍa
HLL'LLLLL ‖ LLL HL|'LL ‖

10ab a$_{\text{ta}}$nanta'nar^{i}ya . garu vīrä sarbìmä 'samu
LHL'LLL ‖ LLHL HLL'LL ‖

10cd ně [jī'vätu paś]*ī*mä cu *rrŏ* [va] jūmä 'aysu 5
LH'LLLHL ‖ LLL HL|'LL ‖

11ab gyastai 'hvāñīndä ma jaḍa *h^{u}v*[ě]' tta 'yana .
HH|'HHL ‖ LLL LLL|'LL ‖

11cd ma ně yanu 'pātcu dīru käḍägā*nä* ['. .]
LLLL'HL ‖ HLLL HL|'LL ‖

12ab [. . . . .] [. . . . .] karma 'h^{u}vě' .
μμμμ'μμμ ‖ μμμμμ HL|'LL ‖

12cd ttausau 'pātcu *u*ysān^{i}yĕ cūḍĕ 'yana 6
HH|'HL ‖ LHLL HL|'LL ‖

13ab nar^{i}yai 'ysaṃthä kyĕ uysànō jsandĕ 'h^{u}vĕ[’]
LLH|'HL ‖ LLL̲H HL|'LL ‖

13cd pā*tc*[u . . . .] [. . . . dukhauttä hä'mätĕ]
HLμ'μμμ ‖ μμμμL HLL'LL ‖

[*fragmentary verses omitted*]

29cd [hvara cu tä] 'haurīmä u ma nĕ brēma 'dukha
LLLL'HHL ‖ LLL HL|'LL ‖

30ab kṣūna u 'ttarrna dukh$_{y}$au haṃthrītä ['. .]
HLL'HL ‖ LHH HL|'LL ‖

30cd [. . . . .] [. . . . . . .] 'puṣṣŏ 5
μμμμ'μμμ ‖ μμμμμ μμμ]|'LL ‖

31ab ttītī 'hūḍĕ tt^{i}yĕ hva’ṃḍä khāysä rä'ṣayä
HH|'HL ‖ LLHL HLL'LL ‖

31cd ysaujsä ma'nā[vä] [. . . . .]
HLL'HL ‖ [

32ab ustamu 'vātcŏ tvī dātu hvāñumä 'aysu
HLL'HL ‖ HHL HLL'LL ‖

32cd tcamnē 'jyārĕ dīra käḍä[gānĕ 'puṣṣŏ]
HH|'HL ‖ HLLL HL|'LL ‖

33ab [khā]ysä nĕ 'hvaḍä śtä cvī [rä]ṣayä hūḍĕ 'naḍĕ
HLL'LLL ‖ HLLL HL|'LL ‖

33cd räṣayī 'hvatĕ sĕ khāysu hvara [. . . . .]
LLH|'LLL ‖ HLLL μμμ'μμ ‖

34ab ttītä pa'jāṣṭĕ *d*[asta haysn]ā*t*ĕ 'śśäru
HLL'HL ‖ HLH HL|'LL ‖

34cd riṣayä nä'ta’stä tvaṃdanī vāt[c]u 'tsu[tĕ]
LLLL'HL ‖ HLH HL|'LL ‖

35ab [räṣayī] 'hvatĕ sĕ hvāña [cu tä dīru] '*y*[ä]ḍu
LLH|'LLL ‖ HLLL HL|'LL ‖

35cd mātaru 'jsataì mä hā pätaru ysurrĕ jsa ['μμ]
HLL'LLL ‖ HLLL LLL|'LL ‖

36ab [. . . .] 'bärstaimä bōdhisatv[ä] 'aysu
μμμμ'HHL ‖ HL HL|'LL ‖

36cd b^{i}ya$_{ta}$nu yä'ḍaimä balysūśtě ṣātě [m]ä 'yiḍä
LLLL'HL || HHL LLL|'LL ||

37ab [ku ttätä sa]'lāva riṣayi b[i]śśä pyūṣṭu 'yiḍě
LLLL'HL || LLLLL HL|'LL ||

37cd ttai hvatě 'asädu käḍě yi[ḍai . . . . .]
HLL'LLL || LLLH μμμ'μμ ||

38ab [dāruṇa] 'käḍägānä dīśa hāḍě 'biśu .
HLL'LLHL || HL HL|'LL ||

38cd cu thu yäḍě 'āyě ō *p*[arstě āyě 'yäḍě]
LLLL'HL || HHL HL|'LL ||

39ab [ttīyä] pu'vai'ttä ṣä naḍě udvirnai 'käḍě
HLL'HL || LLLH HH|'LL ||

39cd kāṣcě jsa 'bistä ha$_{ṃ}$dä*śt*aṃ[. . . . .]
HLL'HL || $\underline{\text{L}}$HH μμμ'μμ ||

40ab [kyau mamä 'trā]yākä hämätě vaṃña du'kh$_{y}$au
HLL'HHL || LLL HLL'H ||

40cd u vīya'n$_{y}$au jsa ku *ma*[mä ārūva . .]
LHL'HL || LLLH HL'μμ ||

Translation

"I committed great evil deeds; I have become just like a burnt bad tree-stump; [2]I do not shine at all here on the earth before people, I will have no lustre at all in the world beyond. [3]Inside the house I have no lustre at all, outside I do not {shine} at all before people. [4]Out of anger I committed evil deeds, therefore I will go into a very bad existence in hell; [5]for another birth I must bear great woes. Where—this I do not know—where am I to come?"

[6]The gods hear what that man's woes (are). He weeps, he laments continually on account of (his) sin: [7]"The world beyond will be {...} without refuge for me, always I must go to hell, must bear woes. [8]Foolish man (that I am), (when) I transmigrate I will bear woes, strong pains, if I have no protector, no refuge at all. [9]Out of sorrow I will abandon life altogether, [because] I killed (my) mother (and) father (and because) I committed these five [10]*ānantarya* (sins); I will climb up upon a mountain; at once I will [abandon life.] Why should I live any more?"

[11]The gods say to him: "Do not do so, foolish man! Do not again commit an evil deed, [12][just because you have previously committed evil] acts, man! Why do you again cause yourself scorching pain? [13](There is) birth in hell for him who kills himself, man! Again [he ... will be distressed]."

In the poorly preserved passage which follows the gods admonish the sinner; they send him to a seer (ṛṣi), *who speaks to him thus:*

[29cd]"[Eat what] I give [you] and do not bewail (your) woes; [30]afflicted by hunger and thirst, by woes, [you will become] altogether [without hope as regards the threefold existence]." [31]Then the *ṛṣi* gave that man food, tasty, delightful ... [32]"Then at the end I will tell you the Law by means of which your evil deeds will be removed [altogether]." [33](But) the man did not eat the food which the *ṛṣi* gave him. The *ṛṣi* said to him: "Eat the food ..." [34]Then he accepted (it and) [washed his hands] well. The *ṛṣi* sat down. Then (the man) went to do reverence to him. [35][The *ṛṣi*] said [to him]: "Tell (me) [what evil] was done [by you]." "I killed (my) mother and (my) father out of anger ...; [36]I destroyed [sanctuaries]; I made an obstacle to enlightenment for a Bodhisattva; this was done by me." [37][When] the *ṛṣi* had heard all [these] words he spoke thus to him: "[You have] done much evil ... [38]But confess completely the [dreadful] deeds which you may have done or [may have ordered to be done]."

[39][Then] the man is afraid, very terrified, pierced by anxiety ... [40]"[Who] will now be [my] protector from woes and pains? Where [will be] my [refuge] ...?"

Notes

3. A 3-mora segment is missing in 3d. Restore perhaps *ysānĕ* "I shine" (cf. Bailey 1979, 96b *s.v. gvāra-*).

5. There seems to be one mora too many in 5c. One should probably delete the second *nĕ*. While the sequence *nĕ nĕ ju* "absolutely not" is common in Z (see above on Text 2, verse 107), the word-order *nĕ ju nĕ* does not seem to be attested.

7. Three morae seem to be missing at the beginning of 7a.

8. The metre requires that the last word of the hemistich should consist of two light syllables. Rather than *stōrĕ* HL "strong" in 8b one should perhaps read *stŏrĕ* LL as a variant spelling or (more probably) mistake for *sturĕ* "heavy." For an alternative suggestion, see now Sims-Williams 2023a, 99.

The ending of *ārūvŏ* in 8d is probably another mistake.[1]

9. Assuming that *jīväta-* "life" was stressed on the second syllable (cf. below on verse 10), the first syllable could be lightened as indicated in the text above.

At first sight *pāda* 9c (*mātaru pätaru jsatä mä* "I killed mother [and] father") seems to be one mora overlong. I suggest reading *p*$_{\text{ät}}$*aru* LL "father" with the common suppression of *-ät-*,[2] cf. Late Khotanese *pyar-*. As an alternative one could read the word for "mother" as *mā*$_{\text{ta}}$*ru* HL "mother," again suppressing one syllable (cf. below on verse

[1] In theory one could read *ārūvō* < *ārūva* + *-u*, but, as noted by Canevascini 1993, 139, note 6, the position of *-u* "and" would be "quite unparalleled."

[2] See Sims-Williams 2022, 41–42, 68–69 with notes 136–137.

35). Either reading gives a 9-mora cadence HLL'LLLLL or perhaps HL'LLLLLL. In Z such cadences are not attested in metre C, but they are occasionally found in metre A.[1]

10. Khotanese *anantanarya-* is an adaptation of Sanskrit *ānantarya-* "(sin) bringing immediate retribution, deadly sin" (Edgerton 1953, 95–6), presumably influenced by *naria-* "hell" (Leumann 1912, 34–5). The intrusive *-ta-* is also found in *byatanu*, verse 36.[2]

The enjambment between 9d and 10a: *ttätä mä paṃjsa yäḍa* || *a*$_{ta}$*nantanar*^{i}*ya* "I committed these five *ānantarya* (sins)" is noteworthy. Even more remarkable is the division of the fixed expression *samu* || *nĕ* "no sooner" = "at once" between the two hemistichs of verse 10.

If Canevascini's restoration *samu nĕ [jīvätu paś]īmä* "at once [I will give up life]" should be correct, this would confirm that *jīväta-* "life" is stressed *jī'väta-* as suggested in Sims-Williams 2022, 68 n. 136. (Cf. above on verse 9). In Z, the 9-mora cadence (type 2) LH'LLLHL is attested twice in metre A though not in metre C.[3]

13. *naryai*, i.e. locative singular *narya* "in hell" + *-i* "for him," is the reading of MS 17, rightly preferred by Canevascini. The older MS 6 has *naryau*, a variant spelling of the alternative locative singular *naryŏ*, which is too short by one mora.

In 13b, *kyĕ uysānō* forms a 5-mora segment, indicating that one unstressed heavy syllable must be lightened. Since there is no evidence that a final long vowel can be shortened, one must read *uysà'nō* L$\underline{\text{L}}$'H, with stress as marked and shortening of the pretonic long vowel.

32. *tcamnē* HH is a Late Khotanese form of *tcamäna* or *tcamna* "by which" + the 2nd person singular enclitic pronoun *tä* or *tĕ*.[4] One could restore an older form such as *tcamäna tä* LLLL or *tcamna tä* HLL, which would scan equally well.

34. This restoration of 34b is suggested by Skjærvø *apud* Emmerick and Vorob'ëva-Desjatovskaja 1995, 60.

35. The most probable reading is *mātaru 'jsataì mä* HLL'LLL, cf. the unambiguous spelling *jsatä mä* in verse 9. A possible alternative is *mā*$_{ta}$*ru jsa'taimä* HLL'HL.

This verse is cited by Maggi (1995, 88–89) in connection with the particle *hā* "and, also."

36. For the intrusive *-ta-* of *byatanu* see on verse 10 above.

37. On the cadence *ttai hvatĕ 'asädu* HLL'LLL see Sims-Williams 2022, 88.

38. For the restoration *[dāruṇa] käḍägānä* in 38a cf. *dāruṇa käḍäyānĕ* "dreadful deeds" in the immediately following passage in metre B (Canevascini 1993, 47, §6 [20]). Similarly my reconstruction of 38cd (adapted from Canevascini's) is based on the metre

[1] See *ibid.*, Table 3 on p. 56 and Table 4 on p. 58.

[2] See Canevascini 1993, 140 n. 17.

[3] See Sims-Williams 2022, Table 4 on p. 58.

[4] Canevascini 1993, 264b.

B hemistich *cu burau̇ aysu yäḍä mä u parstēmä sě yanda* "whatever I did and (whatever) I ordered, (saying): 'Do (it)!'" (*ibid.*, §6 [19]).

39. It is not clear whether this is actually a verse, as it corresponds to a prose passage in the Sanskrit text. No explanation has yet been found for the word or sequence *haṃdäśtaṃ[.*

40. Canevascini (1993, xvii) refers to "the verses [1]–[17]," which suggests that he considers this passage, his "[18]," to be prose. However, it corresponds to a Sanskrit verse, no. 41 in von Hinüber's edition, and can without difficulty be reconstructed as verse. For the proposed restoration of *ārūvā-* "refuge" beside *trāyāka-* "protector" cf. verse 8.

* * * * *

Apart from the passages edited above and those which are known to belong to Z, the only other likely examples of metre C which I have been able to find are very small fragments in the British Library collection: (i) IOL Khot 32/1 (Skjærvø 2002, 245): *pāda* ends with final 'LL (*karä, puña, pharu, aysu*) and L'H (*paḍō*); (ii) IOL Khot 159/3 (*ibid.*, 356), *pāda* beginnings with 7-mora cadences, many LHL'HL (as is characteristic of metre C, see Sims-Williams 2022, 49–50), e.g. *padōṣṭä 'tsīn[d]ä, ku tvī pha'rā[kv̆], khŏ mēri 'pū[rä], tta tvī ha'maṃg[gv̆]*; (iii) IOL Khot 168/1 (Skjærvø 2002, 377), *pāda* beginnings with 7-mora cadences; (iv) perhaps also IOL Khot 20/19 (Skjærvø 2002, 209), verse-ends with final 'LL(?). All of these are amongst the fragments which Skjærvø tentatively assigns to Z.

References

Bailey 1956 H.W. Bailey. *Indo-Scythian Studies, being Khotanese Texts*, Volume III. Cambridge: Cambridge University Press.

1963 *Indo-Scythian Studies, being Khotanese Texts*, Volume V. Cambridge: Cambridge University Press.

1979 *Dictionary of Khotan Saka*, Cambridge: Cambridge University Press.

1981 "Indo-Iranica." *Indologia Taurinensia* 8–9: 15–18.

1982 *The Culture of the Sakas in Ancient Iranian Khotan*. Delmar, New York: Caravan Books.

Canevascini 1993 G. Canevascini. *The Khotanese Saṅghāṭasūtra: A Critical Edition*. Wiesbaden: Reichert Verlag.

Cowell 1895 E.B. Cowell, ed. *The Jātaka or Stories of the Buddha's Former Births*, Vol. 2 (translated by W. H. D. Rouse). Cambridge: Cambridge University Press.

1905 *The Jātaka or Stories of the Buddha's Former Births*, Vol. 5 (translated by H. T. Francis). Cambridge: Cambridge University Press.

Dresden 1955 M. J. Dresden. *The Jātakastava or "Praise of the Buddha's Former Births."* Philadelphia: The American Philosophical Society.

Edgerton 1953 F. Edgerton. *Buddhist Hybrid Sanskrit Grammar and Dictionary*, Volume II: *Dictionary*. New Haven: Yale University Press.

Emmerick 1966 R. E. Emmerick. "The Nine New Fragments from the *Book of Zambasta*." *Asia Major* 12/2: 148–178.

1968 *The Book of Zambasta*. London: Oxford University Press.

1985 "Khotanese *bāljse*." *Münchener Studien zur Sprachwissenschaft* 45: 39–53.

Emmerick and Skjærvø

1987 R. E. Emmerick and P. O. Skjærvø. *Studies in the Vocabulary of Khotanese*, II. Vienna: Verlag der Österreichischen Akademie der Wissenschaften.

1997 *Studies in the Vocabulary of Khotanese*, III. Vienna: Verlag der Österreichischen Akademie der Wissenschaften.

Emmerick and Vorob'ëva-Desjatovskaja

1995 R. E. Emmerick and M. I. Vorob'ëva-Desjatovskaja. *Saka Documents Text Volume III: The St. Petersburg collections*. London: School of Oriental and African Studies.

von Hinüber 2021 O. von Hinüber. *The Saṃghāṭasūtra. A Popular Devotional Buddhist Sanskrit Text, editio maior* (Supplement to the Annual Report of The International Research Institute for Advanced Buddhology at Soka University 24). Tokyo.

Konow 1932 S. Konow. *Saka Studies*. Oslo: Oslo Etnografiske Museum.

Leumann 1912 E. Leumann. *Zur nordarischen Sprache und Literatur*. Straßburg: Trübner.

1920 *Buddhistische Literatur, nordarisch und deutsch*, I: *Nebenstücke*. Leipzig: Brockhaus.

1933–1936 *Das nordarische (sakische) Lehrgedicht des Buddhismus*. Leipzig: Deutsche Morgenländische Gesellschaft.

Leumann 1967 M. Leumann. "Neue Fragmente des altkhotanischen 'Lehrgedichts'." *Zeitschrift der Deutschen Morgenländischen Gesellschaft* 117: 366–375.

Maggi 1995 M. Maggi. *The Khotanese Karmavibhaṅga*. Rome: Istituto Italiano per il Medio ed Estremo Oriente.

1998 Review of Emmerick and Vorob'ëva-Desjatovskaja 1995. *Indo-Iranian Journal* 41: 282–288.

2017 "Annotations on the *Book of Zambasta*, IV: Ronald E. Emmerick's notes." In: *Studia Philologica Iranica. Gherardo Gnoli memorial volume*, 273–291. Rome: Scienze e Lettere.

Maggi and Martini

2014 M. Maggi and G. Martini. "Annotations on the *Book of Zambasta*, III: Chapter 18 no more." *Scripta* 7: 139–158.

Sims-Williams 2022 N. Sims-Williams. *The Book of Zambasta: Metre and Stress in Old Khotanese*. Wiesbaden: Reichert Verlag.

2023a "Metrical Passages in the Khotanese *Saṃghāṭa-sūtra*." *Indo-Iranian Journal* 66: 97–126.

2023b "Two More Fragmentary Folios from the *Book of Zambasta*?" *Journal of Dunhuang and Turfan Studies* 22: 1–13.

Skjærvø 2002 P. O. Skjærvø. *Khotanese Manuscripts from Chinese Turkestan in the British Library. A Complete Catalogue with Texts and Translations*. London: British Library.

Vorob'ëv-Desjatovskij and Vorob'ëva-Desjatovskaja

1965 V. S. Vorob'ëv-Desjatovskij and M. I. Vorob'ëva-Desjatovskaja. *Skazanie o Bxadre*. Moscow: Nauka.

History Writ Backwards*

Asoka and Buddhism

Peter SKILLING

Abstract: The essay discusses the relationship between Emperor Asoka's epigraphic records and the early Indian landscape, especially contemporaneous monumental stupas. It proposes that, while imperial concern and patronage certainly inspirited Buddhism's spread, by Asoka's time the sangha was already well established across much of the Indian subcontinent. The sangha did not follow Asoka: rather, the emperor followed the sangha.

Keywords: Indian history; Asoka; Buddhism; stupas; Mauryan epigraphy

Asoka's portrait

Asoka was generous in thought and deed. He waged war, he saw the terrible suffering it brought, and he renounced it. He rejected the ideal of military and territorial conquest and instead espoused an ethos of success through moral prowess. Even the model monarch, the mythical universal emperor or *cakravartin*, had an army, but the real source of his power and authority was the Dhamma. There can be no conquest without Dhamma; there can be no success without moral principle. Over 2000 years ago, Asoka exemplified ethical standards of governance that are still suited for humankind's present predicaments. It is regrettable that so few people give them any heed.

Peter SKILLING (Bhadra Rujirathat), Chulalongkorn University.

* Throughout her long and productive career, Duan Qing made significant contributions to Indology and Buddhist studies. She guided and inspired students and colleagues in China and abroad. *Ekacittena*, Prof. Duan's friends and colleagues join together to publish this volume as a tribute to her academic accomplishments. The volume was originally intended to celebrate Prof. Duan's seventieth birthday; but by the ineluctable force of impermanence it is now published as a memorial to her fruitful career. I contribute this essay on the relation between Emperor Asoka and stupas at the interface of epigraphy and archaeology.

This is a revised and expanded version of lectures given on several occasions, most recently at The International Buddhist College 15th Anniversary Buddhist Studies Conference, 1 September 2019, Kuala Lumpur, Malaysia. I regret that, not knowing the languages, I am unable to use or refer to research on Asoka in Chinese, Japanese, or Korean. In this essay I follow the early epigraphic and literary sources and use the Prakrit/Pali form of the emperor's name, Asoka, rather than the Sanskrit form, Aśoka (Ashoka). I am never quite certain whether to call this extraordinary monarch "king" or "emperor": neither of the English terms quite seems to fit. In his writings Asoka styles himself simply *rājā*: not *mahārāja* or *mahārājādhirāja* as do later kings. This is something that depends on one's personal understanding and definition of that difficult term "empire."

Asoka's philosophy was influenced by the Buddha and other *samaṇas*, but his thought was original.[1] He propagated his own moral code and ideology. What was the religious landscape like in his time? Did it resemble that described for later periods by Romila Thapar (2016, 15)?

> [...] the period when the gurus, pirs, and sants wandered from place to place, preached their understanding of religion, founded sects and sometimes settled somewhere that became a place of pilgrimage. They were people of every possible religious background and their teachings were often a religious melange that defied identification with a particular religion. [...] Such sects crossed religious and social barriers without a thought and none could stop them because their followings were so large. When they became well established even royal patrons received them cordially. They were the opinion-makers of their times.

The study of Asoka began when James Prinsep (1799–1840) unravelled the puzzle of early Indian writing systems and thereby initiated the study of the "epigraphic Asoka" that continues to this day.[2] The study of writings in Pali, Sanskrit, Chinese, and Tibetan brought the discovery of the "literary" or "legendary Asoka" and his role in Buddhist history and art. Two orders of primary evidence give us two different views of Asoka. This idea is not new; it was already proposed by Robert Lingat (1892–1972).[3] Simply put, there are (at least) two different Asokas:

(1) the evidence of inscriptions, stones, land, and landscape: "epigraphic or archaeological Asoka;"
(2) the evidence of manuscripts, literature and legends: "literary" or "legendary" Asoka.

Our understanding of the great emperor is grounded on these two sources, each of which has its own value for empirical and social research. There is, however, more than this: the two Asokas are regularly conflated to create a third Asoka, born of the synthesis of the two primary sources. Accounts that conflate these sources without distinguishing them are widespread, and we might call the results "everyman's Asoka."[4] This gives us *three* Asokas:

(1) "epigraphic Asoka," based on the evidence of inscribed stones, land and landscape;
(2) "literary Asoka," based on the evidence of words and letters, literature and legends;

---

[1] For the variety of Dharmas in Indian language, thought and religion, see the essays in Olivelle 2009. For Asoka's unique conception of Dhamma, see Hiltebeitel 2010, Chap. 2, "King Aśoka's Dharma" and "Postscript on Aśoka and Dharma as Civil Discourse," 2011, Chap. 2, "Aśoka Maurya" and "Postscript on Aśoka," pp. 683–684.

[2] For a selection of Prinseps' writings, see Prinsep 1858 [1995].

[3] Lingat (1989, 19) writes, "There are in reality two Aśokas—the historical Aśoka whom we know through his inscriptions, and the legendary Aśoka, who is known to us through texts of diverse origins, Pali, Sanskrit, Chinese, and Tibetan." I thank Patrick Olivelle for pointing the passage out to me.

[4] To be socially correct, I ought perhaps to use "everyone's," but I am drawn by "everyman's" time-honoured aura.

(3) "everyman's Asoka," the conflation and synthesis of (1) and (2) to make an idealized Asoka. This Asoka is by and large a fiction that springs from the historical imagination.

Let us suppose that, metaphorically, the Asoka that we know today has three bodies or *kāyas*:

(1) a body or corpus of contemporaneous inscriptions: his *lipikāya*;
(2) a body or canon of later literary compositions: his *avadānakāya*;
(3) a mélange of the two preceding: his *sāmanyakāya*.[1]

My point is that the epigraphic and literary Asokas are different and separate and the habit of combining them only muddles things. Cherry-picking at will from *Mahāvaṃsa*, *Aśokāvadāna*, or other texts produces narratives that are tailored to writers' personal goals or agendas, but stray far into the hazy realms of legend. In this essay, I try to restrict myself to the epigraphic Asoka viewed from the vantage points of archaeological and historical realities. I am especially interested in the interface between Asoka and stupas or caityas—not from the oft-repeated legend that he erected 84,000 stupas or *vihāras* in a single night, but from the archaeological record, from the association of his "messages by the wayside" with stupas and material remains.[2]

Asoka's edicts are well known and well studied. Nonetheless, it strikes me that the relation of his inscriptions to the landscape, and especially their association with and proximity to monumental stupas, has received insufficient attention. By "landscape" I mean both the built or human landscape and the natural or environmental landscape, understanding that the latter is a *chosen* or *designated* landscape, singled out by Asoka and his courtiers as strategic localities to display his royal messages. The natural beauty of the skilfully selected sites frames and invigorates Asoka's thoughts through its aesthetic appeal. The close association with Buddhism is undeniable, as may be seen from the shortlist of sites given below. For this essay, I have chosen to discuss five Asokan records at five different sites. The first of these is in Nepal and the rest are in India:

(1) three Mauryan pillars from lowland Nepal (Rupandehi District, Lumbini Province);
(2) the large Panguraria stupa complex in Central India to the north of the Narmada river (Madhya Pradesh);
(3) the large Boria stupa at Girnar near Junagadh in the Kathiawar peninsula (Gujarat);
(4) the large Sopara stupa on the east coast of the Arabian Sea (Maharashtra);
(5) "Bairāṭ-Calcutta": Asoka's Reading List in the Aravalli mountains of western India (Rajasthan).

[1] I leave aside the Asoka of the Chinese literary sources, including the writings of Faxian and Xuanzang, and the Asoka represented in art, from Kanaganahalli to Santiniketan to modernity.

[2] See Strong 2010, 97–99. The story is recounted in Aśvaghoṣa's *Buddhacarita*, Canṭo XXVIII, vv. 63–65. Could the ritual practice of mass production of miniature stupas have influenced the Asoka legends? This is unlikely since the first evidence for the practice developed several centuries after the Mauryan period.

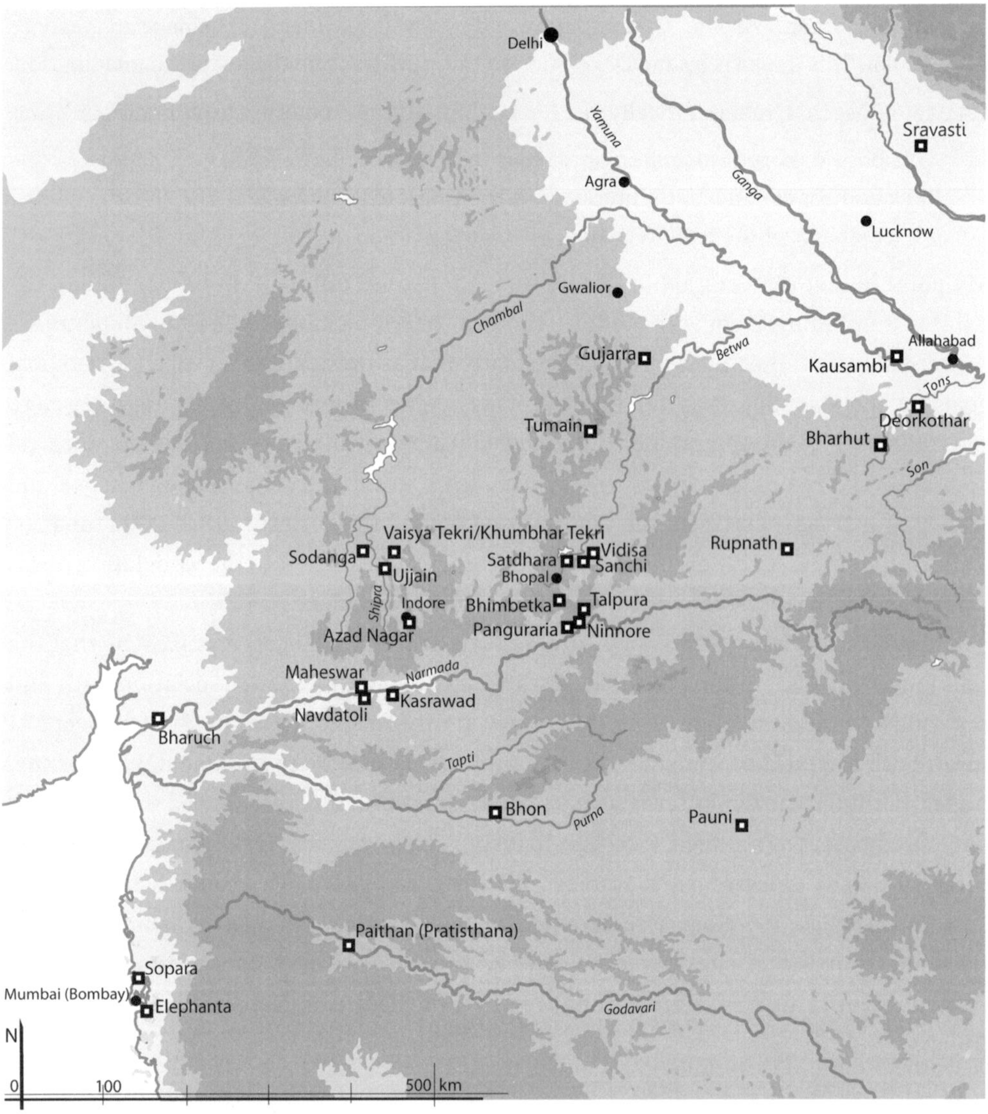

Perspective

Asoka left behind an extraordinary body of writings. These are composed in three languages—Prakrit, Greek, and Aramaic—and indited in four scripts.[1] Greek and Aramaic are written in their respective scripts, while Prakrit is written in either Brāhmī or Kharoṣṭhī letters. All of these writing systems are phonetic. Asoka's messages were recorded on the prepared surfaces of natural boulders or rocks, on the vertical faces of natural rock shelters, and on polished pillars or columns that were surmounted by distinctive capitals. The Asokan evidence is not stable: it continues to grow as new

[1] For the scripts and languages of the Asokan records, see Thapar 2018 and Norman 2012.

records are discovered. "New" MRE I's have been discovered at Bahapur in Delhi itself in 1966, at Ahraura in UP in 1961, and at Panguraria in MP in 1976, to name but a few examples. The old lists and maps need periodic updating. Noteworthy is a "portrait relief carving" of the Emperor at Kanaganahalli (Thapar 2018). As far as I know, the most recently discovered inscription is an MRE I from Ratanpurwa in the Kaimur range, roughly sixty km north of Varanasi on the boundary of Uttar Pradesh and Bihar.[1] Reported 15 January 2009, it was promptly published in Jñāna-Pravāhā, 2009 by distinguished historian and epigrapher Kiran Kumar Thaplyal. He writes (Preface),

> As a young student of history, I used to examine the rocks on the roadside in Garhwal, my native district, with the hope of finding the inscriptions of Asoka. I did not find any. I have the great satisfaction that after my retirement as a Professor of Ancient Indian History and Archaeology I have a good luck of identifying, deciphering and discussing a new and unpublished inscription of the Mauryan king.

The systematic study of Indian inscriptions as a corpus began with Alexander Cunningham's *Corpus Inscriptionum Indicarum I: Inscriptions of Asoka* (1879). This volume was published before photography was enlisted to serve archaeology and it was illustrated with line drawings and hand-drawn facsimiles. In 1925, E. Hultzsch published a new and thoroughly revised edition that was accompanied by estampages; the number of pages went up from 224 to 446. When read in a critical spirit with an eye to new developments, these and other masterworks such as those by Émile Senart, Vincent Smith, D. R. Bhandarkar, Radhakumud Mookerji, Louis de La Vallée Poussin, Jules Bloch, and Romila Thapar, remain invaluable monuments of the intellect. It is not my intention to draw up a current list of Asokan inscriptions, to review previous scholarship, or to attempt to recapitulate the huge bibliography of Asokan studies. That would be futile. In his *Indian Epigraphy*, Richard Salomon (1998, 133–141) gives a lucid summary of the history and state of Mauryan and Asokan epigraphy up to about 1998 (the date of publication), and Harry Falk (2006, 13–54), in his *Aśokan Sites and Artefacts*, gives a forty-page bibliography up to 2006. New studies come out, including monographs like Nayanjot Lahiri's *Ashoka in Ancient India* (2015) or Charles Allen's *Ashoka: The Search for India's Lost Emperor* (2013), along with important collections of essays like *Asoka In History and Historical Memory* (Olivelle 2010) and *Reimagining Aśoka: Memory and History* (Olivelle et al. 2012). New editions come out, such as the third edition of Thapar's *Aśoka and the Decline of the Mauryas* (2012, first edition 1961), or the articles reprinted in the same author's *The Historian and Her Craft*, volume II, *Pre-Mauryan and Mauryan India*

[1] There has been controversy about the discovery and the nature and precise location of the site. I follow Thaplyal's account.

(2018). History and legend are both open. Historians continue to present new evidence and to mould new historiographic myths. It is not easy to keep up with the tide.[1]

A shortlist of Asokan epigraphic sites that are associated with stupas or structural remains includes the following:

Lumbini	Nepal
Bairat	Rajasthan
Junagadh/Girnar/Boria stupa	Gujarat
Sarnath	Uttar Pradesh
Kosambi	Uttar Pradesh
Sanchi	Madhya Pradesh
Panguraria	Madhya Pradesh
Sopara	Maharashtra
Kanaganahalli/Sannati	Karnataka

In this essay, I leave aside the well-known Sarnath, Sanchi, and Kosambi and focus on lesser known sites. My list is by no means exhaustive, and there are important sites that await further exploration and excavation.[2] The Pali chronicles, for example, associate Ujjain with Asoka. No inscriptions have been found there, but Mauryan artefacts, now preserved in the Vikram Kirti Mandir at Vikram University, were recovered from the Sodanga stupa by the ancient city wall. On the outskirts northeast of the modern city, two large stupas nicknamed Vaisya Tekri and Kumar Tekri remain to be excavated.[3]

Not all of Asoka's inscriptions are associated with stupas or structural remains, or with Buddhism. In some cases, the locations seem to have been chosen because they were on trade or pilgrimage routes, or were near sacred sites where people gathered from far and wide for festive occasions determined by autochthonous ritual calendars. Debate continues about whether all of the stone columns were raised by Asoka himself or whether he took advantage of columns that had already been erected by his predecessors and had his messages engraved on them.

[1] In addition, because of the Covid-19 pandemic, over the last two years I did not have access to my library for long periods. This made research difficult.

[2] All of these sites are clearly associated with Buddhism. For Sarnath, see now Barba 2018; Asher 2020.

[3] For the former see Vyas 2001 and Ali et al. 2004; for the latter see Agrawal 2015, 135–136 and pl. CXLIX. See also Skilling 2011 [2015], esp. pp. 157–166. I thank Meera Dass alerting me to these sites, and the Bhopal Circle of ASI for taking me to see them.

So far, there is no way of solving this question. Columns carry their own meanings; a tall column is a powerful statement in itself, and it does not as such need the embellishment of a written text. In one MRE, Asoka himself commands that:[1]

> This matter must be inscribed here and elsewhere on the hills, and wherever there is a stone pillar it is to be engraved on that pillar.

The idea that some columns were erected prior to Asoka's reign raises interesting questions. Of differing sizes and qualities, they are indeed very special artefacts, imperial or royal by nature. If not Asoka, then who erected them? Could some have been raised by earlier Mauryan rulers? Did any of Asoka's predecessors also support or celebrate the teachings of Śākyamuni?[2]

1 Three Mauryan Pillars from Lowland Nepal

At the outset I intended to focus on the relations between Asoka's inscriptions and monumental stupas, but the material evidence is hardly orderly or straightforward. There are inscriptions that are not associated with any stupas or Buddhist relics but nonetheless are indisputedly related to the Buddha and Buddhism. In the Kapilavastu/Lumbini area of Nepal, there once stood three great monoliths. All three of these massive columns were transported to their present locations by water and land, a long distance from their quarries—either Chunar near Varanasi or Pabhosa near Kosambi.[3] Two of them bear inscriptions, and one does not. One of the inscribed pillars is associated with Sākyamuni's birthplace; there is no stupa but there are brick structural remains. Another pillar inscription refers to Buddha Konāgamana's stupa but to date the stupa has not been successfully located. Thapar (2018, 235) points out that "these [two inscribed pillars] were records of actions intended to enhance the merit gained by the king and to impress the Buddhist fraternity [saṅgha]." One pillar bears no inscriptions but is adjacent to a Mauryan stupa.

1.1 Lumbini Pillar Inscription

The Lumbini pillar inscription gives what I consider to be one of the earliest quotes—evocations or paraphrases—of a Buddhist canonical scripture, in India or anywhere else. It even gives the quotation twice. The scripture is the *Sutra on the Great Decease* (*Mahā-parinirvāṇa-sūtra, Mahāparinibbāna-sutta*), which is known is several recensions. The

---

[1] Translation from Thapar 2012, 259 ("a conflation of the various versions").

[2] For a survey of the pillars and their sites, see Falk 2006, 139–153. Pillars with lion and other capitals were integrated into early Buddhist narrative and devotional art from an early date, for example at Bharhut, at the Deccan caves, and at Amaravati. For the last named see Blurton 2022, 49, fig. 2; for Nashik see U. Singh 2022, Fig. 3, relief from Nashik Cave 3: a pair of pillars, one with a lion capital, the other with a *cakra*, flank a stupa.

[3] For these two locations with reference to previous research see Falk 2006, 154–157.

inscribed portion of the pillar was covered by earth for centuries and as a result the tidy letters are well-preserved.[1]

1. devānapiyena piyadasina lājina vīsativasābhisitena
2. atana āgāca mahīyite **hida budhe jāte sakyamunī** ti
3. silāvigaḍabhī cā kālāpita silāthabhe ca usāpāpite
4. **hida bhagavaṃ jāte** ti luṃminigāme ubalike kaṭe
5. aṭhabhāgiye ca

Devānapiya Piyadassī the king / when he had been anointed twenty years / in person came and venerated / thinking, "Here the Buddha was born, Sakyamuni" / He had a stone *vigaḍabhī* made / and had a stone pillar erected /.[2] "Here the Fortunate One was born" / because of this he made the village of Luṃminī tax-free / and aṭṭhabhāgiya /.

I call the phrase **hida bhagavaṃ jāte** a *quote* because of its resemblance to phrases of the *Sutra of the Great Decease*. One may also compare it to the *Avadāna of Kuṇāla*.

Mahāparinibbāna-sutta (Pali) **idha tathāgato jāto**;
Mahāparinirvāṇa-sūtra (Central Asian: Skt) **iha bhagavañ jātaḥ**;
Kunālāvadāna (Nepal: Skt) **asmin** mahārāja **pradeśa bhagavān jātaḥ**.

1.2 Niglihawa Pillar Inscription

The Niglihawa pillar inscription announces that Asoka renovated or expanded the stupa of the (previous) Buddha Konākamana (Pali: Koṇāgamana, Skt.: Kanakamuni).[3] Niglihawa is the *only* Asokan inscription that uses the word *stupa* (Prakrit *thuba*) and it is the *earliest* extant or known record to use the word in South Asian epigraphy (Skilling 2018, 12). But all we have is the *word*: to date no traces of the physical stupa have been located. The pillar is in a marshy area beside a large tank. Can the stupa be somewhere nearby? Or was the heavy pillar moved from elsewhere? If so, from where, by whom, when—and why? Will the stupa ever be found?[4] Portions of the text are abraded.

1. devānaṃpiyena piyadasina lājina codasavasā(bh)i ...(tena)
2. budhasa konākamanasa thube dutiyaṃ vaḍhite
3. .... sābhisitena ca atana āgāca mahīyite
4. .... pāpite

[1] Reading after Bloch 1950, 157. See also text with translation and notes in Salomon 1998, 262–265 with fig. 11, and Deeg 2003, Appendix I, p. 45.

[2] I leave *vigaḍabhī* untranslated. A lot has been written about the term with no resolution of its meaning. It is now popularly identified with the so-called "marker stone" recovered during excavations in 1996, but I find the proposed function of the misshapen stone as an imperial marker farfetched. In his "The Fate of Aśoka's Donation," Harry Falk (2012) proposes that *vigaḍabhī* means "stone railing" and that the railing was later removed to Sarnath where it now stands. The hypothesis is intriguing but it does not convince me. See also Falk 2013 [2017].

[3] According to a shared tradition, Koṇāgamana was the second person to achieve awakening in the present "Auspicious Aeon" (Skt. *bhadrakalpa*, Pali *bhaddakappa*).

[4] One wonders whether Lidar technology might not be helpful.

Following amendments of Hultzsch, Falk, and others, we get the following:

1. devānaṃpiyena piyadasina lājina codasavasā[bhisi]tena
2. budhasa konākamanasa thube dutiyaṃ vaḍhite
3. [vīsativa]sābhisitena ca atana āgāca mahīyite
4. ... [silāthabhe ca usa]pāpite.

Devānaṃpiya Piyadassī the King / fourteen years after he had been anointed / had Buddha Konākamana's *thuba* increased to double in size / when he had been anointed for [twenty] years / in person he came and venerated / ... [and had this pillar] erected.[1]

1.3 Gotihawa Pillar and Stupa

The upper portion of the stone column at Gotihawa is broken and what remains is uninscribed. The pillar's broken stump stands beside a Mauryan stupa. Most stupas and Buddhist sites were rediscovered after centuries of neglect and plunder. By modern standards, early excavations, including the pioneering interventions conducted by Alexander Cunningham, were clumsy, haphazard, and historically irresponsible. Lahiri quotes

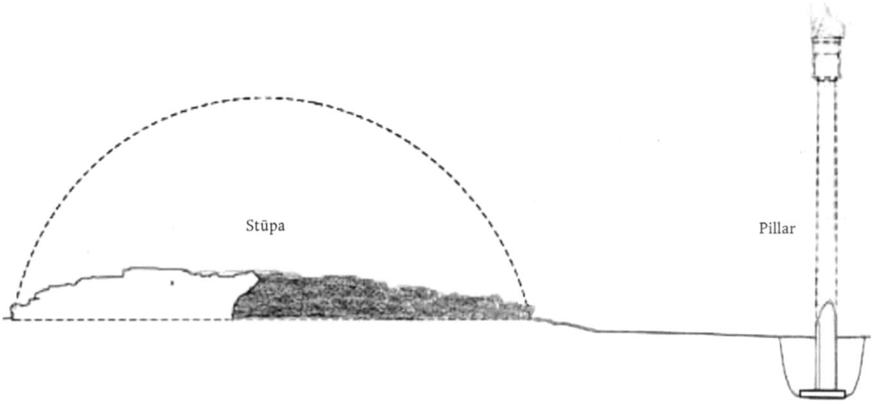

a nineteenth-century British officer's remarks about Cunningham: "a thousand years of time and weather have not done so much injury to the invaluable Topes at Sanchi as was caused by the action of Major-General Cunningham [...] who years ago mined deep into the Topes in the vain search for coins or inscriptions, and never filled in his excavations."[2]

---

[1] For another translation see Falk 2012, 205.

[2] Lahiri 2011. According to K. Singh 2019, n. 28, "This later archaeologist was Lepel Griffin." See also Gibbs 1885–1886.

As archaeological practice and technologies evolved, excavation techniques improved, but still to this day very few stupa complexes have been properly excavated, recorded, or reported. Exceptions include Salihundam (AP), Devnimori (Gujarat), Pauni (Maharashtra), and Ratnagiri (Orissa, where exemplary excavations conducted by Debala Mitra are detailed in an exemplary three-volume report). Giovanni Verardi's exhaustive report on excavations conducted at Gotihawa and Pipri in the Nepalese Terai is a milestone in South Asian archaeology—perhaps the first genuinely scientific and thoroughly comprehensive report on a Mauryan monument, prepared by the specialists of the Nepali-Italian Archaeological Mission.

In the first two inscriptions, the epigraphic Asoka is a pilgrim, a devotee who travels purposefully to the two sites to offer his adoration. The two inscriptions are the earliest written records of pilgrimage in ancient south Asia. Both say that "(the emperor) came in person and venerated." Whether this was also the case for the third site, Gotihawa, cannot be said in the absence of any inscriptions. But it is not unreasonable to suggest that the pillar was set up in homage to the adjacent stupa (which might have been that of a previous Buddha).[1]

Vocabulary

Let us look for a moment at the vocabulary of the two inscriptions.

> *atana āgacca* (*āgācca*). Both Lumbini and Niglihawa state clearly that King Piyadassī came in person a certain number of years after his consecration—twenty for Lumbini, effaced for Niglihawa but taken to be "twenty" on the assumption that Asoka undertook the long journey from the capital to Kapilavastu only once. In the entire corpus of Asokan inscriptions, the phrase *atana āgacca* occurs in these two inscriptions only.
>
> *thuba*. An Asokan Prakrit form equivalent to Gandhari Prakit *thuba*, *thuva*, *thopa*; epigraphic Prakrit *thupa*, *thuba*, *thubha* (only at Kanheri?), *thuva*, *thūpa*; Pali *thūpa*; Skt. *stūpa*. This word occurs only in the Niglihawa pillar inscription and nowhere else in the Asokan corpus. A century or so later, it became frequent in the Western caves. Two thousand years later it was still in local use in northwestern India and entered the English language as "tope."[2]
>
> *silātthabhe ca ussāpāpite*. *silatthabha* (*-thaṃbha*) is used twice elsewhere (Bloch 1950, 150, 172). This is the only inscription that refers to "raising," "setting up," "erecting" a pillar, except for the Niglihawa, where the text is fragmentary but the parallels between the two inscriptions suggest that the emendations are sound.

While on the subject of stūpas, let me note that there is only one (possible) Asokan reference to relics, **budhasa salīle āloḍhe**, in the Ahrauha (Dist. Mirzapur, UP) version of Minor Rock Edict I (MRE I), but the interpretation is difficult and controversial.[3]

---

[1] The final parenthetical statement breaks my rule by taking a hint from Xuanzang.

[2] See Yule and Burnell 1903 [1984], 934–935, s.v. tope, *c*.

[3] Skilling 2018, 12–13. For the text, see e. g., Andersen 1990, §2.1, pp. 16–19.

2 Prince Asoka's Visit to Panguraria (Madhya Pradesh)

Panguraria is in Central India, in Budhni Tehsil, Dist. Sehore, Madhya Pradesh.[1] It lies along an ancient north-south route that is sketched out in the "Introductory Verses" (*vatthu-gāthā*) of the *Parāyana-vagga* of the canonical Pali *Suttanipāta*.[2] Dilip Chakrabarti describes the "communication line coming from the Ganga-Yamuna plain along the Betwa valley" to Panguraria and beyond to "the mound of Ninnore on the northern bank of the Narmada, which marked an old crossing point of the river." He remarks that "Panguraria marks the area of a major archaeological complex: many rock-shelters, stupas, a Mauryan period umbrella and its decorated umbrella shaft, two city-sites (Nadner/Nadnur and Ninnore), one each at the northern and southern limits of the area, and, finally, the MRE itself." [3] His first-hand description presents the early landscape as a coherent network of stupas, Asokan inscriptions, and habitation sites marked by ancient mounds, showing how the ancient landscape was *connected*. In the jargon of today's voracious tourist industry, Panguraria might be described as on a "Buddhist Circuit" that passes from Śrāvastī to the Narmada at Maheshwar and then beyond to the Deccan lands.

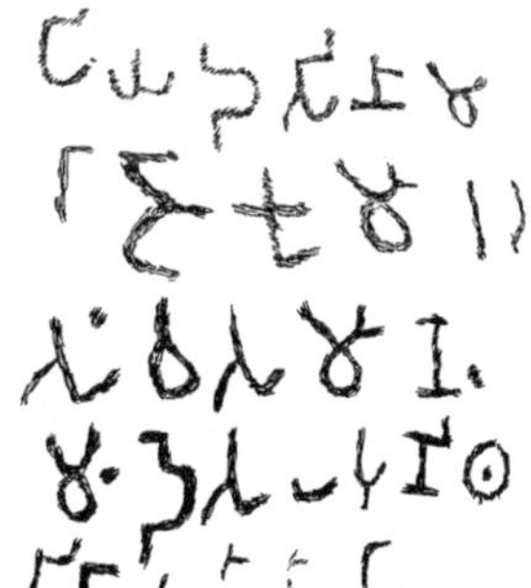

[1] Note that Panguraria is also spelt Pangoraria and Budhni is also spelt Budni. Many Indian place names have more than one spelling; this is the result of different local or regional pronunciation or spellings, historical or official changes, different transliteration systems, and so on.

[2] Trans. Bodhi 2017, 321–328. So far as I know there is no equivalent in the Chinese parallel or in any of the recently discovered Gāndhārī manuscripts. That is, at present the itinerary is known from Pali sources only. The commentary reports that the verses were recited by Ānanda at the first convocation.

[3] For the first, see Trivedi 1984.

At Panguraria the "Western version" of MRE I is inscribed on the vertical face of a rock shelter on the southern slope of the fringes of the Vindhya Mountains where they descend to the Narmada river valley.[1] A short inscription to the side of the MRE states that Asoka visited the site as a prince, a *rājakumāra*. (These statements depend on my understanding of Falk's reading. Sircar's reading gives rise to different ruminations.) We cannot know when this happened, except that since he was a prince it was prior to his coronation. We do not know whether Asoka returned to Panguraria as king, or whether the two epigraphs were engraved at different times.

The majestic site affords stirring views. In front, to the south, stretches the wide and fertile Narmada plain. Behind rises a steep hill tumbling and tangled with vegetation. To the east an abrupt escarpment plunges to the river valley below, as undulations of green hills fade into the distance. Chakrabarti refers to twenty-one "stone-built Satdhara-type stupas, some on platforms" above the level of the rock-shelter. The lush greenery evokes the nature poetry of the early nuns and monks that is preserved in the Pali *Therī*- and *Thera-gāthā*.

It is clear that Panguraria was a major monastic centre in terms of size—it spreads over a large hillside—and numbers of early structures.[2] The local name of the main rock-shelter is Saru-Maru Guphā. Some interpret this as "Cave of Sāriputta and Moggallāna," implying that relics or reliquary stupas of the Buddha's two foremost disciples may once have been worshipped in the area. But there is no epigraphic or other evidence for this (no reliquaries have been discovered so far). The rock-shelter with the inscriptions looks out over the largest stupa, which is 76 m in diameter and is encircled by a raised circumambulatory path (*pradakṣiṇa-patha*). A long shaft or *yaṣṭi* and a stone parasol or *chattra*, both with "Mauryan polish," were discovered nearby.[3] A two-line Prakrit inscription, written in post-Asokan Brāhmī along the length of the shaft, records that the production of this fine parasol was undertaken by a group of nuns:[4]

1. *saṃgharakhitāya bhicchuniya dāna koramaṃkaya atevāsinihi karapitam*
2. *pusaya ca dhamarakhitaya ca arahaya ca etā atevasiniyo karāpikā chatasa*

Donation of Bhicchhuni Saṃgharakhitā at Koramaṃka, caused to be made by the attendant students Pusā, Dhamarakhitā, and Arahā—these attendant students are the makers of the parasol.

---

[1] Sircar 1979 [2000], pp. 94–103, pls. XVI–XVII; Andersen 1990, 72–77; Falk 2006, 89–90; Chakrabarti 2011, 26–30; Agrawal 2015, pp. 129–130, pls. CXLV, CXLVI; Lahiri 2015, 156–160. MRE I is known in sixteen versions (Sarkar 1983, 403).

[2] For a description of the area, see *Indian Archaeology 1975–76, A Review*, pp. 28–30 and pls. XXXVII–XLI. Schopen's portrayal, evidently based on incomplete reports and poor photographs, does not do justice to the site (1994 [2004], 77).

[3] This is reported in *Indian Archaeology 1976–77, A Review*, pp. 32, 60 and pls. XXII*b* and LVIII*c*.

[4] After Sarkar 1983; see also Iyer 1973.

A senior nun, a teacher, organized her nun-disciples to produce a prestige object, an expertly crafted stone parasol with a shaft measuring about 3 metres,[1] to surmount a large stupa near two Asokan records.

This inscription is significant primary evidence for the history of the *bhikkhuṇī-saṅgha*, the Buddhist order of nuns. It adds to our understanding of the networks of nuns in the region that we know from donative inscriptions at Sanchi, Satdhara, and elsewhere as far away as Pauni (Maharashtra). It is regrettable, if not deplorable, that the parasol is not displayed for the considerable public who visit the museum, but is instead locked away in the Sanchi museum storage.[2] Inscribed parasol shafts are rare; an early but somewhat later example is the "Sarnath Umbrella Shaft Inscription of the Time of Kaniṣka."[3]

Adjacent to MRE I is what Sircar (1979 [2000], 96) calls "a kind of preface to the edict proper," Norman (2012, 44–51) a "covering letter," Schopen (1994 [2004], 79[77]) "a cover letter," Thaplyal a "preamble," and Falk (2006, 109–110) a "Separate Edict."[4] I do not know what to call it. It is not an edict, decree or command. "Preface," "preamble," and "cover(ing) letter" imply that the two documents might have been composed or engraved at the same time, but the relative chronology is open to debate. The record is not exactly a "preface" or "preamble," and "covering letter" and "cover letter" sound a bit out of place. Can we find a neutral term, perhaps "subsidiary," "supplementary," or even "side" inscription? Or, perhaps, a "biographical note"?

Officers of the Prehistory Branch, Archaeological Survey of India (ASI), discovered the inscription in January, 1976, and in March of the same year a set of rubbings and photographs was sent to doyen of epigraphers D. C. Sircar. Sircar interprets the inscription to contain three hitherto unattested proper names:

> The king named Priyadarśin (speaks) to **Kumāra Samva** from his march (of pilgrimage) to the **Upunitha-vihāra** (or Opunitha-vihāra) in **Manema-desa** ...

[1] Length according to Iyer 1973, 119.

[2] I was able to visit the storage—a separate building closed to the public, some distance to the back of the museum—through the kind permission of the then Director-General of ASI, Gautam Sengupta.

[3] Text, translation, and notes in Salomon 1998, pp. 270–272 with fig. 15.

[4] Chakrabarti 2005, 99–100; Schopen 1994 [2004], 77; Skilling 2011 [2015], 167–169.

Sircar's reading suggests that the inscription is addressed to a local governor with the curious name "Samva" and that the monastic complex is called Upunitha- or Opunitha-vihāra. His reading and interpretation have been accepted, without, it seems, any questions, despite the fact that, as Falk puts it, "the whole construction is utterly unstable." [1] Falk's careful analysis of the short inscription makes better sense syntactically and yields a more plausible meaning. In comparison. Sircar's reading seems rather fanciful. Falk (1997, 110) reads,

> piyadasi nāma / rajakumāra va / saṃvasamāne i-/ maṃ desaṃ pāpunitha / vihāra(ya)tāy(e)
> Piyadasi by name / as crown prince / while residing[2] / reached this place[3] / on a pleasure tour.

Falk translates:

> The king, who (now after consecration) is called Piyadassi, (once) came to this place on a pleasure tour while he was still a (ruling) prince, living together with his (unwedded) consort).

Chakrabarti (2011, 28) remarks that "Falk's text of the Panguraria edict is completely different from Sircar's version and does not fit in the general range of inscriptions of the period." I am not certain what "general range of inscriptions of the period" means. All of the "inscriptions of the period" emanate from Asoka, and Falk's reading and interpretation seem to fit better than Sircar's, which refers to an unknown locality (*desa*), "Manema," and to a named *vihāra*. The word *vihāra* in the sense of "monastery" qua settled monastic establishment is not found in any other Asokan epigraph, or for that matter in any early-period epigraphs. It is, however, used in the sense of "tour."[4]

Incidentally, there are numerous paintings in the rock-shelters at Panguraria. The nearby UNESCO World Heritage Site of Bhimbetka has around five hundred painted

---

[1] Sircar's reading is followed by S. Subramonia Iyer, Dilip Chakrabarti, Nayanjot Lahiri, K. K. Thaplyal, and Susmita Majumdar, among others. As Falk notes, "Only G. Schopen regarded [Sircar's] interpretation as highly conjectural. Nowhere else was it seriously questioned." See Schopen 1994 [2004], 77. *Indian Archaeology 1975–76, A Review*, p. 29, considers the "preamble" to be a separate inscription and gives a reasonable interpretation: "The cave [...] contains two Asokan inscriptions: one is a version of the Minor Rock Edict I, found in fourteen other places, while the other records the visit of Piyadasi as Maharajakumara to the site."

[2] One of the difficult terms is *saṃvasamāne*, which is discussed at length in Lahiri 2015, 97f.

[3] Forms of *prāp* are regularly used for reaching or arriving at a place. See the examples in Strauch 2012, 2019.

[4] See for example Majumdar 2019, 30. Schopen 1994 [2004], 73–80, gives a useful survey of archaeological evidence for *vihāras* but his primary interest is to date Indian texts that use the term. He overlooks the potential of the rock-shelters as residences for early ascetics (also common in early Sri Lanka); his arguments go off track and his conclusions are off-kilter.

rock shelters. In the same tehsil as Panguraria there are more at Talpur.[1] Talpur is a smaller but prominent stupa complex along the southern flank of the Vindhyas, a few kilometres to the east. Two stupas stand on a high stone terrace, the larger 21, the lesser 10, metres in diameter. Nothing is known about the history of the site. The sole inscription is a one-line donative record reading as *aditaputasa* "in Brāhmī characters of Asokan time." Its relation to the stupas is not known since it was "recovered from a house in the village" about a kilometer from the stupa complex.[2]

In MP paintings are found at Sanchi, and almost everywhere, including Deorkothar and Dhumni far to the east near Rewa. Paintings are also found in Bihar and in other states.[3] The juxtaposition of Buddhist sites and cave shelters with rock paintings leads us to wonder about the relation between the saṅgha and the forest (*aṭavī*) and tribal or indigenous populations. Do we need to factor these non-urban features into our social speculations?

3 Junāgaḍh and Girnar (Gujarat): Boria Stupa

Junagadh is located in the Kathiawar peninsula, which abuts the long coast of the Arabian Sea. In ancient times, the region was known as Saurāṣṭra (Sanskrit) or Soratha (Prakrit). As a modern political formation it is now part of Gujarat. Junagadh ("old or ancient fort," also Junagaḍh, Junagarh) was one of the many princely states that formed the complicated political entity of colonial era Saurāṣṭra. With Independence, after a period of confusion and chaos, Junagarh joined the Republic of India in 1948.

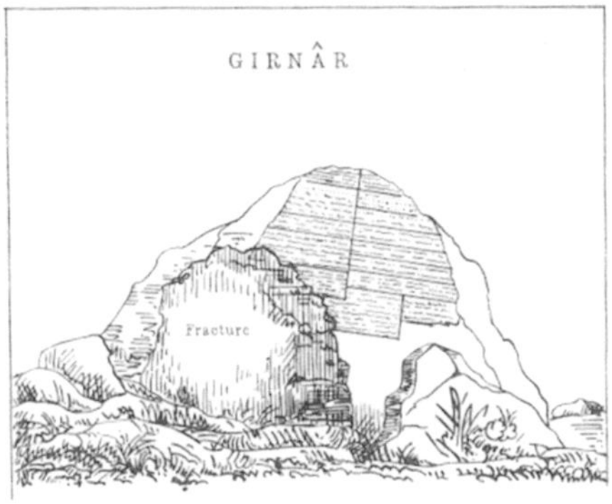

Edict of Asoka, the Buddhist King (third century B.C.).
Engraved on a rock on Mt. Girnar, near Junagadh, in Gujrat.

[1] *Indian Archaeology 1975–76—A Review*, p. 30 and pl. XL*ab*, XLI*a*; Agrawal 2015, pp. 151–152 and pls. CLIX–CLX.

[2] *Indian Archaeology 1975–76—A Review*, pp. 30, 63 and Pl. LXII*d*.

[3] See the remarks on paintings and Panguraria in Lahiri 2015, 156–157. For an eloquent account of field research in central India nearly a hundred years ago, see Ghosh 1932 [1998].

Junagadh is the site of the Girnar inscription, which was noted by the first decades of the nineteenth century.[1] A set of fourteen edicts is engraved on a single boulder that stands along the road to the Girnar mountains. About 6 miles from Junagarh is the massive Boria Stupa, known as Lakha Medi (the abode of Lakha) and the Intwa monastic settlement is about three miles away.[2] In the area are rock-cut monasteries that point to a considerable monastic presence.[3]

J. C. Campbell "opened" the Boria stupa in 1889 and was soon joined by Henry Cousens.[4] A relic coffer was unearthed in February 1889; shortly afterwards it was opened by the two colonial officers. Cousens' report in the *Journal of the Asiatic Society of Bengal* waxes lyrical on the environs and the route to the stupa. Cousens gives a valuable step-by-step description of the opening of the casket.

Henry Cousens (1854–1933) was a Scottish archaeologist who devoted much of his career to the study of the antiquities of the west and northwest (Marshall 1934). He held the position of Superintendent, Archaeological Survey of Western India from 1891 till his retirement in 1910. This was his position during the excavation of the Boria stupa in 1889. As a princely state, Junagarh was not directly administered by the British, and Cousens communicated with the *divan* of Junagarh, Rao Bahadur Haridas Viharidas.[5] Rao Bahadur Haridas Viharidas (1840–1895) was highly regarded by many, including Swami Vivekananda (1863–1902), for his probity and his many contributions to the advancement of the welfare of the State. James McNabb Campbell (1846–1903) was a Scot who came to India in 1869 where he had an illustrious career and rose to high positions.[6] In 1873, at the age of twenty-seven, he was entrusted with the compilation of the *Gazetteer of Bombay Presidency* which when completed counted thirty-four volumes. After his death a gold medal was established in his name to be awarded triennially by the Bombay Branch of the Royal Asiatic Society for work on Indian folklore, history, and anthropology. The first medal was awarded to Sir Aurel Stein in 1909 for his massive 964-page tome, *Ancient Khotan: Detailed Report of Archaeological Explorations in Chinese Turkestan*. Certainly this was appropriate because of the

[1] For the history of modern knowledge of the Girnar inscription, see Dharamasey 2012a, 44–57. I am indebted to Y. S. Rawat (former Director, Directorate of Archaeology & Museums, Gujarat) for illuminating discussions about the Boria stupa.

[2] These sites are poorly documented. For a photo that gives an idea of the size of the Boria stupa, see Rao and Kumaran 2015, pl. 17.

[3] For an enthusiastic overview of the antiquarian history, see Soundara Rajan 1985.

[4] Cousens 1891; Rao and Kumaran 2015, 21. The artefacts are illustrated in Cousens' plate, an important archival sketch that shows the relics as they were found.

[5] The bureaucratic-cum-political circumstances are given in the first paragraph of Cousens' report (p. 17).

[6] Information about Campbell is digested from *Dictionary of National Biography*, 1912 Supplement, vol. I, "Campbell, James Macnabb." Accessed 11 Dec, 2022.

intellectual affinity between the two men whose careers, however, took vary different trajectories. Campbell is little known, or even unknown, to today's "Buddhist studies," while Stein is celebrated for his expeditions to Xinjiang, China and for retrieving artefacts and manuscripts. This shows how the intellectual endeavours of colonial India were interwoven.

The giant stupa was built of bricks measuring 37 x 30 x 5 cm. Remnants of a massive crowning parasol, that unfortunately had broken into several pieces, and at least two sections of stone railing were discovered along with a relic coffer embedded in the brick structure.[1] The square stone coffer has a circular cavity with a circular stone lid. Within the coffer was a "claystone pot;" in this was a set of nested containers, in descending order of size made of copper, silver, and gold. Gems included two corals, and one each emerald, sapphire, ruby, and an aquamarine bead.[2] Located in jungle at the foot of the highest mountain in Gujarat, the Boria stupa is protected by the Gir National Park and Lion Sanctuary, the Asiatic lion's only remaining habitat. The stupa and its surroundings have not yet been properly excavated.[3]

Nearby was a monastic settlement. A baked clay monastic sealing, now in the museum at Junagadh, was found not far away at Intwa. Sanskritist and epigraphist Bahadur Chand Chhabra (born 1908) published the seal in *Epigraphia Indica*.[4] He writes:

> The ancient site of Īnṭwa is situated on a hill, in the midst of a thick jungle, about three miles from the famous rock at Jūnāgaḍh in Saurāshṭra, that contains inscriptions of Aśōka, Rudradāman and Skandagupta. The name Īnṭwa owes its origin to the fact that the site has since long been yielding bricks (*īṇṭs*)[5] in abundance.

The sealing is round in shape, about an inch in diameter. Chhabra reads it as follows:[6]

> *mahārāja-rudrasena-vihāre bhikṣu-saṃghasya.*

---

[1] At present, the whereabouts of the parasol and railing are not known. For an archival photo, see Majmudar 1960, pl. XV(B).

[2] For the relics from the Boria stupa, see Cousens 1891, with plate; for recent colour images see Desai 2010, 56–57.

[3] A recent notice is Lahiri 2011. She writes that the "Lakha Medi stupa in Gujarat is of great archaeological importance. But like many other stupas in India, it lies forgotten and unattended [...]"

[4] Chhabra 1945–1950; 1953 (I thank Virchand Dharamsey for promptly sending me this article [email, 21 Dec. 2022]. For Chhabra's illustrious career, see the "biographical sketch" by Agam Prasad in Ramesh et al. 1984, xiii–xv.

[5] For this word, cp. Pali *iṭṭhaka*, Hybrid Sanskrit *iṣṭakā* and the Thai loan-word *it* อิฐ, common in place names.

[6] Chhabra 1945–1950. The sealing is illustrated in plate facing p. 174 but in the 1985 reprint edition it is not sharp enough to read clearly. See also the small photograph in Majmudar 1960, pl. XVII C.

That is, "Of/belonging to the monastic community of the monastery of Mahārāja Rudrasena." Or, in Chhabra's rendering, it "belongs to the congregation of friars at the Mahārāja Rudrasena Monastery." Chhabra notes that,

> This short record on the sealing is of great historical importance. The Mahārāja Rudrasena spoken of herein is obviously one of those Kshatrapas who were the descendants of Chasṭana and who ruled in Saurāshṭra and in the neighbouring regions from the 2nd to the 4th century A.C. There were four rulers of the name of Rudrasena in this dynasty, and it is not possible at this stage to say definitely as to which one is meant here, though the palaeography of the legend would make him Rudrasena I, who was a son of Rudrasiṃha I and whose reign is known to be 199–222 A.C.

Chhabra remarks that this would be one of the earliest monastic sealings that had been discovered at the time, and I believe that this is still the case.[1]

The government of Saurāshṭra conducted "a small-scale excavation" under the direction of G.V. Acharya who "laid bare remains of a couple of Buddhist monasteries. One finds that their pavements, walls, drains and platforms were all made of bricks of extra-large size. In plan, they closely resemble those exposed at Taxila."[2] Otherwise, the site is neglected.

4 Sopara and the Arabian Sea

The Sopara stupa is a large brick monument that was excavated by Bhagwanlal Indraji in 1882.[3] Its Asokan credentials are established by fragments of two rock edicts found in the vicinity, the first from RE VIII by Bhagwan Lal in 1882, the second from RE IX at the nearby village of Bhuigaon in 1956. Both are kept in the Chhatrapati Shivaji Maharaj Vastu Sangrahalaya (CSMVS), Mumbai; the former is on display while the latter is in storage.

Most ancient stupa ruins are anonymous and unhistoried, and today we have no contemporaneous records of why or when the different sites were chosen. I assume that all major stupas enshrined physical relics, but how and why were their sites chosen? I suspect there must have been multiple reasons, differing from case to case. Some could have commemorated a Buddha's visit or some other event. We simply don't know. Sopara may count as an exception, insofar as its foundation myth can be identified with a fair degree of certainty in Buddhist literature. This is the widely known and popular story of Pūrṇa, one of Gautama the Buddha's direct disciples. There are versions of the

---

[1] For monastic seals see Vogel 1950, 27–32, and Schopen 1994 [2004], 61–62 with extensive bibliography in n. 48. pp. 84–85. For recent examples from West Bengal, see Sanyal 2019.

[2] For Boria, see Rao and Kumaran 2015, 21, for Intwa, idem, 41–42. The Intwa excavations are reported in Acharya 1949 (not seen: summary in Majmudar 1960, 91–92).

[3] For the redoubtable Bhagwanlal, see Dharamsey 2012a. Bhagwanlal was active at three of the sites studied here, Girnar, Bairat, and Sopara. For Sopara, see Dharamsey 2012b, 149–152.

story in the Pali *Majjhima-* and *Saṃyutta-nikāyas* and their commentaries (*aṭṭhakathā*), in Chinese in the *Saṃyukta-āgama* and other sources, and in the Sanskrit *Pūrṇa-avadāna* (*Divyāvadāna*, No. 2), which has a close parallel in the Mūlasarvāstivāda *Vinayavastu* and an eleventh-century verse version in Kṣemendra's *Bodhisatvāvadānakalpalatā*.[1]

At the start of the Pali version, Pūrṇa is dwelling as a monk at Sāvatthī.[2] He takes leave of the Buddha to return to his home-country, Sunāparanta/Aparantaka or western India. His journey home is one of the longest journeys recounted, albeit skeletally, in the early Āgama literature. The details of Pūrṇa's trip and the Buddha's subsequent journey with its crowning event, the offering of a sandalwood pavilion, are not related in the Pali sutta but in the commentary or *Aṭṭhakathā* and cognate narratives These events take place in a port-town that is known in Sanskrit sources as Śūrpāraka. This takes us to today's Nala-Sopara and its Mauryan stupa.[3]

The Sopara stupa and surroundings is an archaeological site of great antiquity and historical significance as a western Indian node of trade, culture, and Buddhist activity. It stands on the cusp of the historical period. The Asokan fragments are the earliest example of the use of writing in Maharashtra. Sopara is, I believe, the only confirmed Mauryan Buddhist site in the Konkan (that is, coastal Maharashtra). The relics from the stupa, carefully preserved in the Asiatic Society of Mumbai, are precious artefacts of several centuries of Indian and Buddhist art. The Sopara stupa and its environs deserve priority for preservation as a heritage site but at present they are threatened by rapidly expanding urban development (Chouhan 2017).

Why did Asoka choose to have his writings engraved in remote places? "Why here?" is a question that needs to be asked for each and every site. Some messages are addressed to the sangha and lay communities, and are engraved in or near Buddhist monastic sites, such as the pillars at Sarnath, Kosambi, and Sanchi, or the rock edicts at Panguraria and Bairat. Some like the Lumbini, Niglihawa, and (possibly) Gotihawa pillars commemorate sites associated with Sākyamuni or other Buddhas. Each case is different. Each message is a deliberate enunciation of policy that was important to Asoka and he chose his words carefully.

What about "remote" places like Rupnath, Ratanpurwa, or Gujjara? What seems remote today was not necessarily so in antiquity. In the vicinity of Rupnath and

---

[1] Pūrṇa must have been a popular name, and in Buddhist literature there are several Pūrṇas. But these are not related to what one might call the "Sopara" or "Aparāntaka" story cycle. They include the Pūrṇa of the first *Avadāna* of the *Hundred Avadānas*, subtitled *Pūrṇa-pramukhāvadānaśataka*, and a Mahāyāna *paripṛcchā* preserved in Tibetan Kanjurs, "The Questions of Pūrṇa," *Ārya-pūrṇa-paripṛccha-nāma-mahāyāna-sūtra* (*Gang pos zhus pa*: Ratnakūṭa Tib, 17): English translation by the Dharmachakra Translation Committee as *The Questions of Pūrṇa* at 84000.com (first published 2020).

[2] For translations of several versions of the story, see Tatelman 2000 [2001].

[3] The narrative and archaeological maps connect this to Kalyan, the Kanheri cave complex, and networks of trade and Buddhist practice from the Konkan to inland central India.

Panguraria, at least, are remains of prehistoric and early historic settlements. Monastic sites are remote by choice because the sangha favoured peace and quiet. Even then, most (or all?) of the sites are located along trade, communication, and pilgrimage channels, and if not at monastic complexes then near centres of commercial or other activities (gold-mining in the South), near ports and near or at local sacred sites. Asoka, or his deputies, chose the sites well. Many locations are striking in their beauty, and to this day are centres of worship. Most are near mountains or commanding rock formations where festivals (*samāja*: cf. Pali, *giri-agga-samāja*) took place and sometimes still take place. By chance (or by divine design?) my own visit to Rupnath (MP) in about 2010 took place on the day of Mahashivaratri.[1] A small fair had set up along the track in front and a stream of (mostly local) devotees paid homage to the deity in the dramatic setting among sharp crags and waterfalls of the Kaimur hills. Ironically, in 1879 Cunningham had written that "an annual *mêla*, or fair, was formerly held here on the Siv-râtri; but this has been discontinued since the time of the mutiny."[2] With reference to Karnataka, Falk (2006, 56) writes,

> How old are these festivals taking place at some MRE sites and elsewhere? Some of the MRE sites on hills and mountains are so impressive by their nature or by the beautiful surroundings or by both that their sanctity must go back to a time much earlier than Asoka or even Buddha. Today, Karnataka is still full of holy places on hills and mountains, visited during a yearly *melā* usually after the harvests either in spring or at the Mahāśivarātrī.

The Asokan sites belonged to an integrated and organic landscape; the emperor's writings are interwoven and point to a network with the Buddhist sanghas, stupas and other edifices, railings and pillars. Asoka's interventions in the landscape developed as packages. Sites and their artefacts are not isolated and separate: they interacted and were in conversation with each other, with their surroundings, with the imperial capital at Pāṭaliputra, or the destinations of long-distance trade routes.

Let us take Junagarh as an example. Today Junagarh, lying in India's far southwestern corner, is remote and isolated. Its isolation is, however, modern, a by-product of the drastic partition of India in 1947. Before partition, busy sea routes linked Bombay, Karachi, and the Indus delta, not to mention of faraway Aden, Cairo, and the Mediterranean, or Colombo, Singapore, Rangoon, and Hong Kong.

Junagarh has a deep history as a centre of communications, trade, and administration, going back to the Mauryan period and much earlier. The Kathiawar peninsula was a node in transregional and long-distance trade networks, exemplified by

---

[1] For at Rupnath (Jabalpur Dist, MP) where an MRE is engraved on a large natural boulder, see Falk 2006, 93–94.

[2] Cunningham, cited in Falk 2006, 94.

Harappan remains, followed by contact with Rome and the Arab lands. Much later still came the encroaching European colonial powers; the Portuguese to set up colonies at Diu, Daman, and Goa, and the British to establish the great port cities, the hubs of imperial commerce of Karachi and Bombay. This is not to speak of the ancient ports of Surat and Bharuch across the gulf of Khambat. Evidence of these contacts have recently been uncovered deep within the Huq cave on the isle of Socotra, which lies on the route from the Arabian to the Red Sea (Strauch 2012; 2019). The names of early visitors from Bharukaccha are inscribed deep in the caves; many of the graffiti link stylistically to western Indian styles. The graffiti as well as drawings of stupas link Socotra to sites in Gujarat and in the high mountains of the Indus valley.[1] The land and water routes were part of a long continuum that flourished for centuries, perhaps millennia. Much nearer to Junagarh, ships sailed from the port of Porbandar around the gulf and to distant maritime destinations.[2]

Rock-cut caves in the area, for example at Bawa Pyara, Khapra Kodia, and Uparkot, attest to the early presence of settled saṅghas.[3] When did Buddhist monastics first settle in the region? At the present state of knowledge, it is not possible to answer, or even to say whether this event was pre- or post-Asokan. Given the size of the stupa at Boria and the size of the Girnar inscription, one might suspect that the sangha was already established before Asoka's time. The caves are much abraded and no inscriptions have been found. Some of them enshrine rock-cut stupas as the centre of cult, like many of the early caves of Konkan and the Deccan.

The large boulder on which Asoka's inscription is engraved stands by an old route that leads from the habitation areas (so little do we know that I dare not say "city centre") to the Boria stupa and the Girnar mountain.[4] The majesty of the enormous stone and the power that emanated from the large letters of Asoka's edicts were such that they inspired two later kings, Mahakṣatrapa Rudradāman (2nd c. CE), and the Gupta emperor Skandagupta (5th c. CE), to add their own records.[5] This gives the stone a remarkable high-profile epigraphic continuity.

[1] For Gujarat, see Sonawane 2013; for the upper Indus valley, see Strauch 2019.

[2] For the rich maritime history of western India and Gujarat, see the essays in Keller and Pearson 2015, and Boussac et al. 2016.

[3] See Burgess [1876] 1998, pp. 139–153 and pls. XVI–XXIX.

[4] See map in Soundara Rajan 1985.

[5] Rudradāman: Burgess [1876] 1998, pp. 128–133 with pl. XIV; Kielhorn 1905; Sircar 1965 [1986], 175–180. For the language see Salomon 1998, 89–90. Skandagupta: Burgess [1876] 1998, pp. 134–138 with pl. XV; Sircar 1965 [1986], 307–316.

5 "Bairāṭ-Calcutta": Aśoka's Reading List (Rajasthan)

In Rajasthan there are not many Buddhist antiquities but one complex of sites, set on a dramatic outcropping of the Aravallis, has been well-known in Buddhist and Indological studies since the mid-nineteenth century.[1] The Asokan inscription found there has gone under various names; here I use one of them, "Bairaṭ-Calcutta." The short epigraph found on the hilltop has been called the "Bairāṭ-Calcutta" inscription because it was recovered near Bairāṭ, near Viratnagar in present-day Rajasthan, and has been kept at the Asiatic Society, Calcutta, since before 1856.[2]

Emperor Asoka's message is extraordinary: he addresses the Buddhist community to express his emphatic reverence for and faith in the Buddha, Dharma, and Saṅgha and his admiration for the Fortunate One's words. He recommends seven titles for monks, nuns, laymen, and laywomen to listen to and reflect on regularly. This unique record gives the earliest known list of titles of Buddhist texts—a "reading list" selected by the Emperor himself. The inscription shows his deep knowledge of the Buddha's Dhamma and gives us a rare glimpse at Buddhist literature by the third or fourth century after the Nirvāṇa (mid-third century BCE).

Early structures on several levels of the hilltop include a cave, a monastic site, and a large circular foundation that is interpreted to be a stupa. Numerous tiny fragments of stone with "Mauryan polish" suggest that a pillar might once have stood at the site but that is only speculation.

In the same area, on the plain below, is a rock edict engraved on a large rock face on "the most prominent hill in the Bairāṭ valley" where an important *melā* is held in spring (Falk 2006, 56, 62–63). In the edict, which is engraved at several other locations, with many variations, Asoka writes about being a lay-follower (*upāsaka*) and his relation to the saṅgha.[3]

---

[1] For the geological and historical background, see Sharma et al. 1984, with pls. I–IV.

[2] Lamotte 1976, 256–259, with reference to earlier research; Warder 1970, 255–257; Falk 2006, 105–108. It was originally known as the "Bhabra inscription," after a village 10 km due north of Bairāṭ (and retained by Bloch 1950, 154, and others like Nikam and McKeon). This was already noted by Hultsch in 1925 (xxv): "the inscription has been styled generally 'the Bhabra edict.' But this name implies a double mistake: the town from which it is derived is not called 'Bhabra,' but Bhābrū, and the latter is twelve miles distant from Bairat, the finding-place of the block."

[3] Inscription at Bloch 1950, 145–149.

*****

According to the standard historical (quasi-historical, pseudohistorical, ahistorical?) narrative, Asoka built stupas and spread the Dhamma across South Asia. This is widely lauded as one of the grand accomplishments of "everyman's Asoka." I suggest that this narrative is *backwards*: that Buddhism was already established, in some places even well- and long-established, and was already expanding, in and to many places—and that it was *Asoka* who, out of his deep respect (*gālava*, Pali *gārava*) for them *followed* the Dhamma and the Saṅgha. He brought new or renewed patronage to already existent Buddhist communities. His inscriptions make it clear that Asoka made sincere efforts to promote the universal values of the Dhamma as he saw it, and that he wanted monks, nuns, laymen, and laywomen to live in harmony and study and practise the Dhamma. Evidently, the saṅgha, including lay communities, was already there.

We should not assume that the Asokan corpora are well studied and that all of the questions have been solved and answered. Far from it. A great deal remains for new generations of researchers to explore. Through the handful of case studies examined here, I hope to have shown how each site is complex and multi-layered, and how, to read Asoka's writings deeply, we need to study their landscapes and contexts. We need to take into account the complexity of Asoka's relationship to Buddhism and the complexity of the relationship of Buddhists to Asoka over the centuries.

Asoka is one of the great moral figures of human history and his message of thoughtfulness, tolerance, and compassion, of human and animal welfare, is relevant to contemporary society and to the problems that we—the troubled and troublesome human race—face today. Asoka's messages become increasingly relevant as intolerance and chauvinism increase. We need to examine the early records to see what they can teach us about the problems of power, ecology, and communication.

Acknowledgements

I am grateful to many colleagues, friends, and institutions for their kind assistance during the protracted period of research that has resulted in this essay. My study has benefited from field visits to Lumbini, Pangoraria, Sopara, Bairat, and other sites. Bearing in mind that all errors, idiosyncrasies, and idiocies are my sole responsibility, it is my pleasure to express my thanks to:

Gautam Sengupta (Centre for Archaeological Studies & Training, Eastern India, Kolkata; DG, ASI, New Delhi); Rakesh Tewari (UP State Archaeology; DG, ASI, New Delhi); Y. S. Rawat (former Director, Directorate of Archaeology & Museums, Gujarat); Meera Dass, (INTACH, Bhopal; National Monuments Authority, New Delhi); Joseph Manuel (ASI, Bhopal); Aparna Bhogal (CSMVS, Mumbai); Dr. Sandrine Gill (Archives Nationale, Paris); Christoph Cüppers (LIRI, Lumbini); Santi Pakdeekham (Royal Society of Thailand, Bangkok); Naman Ahuja (JNU, New Delhi), Jens-Uwe Hartmann (LMU, Munich), Virchand Dharamsey (Mumbai) and many others. Above all, I thank Dzongsar Khyentse Rinpoche for his inspiration and the Khyentse Foundation for their support.

Abbreviations

AP	Andhra Pradesh
EI	Epigraphia Indica
MP	Madhya Pradesh
MRE	Minor Rock Edict
UP	Uttar Pradesh
Skt	Sanskrit

Sources

For a conspectus of inscriptions and published studies, I consult Falk's bibliography (2006) and K. R. Norman's listing (2012). For texts and translations, I turn to the trusty Bloch. For inscriptions discovered post-Bloch, I try to use the most recent and authoritative editions, for example Janert and Anderson.

References

Acharya 1949 G.V. Acharya. "Excavation of a Buddhist Vihāra at Iñṭwā Hill in Girnar at Junagadh." *Gujarat Samachar* (Daily), October.

Agrawal 2015 R.C. Agrawal. *Conservation of Buddhist Monuments in Central India.* Delhi: Sharada Publishing House.

Ali et al. 2004 Rahman Ali, Ashok Trivedi, and Dhirendra Solanki. *Buddhist Remains of Ujjain Region: Excavations at Ṣodaṅga*. Delhi: Sharada Publishing House.

Allen 2013 Charles Allen. *Ashoka: The Search for India's Lost Emperor*. London: Abacus.

Andersen 1990 Paul Kent Andersen. *Studies in the Minor Rock Edicts of Aśoka*, I. *Critical Edition*. Freiburg: Hedwig Falk.

Asher 2020 Frederick M. Asher. *Sarnath: A Critical History of the Place where Buddhism Began*. Los Angeles: The Getty Research Institute.

Barba 2018 Federica Barba. "Sarnath: A Reassessment of the Archaeological Evidence." Appendix 2 In: Giovanni Verardi, *The Gods and the Heretics: Crisis and Ruin of Indian Buddhism*. New Delhi, India and Buenos Aires, Argentina: Aditya Prakashan/ Fundación Bodhiyāna.

Bloch 1950 Jules Bloch. *Les inscriptions d'Asoka traduits et commentées*. Paris: Les Belles Lettres.

Blurton 2022 Richard T. Blurton. *India : A History in Objects*. London: Thames & Hudson/The British Museum.

Bodhi 2017 Bhikkhu Bodhi. *The Suttanipāta: An Ancient Collection of the Buddha's Discourses Together with Its Commentaries Paramatthajotikā II and excerpts from the Niddesa*, Melksham, Wilts (UK) and Somerville, Mass (USA): The Pali Text Society in association with Wisdom Publications.

Boussac et al. 2016 Marie-Françoise Boussac, Jean-François Salles, and Jean-Baptiste Yon, ed. *Ports of the Ancient Indian Ocean*. Delhi: Primus Books.

Burgess

[1876] 1998 James Burgess. *Report on the Antiquities of Kâthiâwâd and Kachh, Being the Result of the Second Season's Operations of the Archaeological Survey of Western India, 1874–75*. London: India Museum. Reprint, New Delhi: Archaeological Survey of India.

Chakrabarti 2005 Dilip K. Chakrabarti. *The Archaeology of the Deccan Routes: The Ancient Routes from the Ganga Plain to the Deccan*. New Delhi: Munshiram Manoharlal Publishers Pvt. Ltd.

2011 *Royal Messages by the Wayside: Historical Geography of the Asokan Edicts*. New Delhi: Aryan Books International.

Chhabra

1945–1950 B. Ch. Chhabra. "Intwa Clay Sealing." *Epigraphia Indica* 28: 174–175.

1953 "Ancient Site of Intwa near Junagarh." *Journal of the Gujarat Research Society* 15/3 & 4 (July–October): 115–116.

Chouhan 2017 Madan Singh Chouhan. *Ancient Soparaka*. New Delhi: Kaveri Books.

Cousens 1891 Henry Cousens. "Boria Stupa of Junagadh." *Journal of the Asiatic Society of Bengal* 60: 17–23.

Deeg 2003 Max Deeg. *The Places Where Siddhārtha Trod: Lumbinī and Kapilavastu*, Occasional Papers 3. Lumbini: Lumbini International Research Institute.

2010 "From the Iron Wheel to Bodhisattvahood." In: Patrick Olivelle, ed., *Asoka in History and Historical Memory*, 109–144. Delhi: Motilal Banarsidass.

2012 "Aśoka: Model Ruler without a Name?" In: Patrick Olivelle, Janice Leoshko, and Himanshu Prabha Ray, eds., *Reimagining Aśoka: Memory and History*, 362–379. New Delhi: Oxford University Press.

Desai 2010 Hemang Desai. *The Buddhist Treasures of Gujarat*. Gandhinagar: Tourism Corporation of Gujarat Ltd.

Dharamsey 2012a Virchand Dharamsey. *Bhagwanlal Indraji, the First Indian Archaeologist: Multi-disciplinary Approaches to the Study of the Past*. Vadodara: Darshak Itihas Nidhi.

2012b "Bhagwanlal Indraji's Pioneering Contribution to Aśokan Studies." In: Patrick Olivelle, Janice Leoshko, and Himanshu Prabha Ray, eds., *Reimagining Aśoka: Memory and History*, 129–154. New Delhi: Oxford University Press.

Falk 1997 Harry Falk. "The Preamble at Pāṅgurāriā." In: Petra Kieffer-Pülz and Jens-Uwe Hartmann, eds., *Bauddhavidyāsudhākaraḥ: Studies in Honour of Heinz Bechert on the Occasion of His 65th Birthday*, Indica et Tibetica 30, 107–121. Swisttal-Odendorf: Indica et Tibetica Verlag.

1998 *The Discovery of Lumbinī*, Occasional Papers 1. Lumbini: Lumbini International Research Institute, 1998.

2006 *Aśokan Sites and Artefacts: A Source-book with Bibliography*. Mainz am Rhein: Verlag Philipp von Zabern.

2012 "The Fate of Aśoka's Donations at Lumbini." In: Patrick Olivelle, Janice Leoshko, and Himanshu Prabha Ray, eds., *Reimagining Aśoka: Memory and History*, 204–216. New Delhi: Oxford University Press.

2013 "Remarks on the Minor Rock Edict of Asoka at Ratanpurwa." *Jñāna-Pravāhā Research Journal* 16: 29–48.

2013 [2017] "The Ashes of the Buddha." *Bulletin of the Asia Institute*, New Series 27: 43–75.

Gibbs 1885–1886 James Gibbs. "The History of Archaeology in India." *Journal of the Royal Society of Arts* 34: 555–564.

Ghosh 1932 [1998] Rai Sahib Manoranjan Ghosh. *Rock-Paintings and Other Antiquities of Prehistoric and Later Times*, Memoirs of the Archaeological Survey of India 24. Reprint, New Delhi: Archaeological Survey of India.

Hiltebeitel 2010 Alf Hiltebeitel. *Dharma*. Honolulu: University of Hawai'i Press, 2010.

2011 *Dharma: Its Early History in Law, Religion, and Narrative*. Oxford: Oxford University Press, 2011.

Hultzsch 1925 E. Hultzsch. *Inscriptions of Asoka*, New Edition, Corpus Inscriptionam Indicarum I. Oxford, 1925.

Iyer 1973 Subrahmonia Iyer. "Panguraria Brahmi Inscription." *Epigraphia Indica* 40: 119–120 and pl.

Janert 1972 Klaus Ludwig Janert. *Abstände und Schlussvokalverzeichnungen in Aśoka-Inschriften*, Wiesbaden: F. Steiner.

Keller and Pearson 2015 Sara Keller and Michael Pearson, ed. *Port Towns of Gujarat*. Delhi: Primus Books.

Kellner 2019 Birgit Kellner, ed. *Buddhism and the Dynamics of Transculturality: New Approaches*. Berlin: De Gruyter.

Kielhorn 1905 F. Kielhorn. "Junagadh Rock Inscription of Rudradaman, Year 72." *Epigraphia Indica* 8: 36-49.

Lahiri 2011 Nayanjot Lahiri. "A Monumental Error." *Hindustan Times*. Updated on Oct 22, 2011, accessed 21 December, 2022.

2015 *Ashoka in Ancient India*. Ranikhet: Permanent Black in association with Ashoka University.

Lamotte 1976 Étienne Lamotte. *Histoire du bouddhisme indien dès origines à l'ére Śaka*. Louvain-la-Neuve: Institut Orientaliste, Université de Louvain.

Lingat 1989 Robert Lingat. *Royautés bouddhiques. Aśoka et la fonction royale a Ceylan*. Paris: Editions de l'Ecole des Hautes Etudes en Science sociales.

Majmudar 1960 M.R. Majmudar, ed. *Historical and Cultural Chronology of Gujarat*. Baroda: Maharaja Sayajirao University of Baroda.

Majumdar 2019 Susumita Basu Majumdar. "Communication, Networks and Imperial Initiatives: Revisiting the Mauryan Inscriptions." In: Kumkum Roy and Naina Dayal, eds., *Questioning Paradigms, Constructing Histories: A Festschrift for Romila Thapar*, 17–31. New Delhi: Aleph Book Company.

Marshall 1934 John Marshall. "Obituary Notice: Henry Cousens." *Journal of the Royal Asiatic Society* 66/3 (July): 644.

Norman 2012 Kenneth Roy Norman. "The Languages of the Composition and Transmission of the Aśokan Inscriptions." In: Patrick Olivelle, Janice Leoshko, and Himanshu Prabha Ray, eds., *Reimagining Aśoka: Memory and History*, 38–62. New Delhi: Oxford University Press.

Olivelle 2009 Patrick Olivelle, ed. *Dharma: Studies in its Semantic, Cultural, and Religious History*. Delhi: Motilal Banarsidass.

2010 ed. *Aśoka in History and Historical Memory*. Delhi: Motilal Banarsidass.

2019 "Ashoka's Writings: New Insights into Ancient Indian Cultural History." In: Kumkum Roy and Naina Dayal, eds., *Questioning Paradigms, Constructing Histories: A Festschrift for Romila Thapar*, 3–16. New Delhi: Aleph Book Company.

Olivelle et al. 2012 Patrick Olivelle, Janice Leoshko, and Himanshu Prabha Ray, ed. *Reimagining Aśoka: Memory and History*. New Delhi: Oxford University Press.

Prinsep 1858 [1995] James Prinsep. *Essays on Indian Antiquities, Historic, Numismatic, and Palaeographic*, edited with notes and additional matter by Edward Thomas, 2 vols. London. Reprint, New Delhi: Asian Educational Services.

Ramesh et al. 1984 K. V. Ramesh, Agam Prasad, and S. P. Tewari, eds. *Svasti Śrī: Dr. B. Ch. Chhabra Felicitation Volume*. Delhi: Agam Kala Prakashan.

Rao and Kumaran 2015 Shivananda V. Rao and R. N. Kumaran. *Excavations in Gujarat*. Delhi: Agam Kala Prakashan.

Reade 2009 Julian Reade, ed. *The Indian Ocean in Antiquity*. London: Routledge.

Salomon 1998 Richard Salomon. *Indian Epigraphy: A Guide to the Study of Inscriptions in Sanskrit, Prakrit, and the Other Indo-Aryan Languages*. New York/Oxford: Oxford University Press.

Sanyal 2019 Rajat Sanyal. "Two Monastic Sealings from Moghalmari." *Pratna Samiksha: A Journal of Archaeology*, New Series 10: 79–93.

Sarkar 1983 H. Sarkar. "A Post-Asokan Inscription from Pangoraria in the Vindhyan Range." In: B.N. Mukherjee et al., eds., *Śrī Dineśacandrikā Studies in Indology (Shri D.C. Sircar Felicitation Volume)*, 403–405, pls. 73–75. Delhi: Sundeep Prakashan.

Schopen 1994 [2004] Gregory Schopen. "Doing Business for the Lord: Lending on Interest and Written Loan Contracts in the Mūlasarvāstivāda-vinaya." *Journal of the American Oriental Society* 114/4: 527–553. Reprinted in: *Buddhist Monks and Business Matters: Still More Papers on Monastic Buddhism in India*. Honolulu: University of Hawai'i Press, 45–90.

Sharma et al. 1984 R.P. Sharma, C. Margabandhu, and B.P. Saxena. "Prehistoric Remains of the Bairat Valley." In: K. V. Ramesh, Agam Prasad, and S. P. Tewari, eds., *Svasti Śrī: Dr. B. Ch. Chhabra Felicitation Volume*, 363–366 and pls. Delhi: Agam Kala Prakashan.

K. Singh 2019 Kavita Singh. "Sanchi, in and out of the Museum." *Sculpture Journal* 28/3: 345–363.

U. Singh 2022 Upinder Singh. *Inscribing Power on the Realm: Royal Ideology and Religious Policy in India c. 200 BCE–300 CE*, 28th J. Gonda Lecture 2022. Royal Netherlands Amsterdam: Academy of Arts and Sciences.

Sircar 1965 [1986] Dinesh Chandra Sircar. *Select Inscriptions Bearing on Indian History and Civilization*, Vol. I, *From the Sixth Century B. C. to the Sixth Century A. D.* Second Edition. Calcutta, 1965. Reprint, Delhi-Madras: Asian Humanities Press.

1979 [2000] *Aśokan Studies*. Calcutta: Indian Museum.

Skilling 2011 [2015] Peter Skilling. "Stūpas, Aśoka, and Buddhist Nuns: Early Buddhism in Ujjain and Malwa." *Bulletin of the Asia Institute*, New Series 25: 157–173.

2018 "Relics: The Heart of Buddhist Veneration." In: Janice Stargardt and Michael Willis, eds., *Relics and Relic Worship in Early Buddhism: India, Afghanistan, Sri Lanka and Burma*, British Museum Research Publication 218, 4–17. London.

Sompura 1969 Kantilal F. Sompura. *Buddhist Monuments and Sculptures in Gujarat: A Historical Survey*. Hoshiarpur: Vishveshvaranand Institute.

Sonawane 2013 V. H. Sonawane. "Rock Paintings Depicting Stupas in Gujarat, India." *Bulletin of the Asia Institute*, New Series 27: 91–97.

Soundara Rajan
1985 K.V. Soundara Rajan. *Junagadh*. New Delhi: Archaeological Survey of India.

Strauch 2012 Ingo Strauch, ed. *Foreign Sailors on Socotra: The Inscriptions and Drawings from the Cave Hoq*. Bremen: Hempen Verlag.

2019 "Buddhism in the West? Buddhist Indian Sailors on Socotra (Yemen) and the Role of Trade Contacts in the Spread of Buddhism," In: Birgit Kellner, ed., *Buddhism and the Dynamics of Transculturality: New Approaches*, 15–51. Berlin: De Gruyter.

Strong 2010 John Strong. "Aśoka and the Lotus Sūtra." In Patrick Olivelle, ed. *Aśoka In History and Historical Memory*. Delhi: Motilal Banarsidass, 95–102.

Tatelman
2000 [2001] Joel Tatelman. *The Glorious Deeds of Pūrṇa: A Translation and Study of the Pūrṇāvadāna*. Richmond, Surrey: Curzon Press. Reprint, Delhi: Motilal Banarsidass.

2005 trans. *The Heavenly Exploits: Buddhist Biographies from the Divyāvadāna*, vol. 1. New York University Press/JJC Foundation.

Thapar 2012 Romila Thapar. *Aśoka and the Decline of the Mauryas, with a New Afterword, Bibliography and Index*, 3rd edition. Delhi: Oxford University Press (first published 1973).

2016 "Reflections on Nationalism and History." In: Romila Thapar, A.G. Noorani, and Sadanand Menon, *On Nationalism*, 1–58. New Delhi: Aleph.

2018 *The Historian and Her Craft*, vol. II. Edited by Kumkum Roy. New Delhi: Oxford University Press.

Thaplyal 2009 Kiran Kumar Thaplyal. *A New Aśokan Inscription from Ratanpurwa*. Varanasi: Jñāna-Pravāhā.

2012 *Aśoka: The King and the Man*. New Delhi: Aryan Books International.

Tripati 2015 Sila Tripati, ed. *Maritime Contacts of the Past: Deciphering Connections Amongst Communities*. New Delhi: Delta Book World.

Trivedi 1984 C.B. Trivedi. "Identification of Nandinagar and Naṃdinagar." In: K. V. Ramesh, Agam Prasad, and S. P. Tewari, eds., *Svasti Śrī: Dr. B. Ch. Chhabra Felicitation Volume*, 325–328. Delhi: Agam Kala Prakashan.

Verardi 2002 Giovanni Verardi. *Excavations at Gotihawa and a Territorial Survey in Kapilavastu District of Nepal: A Preliminary Report*, Occasional Papers 2. Lumbini: Lumbini International Research Institute.

2007 *Excavations at Gotihawa and Pipri, Kapilbastu District, Nepal*. Rome: Istituto Italiano per l'Africa e l'Oriente.

2018 *The Gods and the Heretics: Crisis and Ruin of Indian Buddhism*. New Delhi, India and Buenos Aires, Argentina: Aditya Prakashan/Fundación Bodhiyāna.

Vogel 1950 J. Ph. Vogel. "Seals of Buddhist Monasteries in Ancient India." *Journal of the Ceylon Branch of the Royal Asiatic Society of Great Britain & Ireland, New Series* 1 (Centenary Volume [1845–1945]): 27–32.

Vyas 2001 Narayan Vyas. "Ancient Remains of a Stupa at Ujjain (M.P.)." In: A. V. Narasimha Murthy, K. M. Suresh, K. P. Poonacha, and K. R. Basavaraj, eds., *Hemakuta: Recent Researches in Archaeology and Museology (Shri C.T.M. Kotraiah Felicitation Volume)*, vol. 1, 126–128. Delhi: Bharatiya Kala Prakashan.

Warder 1970 A.K. Warder. *Indian Buddhism*. Delhi: Motilal Banarsidass, 1970.

Yule and Burnell
1903 [1984] Colonel Henry Yule, and A.C. Burnell. *Hobson-Jobson: A Glossary of Colloquial Anglo-Indian Words and Phrases, and of Kindred Terms, Etymological, Historical, Geographical and Discursive*, new edition edited by William Crooke. London: John Murray, 1903. Reprint, New Delhi: Munshiram Manoharlal, 1984.

Modelling Xuanzang*

Master Wuqian and His Journey to India

Zhang Xing

Abstract: Master Wuqian was an important figure in the history of Buddhist interactions between China and India. Probably influenced by the writings of Xuanzang, Wuqian studied Consciousness-only philosophy in addition to other major schools of Chinese Buddhist thought. Master Wuqian also became one of the few Chinese Buddhists from central China to receive systematic training in Tibetan Buddhist Tantric rituals. He went to India in the middle of the 20th century and dedicated his life to the revival of Buddhist thought there. He played a key role in promoting Chinese Buddhism in Calcutta by establishing Buddhist institutions, managing Buddhist sites, organizing Buddhist activities, and building the Xuanzang Temple. In his later years, he devoted himself to facilitating mutual Buddhist exchanges and monastic visits between Buddhist organizations in China and India. He is reported to have presented two relics to the Daci'en Temple in Xi'an in emulation of Xuanzang's legacy. Moreover, at the Xuanzang Temple in Calcutta, Wuqian established the Institute of Buddhist Studies and organized the translation of many important Buddhist texts to promote China-India interactions, which reflects his intention of following the spirit of Xuanzang to contribute to Sino-Indian Buddhist exchanges.

Keywords: Wuqian, Buddhism, Consciousness-only, Xuanzang, China-India interactions

Buddhist exchanges between China and India during the twentieth century remains a relatively unexplored topic. This is especially true for the post-1949 period that witnessed significant growth in cross-cultural exchanges during the 1950s but then a rapid collapse of such interactions after the China-India conflict of 1962. Contemporary scholarship on Sino-Indian cultural and religious relations has focused heavily on the pre-modern periods, especially the experiences of Indian Buddhist missionaries in China and Chinese pilgrims in India in the medieval era. However, in the past two decades, we have witnessed the flourishing of the study of the twentieth century. Indeed, though India and China suffered a turbulent century, they shared similar revivals and restorations in political and cultural domains. As Ji Xianlin 季羡林 (1911–2009) pointed

Zhang Xing, Research Center of Eastern Literature and Department of South Asian Studies, Peking University.

* This paper is derived from my presentation at an international conference organized by the Institute of Southeast Asian Studies in Singapore in 2009, the first international conference Professor Duan Qing 段晴 and I attended together. At that conference, I briefly mentioned Master Wuqian in my paper on the Buddhist practices and institutions of the Chinese community in Calcutta. Professor Duan was among my audience and encouraged me to explore the issue further. Professor Duan's encouragement and guidance have fostered my intellectual life for nearly two decades. This paper is dedicated to the memory of Professor Duan with my deep gratitude.

out, Buddhism certainly played a most important role in bridging these two unique cultures in Asia (Ji 1996).[1] Nevertheless, some figures in the history of Sino-Indian relations during the twentieth century attracted more attention from contemporary scholars than others, who have remained obscure. For example, Taixu 太虚 (1890–1947), one of the most important Buddhist masters and monastic reformers in Chinese history, left numerous material for scholars to explore. In contrast, Wuqian 悟謙 (1922–2010), a master who was the most important monastic leader of the Chinese Buddhist community in India in the second half of the twentieth century, is less well-known to scholars, though he was well respected and well known to numerous Buddhist monastics and laypeople across Asia. A detailed account of his life and journey to India will help us better understand the sophisticated Sino-Indian relations and broaden the horizon of Buddhist history in Asia.

In the published research, only limited attention has been given to this important master. For example, my previous paper on the Buddhist practices and institutions of the Chinese community in Calcutta documented his activities in helping establish Chinese temples (Zhang 2014, 429–457). Li Yuzhen (Yu-Chen Li) 李玉珍 briefly noted that Wuqian was involved in the international full ordination ceremony in 1998 (Li 2013, 168–198). However, there are some misunderstandings about him. In a study on English-language scholarship on Asian Buddhism, he was misunderstood as a Foguangshan 佛光山 Buddhist missionary (Geary 2017, 205; 2007, 192). Wuqian was an important figure, for he was a Chinese monk who lived in India for nearly half a century, fostering the revival of Buddhism and maintaining an active Chinese Buddhist community in Calcutta. There are, of course, difficulties in studying him. Unlike Taixu and other leading Buddhist masters, he was not a prolific writer and did not leave many writings. This lack contributes to the difficulty of studying his Buddhist thought and teachings from the perspective of intellectual history. In fact he was primarily a Buddhist organizer, manager, and practitioner, spending most of his time organizing activities and managing the monastic community, activities that should be considered in writing a socio-cultural history of the Buddhist community. Many of his contemporary peer masters mentioned him, often briefly. His long stay in India may have hindered him from communicating with other Buddhist monks in mainland China. After his passing in 2010, more and more material, such as letters, memoirs, travelogues, and short commemorative essays, appeared, enabling us to gain a better picture of the

[1] Ji Xianlin first received his initial training from Chen Yinke (1890–1969) at Tsinghua University in the 1930s and was inspired by Chen to study Indology in Germany. Ji made significant contributions to the Chinese understanding of Indian Buddhism and culture, ranging from early Buddhist literature, including Tocharian manuscripts, Buddhist material culture, such as the cultural history of sugar, and Buddhist history. For his contributions, see *Ji Xianlin wenji* 季羡林文集 [A Collections of Ji Xianlin's Writings] in 24 volumes by Jiangxi Educational Press in 1996.

man and his activities. [1] Since Master Wuqian was intimately involved in temple-building and ordination activities as well as in the people and material exchanges between China and India from the late-1950s to 2010, it is important, as this paper argues, that more attention be paid to his contributions and several aspects of inter-Asian and Sino-Indian interactions that he fostered.

1 Early Monastic Education and Training in China

Wuqian was among the few Chinese masters trained in Chinese and Tibetan Buddhist traditions. He spent more time in India than in China. Since he passed away in Hong Kong on December 8, 2010, his followers in Hong Kong issued a short obituary that briefly included his biography. However, some of his followers published memoirs on him in both printed materials and on websites of Buddhist organizations, such as the Buddhist magazine *Buddhist in Hong Kong (Monthly)* (Xianggang fojiao yuekan 香港佛教月刊)[2] and the website of the Hong Kong Vajrayana Association (Xianggang jingangcheng xuehui 香港金剛乘學會).[3] Many personal communications between Wuqian and his friends also gradually surfaced. Thanks to these new sources, we can now draw a portrait of Wuqian. His Buddhist life could be divided into three periods: in 1937–1947, he mainly lived in the Sinitic Buddhist tradition centred on several temples in Shaanxi; in 1947–1958, he travelled to Sichuan, Qinghai, and Xizang to seek a teacher and learn about Tibetan Buddhism; in 1958–2010 he was active in India but stayed connected with Buddhists in the greater China region. While in Shaanxi, he was exposed to many Buddhist traditions, including Chan, Consciousness-only thoughts, and Tantrism, which laid the foundation for his future experience in Xizang, China and India. He models Xuanzang in many ways, such as seeking a new adventure in his middle age in India and focusing on Buddhist translations in his later years. The following discussion in this section attempts to reveal his karmic affinity for Buddhist learning for his future career in India.

Wuqian was born on July 24, 1922, in the historic town of Xianyang in the Shaanxi province of China. His original surname was Kong. His family was struggling with poverty when he was born. At fifteen, he went to Chongren Temple (Chongren si 崇仁寺) to become a novice monk, studying with Master Chunde 純德/淳德. When he reached seventeen, he moved to Daxingshan Temple (Daxingshan si 大興善寺) and

[1] As this paper will show, Wuqian's fellow masters, disciples, and friends left many notes on him and his activities in India and China.

[2] https://www.hkbuddhist.org/zh/page.php?p=booklet&cid=7&scid=6&kid=2 all materials of this monthly magazine have been online available.

[3] http://www.vajrayana.org.hk/ it offers numerous materials for the history of this organisation and its associated masters.

received full ordination there from Master Xindao 心道 (1905–1968). Xindao was not an ordinary master but belonged to the new generation of Buddhist masters who received modern Buddhist education. In Xindao's youth in the 1920s, he travelled to many temples in Zhenjiang, Changzhou, Shanghai and Ningbo to study numerous Buddhist teachings from the traditional monastic perspective. Eventually, he ended up at Minnan Buddhist College (Minnan foxueyuan 閩南佛學院) for modern monastic education. He then served as a faculty member and lectured on Pure Land Buddhism. In 1934, Xindao went to Qinghai to study Tibetan Tantrism. He received the Kālacakravajra abhiṣeka 時輪金剛大灌頂 from the 9th Panchen Lama 九世班禪 (Thubten Choekyi Nyima, 1883–1937) at Kumbum (Ta'er 塔爾) Temple in Xining and a title of Pandita from Tibetan Buddhist master Dngul chu 恩久活佛. Thereafter, he stayed in the north-western regions to study and preach Buddhism. In 1937, he was invited by Master Taixu to lecture at Wanshou Temple (Wanshou si 萬壽寺) in Nanjing for the Chinese Buddhist Association. The next year, he was invited by Kang Jiyao 康寄遥 (1880–1968) to lecture on the *Diamond Sutra* in Shaanxi.[1] Both monastic and lay Buddhists supported him in heading Daxingshan Temple. As Wuqian's first official master, Xindao's rich experience of learning and lecturing on both Chinese and Tibetan Buddhist traditions significantly impacted Wuqian's career path. Under his tutelage Wuqian must have become interested in both traditions.

Besides Xindao, three other notable Buddhist masters also taught and trained the newly ordained monk Wuqian: Hanjing 含静 taught him Chan Buddhism, Miaokuo 妙闊 (1878–1960) taught him the Consciousness-only tradition, and Nenghai 能海 (1886–1967) taught him precepts and Tantrism. Miaokuo and Nenghai were even more instrumental in Wuqian's spiritual and monastic journey in the future. Hanjing was an abbot of Damaopeng Temple (Damaopeng si 大茅篷寺) in Mount Zhongnan. As a master of teaching meditation, Hanjing kept a low profile, leading a very private life in obscurity. Unlike Hanjing, Miaokuo and Nenghai had greater visibility in the Buddhist community. Miaokuo was invited to Shaanxi in 1922 to preach Buddhism. Miaokuo became the abbot of Xingjiao Temple (Xingjiao si 興教寺) under the support of Kang Jiyao and other leading laypeople. Xingjiao Temple was a memorial site for the legendary pilgrim and translator Xuanzang and his leading disciples. Xuanzang's relics were housed and honoured at this temple.

Miaokuo, originally from the renowned Mount Wutai region in Shanxi, commenced his monastic career in Shanxi before discovering a profound interest in Consciousness-only Buddhism while pursuing studies at Zifu Temple (Zifu si 資福寺) near Beijing. After 1906, he travelled to South China and studied at various traditional Buddhist temples in Nanjing, Shanghai, Hangzhou, and Wuhan as well as Huayan

[1] Kang was a leading lay Buddhist who sponsored the trip of Taixu to Shaanxi and wrote a detailed record of Taixu's journey (Kang 1997).

University, a modern Buddhist college based in Shanghai. In 1922, the Buddhist community in Shaanxi requested Taixu to teach Buddhism there. However, recognizing the potential of his disciple, Taixu proposed that Miaokuo assume the responsibility of teaching Buddhism in Shaanxi instead. Miaokuo answered the call and lectured on the *Treatise on the Awakening of Faith according to the Mahāyāna* (*Dacheng qixing lun* 大乘起信論) for the Shaanxi Buddhist Association. Because of his successful lecture, he was convinced to stay to head Xingjiao Temple. He then moved there and lectured on the Consciousness-only tradition. With these lectures Miaokuo played a crucial role in reviving Xuanzang's legacy in this commemorative temple (Miaokuo 1931, 178–179; Scott 2020, 232). In 1931, Master Taixu eventually visited Shaanxi for a lecture tour focusing on Consciousness-only teaching. In the following years, this tradition was revived and flourished again in Shaanxi. In 1941, Taixu helped Miaokuo organize the World Buddhist College at Daxingshan Temple and established a Pali Tripitika division. Wuqian developed as a newly ordained Buddhist monk in this institutional context. He studied with Miaokuo on the Consciousness-only tradition and also learned about Taixu's teachings. He must also have been aware of the World Buddhist College and its division of studying Pali texts. It would have been natural for Wuqian to think about making a pilgrimage trip to India after learning about Xuanzang and his legacy of the Consciousness-only tradition from Miaokuo during this period.

Wuqian's other master Nenghai was influential in introducing him to Tantric Buddhism. Nenghai was a native of Sichuan and began his career as a low-ranking military officer in the Qing troops. While struggling with the chaotic situation in Sichuan in the early Republican era, Nenghai turned to Buddhism for help in 1914 when he accidentally listened to Master Foyuan's 佛源 (1923–2009) dharma talk in Chengdu. In 1915, he went to Japan for a business trip and came into contact with Japanese Buddhism. After he came back, he devoted himself to Buddhist learning, especially studying the Consciousness-only tradition with Zhang Kecheng 張克誠 (1865–1922) at Peking University, which reflected the popularity of the Consciousness-only tradition among intellectuals at that time.[1] In 1924, having deliberated for many years, he eventually received ordination from Master Guanyi 貫一 (1875–1954) and became a monk at Mañjuśrī Temple (Wenshu yuan 文殊院) in Chengdu. While living in Western Sichuan bordering the Tibetan region in China, Nenghai realized the importance of Tibetan Buddhism. He went to Kangding to study the Tibetan language with a local lama. In 1928, Nenghai started his journey along with three monks to Lhasa. He received Tibetan Buddhist teachings from Master Khang-gsar 康薩 (1888–1941) Rinpoche at

[1] At Peking University, Zhang Kecheng was the first Buddhist to introduce the Consciousness-only school of thought. Many Chinese intellectuals developed an interest in Consciousness-only philosophy in the 1910s and 1920s (Makeham 2014).

Drepung Monastery 哲蚌寺 in Lhasa for nearly ten years.[1] In 1936, Nenghai left China and travelled to Nepal and India. In 1937, he reached Mañjuśrī Temple and established a ritual platform for teaching Tantric Buddhism. As the first ritual platform for teaching Tibetan Tantric Buddhism in Chengdu, it attracted numerous Buddhists from the Central Plains. Wuqian was one of the Buddhists who wanted to study with Nenghai. In the early 1940s, Wuqian went to Chengdu and studied Tantric Buddhism with Nenghai. Nenghai's teacher, Master Khang-gsar Rinpoche was a well-respected monk in the Gelugpa 格魯 sect of Tibetan Buddhism. He received his Geshe degree at Drepung Temple, and later he was regarded as the 27th generation of Je Tsongkhapa 宗喀巴 (1357–1419). As his student, Nenghai was a direct dharma descendant of the Gelugpa sect based on the lineage of Je Tsongkhapa at Drepung Monastery (Qiu 2016; Tan 2008). Given this transmission, it should not be surprising that Wuqian eventually also studied at Drepung Monastery (Nenghai 1994). As Esther Bianchi noted, Nenghai advocated the simultaneous practice of Vinaya and tantra from the perspective of exoteric and esoteric combined practice following a Gelugpa model (Bianchi 2021, 225–252; Bianchi 2017, 300–318; Bianchi 2009, 295–346; Bianchi 2003), which exactly matched what Wuqian was trained to do in the course of his monastic journey.

After learning Tantric Buddhism for some time with Nenghai, Wuqian planned to follow Nenghai's steps to Lhasa. In 1946, Wuqian travelled to Xizang via Sichuan and Qinghai. Just as Nenghai, he aimed to study at Drepung Monastery. Fortunately, he was accepted by Blo bzang Smon lam (1898–1989) Rinpoche at Drepung Monastery, who was the Jé Khenpo 杰巴堪布 of a monastic college (Dratsang Jé 杰巴扎倉) there. Wuqian focused on Tibetan Buddhist logic and the *Ornament of/for Realization*[s] (*Abhisamayālaṅkāra* 現觀莊嚴論). He stayed in Lhasa for nine years, similar to the length of time of his master Nenghai at Drepung Monastery.

2 Propagating and Networking Buddhism in India

It is only within the last two decades that scholars have started the study of Sino-Indian Buddhist exchanges during the latter half of the twentieth century. Although in the 1950s, with the founding of the People's Republic of China and the independence of the Republic of India, there were frequent political and cultural connections between these two nations, subsequently, these connections were disrupted following the Sino-Indian military conflicts over the border dispute in 1962. Some significant Chinese Buddhist figures such as Taixu, Xudan 許丹 (1891–1953) and Wanhui 萬慧 (1889–1959) made visits to India in the 1940s. Yet, since the 1950s, the Chinese Buddhist community in

[1] Khangsar, meaning "new house," is a family of the Begu clan, a branch of the Gyer clan. They are based in the Ganze region of Kham. See https://treasuryoflives.org/zh/institution/Khangsar (accessed on March 2, 2023). He was born in the year of rat in the Tibeatan calendar, and he received his Geshe degree in 1904; see https://fofars.com/1034.html (accessed on March 6, 2023).

India, mainly in Calcutta, has suffered political turmoil. A few books and articles have offered some preliminary study on the Buddhist activities of the Chinese diasporic community in India, including those of eminent scholar Tan Yunshan 譚雲山 (1898–1983) and Master Fafang 法舫 (1904–1951), as well as the monastic members of the Chinese Indian communities in Calcutta (Zhang 2014). As one of the Buddhist leaders who stayed in India for the longest time, more than half a century, Master Wuqian played a vital role and made tremendous contributions to Buddhist interactions across India, bridging India and China and connecting with Taiwan and Hong Kong of China. He has been ignored by mainstream scholarship on modern Buddhism and China-India studies. By concentrating on Wuqian's actions in India, on his contributions to reconstructing the Chinese monastic community in Calcutta and revitalizing Chinese Buddhism in India and beyond, this section will restore a lost chapter of Sino-Indian Buddhist links in the second half of the twentieth century.

In 1958, Wuqian left for India and arrived in Kalimpong. He arrived in this region with his Chinese friend Liu Ruizhi 劉鋭之 (1914–1997). When Liu first decided to travel to India, Yogi Chen (Chen Jianmin 陳健民, 1903–1987) suggested that Wuqian serve as Liu's interpreter because Liu's Tibetan language was insufficient. Liu studied with Dudjom 敦珠 Rinpoche (Jikdrel Yeshe Dorje, 1904–1987) in Kalimpong, and Wuqian served to facilitate communication between Dudjom and Liu. When Wuqian had just arrived in Kalimpong and was translating for Dudjom, Dudjom was focusing on teaching *Bdud-'joms 'Jigs-bral-ye-śes-rdo*-rje 大幻化網導引法. In the beginning, Wuqian could only understand half of Dubjom's teachings. One month later, he could understand more than 90 percent of Dudjom's teachings. Liu later translated this teaching into Chinese, based mainly on Wuqian's translation. Liu also received the Narak Dong-truk Tantra and the title of Lama Sonam Chokyi Gyaltsan from his master. Upon Liu's return to Hong Kong, he committed himself to the propagation and advancement of Vajrayana teachings.[1]

During that time, there were also some British Buddhists who were studying under the guidance of Dudjom Rinpoche in Kalimpong. On April 18, 1959, along with three British Buddhists and Liu, Wuqian received the bestowing of the Tibetan *Consecration Ritual of the Vajrasatva with a Hundred peaceful and wrathful deities* 金剛薩埵寂忿百尊灌頂 from Dudjom Rinpoche, which was the first time this ritual was performed for non-Tibetan Buddhists. These three British Buddhists included monk Sangharakshita (born Dennis Philip Edward Lingwood, 1925–2018) and two laypeople, John Driver and John

[1] Later, he played a key role in advancing Vajrayana in Hong Kong. He also exchanged Tantric Studies with some preeminent Tibetologists in mainland China including Chen Qingying 陳慶英 and Wang Yao 王堯 (Chen 2006, 269).

Blofeld.[1] In his memoir, Sangharakshita often mentioned Wuqian as his friend studying in Kalimpong (Sangharakshita 1997; Viehbeck 2017). Sangharakshita was a close associate of Bhimrao Ramji Ambedkar (1891–1956), who contributed considerably to the revival of Buddhism in India (Sangharakshita 2007). John Blofeld was a little bit different. He was interested in many various aspects of Eastern culture. Although he claimed himself to be a Buddhist, he became a crucial translator of translating different Chinese religious texts into English, not limited to Buddhist texts (Blofeld 1988; Blofeld 2002).

Even before the People's Republic of China and the Republic of India established formal diplomatic relations in 1950, there were already thousands of Chinese settlers in Calcutta and other towns and cities of India. These Chinese migrants, who first arrived in the last quarter of the eighteenth century, brought to India a diverse set of local religious traditions, including the veneration of female Bodhisattva Guanyin 觀音 and other local deities associated with Chinese Buddhism (Zhang 2015). These deities were usually housed within the *Huiguan* 會館 (Native-Place Association) buildings, where migrants from specific regions of China congregated. Buddhist temples specifically for the Chinese communities were set up in Sarnath in 1921, Chinese Buddhist Temple (Zhonghua fosi 中華佛寺), in Bodhgaya in 1923, Mahabodhi Chinese Temple (Zhonghua dajue si 中華大覺寺), in Balrampur in 1923, Temple of Chinese Light (Huaguang si 華光寺), in Gorakhpur in 1927, Twin Grove Temple (Shuanglin si 雙林寺), and at Nalanda in 1931, China Temple (Zhongguo miao 中國廟). Additionally, the Buddhist Association of the Chinese in India (Yindu Huaren fojiaohui 印度華人佛教會) was established in Ajmer in 1932 (Zhang 2008, 56; Zhang 2014, 433). After Wuqian arrived in India, he became active in several of these organizations, significantly impacting the Indian Chinese communities.

Wuqian arrived in India when the Sino-Indian cultural exchanges peaked. After the Chinese premier Zhou Enlai visited India in 1956, the Chinese government also donated money to build the Xuanzang Memorial Hall at Nalanda. Tan Yunshan, the director of Cheena Bhavana in Santiniketan, had proposed to the Indian government that the Xuanzang Memorial Hall at Nalanda could be utilized as a Chinese Buddhist Research Institute "with a specific task of study of and research in Chinese Buddhism, its background, introduction, development and spreading."[2] In the 1930s and 1940s, Tan, himself a lay Buddhist, brought Chinese Buddhist monks such as Fafang and Wang Pachow 巴宙 (1918–2017) to Santiniketan. Tan was also deeply involved with the monk

[1] Sangharakshita was among the few Western individuals ordained as Theravadin Bhikkhus in the post-World War II era. He devoted over 20 years to residing in Asia, during which he received teachings from several Tibetan Buddhist masters. He was the founder of the Western Buddhist Order and the Friends of the Western Buddhist Order.

[2] National Archives of India, Ministry of Education. "Hiuen Tsang Memorial Hall: Proposal for Developing it into a Center for Sino-Indian Studies." File No. 3-194/57 C1.

Taixu's visit to India in 1940. After retirement, Tan settled in Bodhgaya. While Tan Yunshan seems to have been more interested in the academic study of Chinese Buddhism, Master Wuqian engaged with the practice of Buddhism and promulgated it among the Chinese migrants in India.

In the late 1950s and early 1960s, the Chinese Buddhist community remained a marginal minority group, politically, religiously, and culturally powerless. In Calcutta, particularly, the Chinese Buddhist community had to face challenges from both the Hindu and Islamic communities. The first challenge was the need for more institutional establishments. After all, the monks and nuns needed their institutional foundation for spiritual cultivation and ritual performance, and the laypeople needed a monastic community to practice as lay Buddhists. Therefore, Wuqian spent most of his time planning and founding temples for the diasporic Chinese Buddhists, which was very important for preserving the identity of the Chinese Buddhist community. In the 1960s, Wuqian served as the abbot of the Twin Grove Temple in Gorakhpur and the Chinese Temple in Sarnath. In 1966, Wuqian established the Buddhist Sangha Council and functioned as its president. He also attended a meeting of the Chinese Buddhist Society as a representative of the Chinese Buddhist monks residing in India (Zhang 2014, 225–253). In 1967, when he was the abbot at Sarnath, Wuqian started planning for the Xuanzang Temple in Calcutta. Since all the Chinese Buddhist temples in India were built by lay Chinese immigrants, Wuqian thought Chinese monks should also have their own monastery. He soon purchased 70,000 sq. ft of land about 5 km from Tangra, one of the areas where the Chinese, especially the Hakka community, had settled in Calcutta. Due to insufficient funds, the construction progressed slowly. In 1971, while supervising the construction work, Wuqian was robbed at gunpoint and lost all the money and his ribs broken. Despite all the difficulties, his faith in building the temple remained unaffected. The main building of the temple was finally completed towards the end of the 1970s (Zhang 2014). Master Dongchu 東初 (1908–1977) from Taiwan, China, who visited India in the late 1960s and the early 1970s, met with Master Wuqian and wrote a detailed account of Buddhist interactions between China and India called *ZhongYin fojiao jiaotong shi* 中印佛教交通史 (History of Buddhist Exchanges between China and India). He noted that Xuanzang Temple was built to commemorate the monk Xuanzang as the leading contributor to China-India cultural exchange, as well as in the hope of promoting friendship between China and India in the future (Dongchu 1985, 522).

Wuqian established the above-mentioned temple in honour of the great pilgrim Xuanzang and named this temple after Xuanzang. As the preface written by Wuqian's friend dedicated to the founding of this temple indicates, at that time the political turbulence disturbed the Chinese Buddhist community in India, leading many to believe that they were living in the age of the final Dharma. The age of the end of the Dharma is thought to come not only from natural disasters but also from human misfortune.

Wuqian aimed to transform this situation by expounding Buddhist teachings. For Wuqian, Buddhism was instrumental in rebuilding morality to save sentient beings from the corrupted and decaying worldly realm. In 1971, during his visit in Calcutta, Master Dongchu gave a speech at Xuanzang Temple, explaining Buddhist developments in Taiwan and describing the journey of the skull relics of Xuanzang from Japan to Taiwan, China. He also reported that at a celebration attended by over 1000 local Chinese and Indian residents, a plaque with the name of the Xuanzang Temple calligraphy was presented to Master Wuqian by Ye Ganzhong 葉幹中, one of the local Chinese community leaders (Dongchu 1985, 522–523). Nowadays, entering through the Chinese-style gate is an open field where the main structure of the two-story Xuanzang Temple can be seen. On both floors, prayer halls are dedicated to Śākyamuni Buddha and Guanyin and Maitreya Buddha. The hall on the ground floor is decorated with brightly painted frescoes. Next to the temple is also the Xuanzang Memorial Hall, where a golden statue of Xuanzang, covered in glass, is placed in the centre. This hall also doubles as a library, housing a collection of Buddhist scriptures and rare Chinese religious books neatly arranged on shelves. In the courtyard is a statue of the White Guanyin and a small fountain, and a small Chinese cemetery is adjacent to the monastic complex.

The Xuanzang temple was built in Calcutta at a time when ties between China and India were at their worst. The 1962 Sino-Indian confrontation led to ongoing hostility between the two nations. The Chinese community in India witnessed various persecutions, including restrictions on movement within India and forced deportation (Zhang 2015). This temple was built specifically for Chinese Buddhists and Master Wuqian continued to spread Chinese Buddhism during this period of political conflict between China and India. It is most likely because of the presence of Dongchu during this time that Master Wuqian also established links with Buddhist monks and institutions in Taiwan, China (Xiao 2023). Master Wuqian began managing the Bodhimandala at the Mahabodhi Chinese Temple in Bodhgaya in 1983. He also renovated the Mahavira Hall and the residence for monks at the temple. When the General Association for Chinese Buddhists in India (Yindu Huaqiao fojiao zonghui 印度華僑佛教總會) was founded in 1985, Wuqian was elected to become the first president and was also elected to become chair of the executive board. Wuqian organized lecture on the *Kṣitigarbha Sūtra* (*Dizang jing* 地藏經). He considered that the weather in Calcutta was humid and hot and that there weren't enough crops to eat in India, particularly in Calcutta, which led to heat death and famine. Numerous of the dead were not allowed to rest in peace, leading the locals to seek assistance from the Buddhist masters. Wuqian thought that talks on this sutra which dealt with assisting the dead would be advantageous to the community.

During his visit to Bodhgaya in 1989, Master Sheng Yen 聖嚴 (1931–2009) expressed admiration for the Buddhist endeavors undertaken by Master Wuqian in Calcutta and

Bodhgaya. In his travelogue, Master Sheng Yen points out that Master Wuqian had taken over the responsibilities of administering the Mahabodhi Chinese Temple from a Tibetan monk (Sheng Yen 2014, 106–108). This Tibetan monk was most likely Fujin Lama, who in 1967 had presented Master Dongchu with three pieces of relics when the latter, accompanied by Master Wuqian, paid a visit to the temple in Bodhgaya. These relics are preserved at the Chung-Hwa Institute of Buddhist Culture in Taipei. After Master Wuqian took charge of the Mahabodhi Chinese Temple, the new hall that he built inside the temple started accommodating 200 to 300 people (Sheng Yen 2014, 106–108). Through this temple, Master Wuqian seems to have played an important role in furthering ordination activities for monks and nuns from different parts of Asia. In 1998, for example, Master Wuqian, in collaboration with the Foguangshan organization in Taiwan, China, organized a pilgrimage for about 1200 lay Buddhists and 300 monks and nuns to Bodhgaya. Master Wuqian from India, Master Yongxing 永惺 (1926–2016) from Hong Kong, China, the President of the Hong Kong Buddhist Association, and Master Xingyun 星雲 (1927–2023) from Taiwan China, the founding abbot of the Foguangshan order, presided over the activities of these participants. In her study on Taiwanese nuns, Li Yuzhen documented Wuqian's participation in the full ordination ceremony in Bodhgaya. According to Li, she learned from the Foguangshan members about the plan to conduct an international full ordination ceremony in February 1998. She arrived in Calcutta with about 40 ordination candidates. They travelled with a large group of lay pilgrims from Foguangshan. Following the Chinese Buddhist tradition, three leading precept masters officiated at this full ordination ceremony: Xingyun as sīla-upādhyāya (precept-teacher), Wuqian as dharma-ācārya (preceptor of teachings), and Yongxing as the instructing ācārya (instructing preceptor). Li pointed out that Xingyun was the leading proponent of this international ordination ceremony for women. Li noted that Wuqian was the abbot of the Xuanzang Temple in Calcutta and the abbot of the Chinese Buddhist Temple in Bodhgaya. Taiwanese nuns regarded him as a remarkable figure and well-respected monk who devoted himself to Buddhist missionary activities in India by overcoming immeasurable difficulties in India. Wuqian's leadership brought Chinese temples to life with the support of the overseas Chinese community in Calcutta.[1] (Li 2013, 172, 194)

Master Wuqian, in contrast to Xuanzang, was not a prolific translator or writer of Buddhist texts. But he was a devoted administrator, supporter, and practitioner of Buddhism. While Wuqian was indeed trained in many Buddhist traditions in the central

[1] Other notable Buddhist monks from South Asia and other parts of the world were also there. Information about this historical event, which included lectures and the ordination of candidates at the Mahabodhi Chinese Temple, can be found in Li Yuzhen (Yu-Chen Li)'s (2000) dissertation, "Crafting Women's Religious Experience in a Patrilineal Society: Taiwanese Buddhist Nuns in Action (1945–1999)," as well as other articles.

and Tibetan regions of China as well as India, when he found himself in India, the political and religious environment was complicated and might not have allowed him to devote himself to writing commentaries and works, even though he attempted to model himself on Xuanzang.[1] Instead, he devoted himself to maintaining Buddhist teachings and stabilizing the local Chinese Buddhist community in India, as well as focusing on Buddhist interactions between China and India.

3 Building Buddhist Exchanges between India and China in Later Years

Master Wuqian nurtured enduring connections with Buddhist institutions and groups across the greater China region. Having resided in India for more than five decades, he should be acknowledged as a pivotal figure in fostering Buddhist networks within and beyond India during the latter half of the twentieth century. Master Moru 默如 (1905–1991), a leading master from Taiwan, China recounted his pilgrimage to India in a memoir, describing his encounter with Wuqian and his significant role in the Chinese Buddhist community in India. As a discipline of Master Taixu, Moru inherited the modern Buddhist legacy from Taixu and subsequently received his early monastic education at Minnan Buddhist College. He later moved to Taipei and spent most of his later life at Fayun Temple (Fayun si 法雲寺) in Taipei. In 1984, Moru undertook a pilgrimage trip to India, where he had the opportunity to visit the Xuanzang Temple in Calcutta. He recollected that the abbot of Xuanzang Temple, Wuqian, was a preeminent monastic leader with a clear mind and broad vision. He made a detailed plan for all the pilgrims. According to Moru, Wuqian was devoted to expanding the influence of Xuangzang Temple, often offering dharma talks and bestowing precepts on local Buddhists (Moru 1990).

Aside from his connections with Buddhist institutions in Taiwan, China, Master Wuqian re-established his links with Buddhist temples and organizations in mainland China during the late 1980s and began hosting visitors from mainland China. In May 1992, Wuqian hosted Professor Dong Shuangchang 董雙長 and his wife, who lived at Mahabodhi Chinese Temple for over a month. Dong was a professor from Hebei Medical College and was sponsored by a government grant to India. In October, Wuqian met Zheng Weihong, a professor focused on Buddhist logic. Wuqian noted that the young generation should learn Buddhist and non-Buddhist logic. Later when he was interested in translating Buddhist logic works into Chinese, he also read works by Chinese scholars. In the meantime, he invited Chinese Buddhist logic scholars to India for scholarly exchanges. (Zheng 2019, 477). Later, on June 10, 1998, Master Wuqian gifted two relics to the Daci'en Temple (Daci'en si 大慈恩寺) in Xi'an. This is the temple where Xuanzang

[1] Many scholars have written about the Sino-Indian relations in this period; see Lüthi 2012, 95–119; Ghosh 2017, 697–727.

was engaged in translation activity after his return from India in the mid-seventh century. The relics that Master Wuqian gifted were housed in the central arena of the third floor of the Giant Wild Goose Pagoda (Dayan ta 大雁塔) at the temple. [1]

The enduring friendship between Master Jingtian 净天 (1925–2004) and Master Wuqian, spanning over half a century, and their connection between China and India is also noteworthy. Jingtian was Wuqian's dharma brother back in the Republican era, and he was three years younger than Wuqian. He also received his full ordination from Master Xindao in 1942. Jingtian later studied the Consciousness-only tradition with Miaokuo and Tantric Buddhism with Nenghai. Therefore, Jingtian shared the same master-disciple relations with Xindao, Miaokuo, and Nenghai as Wuqian. In 1991, when the Xuanzang Memorial Hall was completed in Calcutta, Wuqian invited the Chinese Buddhist Association to send a delegation to participate in the ceremony. The Chinese Buddhist Association sent a delegation to Xuanzang Temple, and Jingtian was one of the delegation members. Wuqian noted in his letter to Jingtian that this was their first meeting in forty-five years since they had parted in 1946. In the letter, Wuqian recollected that Jingtian and he discussed Buddhist teachings for more than one month untill Jingtian was troubled by the hot and humid weather in India and returned to China via Thailand. After that, they did not communicate for more than a decade until May 2004, Wuqian and Jingtian met again at the newly opened Xifang Temple (Xifang si 西方寺) in Hong Kong. Then they went to Famen Temple in Shaanxi together to welcome the Buddha's finger relics to Hong Kong. They attended the ceremony to pay homage to the relics together. They also practised the ritual of bathing the Buddha's statue in Hong Kong during the Buddha's birthday celebration on May 26. However, on this day, Jingtian fell ill and collapsed. He passed away the next day. On May 28, Wuqian made a poignant visit to Hongfa Temple (Hongfa si 弘法寺) to offer a final tribute to Jingtian, a fellow monk who shared the same Dharma lineage.[2]

Wuqian also actively sought collaborations with Buddhist institutions in Hong Kong and southern China. On November 24, 2010, Wuqian conducted a Buddhist ceremony in Bodhgaya in collaboration with Buddhist organisations from Hong Kong and Guangdong province. He invited Master Rizhao 日照 (1971–), abbot of Lifo Temple (Lifo chansi 禮佛禪寺) in Guangdong, to perform the Chinese tradition of the Buddhist Rite for Deliverance of Creatures of Water and Land (Handi shuilu fahui 漢地水陸法會). This ritual performance turned out to be very successful, and it attracted many Buddhists in the local community. Unfortunately, less than a month after this ceremony, Master Wuqian passed away in Hong Kong on December 8 at the age of 88. Prior to his

---

[1] See Wuqian's letter to Jingtian on 1 July 2010, reprinted in Liu Yaowu's 劉耀武 edited volume dedicated to Jingtian in 2020.

[2] Wuqian's obituary of Master Jingtian, June 19, 2004, reprinted in a volume in memory of Jingtian edited by Liu Yaowu in 2020.

death, he invited Rizhao to succeed him as the abbot of the Mahabodhi Chinese Temple in India. Master Wuqian's body was transported to Nanhua Temple (Nanhua si 南華寺) in Guangzhou for cremation, a solemn ceremony that occurred on December 17, 2010. The cremation and burial rites were overseen by Master Rizhao, the new abbot of Mahabodhi Chinese Temple.[1]

Master Wuqian's many contributions also included the setting up of the Buddhist Studies Institute at the Xuanzang Temple in 2000 and an initiative to translate Buddhist texts that he launched in 2002 to revive Xuanzang's legacy of translating Indian Buddhist texts into the Chinese language. Most translations in this project focused on Buddhist logic. However, soon this project was paused due to financial difficulty. Wuqian visited Hong Kong in pursuit of additional resources to continue this ongoing translation project. During his time there, he went on to complete the translation of three major works, including the Hetuvidyā texts, which were first introduced to China from India by Xuanzang.

4 Conclusion

In conclusion, it is evident from the preceding discussions that Wuqian was among the most significant Chinese Buddhist masters of the twentieth century. Some of the most eminent figures in Chinese Buddhism, including Miaokuo and Nenghai, nurtured his early intellectual development in Buddhism. Although originally Wuqian was ordained in a traditional Buddhist temple, he received monastic education in both traditional and modern ways. Wuqian embraced both Chinese and Tibetan traditions. On the one hand, he received training in the most dominant Chan tradition. On the other hand, while receiving his education at the Daxingshan Temple, he was inspired by Xuanzang's legacy of learning Consciousness-only teaching. His two masters, Miaokuo and Nenghai, introduced him to the Consciousness-only and the Tantric traditions.

Wuqian stood out as a pioneering figure among his generation of Chinese monks for his unwavering commitment to studying Tibetan Buddhism directly and intensively in Xizang. His study of nearly a decade at Drepung Monastery enabled him to understand Tibetan Buddhism, especially the Gelugpa sect comprehensively. His knowledge of Buddhist logic was made possible by his stay there. In the interim, Liu Ruizhi, a fellow Chinese Buddhist, greatly benefited from Wuqian's interpretation of Tibetan teachings. To a great extent, Liu Ruizhi's translation of Tantric ritual resulted from Wuqian's assistance. Wuqian's other fellow Buddhist learners include three British Buddhists who later became influential advocators of Tibetan Buddhism in the West.

[1] After the passing of Master Wuqian, his appointed Dharma heir of Mahabodhi Chinese Temple Master Rizhao wrote an obituary for him, which was published along with a brief introduction of his biography in *Buddhist in Hong Kong (Monthly)*, no. 608, in January 2011.

It is evident from the evidence we have that Master Wuqian was one of the key figures involved with the practice of Chinese Buddhism in India for over five decades. He was instrumental in administering and setting up important Chinese Buddhist temples in different regions of India. He also significantly organized pilgrimage and ordination activities for Chinese monks, nuns, and lay followers at sacred Buddhist sites in India. Xuanzang Temple, which he helped found, became a hub of Chinese Buddhism and culture in South Asia. It hosted numerous pilgrims from mainland China, Taiwan, Hong Kong, and other Chinese communities across Asia. In addition, he organized to bring Chinese masters to perform many Chinese Buddhist rituals at Xuanzang Temple in the 1990s, which helped the revival of Buddhism in the local region.

Master Wuqian's additional contributions include starting the translation initiative to make numerous works on Buddhist logic accessible to a Chinese audience. He also presented two relics to the Daci'en Temple, in emulation of Xuanzang's legacy. He hosted many Chinese visitors, including pilgrims and scholars, to promote Buddhism and Buddhist scholarship. These all reflect his modelling of Xuanzang and his adherence to the spirit of Xuanzang, contributing significantly to various aspects of fostering intercultural and interreligious interactions in Asia, particularly between China and India. In sum, tracing his legacy in the history of twentieth-century Buddhism holds great significance.

References

Bianchi 2003 Esther Bianchi. "L'insegnamento tantrico del 'lama cinese' Nenghai (1886–1967): Inquadramento storico e analisi testuale del corpus di Yamāntaka-Vajrabhairava." Ph.D. dissertation, Paris/Venice: Università Ca'Foscari di Venezia and École Pratique des Hautes Études.

2009 "The 'Chinese Lama' Nenghai (1886–1967): Doctrinal Tradition and Teaching Strategies of a Gelugpa Master in Republican China." In: Matthew T. Kapstein, ed., 295–346. Boston: Wisdom Publishers.

2017 "Sino-Tibetan Buddhism: Continuities and Discontinuities. The Case of Nenghai's 能海 Legacy in the Contemporary Era." In: Yael Bentor and Meir Shahar, eds., *Chinese and Tibetan Esoteric Buddhism*, 300–318. Leiden: Brill.

2021 "The Combined Practice of Vinaya and Tantra in Nenghai's Path to Liberation." In: Esther Bianchi and Shen Weirong, eds., *Sino-Tibetan Buddhism across the Ages*, 225–252. Leiden: Brill.

Blofeld 1988 John Blofeld.. *The Wheel of Life: The Autobiography of a Western Buddhist*. Amherst: Shambhala.

2002 *The Tantric Mysticism of Tibet*. Charleston: Charleston Buddhist Fellowship.

Chen 2006 Chen Qingying 陳慶英. *Chen Qingying zangxue lunwenji* 陳慶英藏學論文集 [Collected Papers on Tibetology by Chen Qingying]. Beijing: Zhongguo zangxue chubanshe.

Dongchu 1985 Dongchu 東初. *ZhongYin fojiao jiaotong shi* 中印佛教交通史 [History of Buddhist Exchanges between China and India]. Taipei: Dongchu chubanshe.

Geary 2007 David Geary. "Raising the Status of Nuns: The Controversy over Bhikkuni Ordination." In: Sarah LeVine and David N. Gellner, ed. *Rebuilding Buddhism: The Theravada Movement in Twentieth-Century Nepal*, 171–206. Cambridge, MA: Harvard University Press.

2017 *The Rebirth of Bodh Gaya: Buddhism and the Making of a World Heritage Site*. Seattle: University of Washington Press.

Ghosh 2017 Arunabh Ghosh. "Before 1962: The Case for 1950s China-India History." *Journal of Asian Studies* 76/3: 697–727.

Guoche 1988 Guoche 果徹. "Dongchu laoren jianpu 東初老人簡譜 [A Preliminary Chronicle of Elder Dongchu]." *Zhonghua foxue yanjiu* 中華佛學研究 [Chinese Buddhist Studies], vol. 2: 1–48.

Ji 1996 Ji, Xianlin 季羡林. *Fojiao yu Zhong Yin wenhua jiaoliu* 佛教與中印文化交流 [Buddhism and the Sino-Indian Cultural Exchanges]. Nanchang: Jiangxi jiaoyu chubanshe.

Kang 1997 Kang Jiyao 康寄遥. *Taixu dashi hongfa ji* 太虛大師弘法記 [A Record of Master Taixu's Preaching the Buddhist Dharma]. Zhengzhou: Henan Renmin chubanshe.

Li 2000 Li Yu-chen (Li Yuzhen) 李玉珍. "Crafting Women's Religious Experience in a Patrilineal Society: Taiwanese Buddhist Nuns in Action (1945–1999)." PhD dissertation, Cornell University.

2013 "Ordination, Legitimacy, and Sisterhood: The International Full Ordination Ceremony in Bodhgaya." In: Karma Lekshe Tsomo, ed., *Innovative Buddhist Women: Swimming against the Stream*, 168–198. London and New York: Routledge.

Lüthi 2012 Lorenz Lüthi. "Sino-Indian Relations, 1954–1962." *Eurasia Border Review*, vol. 3, Special Issue on China's Post-Revolutionary Borders, the 1940s–1960s, 95–119.

Makeham 2014 John Makeham ed. *Transforming Consciousness: Yogacara Thought in Modern China*. London: Routledge.

Miaokuo 1931[2006] Miaokuo 妙闊. "Zhongnanshan Xingjiao si ji 終南山興教寺記 [A Record of Xingjiao Monastery in Mount Zhongnan]." *Haichaoyin* 海潮音 [The Sound of Sea Tide] 12/6 (2013). Reprinted in *Minguo fojiao qikan jicheng* 民國佛教期刊集成[A Complete Collection of Buddhist Periodicals in the Reppublican Era]. Beijing: Quanguo tushuguan wenxian suowei zhongxin, 2006, 178–179.

Moru 1990 Moru 默如. *Moru congshu* 默如叢書 [Collection of Master Moru]. Taipei: Xinwenfeng chuban gongsi.

Nenghai 1994 Nenghai 能海. *Kangsa renboqing xingjiji chugao* 康薩仁波卿行迹記初稿 [A Draft of the Record of Journey of Khang-gsar Rinpoche]. *Xianmi wenku* 顯密文庫. http://read.goodweb.net.cn/news/news_view.asp?newsid=22200 (accessed on March 2, 2023).

Qiu 2016 Qiu, Yihua 邱熠華. "Kangsa renboqie yu Nenghai fashi de shitu wangshi: jianlun minguo shiqi hanzang fojiao wenhua jiaoliu 康薩仁波切與能海法師的師徒往事——兼論民國時期漢藏佛教文化交流 [The Story of Khang Gsar Rinpoche and Neng Hai Lama, View on the Buddhist Cultural Communication between Han and Tibetan during the Republic of China]." *Xiazang yanjiu* [Tibetan Studies], no. 6: 17–27.

Rizhao 2011a Rizhao 日照. "Daonian Wuqian zhanglao 悼念悟謙長老 [An Obituary of Master Wuqian]." *Xianggang fojiao yuekan* 香港佛教月刊 [Buddhist in Hong Kong (Monthly)] no. 608, January 2011.

2011b "Wuqian zhanglao shengping 悟謙長老生平 [The Life of Master Wuqian]." *Xianggang fojiao yuekan* 香港佛教月刊 [Buddhist in Hong Kong (Monthly)] no. 608, January 2011.

Sangharakshita
2007 Sangharakshita. *Precious Teachers: Indian Memoirs of an English Buddhist*. Cambridge: Windhorse Publications.

1997 *The Rainbow Road: From Tooting Broadway to Kalimpong, Memoirs of an English Buddhist*. Cambridge: Windhorse Publications.

Scott 2020 Gregory Adam Scott. *Building the Buddhist Revival: Reconstructing Monasteries in Modern China*. Oxford: Oxford University Press.

Sheng Yen 2014 Sheng Yen 聖嚴. *Foguo zhi lü* 佛國之旅 [Journey to the Land of Buddha]. Jinshan: Caituanfaren Fagushan wenjiao jijinhui 財團法人法鼓山文教基金會.

Tan 2008 Tan Tian 譚天. *Nenghai shangshi zhuan* 能海上師傳 [A Biography of Master Nenghai], Beijing: Zhongyang wenxian chubanshe.

Viehbeck 2017 Markus Viehbeck, ed. 2017. *Transcultural Encounters in the Himalayan Borderlands: Kalimpong as a Contact Zone*. Heidelberg: Heidelberg University Publishing.

Wuqian 2020 Wuqian 悟謙. "Daonian Jingtian fashi 悼念净天法師 [An Obituary of Master Jintian]." In: Liu Yaowu 劉耀武, ed., 慈意永流無盡意: 追憶净天長老 [Compassion Flows Everlastingly and Endlessly: Reminiscing about Elder Jingtian], 84–86. Beijing: Zongjiao wenhua chubanshe.

Xiao 2023 Xiao, Qingqiu 蕭慶秋. "Wuqian fashi canfang jianwen suiji 悟謙法師參訪見聞隨記 [A Note on Master Wuqian's Visit]." on the Website of Vajrayana Association 金剛乘學會 https://vajrayana.org.tw/%E6%82%9F%E8%AC%99%E6%B3%95%E5%B8%AB%E5%8F%83%E8%A8%AA%E8%A6%8B%E8%81%9E%E9%9A%A8%E8%A8%98/ (accessed on March 2, 2023).

Zhang 2008 Zhang, Xing 張幸. "Wenhua rentong de chuancheng yu chuangxin: Yindu Jia'ergeda huaren de duoyuanhua zongjiao xinyang yanjiu 文化認同的傳承與創新: 印度加爾各答華人的多元化宗教信仰研究 [Inheritance and Innovations as Factors of Cultural Identity: India-related Religious Practices Among the Chinese Community in Calcutta]." *Huaqiao Huaren lishi yanjiu* 華僑華人歷史研究 [Studies in Overseas Chinese] 84/4: 49–58.

2014 "Buddhist Practices and Institutions of the Chinese Community in Kolkata, India." In: Tansen Sen, ed., *Buddhism Across Asia: Networks of Material, Intellectual and Cultural Exchange*, 429–457. Singapore: Institute of Southeast Asian Studies.

2015 *The Chinese Community in Calcutta: Preservation and Change*. Halle: Univeritätsverlag Halle-Wittenberg.

Zheng 2019 Zheng, Weihong 鄭偉宏. *Quwei luoji zongheng tan* 趣味邏輯縱橫談 [An Overview on the Interesting Logic]. Hong Kong: Zhonghe chubanshe.

On Sanskrit Epistolary Literature, Kharoṣṭhī Letters and a Letter from *Prajñādeva to Xuanzang

BANDENG (Shenyang Falun Temple)

This paper is divided into three parts. The first part introduces three texts of Sanskrit epistolary literature: The *Patrakaumudī*, the *Lekhapaddhati* and the *Yāvana-paripāṭī-anukrama*. The second part introduces the general format of letters in the Kharoṣṭhī script from the Niya region. The third part, takes as its object a letter from *Prajñādeva (Ch. *Huitian*/慧天) to Xuanzang. I explain the letter's contents in detail and analyse the relationship between this letter, Sanskrit epistolary literature and the Kharosthi letters. In particular, I note that the phrase "ask for the infinite number of health and non-annoyances" is almost identical to a direct translation of the phrase "*arogi preṣeti bahu aprameyo*" in the Kharoṣṭhī letters, a phrase which is not found in the Sanskrit letters. It is also noted that the format of *Prajñādeva's letter is very different from the structure of the letters in the *Patrakaumudī*. From this fact, I speculate that in Xuanzang's time and earlier, a simpler form of the Sanskrit epistolary formula was prevalent in India and the surrounding areas.

Keywords: Sanskrit epistolary literature; Kharoṣṭhī; Xuanzang

The *Pūrṇāvadāna* in Sanskrit, Tibetan, and Chinese

A Newly Discovered Manuscript of Staël-Holstein's Sanskrit Textbook for a Reading Seminar at Peking University

CHEN Ming (Peking University) and LUO Hong (Peking University)

This paper focuses on a manuscript of a newly surfaced booklet prepared by Alexander Wilhelm von Staël-Holstein (1877–1937) as the textbook for a class which he conducted at Peking University during the academic year 1929 to 1930. Staël-Holstein selected, collated, and annotated trilingual passages of the *Pūrṇāvadāna* for a special reading seminar held weekly at his house. This seminar—which hosted established scholars as well as future giants in the field of Oriental Studies—and the textbook specifically designed for it, deserve a special mention in the history of Oriental Studies in China. As general background, this paper also highlights how Staël-Holstein gradually developed the teaching program of Sanskrit at Peking University from the spring semester of 1920 until his demise in 1937.

Keywords: Staël-Holstein; Oriental studies; *Pūrṇāvadāna*; Sanskrit textbook

A Sanskrit Manuscript of the *Arapacanamañjunāthapūjāvidhi* from Xizang

DAWA CHOEZOM (Tibetan Academy of Social Sciences)

The Sanskrit manuscript of the so-catalogued *Arapacanasādhana* from Xizang comprises five texts. This article focuses on the first text, the *Arapacanamañjunāthapūjāvidhi*, presenting a collation of the Tibetan translation found in the Tanjur, along with a transcription and preliminary investigation of the manuscript.

Key words: *Arapacanamañjunāthapūjāvidhi*; Sanskrit version; Tibetan version

Puñargaṃ's Life Recorded in the Khotanese Documents Kept in the Museum of Renmin University of China

FAN Jingjing (Peking University)

In the manuscripts from the Western Region kept in the Museum of Renmin University of China (MRUC), the name Puñargaṃ appears quite often. Nevertheless, given that most of the documents mention him only in passing, and that the manuscripts are rather fragmentary, we know very little about his life. This paper will publish five Khotanese documents about Puñargaṃ kept in the MRUC: GXW0399, GXW0407, GXW0406, GXW2049, GXW2059. Focusing on these materials, this paper reveals Puñargaṃ's life more clearly by making a thorough survey of the manuscripts which refer to this figure. Puñargaṃ used to be the head (Khotanese *auva haṃdasta*) of the Gaysāta village, probably as a successor, (or predecessor), of Sīḍaka. During the period from about 780 to 790 CE, he took charge of collecting taxes paid in grain (Ch. shuiliang/税粮) in Gaysāta, as is recorded in Chinese documents. He also supervised the collection of taxes paid in textiles, sesame, hempseed, sheep skins, money, etc., as is recorded (primarily) in Khotanese documents.

Keywords: Puñargaṃ; Museum of Renmin University of China; Khotanese documents

Case for the Translation of Buddhist Scriptures and the Evolution of Chinese Language

JIANG Nan (Chinese Academy of Social Sciences)

The introduction of Buddhism into China initiated a cultural exchange between the two ancient civilizations of China and India for more than a thousand years. This exchange left behind a huge volume of Chinese Buddhist scriptures. These materials are not only essential for the study of medieval Chinese language, but also invaluable for the historical exploration of Sino-Indian language contact, and its influence on the development of Chinese language itself. The purpose of this paper is to expose these influences from the perspective of grammar, which reflects the core features of a language.

First, I examine the direct influence of the source language and I take the addition of topic-shift markers as an example. Based on a comparative analysis of the *Lotus Sutra* in Sanskrit and in various Chinese translations, I found that topic markers such as *ershi* (尔时), *jin(zhe/ri)* (今者/日), *fuci/cifu* (復次/次復), and *(fu)you* (復有/復) were always added at the beginning of a sentence to initiate a new topic, even though there was no counterpart in the original Sanskrit text. This practice was increasingly favoured by the Chinese translators because it indicated distinct boundaries between sentences or clauses. As a topic-prominent language, Chinese has an intrinsic demand for projecting the topic in discourse. Adding topic-shift markers in the translations highlights the direct influence of a typological property of Chinese in the process of translation.

Second, I refer to the indirect influence of the source language. For example, *wei* (爲) had become a mature copula in ancient Chinese which can lead to both substantive and declarative ingredients acting as the predicate, but the declarative ones must be referential in the predicate position. After the middle ages—especially in the Chinese-translated Buddhist Scriptures—*wei* expanded its meaning because there were a large number of existential verbs in the original Sanskrit texts to be rendered. *Wei* may modify a declarative predicate, but may also help constitute the passive voice. In may indicate an interrogative sentence or strengthen mood. Here, I show the distinctive and comprehensive attributes of this auxiliary verb, which laid an important syntactic and semantic foundation for further evolution into modal adverbs and alternative conjunctions.

Third, I turn to word innovation in translation. For instance, I discuss the new comparative structure *ru*(如)...*deng/xu* (等/許) indicating equality, that was often used in the Chinese translations of Buddhist Scriptures. With plenty of examples from Chinese Buddhist scripture and Sanskrit-Chinese comparative materials, I provide a preliminary demonstration that this equal-comparative marker is a discontinuous construction temporarily composed of the preposition *ru* and the postposition *deng*/*xu* and is based on the calque of the equal-comparative structure in the original text. Meanwhile, the lexical calque also occurred through translations, further promoting the development from the equal-comparative marker to the morpheme within a word.

Keywords: Translation of Buddhist scripture; the Evolution of Chinese language; Language contact

Early Jātaka Images of Mainland Southeast Asia

Reliefs from the Dvāravatī Period at Cula Pathon Cetiya

Chakhrit LAEMMUANG (DCI Center for Buddhist Studies)

There are many early Jataka (Skt. *jātaka*) images representing mainland Southeast Asia which have been found in the central region of Thailand. These images were made during the Dvāravatī period, and were placed on the bases of the walls of pagodas or cetiyas (Skt. *caitiya*; Thai. *chedī*). This paper focuses on Jataka images constructed from the 7th to 9th century CE from Cula Pathon Cetiya in Nakhon Pathom Province. A defining characteristic of these images is the use of terracotta or stucco to create the reliefs, as these were materials readily available in the local area. Moreover, during that period, this cetiya was located near a port that served as a trade center.

Previous researchers have identified the images of twelve Jataka stories on these reliefs, and two images of other stories have been newly identified in this paper. These Jataka images are generally based on Sanskrit Buddhist texts, but some display details from Pali Buddhist texts. There are images of five Jatakas that do not correspond to the Pali Canon, viz. *Candraprabha*, *Kacchapa*, *Śibi*, *Surūpa*, and *Hastin*. Later monks in northern Thailand paid much attention to the stories of *Kacchapa* and *Surūpa* and even incorporated parts of these stories into the *Paññāsajātaka*, which is non-canonical Pali literature. In addition, the Jataka images from Cula Pathon Cetiya include images which reflect the customs and lifestyle of the Dvāravatī people, depicting maritime objects, and animals used for riding.

Keywords: Dvāravatī, Jataka; Terracotta; Stucco; Southeast Asian history

Notes on the *Mahāmayūri-vidyārājñī-dhāraṇī* Transcribed by Amoghavajra

Li Jianqiang (Renmin University of China), Guo Yutong (Peking University) and Zhao Wenbo (Renmin University of China)

In previous research on Sanskrit-Chinese transcriptions, critical works on mantra have rarely been published. In this article, we seek to redress this omission by creating a critical edition of a mantra text from the Chinese. By reconstructing a Sanskrit mantra text from its Chinese version, we can contribute to and greatly enrich the wider study of Sanskrit literature. Our reconstruction conforms to the phonetic rules of Sanskrit-Chinese transcriptions and the Sanskrit grammar, occasionally referring to Tibetan texts when appropriate. This paper will present some examples from *Mahāmayūri-vidyārājñī-dhāraṇī* transcribed by Amoghavajra.

Keywords: Sanskrit-Chinese transcriptions; Mantra; Collation

Exegetical Approaches to the Dunhuang Commentaries of the *Lotus Sutra*

Li Silong (Peking University)

The Buddhist manuscripts preserved in the Dunhuang caves have had great impact on the study of ancient Chinese Buddhism. They contain a large number of Chinese Buddhist exegetical documents and are of significant academic value in the field of medieval Chinese Buddhist philosophy. The Dunhuang manuscripts involving the *Lotus Sutra* have been meticulously catalogued and organised. This article attempts to interpret their philosophical value from the perspective of Buddhist exegetical methods. There are five aspects of this method: explaining the meaning of classic titles; analysing textual structures; revealing the essence of Buddhist texts; interpreting the means of argumentation; and classifying the Buddha's teachings. This article examines these five aspects of exegetical method and also explores the *Lotus Sutra* in the context of the intellectual world of medieval northern China.

Keywords: Chinese Buddhist exegetical documents; Dunhuang manuscripts; Buddhist exegesis

A Survey of a Newly Found Sanskrit Manuscript of the *Gāthādvayavyākhyāna* and Other Texts

Li Xuezhu (China Tibetology Research Center)

This article presents a survey of case 37 of the Sanskrit palm leaf manuscripts housed in the China Tibetology Research Center. The survey reveals that the case contains, in total, seven exoteric and esoteric scriptures and treatises—of which three are esoteric Buddhist and four are exoteric Buddhist scriptures. One of the esoteric Buddhist works, *Śrīmadraktayamāritantrarāja*, situated in the *Yamāri* system of tantra, is a very rare Sanskrit manuscript. It is an important text for the study of the *Tantra of Red Yamāri* (Skt. *raktayamāritantra*). The three treatises of exoteric Buddhism found in case 37—*Gāthādvayavyākhyāna*, **Madhyamakayogācārabalābalaparīkṣā*, and *Āryabhadracaryāpraṇidhānaṭīkā*—are the only extant Sanskrit manuscripts of these texts. Collectively, the texts in case 37 are an invaluable resource for the study of Mahāyāna Buddhist teachings, tantric ritual, and Pure Land thought.

Keywords: Sanskrit manuscript; *Gāthādvayavyākhyāna*; *Āryabhadracaryāpraṇidhānaṭīkā*

A Brief Introduction and Selected Translation of the *Mayamatam*

Li Ying (Beijing Foreign Studies University)

Among the series of Indian treaties on the principles of arts and architecture classified as *vāstuśāstra*, the *Mayamatam* is acknowledged as one of the most significant texts. It shares common general themes as housing, architecture and iconography with other *vāstuśāstras*. However, there are also notable differences: it comes from a regional source; has religious sectarian features; deals with specific topics; and employs distinctive interpretations of certain terms. These differences manifest the characteristics of Dravidian art and architectural culture within their historical context.

Current domestic research on the *Mayamatam* is still in its beginning phase. This article provides a translation of the text and a necessary introduction to relevant works. In doing so, this article aims to sketch an outline of *Mayamatam* by giving a brief introduction to the general features of the treatise and a translation of the first chapter of *Mayamatam* (from its original Sanskrit text into Chinese). The chapter being translated here is basically a summary of the treatise, dealing firstly with Maya, the auditor of the Lord of the Universe and the author of the treatise, and then the concise account of the treatise's contents, and finally its divine origin and some specific instructions on the making of shrines and human dwellings.

Keywords: Indian art; Indian architecture; *Vāstuśāstra*; *Mayamatam*

The Layouts of Gandhāran Buddhist Temples

Focusing on Taxila, Peshawar and Swat Regions

LIAO Zhitang (Chinese Academy of Social Sciences)
and LI Xiao (Renmin University of China)

In this article, we conduct a cross-regional analysis of the layouts and developments of Gandhāran Buddhist temples, taking examples from the regions of Taxila, Peshawar and Swat. Although the temples maintained distinct local characteristics, the layouts of Buddhist temples from these three areas shared similarities, at least in later developmental stages. These shared elements were based on early Indian Buddhist temple features such as a round stupa base; linear-formed monastic cells; and an apsidal temple.

Despite various differences, Buddhist temples from all three of these regions (in their later manifestations) demonstrated a basic combination of a square stupa courtyard and a square *vihāra* courtyard. The architecture usually became more complex as votive stupas, shrines and so on, were added to the temples. Furthermore, certain differences in temple configuration may be accounted for by reference to differences between various doctrinal sects. Some Buddhist temples were located within clearly defined locations, possibly because they belonged to wider Buddhist settlements.

But the common practice of employing a binary layout in Gandhāran Buddhist temples—the division of the temple into the stupa and the *vihāra* courtyard sections of the complex—was distinctive and widespread. It is also evidenced in findings of mural paintings and coins from the region. Furthermore, this architecture had a profound impact on the process of dissemination of Buddhism and influenced Buddhist temples in northern Central Asia; in the western regions; and in the Central Plains of ancient China. It even informed the layout of later Indian Buddhist temples. The influence of this feature serves as a powerful reminder of the long-distance cultural communication between East and West along the Silk Road.

Keywords: Gandhāra; Layout of Buddhist temples; Taxila; Peshawar; Swat

A Preliminary Report on a Saindhavī Manuscript of the *Dīrghāgama* of the Sāṃmitīyas

PHURTSAM (Tibetan Academy of Social Sciences)

This paper presents a preliminary report on the principal contents of the text catalogued as the *Bṛhmajālasūtra* manuscript, which is preserved in the Lhokha Museum in Xizang. I establish that the manuscript comprises at least eight sutras with corresponding texts found in the Pali *Dīghanikāya* of the Theravādin school of Buddhism, and the Chinese *Dīrghāgama* (Ch. *Cháng āhán jīng*). Through an examination of the script and the use of language employed in the manuscript, I confirm that the text pertains to the contents of the *Dīrghāgama* of the Sāṃmitīya school.

Keywords: Bhaikṣukī script; Saindhavī script; *Bṛhmajālasūtra*; *Dīrghāgama*

Khotanese Names in Chinese Documents

Examining a New Set of Inhabitants in Gaysāta

RONG Xinjiang (Peking University) and CHING Chao-jung (Kyoto University)

Thanks to the collaboration between R. E. Emmerick and M. I. Vorobyova-Desyatovskaya, the study of Khotanese documents progressed in the 20th century. Furtheremore, the catalogisation of the British Collection by P. O. Skjærvø and U. Sims-Williams at the turn of the 21st century was a milestone in the field. In 2006, referring to H. Kumamoto's review (1996) on the research of Vorobyova-Desyatovskaya, Y. Yoshida emphasized the importance of prosographical analysis and the value of Chinese and Tibetan texts. In fact, on the basis of H. W. Bailey's study, Zhang Guangda and Rong Xinjiang (1997) proposed a biographical chronology of Sīḍaka and the chronicle of the king, Viśa' Vāhaṃ. In accordance with this tradition, our paper examines inhabitants of late 8th-century Gaysāta (today known as Dandan Uilik), such as Puñargaṃ (Ch. Boyanyang 勃延仰) found in the bilingual contract Дх.18926 + SI P 93.22 + Дх.18928. We use this text to elucidate some important sets of personal names and social relationships.

In particular, we focus on BH1-3 (81.8 × 29 cm, National Library of China), a scroll in the group of Chinese documents from Khotan recently analyzed in a series of our research papers (Ching and Rong 2022a, 2022b, 2022c). Written in 790CE, it is a list of thirty individuals concerning tax collection. According to our analysis, the individuals mentioned were local inhabitants (*baixing*, 百姓, transcribed in Khotanese *pa'kisina*) of Gaysāta who paid a specific kind of tax called *shuiliang* (税糧, lit. "tax-grain") to the Tang military office at Gaysāta. The text provides some hints to clarify what is referred to as the "archive of Gaysāta," initially supposed by Vorobyova-Desyatovskaya.

Keywords: Khotan; Jiexie/Gaysāta; Khotanese; Prosographical analysis; Dandan Uilik

Notes on the *Ratnaketuparivarta*

SAERJI (Peking University)

The *Ratnaketuparivarta* is one of the most popular Mahāyāna texts from the late period of Mahāyāna Buddhism. Many Sanskrit fragments from Gilgit, Bamiyan, and Central Asia, verify its popularity in history. In the tradition of Chinese Buddhism, the *Ratnaketuparivarta* is at first embedded in the Mahāyāna Buddhist collection of the *Mahāvaipulya-mahāsamnipātasūtra*, and translated by Dharmakṣema. Later, as an independent text, it is translated again by Prabhākaramitra during the Tang dynasty.

According to Tibetan Buddhist sources, the *Ratnaketuparivarta* is one of the Mahāyāna texts brought back from India to Xizang, China by Thonmi Sambhoṭa (who invented the Tibetan Script) in the early-to-mid-7th century CE. Recently discovered Tibetan manuscripts that were circulated independently also attest to its popularity. This paper analyses the title and mantras of the text. I especially examine the different colophons which are preserved not only in the Gilgit Sanskrit manuscripts, but also in the Tibetan manuscripts, (now housed in the Newark Museum, USA, and in Western Xizang, China). Through such analysis, this paper aims at deepening our understand of the *Ratnaketuparivarta*, especially the text's influence on communicating exoteric and esoteric Buddhism, Buddhist ritual and the aspects of Buddhism as cult.

Keywords: *Ratnaketuparivarta*; Title; Mantra; Colophon

The Recognition of Spiritual Civilizations in Ancient India and China

A Comparative Study of the *Siṅgālovādasūtra*

Wilaiporn SUCHARITATHAMMAKUL (Kasetsart University)

This article highlights the crucial importance of the exchange between China and India, two ancient spiritual civilizations. In particular, I focus on the *Siṅgālovādasūtra*, a Buddhist sutra that was transmitted from India to China sometime between the 1st and 5th centuries CE. In the present era, five ancient Chinese versions of the *Siṅgālovādasūtra*, have been found: the *Sutra Spoken by the Buddha to Sigālaka on the Worship of the Six Directions*; the *Sutra of the Son of Shansheng*; the *Shansheng Sutra of the Madhyamāgama*; the *Shansheng Sutra of the Dīrghāgama*; and the *Sutra of Upāsakasīla*.

Despite the differences between the translated texts, the main idea is the same and there are few differences. One difference of note concerns the relationship of married couples and the relationship between a master and a subordinate. There is a significant amount of focus on these relationships in some texts. Remarkably, some editions contain double the amount of text concerned with similar material, such as the *Sutra of the Son of Shansheng*; the *Shansheng Sutra of the Madhyamāgama*; and the *Sutra of Upāsakasīla*. This article is concerned with explaining these differences.

Keywords: Ancient India; China; Spiritual civilization; *Siṅgālovāda*; Shansheng

The *Lipiśālāsaṃdarśanaparivarta* in the *Lalitavistara*

WANG Bangwei (Peking University)

This paper discusses the *Lipiśālāsaṃdarśanaparivarta* in the *Lalitavistara*, a well-known Biographical text of the Buddha. While accounting for the distinguishing stylistic features of the story as a whole, I focus particularly on the origins of the words *cīnalipi, hūṇalipi, khāṣyalipi,* and *yavani*, which are mentioned in various versions of the *Lipiśālāsaṃdarśanaparivarta*. In doing so, in this paper I provide some new understandings of both the Sanskrit and the Chinese versions of this text.

Keywords: *Lalitavistara*; *Lipiśālāsaṃdarśanaparivarta*; *Cīnalipi; Khāṣyalipi*; *Yavani*

The Two Springs of the Sea

A Set of Sacred Lakes and Fire Temples in Sasanian Iran

WU Yunpei (Shanghai Academy of Social Sciences)

The paper is a discussion on the two sacred lakes, Čēčast and Sōwar, mentioned in the Middle Persian texts as the two Springs of the Sea. It sets off with a definition on three related words, i.e. *čašmag* "spring", *war* "lake" and *zrēh* "sea", as well as three mythological accounts on the origin of water, i.e. the myths of Tištar, Anāhīd and *xwarrah,* in order to provide a partial description on the Middle Iranian imagination of the world water system. It then proceeds to discuss the classification of the two lakes into one special category in the Sasanian dynasty, analyzing how they were interwoven with the construction or transformation of two Fire Temples, Ādur Gušnasp and Ādur Burzēnmihr, as well as with the legends of Kayanian king Khusrow and Sasanian king Yazdegerd I, which belonging to the imperial ideological narrative, the *Xwadāy-nāmag* tradition in the making, imparted a newly-defined sanctity and legality to both the lakes and the fire temples. The paper proposes that the two sacred lakes, along with the two fire temples, invoke an image of two eyes of the world, a symbolism of the twofold kingship manifested in the east and the west.

Keywords: Spring; Lake; Fire temple; *Xwadāy-nāmag*; Sasanian Iran

A Review on *Biluo*

YANG Xi (Chinese Academy of Social Sciences)

Biluo is a kind of food which was well known in Tang and Song Dynasties in China but which fell out of circulation in the late imperial period. There has been much discussion by modern scholars about its origin and form. This article considers a number of Central Asian foods that have similar sounding names to "*biluo*" in Middle Chinese and resemble its form in the historical records. Here, I develop upon the discussion about *biluo* in modern scholarship and comment upon the methodology in the field of historical studies about ancient cultural exchange.

Keywords: *Biluo*; Central Asia; Cultural exchange; History of cultural exchange; Methodology

Nāgārjuna's Life and Legend

An Overview of Materials and Studies

YE Shaoyong (Peking University)

Nāgārjuna is generally believed to have flourished in India in the 2nd-3rd century CE. His magnum opus, the *Mūlamadhyamakakārikā*, laid the theoretical foundation for the exposition of emptiness in Mahāyāna Buddhism, significantly impacting doctrinal studies and sectarian development in both Xizang and the Central Plains of China. Descriptions of Nāgārjuna in various ancient texts are imbued with mythological elements, and later periods witnessed a plethora of esoteric, medical, and alchemical works attributed to him. However, details regarding Nāgārjuna's era and life remain unclear in modern scholarship. This paper provides an overview of accounts of Nāgārjuna's life found in Chinese, Sanskrit, and Tibetan sources. Additionally, it reviews modern scholars' perspectives, which are based on these materials.

Keywords: Nāgārjuna; Madhyamaka; Mahāyāna Buddhism

An Examination of the Chinese Translation of the Tibetan Terms, *Rang rgyud pa* and *Thal 'gyur ba*

YONTAN (Shenyang Falun Temple)

The Tibetan terms *rang rgyud pa* (Skt. *svātantrika*) and *thal 'gyur ba* (Skt. *prāsaṅgika*) are frequently used to denote the two major branches of the Madhyamaka school of Buddhism. The former has been translated into Chinese as *zi xu pai, zi li liang pai, zi zai lun zheng pai, zi li pai*, etc. The latter is rendered as *ying cheng pai, sui ying po pai, gui miu pai, gui miu lun zheng pai*, etc.

After analysis, I argue here that translating these Tibetan terms as *zi li liang pai* and *sui ying po pai* respectively, can lead to the misunderstanding that a proponent of the *thal 'gyur ba* veiw has no philosophical position. These terms also imply that he does not use any formal reasoning (Skt. *anumāna*). Conversely, the translation of the terms as *zi zai lun zheng pai/zi li pai* and *gui miu pai/gui miu lun zheng pai* respectively may lead to the misunderstanding that the *thal 'gyur ba* fails to make positive arguments and only employs reductio ad absurdum arguments. These terms in Chinese also suggest that the word *thal 'gyur* is not completely equivalent to "reductio ad absurdum." Therefore, the translation, *zi xu pai* and *ying cheng pai* should be preferred to the other terms mentioned above.

Keywords: *Rang rgyud pa* (*svātantrika*); *Thal 'gyur ba* (*prāsaṅgika*); *Sui ying po pai*; *Zi li liang pai*; *Gui miu pai*; *Gui miu lun zheng pai*; *Prasaṅga*; *Svatantra*

Iconography of Buddhist Demons, Deities and Dharma Protectors in Khotan

Study on the Textual and Pictorial Materials of the Four-armed, Beast-headed *Yakṣī*-goddess

ZHANG Huiming (China National Academy of Painting)

Yakṣa (Ch. *yecha*/夜叉) is the name of a large class of nature spirits, usually benevolent, who are the guardians of natural treasures hidden beneath the earth. They appear in Hindu, Jain and Buddhist mythology as deities and celestial beings. The feminine form of the word in Sanskrit is *yakṣī* or *yakṣiṇī*.

In Hindu, Jain and Buddhist mythologies, *yakṣa* have a dual personality. On the one hand, they are fairies with a harmless nature. But there is a much darker version of these spirits. They also appear as a kind of ogre, ghost, or anthropophagous demon that haunts the wilderness, and who attacks and devours travellers. On this account, a *yakṣa*, who occupies an important place in the Indian pantheon, is a half-god and half-demon with the dual character of mercy and evil.

The *yakṣa* were believed to be Dharma protectors in early Mahāyāna Buddhist and tantric Buddhist imagery that was popular in the Western regions (Northwest India, Central Asia, and Xinjiang, China) from the 3rd to the 9th centuries CE. Khotan was an important location where Indian Buddhism spread from the east to the Western regions and in Khotan there are images of the creatures as Buddhist Dharma protectors, local protectors, ghosts and gods. One of these is the Beast-headed Yakṣa/Yakṣī image which was an important theme in the murals of local temples. Our focus in this article is the fragment of a wall painting of a four-armed, Beast-headed Yakṣī-goddess (Ta. 008), found by A. Stein at the Tarishlak site (Ta.i) in Hetian in the early 20th century.

Based on previous research, we make a preliminary review of the textual and pictorial materials related to the Beast-headed Yakṣī-goddess in Khotan. We then discuss whether the remnant painting of the four-armed goddess at the Ta.i could be identified as the Hindu goddess, Revatī. In addition, we explore the relationship (in the literature and iconography) between the image of the Beast-headed Yakṣī protecting the dharma of Khotanese Buddhism in the 6th-7th century CE, and a sculpture with the motif of Mathura Mātṛkās in the Kushan period in India.

Keywords: Yakṣī; Revatī; Khotan; Mātṛkās; Mathura

The Past Life Story of the *Śārdūlakarṇāvadāna* Reflected in the Sanskrit Manuscript in the Bodleian Library, Oxford

ZHOU Liqun (Beijing Foreign Studies University)
BANDENG (Shenyang Falun Temple)

The manuscript identified as MS. Sansk.e.23(P) in the Oxford Sanskrit Collection, includes the Central Asian Sanskrit text, the *Śārdūlakarṇāvadāna*. The text consists of a total of nine palm leaves, written in Brāhmī script. This article transliterates the first part of the manuscript from digital photographs of the text of the story of Prince Tiger-ear's past life for the first time.

We also analyze the characters in the story—such as Puṣkasārin, Prakṛti, Triśaṅku and Śārdūlakarṇa—in terms of their cultural and linguistic relevance. For example, the name of the great Brahmin Puṣkasārin is associated with the Puṣkasārin script, and the name of his daughter Prakṛti, is associated with the Prakrit languages. The Caṇḍala king Triśaṅku is associated with the mythical king Triśaṅku who levitated in the air and became the Southern Cross. His son Śārdūlakarṇa, i.e. Tiger-ear, may be related to the Bengal tiger in South Asia. The Caṇḍala caste was born of a Śudra man and a Brahmin woman and was thus considered to be a low social status. The cultural image of the Mātaṅga tribe in this text may be associated with the goddess Mother Mātaṅgī in East India. She is associated with the knowledge of language, the art of music, but also with pollution, inauspiciousness, otherness and the margins of Hindu society. Overall, it appears that the figures in the *Śārdūlakarṇāvadāna* have strong connections with the nature, history and religion of northern India. However, whether this leads to the conclusion that the composition of the *Śārdūlakarṇāvadāna* was completed in northern India is worthy of further exploration.

Keywords: *Śārdūlakarṇāvadāna*; Sanskrit manuscript; Oxford

The Restoration of the Beginning of Huida's *Zhaolunshu*

ZHOU Xuenong (Peking University)

This article examines a textual misplacement at the beginning of Huida's *Zhaolunshu*. The first page, which is believed to be lost, can be found in a later paragraph. However, this restored version, which might belong to an early but incomplete manuscript, still can't present the original form.

Key words: Huida; *Zhaolunshu* [Commentary on the *Theses of Sengzhao*]; Sengzhao; *Zhaolun* [*Theses of Sengzhao*]

Sāṃkhya Philosophy and its Impact on Natural Knowledge and Technology in Post-Vedic India

ZHU Chengming (Chongqing University)

Cosmological myth and revelation-centered mytho-speculation are the two principal forms of knowledge in Vedic India, and the practical teaching of both focuses on divine-human and inter-human relationships. In this religion-oriented intellectual context, natural knowledge and technology in Vedic India had little chance of independent development. They were almost entirely subject to the influence of religious and socio-political concerns. The rise of Sāṃkhya philosophy, however, with its evocation of a disenchanted, disassociated cosmos (with gods "expelled"); rejection of mythical elements in the enterprise of knowledge acquisition; upholding of autonomous human reason in spiritual orientation; and equipping of man with a "logical" instrument (i.e., *ānvīkṣikī*), largely facilitated the ground-breaking leap in natural knowledge and technology in post-Vedic India, partially severing it from its religious and mythical dependence.

Keywords: Sāṃkhya; Vedic India; Post-Vedic India; Natural knowledge; Natural technology

Some Buddhist Elements in Tao Yuanming's Literary Vocabulary

A Case Study of the Contribution of Buddhism including the Chinese Translation of Buddhist Scriptures to the Chinese Classical Literary Language

ZHU Qingzhi (The Education University of Hong Kong)

The transmission of Indian Buddhism (including the translation and spread of Buddhist scriptures) made significant contributions to the development of Chinese literature. Not only did it exert an influence on literary content, but it also affected its vocabulary. Scholars have done much work on this topic. For example, the author himself (Qingzhi Zhu, 1992) has discussed the interaction between the vocabulary of Dunhuang transformation (Ch. bianwen/變文) texts and the Chinese translation of Buddhist scriptures. However, most previous studies in this field contain only superficial descriptive analyses and they lack sufficient monographic and quantitative research.

This article seeks to explicate the relationship between the Buddhist concept of chen (塵, lit. dust, Budd. worldly, mundane), and how the eight words containing chen are used in the poems of Tao Yuanming (陶淵明)—a great poet during the Eastern Jin Dynasty. Chen is a term which has a strong Buddhist flavor in medieval Chinese. In Tao Yuanming's poems, there are eight compound words containing chen, viz., chenji (塵羈, lit. detaining by dust, earthly bondage), chenjue (塵爵, lit. dust vessel, nobility in seclusion), chenshi (塵事, lit. affairs of dust, mundane affairs), chenwang (塵網, lit. dust net, earthly bondage), chenxiao (塵囂, lit. a hubbub of dust, hustle and bustle), chenxiang (塵想, lit. thinking of dust, worldly perception), liuchen (流塵, lit. flowing dust), and moshangchen (陌上塵, lit. dust on the road). The first step of this article is to discuss the use of chen and words containing chen as a word-forming element in the Buddhist scriptures translated from the Eastern Han to Eastern Jin period. Based on this, the second step of this article is to investigate the origin of chen-related words presented in Tao's poems. Finally, this article examines the use of those words in the literature of later ages.

The main achievement of this article is to use digital research tools, such as "CBETA" and "Souyun", to obtain a large amount of first-hand information, conduct quantitative analysis on it, and obtain the following new understandings: First, Tao Yuanming's poetic language not only absorbed Buddhist vocabulary, but also used Buddhist terminology to create new words. This deepens our understanding of the relationship between Tao Yuanming and Buddhism. Second, most of these Buddhistic words used or created by Tao Yuanming, together with other Buddhist words, were not only used by later poets, but also introduced different types of innovations, injecting vitality into the creativity of Chinese literature. This also deepens our understanding of Buddhism, especially the contribution of the Chinese translation of Indian Buddhist scripture to the enrichment and development of ancient Chinese literary vocabulary.

The paper sets out to study the poems of Tao Yuanming for the following reasons: Tao Yuanming is widely considered an icon of Chinese literature during the Six Dynasties period, and an essential writer in the history of Classical Chinese literature. Modern scholars have paid close attention to how religion played a role in shaping Tao Yuanming's thought and style of poetry. There is no agreement between Chen Yinke's theory of the Way of the Celestial Masters (Tianshi Taoism) of the Xi people; the teachings of the Confucian ethical code and nature; and Buddhism. The author has no intention in this paper of joining the discussion about these disagreements. Instead, this paper upholds the idea that since Tao lived in the era when Buddhism was becoming prevalent throughout Chinese society, his speech and writing—as well as those of his contemporary literatus and intellectuals—would inevitably show Buddhist features. It is an indisputable fact that Tao Yuanming's poems contain many Buddhinised words. By clarifying the etymology of chen, we see convincing proof of the influence of Buddhism on the language and vocabulary of Chinese literature.

Keywords: Buddhism; Tao Yuanming (陶淵明); Literary vocabulary; History of Chinese literature; Digital research tool and Digital Humanity; Quantitative study